144

32 20 sq ft

4. Jones

32 | 120

ZONDERVAN

DICTIONARY of
BIBLICAL IMAGERY

ZONDERVAN

DICTIONARY of BIBLICAL IMAGERY

General Editor

John A. Beck

ZONDERVAN®

ZONDERVAN.com/
AUTHORTRACKER
follow your favorite authors

ZONDERVAN

Zondervan Dictionary of Biblical Imagery
Copyright © 2011 by John A. Beck

This title is also available as a Zondervan ebook. Visit www.zondervan.com/ebooks.

Requests for information should be addressed to:

Zondervan, *Grand Rapids, Michigan 49530*

Library of Congress Cataloging-in-Publication Data

Beck, James R.
    Zondervan dictionary of biblical imagery / Jack Beck.
    p. cm.
    ISBN 978-0-310-29285-2 (hardcover, printed) 1. Bible — Language, style — Dictionaries. 2. Symbolism in the Bible —
  Dictionaries. I. Title. II. Title: Dictionary of biblical imagery.
  BS537.B43 2011
  220.6′403 — dc22   2010010932

Cover and interior design by Kirk DouPonce

Printed in the United States of America

10 11 12 13 14 15 16 17 18 19 20 /DCI/ 23 22 21 20 19 18 17 16 15 14 13 12 11 10 9 8 7 6 5 4 3 2 1

For Marmy,
my soul mate and coadventurer

PREFACE

Why should you take the time to learn more about the culture and land of the biblical world when you find yourself overwhelmed by the increasing complexity of your own world? The answer is simple: doing so will revolutionize what you see when reading your Bible.

As the Holy Spirit led the inspired authors of the Bible to write, he also led them to fill the pages of the Bible with vibrant images drawn from the culture, natural history, and landscape around them. Using such vivid imagery as looms, donkeys, water cisterns, grapes, sackcloth, and shepherds makes what they say both more beautiful and more memorable. These images stimulate our imagination, animate our interest, and make the abstract clearer. In short, the biblical authors used the reality around them to enhance the rhetorical impact of what they wrote.

Unfortunately, the full impact of this imagery can be lost on modern readers. Just as the ancients knew nothing of iPhones and airplanes, modern readers are likely to know next to nothing about threshing sledges and desert locusts. What is more, we are in the dark about the connotations that attend such cultural images. What did a threshing floor look like, and how did it function? What habits of the fox distinguished it from other predators? What is it like at the Dead Sea or in the Jezreel Valley? The biblical authors knew the answers to such questions, and they presumed their readers did as well. To the degree that we have lost touch with the culture, natural history, and landscape of Bible times, we will miss some of what God wishes to share with us in his Word.

This dictionary attempts to fill that gap in our understanding. Each entry focuses on a particular biblical image, starting with the reality that lies behind the word. Appearance, distinctive characteristics, and cultural use are addressed, using clear descriptions, photographs, and maps. Each entry also investigates the cultural connotations linked to the image, recognizing that a particular image may arouse an emotional response from one who sees it or hears it mentioned. At times the connotation of a familiar image may solicit exactly the opposite response from us that it did from the ancients. For example, dogs, which are likely to stimulate very positive feelings in us, generated very negative feelings in ancient Israel. Once both the reality of an image and its connotations are presented, the entry then surveys the use of that image in the Bible to illustrate how it is put to work by the divine wordsmith.

As you take time to learn about ancient culture, your Bible reading will radically change. You will know why God's people kept goats and why the goat became the symbol of the lost. You will know why Jesus called Herod a fox and how the Mount of Olives contributed to Jesus' struggle in prayer. You will know why people mixed salt with manure and appreciate why Jesus called for us to become the salt of the earth. Expect new insights each time you turn the page in this book — insights that will forever change the way you interact with the pages of your Bible.

A

Altar

In a landscape that was peppered with pagan altars, the Lord was very particular about how his altars were constructed and used. The first divinely approved altars were fashioned from the soil itself or undressed fieldstones (Ex. 20:24–26; Deut. 27:5–6). But in time the Lord directed Israel to construct larger and more ornate altars associated with the tabernacle and temple. These square altars had a wooden frame overlaid with metal (Ex. 27:1–8; 30:1–5; 1 Kings 8:64; 2 Chron. 4:1). They also had horns, projections from each of the four upper corners, which may have been designed to hold up a grate that separated the fire proper from the sacrifice (Ex. 29:12). The exact function of the horns remains something of a mystery, but Amos tells us that an altar whose horns were removed could no longer be used (Amos 3:14). The largest and most stunning altar mentioned in the Old Testament is the one anticipated by Ezekiel. He writes of an altar composed of three tiers, rising more than twenty feet from its foundation (Ezek. 43:13–17). From this description we detect a trajectory in the divine plan for altar construction— from the simple rock or earthen mound altar to a future altar that rests within the throne room of the Lord, an altar we glimpse briefly through the eyes of Isaiah and John (Isa. 6:6; Rev. 8:3; 9:13; 16:7).

Altars functioned in a variety of ways. Noah, Abraham, and Moses built altars both as worship tools and as memorials marking enduring covenants that God had made with them (Gen. 8:20–22; 12:6–7; Ex. 24:1–4). While these particular memorial altars were used for sacrifice, other memorial altars were not. As Reuben, Gad, and the half-tribe of Manasseh concluded their time with Joshua on the west side of the Jordan River, their trip home to their families on the east side of the river precipitated a concern. Fearing that their connection to God's promises might be compromised, they built an imposing altar by the Jordan as a symbol of their connection to the tribes west of the Jordan and to the promises that God had given to all Israel (Josh. 22:10–29). Kings in Bible times also founded altars in their capital cities to champion a particular deity and link that deity to their nation.

A four-horned altar at Beersheba.

In that spirit, Solomon established the great altar at the temple in Jerusalem (1 Kings 6:20). The smoke rising from this altar reminded Israel of their special status as God's people as they made sacrifices praising God for his blessings or seeking assurance of their forgiveness.

The biblical authors work to shape our understanding and perceptions by mentioning altars more than four hundred times. In these cases, the altar is a place to express one's faith in the Lord, to develop one's faith, and to proclaim that faith. Consider the following examples. Throughout the book of Genesis, we read that Abraham and his family built memorial altars in one place after the next in locations along the Ridge Route, the well-worn path that became the main north-sound road through the interior of the Promised Land (Gen. 12:7–8; 13:18; 26:25; 33:20; 35:7). These altars were typically established in connection with a theophany that reviewed covenant promises personally given to Abraham, Isaac, and Jacob. Subsequently, as members of Abraham's family traveled north and south through the land seeking pasture for their animals, they came upon these memorial altars, which provided an opportunity for education, worship, and recommitment to God's plan for them.

The covenant made with Abraham's descendants via Moses was also marked by the construction of altars. Moses built an altar at the foot of Mount Horeb (Ex. 24:4) where the Law was given, and Joshua built a complimentary altar when Israel reached the Promised Land. That altar was built on Mount Ebal in connection with the covenant renewal ceremonies held there (Josh. 8:30–31).

The Lord not only spoke about altars dedicated to him, but also about how Israel was to react to altars established to honor false gods. His language is clear and uncompromising. The Israelites were to prove their full commitment to the Lord by destroying all the pagan altars in the Promised Land (Ex. 34:13; Deut. 7:5; 12:3). The most glaring failure to do so during the days of the judges is illustrated in the life of Gideon's father who had actually built an altar in devotion to Baal (Judg. 6:25). The darkest days in Israel's history are marked not just by a failure to destroy pagan altars but by a commitment to build them. When Solomon's kingdom split, King Jeroboam I established rival altars associated with the calf worship sites at Bethel and Dan (1 Kings 12:28–33). King Ahab took matters a step further by championing Baal as his national deity and building an altar to Baal in his capital city (1 Kings 16:32). And when King Ahaz of Judah made a treaty with Assyria, he showed where his allegiance lay by replacing the great altar at the temple with an altar that resembled one he had seen in Damascus (2 Kings 16:10–15).

These darker days of the divided kingdom were punctuated by times of reformation. Elijah used an altar on Mount Carmel (1 Kings 18:30) to put Baal in his place, while Hezekiah and Josiah removed the altars to foreign gods as they led God's people to recommit themselves to the Lord (2 Kings 18:22; 23:20). But in the end, the rebuilding of altars to foreign gods under the likes of Manasseh (2 Kings 21:3) and others spelled exile for the nation of Israel. Yet when they returned with hearts dedicated to the Lord's promises, the first thing they did was rebuild the altar in Jerusalem (Ezra 3:3).

The New Testament authors mention altars less frequently than the Old Testament authors. In most instances when an altar is mentioned, it is the great altar in Jerusalem that is in view. But one instance in the book of Acts stands out. As Paul walked the streets of Athens, he was surrounded by the pagan idols and altars that filled that city's streets. It was one of those pagan altars, the one dedicated "TO AN UNKNOWN GOD," that opened the door for Paul to preach the gospel there (Acts 17:23).

Arrow

The arrow was well known throughout Bible times and was as likely to be found in the hands of a common shepherd (Gen. 48:22) as in the hands of the king's son (1 Sam. 20:20 – 38). In general the arrow of the ancient world resembled the arrow of today, with a head, shaft, and fetching. The fetching at the rear of the shaft was typically composed from the feathers of an eagle or vulture. Its purpose was to stabilize the flight path of the arrow when fired. A wooden or reed shaft approximately thirty inches in length separated the fetching from the pointed head—the part of the arrow that went through the most design changes in its flight through history. Arrowheads were first made of flint then bronze and then iron. Their shape and composition were continually addressed in a bid to improve their aerodynamic profile and thus their contribution to the velocity, range, and accuracy of the weapon. In some instances arrowheads had a hole bored through them so that tufts of wool might be loaded and ignited to create flaming arrows that could be fired into an enemy compound.

The Bible knows of at least three uses for the arrow. Esau picked up his bow and arrow to hunt the wild game that was his father's favorite food (Gen. 27:3). Aside from hunting, an arrow might be used when seeking an omen from the gods. When the campaigning king of Babylon came to a crossroads, he called for arrows in order to learn which way he should turn. Ezekiel says this king "cast lots with arrows" as part of the ritual that led him to select Jerusalem as his military target (Ezek. 21:21). But most commonly we find the arrow being used when people are at war. As a weapon, the arrow distinguished itself by delivering a sudden and unexpected blow from a distance of over 225 yards, well outside the range of other weapons.

The arrow thus became a symbol of dominance in the ancient world. That is likely why Elisha included arrows in the enacted message for Jehoash king of Israel. Elisha instructed this king to shoot an arrow out a window and then to bang the collection of arrows in his hand on the ground. In both instances, Elisha linked the actions of the king to the military success or failure he would find in his fight against Aram (2 Kings 13:15 – 19). In that light, the inability to fire an arrow was a sign of impotence. When King Hezekiah of Judah expressed his concern over the impending approach of the strong Assyrian army, Isaiah assured him that the Assyrian king would not so much as shoot an arrow in Jerusalem (2 Kings 19:32; Isa. 37:33).

The arrow also flies onto the pages of our Bible in a variety of metaphors. The poet of Psalm 127 likens the blessing of having sons to the advantage owned by the soldier whose quiver

An iron arrowhead from Tel Miqne (the biblical Ekron).
Copyright 1995-2011 Phoenix Data Systems

is packed full of arrows (Ps. 127:4 – 5). Given the similarities between lightning and an arrow, it is no surprise that the arrow is also used as a metaphor for this meteorological phenomenon (2 Sam. 22:15; Pss. 18:14; 144:6). Both make their appearance suddenly and unexpectedly. Both dart across the sky at incredible speed. And both arrive on the scene with lethal power.

Arrows are also likened to words, which have the power to build up or tear down. When the latter is the case, the words that fly through the air are like destructive arrows that ambush the innocent (Ps. 64:3–4) and ruin reputations with false testimony (Prov. 25:18). Furthermore, arrows represent the calculated harm the wicked bring to our lives through their actions: "For look, the wicked bend their bows; they set their arrows against the strings to shoot from the shadows at the upright in heart" (Ps. 11:2). And we may add to that list the sinister desires of the Evil One who is more than willing to send flaming arrows in our direction. Paul offers the comforting reminder that our defense is the shield of faith with which we can "extinguish all the flaming arrows of the evil one" (Eph. 6:16).

Divine judgment is also linked to the arrow. Moses made it clear that no one was to touch Mount Sinai when the Lord appeared there to give the Law. Those who violated this command were to be executed without being physically touched. The arrow is specifically mentioned as one tool for rendering divine judgment in this instance (Ex. 19:13). In subsequent passages of Scripture, the arrow continues as a metaphor for divine judgment. When the inspired poets of the Bible felt the press of God's judgment, they often described their experiences in terms of being pierced by divine arrows (Ps. 38:2) or poisoned by arrows of the Almighty (Job 6:4). It is no surprise then that the arrow also is used as a metaphor for famine, plague, and other misfortune God would direct against Israel when they betrayed him (Deut. 32:23–26).

But in the end, it is not God's judgment but his protection that most comforts our hearts.

Given the speed, range, and accuracy of the arrow, it was truly a weapon that induced fear. Only when we appreciate the terrible dread associated with the arrow will we appreciate what it means to dwell in the shelter of the Most High, not fearing "the terror of night, nor the arrow that flies by day" (Ps. 91:5).

Assyria

The Promised Land enjoyed not only the attention of the Lord but also the attention of the empires that came to power on the stage of ancient history. Its strategic location at the crossroads of Asia, Africa, and Europe beckoned to those empires with the twin promises of military supremacy and untold wealth. Assyria was among the nations that answered the call.

The heartland of ancient Assyria straddles the upper course of the Tigris River in northern Iraq. In time the sleepy agricultural villages of this region became the powerful empire of Assyria whose reach extended across the Fertile Crescent from the Persian Gulf to Egypt and the Nile. During the middle of the ninth century BC, Shalmaneser V pushed west, drawn by the timber, minerals, and trade benefits associated with the eastern Mediterranean. But it was not until the middle of the eighth century that hit-and-run campaigns designed to collect tribute were replaced by extensive military campaigns bent on conquest and occupation of those lands.

Tiglath-Pileser III (Pul), Shalmaneser V, Sargon II, and Sennacherib were among the Assyrian kings whose empire-building dreams brought them into contact with God's people and the Promised Land. The Assyrian kings' dreams to expand Assyrian control brought the kings of Israel and Judah to a crossroads of their own. They could either declare their allegiance to Assyria and pay tribute or save their money and face military conquest. Kings Menahem and Pekah illustrate the choice and consequences. When Tiglath-Pileser III came calling, Menahem dug deep into the royal treasury, temporarily purchasing Israel's freedom with tons of silver (2 Kings 15:19). Years later Pekah withheld tribute, faced conquest, and ended up losing nearly all of his land holdings and many of his citizens (15:29). When Hoshea, the last king of the northern kingdom, followed the same rebellious path, Shalmaneser V began a three-year siege of Samaria, the capital city of Hoshea. The capital fell, and the remaining subjects of the kingdom were exiled (17:1–6).

The kings of Judah faced the same choice in the face of the growing Assyrian threat. King Ahaz offered to become both a "servant and vassal" to Tiglath-Pileser III, stripping both the royal and temple treasuries to compose a gift to sweeten his offer (2 Kings 16:7–8). Ahaz's efforts won the southern kingdom a reprieve from conquest but also came with a bitter price; Ahaz surrendered the religious autonomy of Judah and had to relinquish symbols of his political authority in deference to the king of Assyria (16:10–18). From Jerusalem Ahab's son and successor, Hezekiah, watched the siege and fall of Samaria together with the deportation of its citizens, a process that began under Shalmaneser V and concluded under Sargon II (18:9–11). But he waited for the less stable moment in Assyrian politics marked by the change in leadership from Sargon II to Sennacherib to mount his own independence campaign. Sennacherib responded with a military campaign of his own that put dozens of Judah's fortified cities, including Jerusalem, in harm's way (2 Kings 18:13). Nevertheless, the good character and humble prayers of King Hezekiah were rewarded. Sennacherib exited the region,

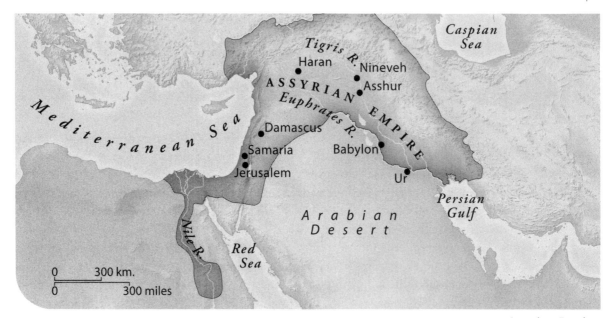

Assyrian Empire.

leaving Jerusalem intact and Judah's population untouched by exile (2 Kings 18–19).

The presence of Assyria played a very real role in the lives of ordinary people in Israel. When their kings elected to pay tribute to the Assyrian monarchs, household budgets were touched as the king's messengers came asking for more than the usual tax payment (2 Kings 15:20). It also meant that ordinary families would find their lives disrupted by the presence of occupying soldiers who put pressure on the locals to supply them with food and water. And given the Assyrian soldiers' reputation for cruelty, the pain of occupation was likely more than just economic. The alternative path was even more threatening. If the king withheld payment, the people of the land faced the very real risk of deportation, an Assyrian policy that began with Tiglath-Pileser III and continued with his successors.

Given all the above, Assyria was not just an empire; it became a symbol for the biblical authors. First, Assyria was a symbol of God's anger at the high treason of his people, treason associated with their excursions into the worship of other gods. The Lord fostered the growth of Assyria on the stage of history so that this nation might become the rod of his anger and the club of his wrath directed at the rebellion of his people in the Promised Land (Isa. 10:5). When the kings of God's people sought alliance with Assyria rather than answering the call to repent (Hos. 5:13; 7:11), Assyria delivered the divine response (2 Kings 17:7–23). Second, Assyria joined Egypt as a symbol of what a nation might face when its national pride blocked the door of divine intentions. Hezekiah urged his people to trust in the Lord even as the Assyrian king threatened Jerusalem, "for there is a greater power with us than with him" (2 Chron. 32:7–8). The entire book of Nahum delivers that message, illustrating how the Lord would sweep the powerful empire of Assyria from the stage of history.

B

Babylon

In the Old Testament, Babylon may either refer to the great empire that formed in the southeastern segment of the Fertile Crescent or to the capital city of that empire. In many cases, the two merge into one, representing the intrusive force that made its presence felt in Israel, a force that disrupted the lives of God's people both physically and spiritually.

The heartland of the Babylonian Empire lies within modern Iraq, just south of Baghdad where the Tigris and Euphrates rivers enclose an alluvial plain. For a time the throne of the early Neo-Babylonian kingdom bounced back and forth between Assyrian and Chaldean monarchs. Then Nebuchadnezzar II (604–562 BC) seized that throne and established an enduring Babylonian Empire. Like the Egyptian and Assyrian rulers that preceded him, Nebuchadnezzar had a vital interest in controlling the Promised Land because of the strategic and economic benefits it promised.

With significant victories over Assyria and Egypt in his wake, Nebuchadnezzar invaded the land the Lord had set aside for his people in the fourth year of King Jehoiakim (Jer. 46:2). At first this king of Judah yielded to Babylon. But within three years Jehoiakim rebelled, perhaps finding hope in Egypt's recent success against Babylon and hoping that Egypt would rally to Judah's side should it join the resistance movement (2 Kings 24:1). But when the king of Babylon came to address the matter, Egypt stayed home (24:7). The very month that the king of Babylon was to arrive in Jerusalem, Jehoiakim died, leaving his son of a similar-sounding name, Jehoiakin, to face the brunt of the attack.

The Babylonian siege of Jerusalem lasted about as long as King Jehoiakin ruled, three months. In the end the city surrendered to the attack. The treasury of the palace and temple was emptied. The royal family, military leaders, craftsmen, and artisans were deported from the land with the exception of one royal family member, Zedekiah, who was assigned to govern the newly humbled Judah under the oversight of Babylon (2 Kings 24:10–17).

Rather than settle into this new arrangement, Zedekiah invited the kings of Edom, Moab, Ammon, Tyre, and Sidon for a war council (Jer. 27:3). But their ill-conceived rebellion enraged Babylon all the more. By Zedekiah's ninth year, Jerusalem was again under siege (2 Kings 25:1). The walls of the city were compromised as the food within the walls was running out. Then Babylon repaid rebellion with rampant destruction and looting. They set fire to the temple, royal palace, and homes of the city. They deported thousands more to Babylon, leaving only the poorest people in Judah. They blinded the king, took the high priest captive, and confiscated all the items required for worship at the temple (2 Kings 25:9–21).

So what did Babylon signify for God's people? First, it signified profound disruption of their personal lives and robbed their hope. Every invasion,

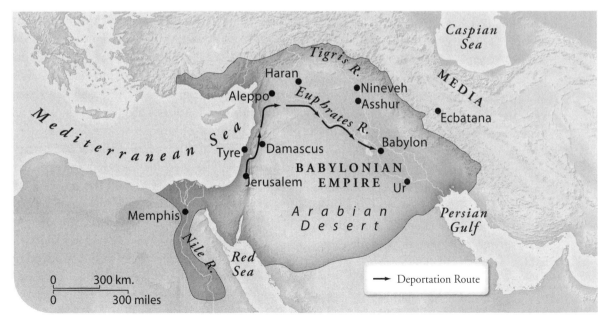

Babylonian Empire.

conquest, and occupation brought hardship. As uncertain as daily life can be under normal conditions, it becomes even more uncertain when faced with repeated invasions. What is more, the loss of the king, high priest, and temple marks the low point in the history of the Old Testament. With hope all but lost, it is no wonder the inspired poet lamented, "By the rivers of Babylon we sat and wept when we remembered Zion" (Ps. 137:1). This became such a powerful milestone in the history of God's people that it became a time marker that appears in the genealogy of Jesus (Matt. 1:11, 12, 17).

In addition to all the personal pain that Babylon brought to God's people, their presence was a reminder that they had brought all this pain upon themselves. The Lord had sent this misfortune into their lives because they and their leaders had failed to be the people God had called them to be (2 Kings 24:3 – 4, 20). They had failed to heed the early warning of the prophets and now added the pain of guilt to the pain of misfortune (2 Chron. 36:15 – 19; Jer. 20:4 – 5; 25:8 – 11). Thus Babylon also symbolized the Israelites' failing as God's people.

The Lord, of course, remained in control. And when Babylon's pride pushed this empire to overstep its divine mission, God decreed that this empire would fall (Isa. 13:19; 14:22; Jer. 25:12). Even while Babylon was riding high, various events preserved in Daniel compare and contrast Daniel with the great King Nebuchadnezzar and the court of Babylon. In every area, whether it be diet, wisdom, or worship, Daniel and his colleagues thrived while the king and his court suffered indignities (Dan. 1 – 4).

Given both the power and frailty of Babylon, it is no wonder that the inspired writers of the New Testament saw Babylon as a symbol for Rome. That is the most likely explanation for the peculiar language that closes Peter's letter to believers in Asia Minor, as he sends his greetings from "Babylon" (1 Peter 5:13). The extraordinary revelation received by John also makes reference to Babylon six times (Rev. 14:8; 16:19; 17:5; 18:2, 10, 21). In each case, the reference is a reference to Rome, the powers that are opposed to the coming of God's kingdom, or both.

Barley. *See* Grain.

Barn

The function of a barn in the Bible is much closer to the function of a modern silo than that of a modern barn. It is not a place to keep one's animals but chiefly a place in which to store grain. The physical appearance of such a barn is not provided for us in the Bible, but archaeology in Egypt and Israel has produced examples that allow us to see what a barn looked like. These grain storage units began as round pits lined with fieldstones or brick. Brick superstructures might then be built over the top of these underground pits, rising above ground level to form conical domes that covered the granaries. The size of such a barn depended on the size of the population using it. Some barns, like the one discovered at Megiddo, were over thirty-five feet in diameter and twenty feet deep. The Megiddo barn was so large that stairs were constructed around the perimeter of this underground silo so that one could simply walk to the level of the grain as the stored grain was consumed. In contrast Tel el-Hesi contains examples of granaries that were considerably smaller, only a bit over six feet wide and six feet deep. No matter what the size, the goal of the barn was the same — to protect the harvested crop against loss to moisture or animals.

The best way to appreciate the importance of such a barn is to appreciate the importance of grain in the ancient diet as well as the risks associated with the harvest itself. Wheat was a staple in the diet during Bible times. It provided a significant portion of the protein and calories that were consumed on any day. Consequently, the risk of drought and foreign invasion required the residents of this land to design a grain-consumption strategy. Given the uncertainty of future harvests, one always ate the grain that was harvested the previous year, while the grain harvested during the current growing season was stored away

The public "barn," a grain-storage silo at Megiddo.

as a buffer against future crop loss. This reality reveals how critical the grain storage barns were to the people of Bible times.

The barn appears in the symbolic language of both the Old and New Testaments; full barns are contrasted with empty barns. The invasion of enemy soldiers could cause barns to be emptied; consequently, the king prayed for deliverance from those enemies so that "our barns will be filled with every kind of provision" (Ps. 144:13). Full barns are also linked with the obedience of God's people. Once he laid out the directives of Deuteronomy, Moses conditioned a successful harvest on covenant faithfulness: "The LORD will send a blessing on your barns and on everything you put your hand to" (Deut. 28:8). Simi-larly, the giving of firstfruits, which might at first appear to compromise the status of the harvest, would instead produce barns filled to overflow-ing (Prov. 3:10). In contrast an empty barn sum-moned one to reflection. When those returning from the Babylonian captivity gave their first attention to rebuilding their own homes rather than the temple, the Lord expressed his displeasure by allowing a drought to strike the region (Hag. 1:7 – 11). Haggai called attention to the misplaced priori-ties of God's people with this rhetorical question: "Is there yet any seed left in the barn?" (2:19).

In the New Testament, the image of the barn is associated with the final judgment. When Pharisees and Sadducees approached John the Baptist, seeking baptism for themselves, John unleashed a powerful call to repentance, a call that clearly laid bare the consequences of the coming judgment. One would either be gathered like wheat into the barn or burned up like chaff (Matt. 3:12). Exactly the same image appears just ten chapters later in Matthew as Jesus tells the parable of the weeds, which, too, is designed to teach about the final judgment. In this par-able the servants are told to allow the wheat and the weeds to grow together until the harvest. At that time the weeds will be tied in bundles and burned while the wheat will be brought into the barn (13:30). In both cases the image of the grain being stored securely in barns presents the comforting picture of God's children safely preserved with him for eternity.

The image of the barn also appears in back-to-back discourses in Luke 12 that address the twin topics of wealth and worry. The first encounter with a barn in this chapter is found in the parable of the rich fool. Here we meet a wealthy man whose fields produced a bumper crop, so much in fact he would have to replace his older storage silos with new ones (Luke 12:18). Full barns in the Old Testament typically symbolize godly attitudes and actions, but not so here. The blessing of the full barn is used to illustrate this man's shortsightedness. His barns were a symbol of his misplaced priorities. He had built barns rather than building a relationship

Woman weaving coiled reed baskets.
Library of Congress, LC-matpc-04633/www.LifeintheHolyLand.com

with his God; true wealth is defined by the latter rather than by the former. The fact of the matter is that security may well be found in having no barns! That part of the lesson comes quickly as we move to Jesus' discourse on worry, which immediately follows the parable of the rich fool.

The rich man had failed to be concerned about his relationship with God. But if we have taken care of that dimension of our life, we can live like the birds: "Consider the ravens: They do not sow or reap, they have no storeroom or barn; yet God feeds them" (Luke 12:24).

Basket

The basket was among the most common and most versatile items in the home, a reality underscored by the fact that no less than ten different Hebrew and Greek words have been translated "basket" in the English versions of our Bible. The ubiquitous basket of the Bible world was made from straight strips of flexible organic material. The crafters of these baskets employed palm fronds, reeds, grasses, and leather as the base building materials. Two techniques were used for fabricating baskets. In the first, straight lengths of the base material were wrapped together with a thread and then coiled around one another in concentric circles to form the base and walls of the basket. This wrapping method produced small round- or oval-shaped baskets. The other technique required the base material to be woven horizontally around vertical components like the wicker baskets of today. This technique was used to produce larger square-shaped baskets.

The size of a basket and the additions to it were driven by application. Some baskets resembled a large plate. Such a basket could be used to carry bread on one's head (Gen. 40:16–18) or used to hold the bread associated with the ritual of ordaining the Israelite clergy (Ex. 29:23, 32; Lev. 8:2, 26, 31). Other baskets used around the home were shaped like small bowls. It was unthinkable to put such a basket over an oil lamp, but the possibility is raised in Jesus' illustration on faith (Matt. 5:15; Mark 4:21; NIV "bowl"). And then there were the much larger and deeper baskets fashioned with handles and/or covers that were used to carry harvested grain, produce, or heavy building materials like bricks (Ps. 81:6; Jer. 24:1, 2; Amos 8:1, 2).

These various types of baskets that dominated daily living also rose to become symbols of something more under the hand of the inspired authors. For example, a basket could be the indicator of a fresh and promising start. The mother of Moses, fearing for her son's life, decided to hide him among the reeds of the river in a basket (Ex. 2:3). The Israelites had seen more than enough baskets, because Egyptian overlords had forced them to carry bricks in baskets (Ps. 81:6). But in Exodus 2 we find a very unusual word for basket. It is exactly the same Hebrew word used throughout Genesis 6–9 for the massive ark that brought Noah and his family safely through the deluge, a very special "basket" that meant that the world would get a fresh start. In that light the basket (ark) in which the child Moses floated symbolized not harsh labor but the hope of a new and promising start under Moses' leadership.

The very large baskets used to gather grain and fruit became a symbol for the agricultural harvest. Such a harvest in the Promised Land was connected to divine provision, which in turn was linked to the obedience of God's people to the Law. As Moses announced the blessings that would accompany obedience to the Law and curses that would attend disobedience, the harvest basket is center stage as a representative of the harvest. Obey and your basket will be blessed; rebel and your basket will be cursed (Deut. 28:5, 17).

But the most striking symbolism associated with baskets may be the one that is introduced through the two miraculous feedings in the Gospels. There are many similarities between the feeding of the five thousand and the feeding of the four thousand (Matt. 14:13–21; Mark 6:30–44; Luke 9:10–17; John 6:1–15). Not least of these similarities is the fact that multiple baskets of food were collected after everyone had eaten their fill. But the enduring lesson is found in the differences. Jesus urged the disciples to look at the different kinds of baskets used to collect the food and the different number of baskets collected (Matt. 16:9–10; Mark 8:19–21). After the feeding of the five thousand Jews, the disciples collected twelve baskets (*kophivous*) of leftover food, a number associated with Judaism (Gen. 49:28; et al.). In contrast the feeding of the four thousand Gentiles ended with the collection of seven baskets (*spyridas*), a number associated with the Gentiles (Deut. 7:1; Acts 13:19). The point Jesus made is clear. Both Jews and Gentiles were welcome in the kingdom he had come to establish. But from this time on, the two words for baskets also have a link to two different ethnic groups, *kophivous* with Jews and *spyridas* with Gentiles.

This distinction may well play a role in our understanding of Acts 9:25. The recently converted Paul was preaching aggressively in the synagogues of Damascus. Certain Jews opposed to his teaching formed a conspiracy and pursued a plan to have him executed, so his closest followers lowered him in a basket through an opening in the wall. Recounting this moment in 2 Corinthians, Paul uses a Greek word used only here in the New Testament to call to mind a large rope basket (11:33). But in Acts, Paul's escape is said to be via *spyridi*, the same kind of basket associated with the Gentiles in the gospel accounts noted above. Perhaps the author of Acts selected this word because it associated this moment in Paul's life with the new direction his life was taking. He would take the good news of Jesus to the Gentiles.

Bear

When we meet a bear face-to-face, it typically is a meeting safeguarded by barriers. Not so for the residents of the Bible's world who would have had unprotected encounters with bears while traveling or working in the countryside. The bear of the Bible is likely the Syrian brown bear, which has a dull yellow coat. The diet of this omnivore included plants, insects, and carrion, which multiplied the bulk of the bear to a final weight nearing or exceeding five hundred pounds. Although the last sighting of a Syrian brown bear in Israel was in the mid-1900s, we know that a healthy population of them was native to all of western Asia including the Promised Land during the biblical period.

Travelers and shepherds walking the back-country paths of Palestine were destined to wander through the woods and rocky ridges that were the primary habitat of bears. And although these bears generally preferred to flee rather than fight with humans, hunger and fear could compel their contact with mortals and their livestock. If encountered, a bear might charge to bluff and scare off the intruder. But if this charge was not a ruse, it could become deadly, ending with the sudden sweep of a powerful paw. Escaping a charging bear was nearly impossible, because these bears were capable of charging with speeds nearing thirty-five miles per hour. Of all the bears that might be encountered, people living in Bible times knew that sows were particularly dangerous when their cubs were with them. The unpredictable nature of the bear became even more unpredictable under such circumstances. We can put such encounters into perspective when we consider that the most likely explanation for a bloodstained garment found in the open country was that an unfortunate person had been waylaid by a wild animal (Gen. 37:33).

A Syrian brown bear.
© Christian Riedel/www.istockphoto.com

Because the bear was part of the natural history of the biblical world, it and its qualities make an appearance on the pages of our Bible. The bear was a symbol of strength and military proficiency. In addressing Saul's reservations about his abilities to fight Goliath, David told Saul of his encounters with bears. After a bear had taken an animal from his flock, David pursued the bear, struck it, and killed it. The Lord's presence would allow him to do the same to the Philistine giant (1 Sam. 17:34–37). Later in his life, David was compared to a bear. When Absalom had driven his father from the throne in Jerusalem, he was faced with a decision; Absalom could pursue David immediately or wait. Hushai advised Absalom to wait for David and his men to cool down a bit because they were "as fierce as a wild bear robbed of her cubs" (2 Sam. 17:8). The same image of military proficiency lies behind the image of the bear in the visions of Daniel and John (Dan. 7:5; Rev. 13:2).

The bear further became a symbol of divine judgment in the language of the prophets. Elisha urged the Israelites of his day to abandon their rebellion and return to the Lord. When he met a gang of youth who made fun both of him and the Lord, Elisha's curse brought two bears out of the woods who mauled forty-two of the youths (2 Kings 2:23–24). Hosea's diatribe against the rebellion of Israel anticipated divine judgment. Despite the care and concern the Lord had shown his people again and again, Israel had revolted (Hos. 13:5–6). Consequently, Hosea likened the Lord to a bear robbed of her cubs who was ready to attack and rip them open (13:8). Amos also included mention of a bear when describing the coming day of the Lord. For some, this will be an era of dark trouble: "It will be as though a man fled from a lion only to meet a bear" (Amos 5:19). Given that the bear is a less predictable aggressor than the lion, this metaphor speaks of life going from bad to worse. As the days that witnessed the disastrous fall of Jerusalem to the Babylonians were bemoaned in Lamentations, the inspired poet compared the heavy hand of the Lord's judgment to the experience of being waylaid by a bear, dragged from the path, mangled, and left without help (Lam. 3:10–11).

The book of Proverbs also finds bears among its verses. The fool characterized so many ways in this book is said to be more dangerous than a bear that has lost her cubs (Prov. 17:12). And subjects forced to live under the whims of a wicked ruler are said to be as helpless in their predicament as one who is facing the charge of a bear (28:15).

Finally, there is good news for those who are awaiting the coming of the Messiah and are eager for the age that will attend his coming. Isaiah proclaimed this as a time of unimaginable peace. His listeners knew all too well the risk that bears posed to their domestic livestock; so the following image was particularly meaningful for them. In the coming age, "The cow will feed with the bear, their young will lie down together" (Isa. 11:7).

Beard

Throughout most reaches of society today, a man's decision to wear a beard or mustache, or to shave every morning grows from a personal grooming choice. That was not the case in the biblical world. Particularly during Old Testament times the beard was the norm, and its absence sent an important social signal that things were not all they should or could be.

If the various art pieces from the ancient world accurately picture society as it was, men with beards were the norm among all the cultures associated with the Old Testament, whether Canaanite, Assyrian, Egyptian, or Babylonian. That does not change until we see the clean-shaven look worn in the Greek and Roman cultures. Yet in the Old Testament legislation, the beard receives special attention that suggests it played a unique role in defining God's chosen people. In Leviticus the Lord established a wide range of directives that were in part designed to separate Israel from the cultures around them (Lev. 19:2). And just a few verses away from God's call for Israel to be holy, we find this requirement: "Do not cut the hair at the sides of your head or clip off the edges of your beard" (19:27). This is joined a couple of chapters later with a reminder for the priests that this applied to them in particular (21:5); their beards could be trimmed but not cut (Ezek. 44:20). How are we to understand this call to be unique when having a beard was the norm in the ancient cultures in contact with Israel? Apparently there was some form of pagan ritual that required men of the ancient world to shave their beards. This law directed Israelite men to avoid any association with this pagan ritual, whether real or implied, by maintaining their beards.

Consequently, an Israelite man wearing a beard was sending the cultural message that life was fine as well as expressing his singular devotion to the Lord. Given these subtle but important messages, the beard appears to have played a role in the greeting ritual. Israelite men who were greeting one another might grasp the other's beard during the greeting process, a signal that Joab used to put Amasa at ease just before plunging a dagger into his belly (2 Sam. 20:9 – 10).

If a man appeared in public without a beard, this sent the signal that life had been disturbed in some way or had now settled into a more disturbing place. The message sent depended in part on whether one shaved his own beard or had it done to him. For example, a man might shave his own beard as part of the ritual cleansing ceremony following contraction of an infectious skin disease. Once a man was certified as healed by the priest, the man was to remove all the hair from his body, including his beard (Lev. 14:9). A man might also shave his own beard to signal that he was in a state of deep grief. Men from the defunct northern kingdom who were bringing offerings to the site of the defunct temple complex in Jerusalem expressed their grief over all that had happened by traveling toward Jerusalem with their beards shaved off (Jer. 41:5). Grief is likely in the mix during the enacted prophecy of Ezekiel in which he is directed to shave both his head and his beard (Ezek. 5:1). Isaiah and Jeremiah include a prophecy against Moab predicting that things would get so bad in their major cities that every beard would be cut off (Isa. 15:2; Jer. 48:37). And when the Israelites who had just returned from the imposed Babylonian exile began to return to the old ways of living that had landed them in trouble in the first place, Ezra "pulled hair from [his] head and beard" as a signal of his deep grief (Ezra 9:3).

In contrast, if one forcefully removed a man's beard, it was a way of degrading and humiliating the victim. David had developed a good political relationship with Nahash, king of Ammon. When this Ammonite leader passed away, David

Among the Israelites, wearing a full beard expressed one's singular devotion to the Lord.
© Paul Prescott/www.BigStockPhoto.com

sent a delegation to express his kingdom's sympathy to Hanun, the king's son. The nobles of Ammon convinced Hanun that David had another agenda; these men were sent to search out the weaknesses of the kingdom during this time of political transition. Consequently, the men in the Israelite delegation were seized and humiliated by shaving off half their garments and half their beards. Of course the clothing situation was easily rectified. But rather than having them shave off the remainder of their beards, David directed these men to wait in Jericho until their beards had grown back (2 Sam. 10:1 – 5). The same indignity was imposed on the Servant of the Lord. Isaiah describes the humble suffering of the Servant in many different ways, including this one: "I offered my back to those who beat me, my cheeks to those who pulled out my beard" (Isa. 50:6). Thus the presence of a man's beard signals that life is moving positively, while the absence of a beard urges us to look for the difficulty that has beset him.

Bed

The biblical authors make mention of a bed with some frequency as they speak to us from the pages of their books, but there is no single image that does justice to the wide array of bed designs this word can conjure. Beds varied in composition and appearance throughout Bible times and through the various socioeconomic strata of society. At base, a bed was a mat. This mat was composed of reeds, straw, or animal hide, which provided only a modicum of separation from the ground or floor as its owner pursued a good night's sleep. It could easily be folded up and carried from one encampment to the next, or it could be folded and stored on a shelf in the home, allowing the floor space it occupied to be

used for something else. For those whose budget would allow for more than a sleeping mat, a bed looked closer to what this word brings to mind today. This bed had a wood frame and a suspension made from woven rope or fabric that softened the sleeping surface by putting something flexible between the sleeper and hard floor. This may be the kind of bed that is mentioned in a list of furnishings that the well-to-do woman of Shunem wished to provide for Elisha (2 Kings 4:10). Even the most ornate beds owned by the wealthiest and most powerful members of society had wood frames. The metal bed of Og gets special mention in Deuteronomy because it was made of iron (Deut. 3:11). But the most well-developed beds went well beyond the basics. Such beds were designed with ivory inlay (Amos 6:4), covered with linens, perfumed (Prov. 7:16 – 17), and even

A woman weaving papyrus mats of reeds, the most common kind of bed of Bible times.

decorated with jeweled canopies (Judith 10:21).

As today, the bed was used most frequently for sleeping. But a variety of other conditions and activities are closely linked to the bed in the

Bible. We often meet those who are sick, injured, or stricken by paralysis while they are lying in a bed (Gen. 48:1–2; 2 Kings 1:1–4; Ps. 41:3). In the New Testament this is particularly true of those about to receive miraculous healing (Matt. 8:14; 9:2, 6; Luke 5:18, 19, 24; Acts 9:34; 28:8). Those who are dying or who have already died may be lying on a bed (Gen. 49:33; 1 Kings 1:47; 2 Kings 4:21). And depression over the disappointments in life may delay one's rising from bed for extended periods of time. When King Ahab was unable to persuade Naboth to sell his vineyard, this king of Israel sulked in his bed and refused to eat (1 Kings 21:4). The bed is further pictured as a private place in which to explore the great intimacies of life and of the mind. As today, the bed was the place of choice for making love. And in certain passages, going to bed or the bed itself becomes the equivalent of sexual intercourse (Gen. 49:4; 1 Chron. 5:1; Song 1:16; Heb. 13:4). Ezekiel extends this image, addressing foreign alliances as falling into the "bed of love" (Ezek. 23:17). Alternatively, the bed can be the place where serious, private reflection occurs (Ps. 4:4). This reflection can take a more ominous tone as the bed becomes the place for planning evil (Ps. 36:4; Mic. 2:1). Or such reflection can lead to disabling feelings of guilt that compel one to flood the bed with tears of remorse (Ps. 6:6). But the bed is also a place to reflect on the greater hope that comes from remembering the Lord (Ps. 63:6). And particularly in Daniel when a person goes to bed, we can expect that the Lord will use this opportunity to reveal a message, as he did to the Babylonian king (Dan. 2:28–30; 4:5–13) and to Daniel himself (7:1).

Certain expectations were associated with the bed. The bed was to be a place of comfort that offered respite from the trials of life, something that it did not do for Job (Job 7:13). And

once one took leave of life to lie down in bed, there was every expectation that one would not be disturbed even by the hospitality needs of a friend (Luke 11:7). Against this backdrop, it is unthinkable that one should face harm or death while sleeping in his or her own bed, so exceptions are strongly noted in the Bible (2 Sam. 4:11; 2 Chron. 24:25). This sends more than a subtle message about Saul who demanded, "Bring him [David] up to me in his bed so that I may kill him" (1 Sam. 19:15). And it clearly informs Jesus' statement regarding the end times: "I tell you, on that night two people will be in one bed; one will be taken and the other left" (Luke 17:34).

The biblical authors also use the bed as a symbol. In crusading for social justice among a people who had lost their affection for the Lord, Amos saw the extravagant bed inlaid with ivory as a symbol of those who had profoundly lost their way (Amos 6:4). The bed was also a symbol for home, the place where one's roots were (Ps. 139:8; Ezek. 32:25). And because pagan worship rites often had a sexual dimension, the bed was sometimes a symbol of illicit worship. Isaiah criticized God's people for their reckless worship of false gods by saying, "You have made your bed on a high and lofty hill; there you went up to offer your sacrifices. Behind your doors and your doorposts you have put your pagan symbols. Forsaking me, you uncovered your bed, you climbed into it and opened it wide" (Isa. 57:7–8).

Beersheba

Within every geographical region there are always places so well known by the locals that their location and character are instantly recognized. Within the land of the Bible, Beersheba is just such a place. It lies in the southern reaches of the Promised Land, south of Jerusalem and the

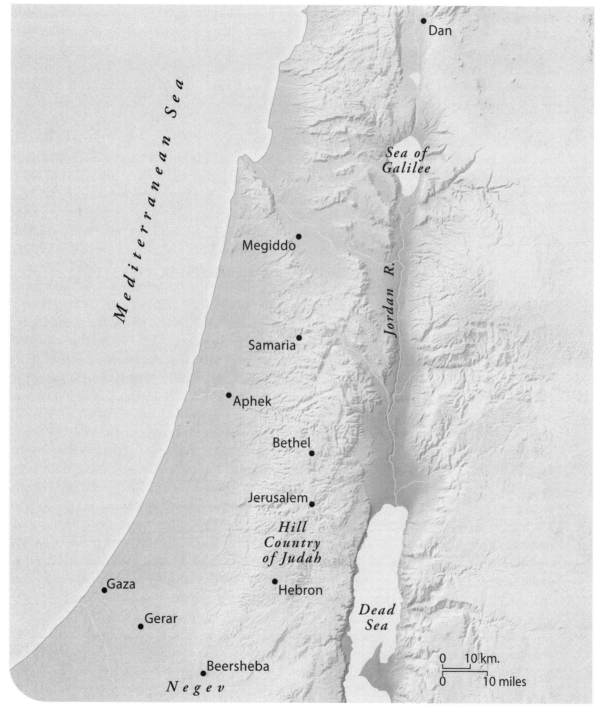

Beersheba.

well-populated Judean hill country but north of the desolate Wilderness of Zin. Beersheba resides in a wide basin that is surrounded by low, round hills. The soil in the basin has a yellow-brown cast to it that appears to offer little hope for growing field crops. But when the winter and spring rains arrive, they can quickly green the grain fields and pastures, and the runoff water cuts the basin into a maze of shallow gulches and ravines called wadis. Unfortunately, the amount of rain necessary to grow grain occurs only once every three to four years. More often than not, grain fields fail and wadis go dry. This leaves the local residents to dig for water, sinking wells into the dry streambeds. Wells like these and the water rights associated with them provide a name for this location (Gen. 21:31; 26:32–33), for in Hebrew *Beersheba* means "well of the seven" or "well of the oath."

The lack of seasonal rainfall dictated that the Negev region in general and Beersheba in particular would be characterized by the presence of shepherds and herdsmen. When the pastures were green, the families connected to Beersheba would remain in the basin. But as the summer season saw those pastures fade, they would be forced to do what we see the families of Abraham, Isaac, and Jacob do so often—move north where more substantial seasonal rainfall promised green pastures.

The earliest families of the Bible knew Beersheba as a living space, but in time this living space developed into a village and then a city. This change was propelled by two geographical realities. First, Beersheba lay at a very unique confluence of north-south and east-west roadways. Trade goods moving from Arabia to Gaza on the Mediterranean Sea would follow the travel-friendly topography that led them past Beersheba. But trade was not the only reason

Beersheba grew to become a respectable city during the days of the united kingdom. Beersheba joined with Arad in guarding the southern frontier of the Promised Land. These two fortified cities became the security gates that protected the routes that traveled north into the interior of the country. Thus Beersheba's population and city plan grew as it assumed the role of military outpost and administrative center. Although they did a poor job, Samuel's two sons served as judges in this city (1 Sam. 8:1–3).

The biblical authors most often use the name Beersheba in two settings. One is worship and the other is within a geographical merism. Beersheba was among the first locations closely linked to the promises that God made to Abraham's family and to the worship life of this family. Abraham "called upon the name of the Lord, the Eternal God" at Beersheba (Gen. 21:33). That same God appeared to Isaac in this location, confirming for him the importance of remaining in the Promised Land so that the promises made to this family might be fulfilled. In response, Isaac built an altar there and "called on the name of the Lord" (Gen. 26:25). And while en route to Egypt where he would find escape from the perils of famine as well as reunion with his son Joseph, Jacob offered sacrifices and heard the promises of God echo over this basin (Gen. 46:1–4). Given the close connection between worship of the one true God and Beersheba, it is ironic that during the time of the divided kingdom this city became a pagan worship site. Amos listed Beersheba along with the notorious sites of Samaria, Bethel, and Dan as places linked to Israelite apostasy. The Lord urged his people to come to him rather than going to Beersheba (Amos 5:5), and he warned of coming judgment against those who said, "As surely as the god of Beersheba lives" (8:14).

Perhaps the most common mention of

Beersheba is in the geographical merism found throughout the historical books of the Old Testament. A merism is a literary device by which two opposite extremes are named with the intention of communicating the whole. Beersheba appears frequently in the geographical merism "from Dan to Beersheba." By listing the northernmost and southernmost cities of the Promised Land, the writer is creatively calling our attention to the entire land. Thus "from Dan to Beersheba" is the equivalent of all the land of Israel. This merism surfaces in two contexts associated with the assembly or counting of men eligible for war. In Judges 20 the Israelites gather from Dan to Beersheba to address the wrong perpetrated by Benjamin (Judg. 20:1). And in a moment of weakness, David directs Joab to count all those eligible for military service between Dan and Beersheba (2 Sam. 24:2; 1 Chron. 21:2). Additionally, when the biblical authors wished to express the notion of kingdom unity at the time of Samuel, David, Absalom, Solomon, or Hezekiah, whether it was unity evident, being realized, or longed for, they used "from Dan to Beersheba" to mark the extent of that kingdom (1 Sam. 3:20; 2 Sam. 3:10; 17:11; 1 Kings 4:25; 2 Chron. 30:5).

Bethel

After Jerusalem, the most frequently mentioned city in the Bible is Bethel. It appears on the pages of the Old Testament more than seventy times, evoking both very positive and very negative connotations. Biblical Bethel is associated with the modern city of Beitin, which is located about twelve miles north of Jerusalem, astride the ancient Ridge Route and on the border between the tribal territories of Ephraim and Benjamin (Josh. 16:1–2; 18:13). Here rich soil,

ample rainfall, good wells, pastureland, and farm fields combine to meet the basic needs of life. Bethel was further blessed by virtue of its location near the important internal crossroads of the Promised Land. East-west traffic moved between the Jordan Valley and the coastal plain by taking advantage of the plateau that lay just south of Bethel, while travelers on the primary north-

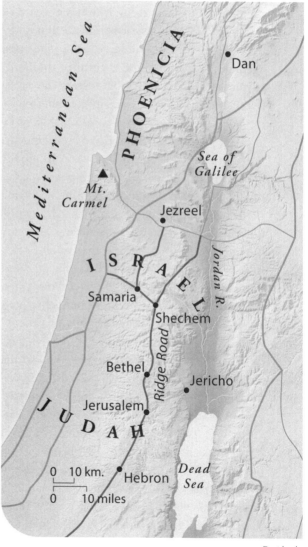

Bethel.

south roadway, the so-called Ridge Route, picked their way along the central ridge near Bethel (Judg. 21:19). These transportation arteries that cross near this city made it a natural stopping place for those traveling on business or pleasure. And after God appeared to Jacob in Bethel, it became a spiritual destination, a pilgrimage site, for those who wished to worship.

But of all the worship centers mentioned in the Bible, Bethel has the most uneven record of orthodoxy. In the earliest periods of Bible history, Bethel was a premier worship site used again and again by those faithful to the Lord. In the later periods of Bible history, however, Bethel became a pagan worship site abhorred by the prophets and consigned to ruin in the wake of divine judgment. Abraham had built a memorial altar here (Gen. 12:8), but it was Jacob, his grandson, whose experiences really put this sanctuary on the map. The location of Bethel astride the Ridge Route makes it likely that Jacob visited this location many times during his years of seasonal migration behind the family flocks. But none of those earlier visits had fully prepared him for what happened on the fateful day when he arrived near Luz, running from his brother's anger and fatigued by his flight. As exhaustion mingled with worry over his future, Jacob collapsed into a deep slumber. Here he had his famous dream with a stairway that led heavenward into the presence of the Lord, who quieted his fears and gave direction to his future (Gen. 28:10 – 15). When Jacob awakened, he said, "How awesome is this place! This is none other than the house of God; this is the gate of heaven" (v. 17). In that spirit Luz was given a new name, Bethel, Hebrew for "house of God" (v. 19). From this time until the days of Solomon, wholesome connotations are overwhelmingly linked with Bethel. Deborah offered guidance from the base

of a palm tree near Bethel (Judg. 4:5). All Israel gathered here before the ark of the covenant to worship and seek God's guidance during a time of national crisis (Judg. 20:26 – 27; 21:2). And Samuel put Bethel on the list of cities he visited on a regular basis (1 Sam. 7:16). Thus Bethel was a place where God revealed his promises, a place of altars and memorial stones, a place for worship, and a place for seeking divine guidance. Prior to Samuel's day, the only time we find Bethel mentioned in a negative light is in the book of Joshua where this city is among those who resisted the entry of God's people into the Promised Land only to join the list of those defeated (Josh. 12:16).

But these positive connotations take a dark and terrible turn shortly after the death of Solomon. When the united kingdom ruled by Solomon split in two, Jeroboam became king of the northern portion of that formerly unified kingdom. Of course, the temple designed by the Lord himself remained in the south at Jerusalem. Jeroboam was concerned that if the citizens of his new kingdom traveled to that old place of worship, they would be inclined toward reunification under Solomon's son. Consequently, he designed two border sanctuaries of his own, one at Bethel and the other at Dan, fully stocked with his own chosen priests who were ready to teach people how to worship before the golden calves, the symbol of his new nation's national religion (1 Kings 12:28 – 33). For almost anyone living in the new northern kingdom, a trip to Jerusalem would have meant a longer journey and one that would have brought the traveler right past this worship site at Bethel. Clearly the site of Jeroboam's national shrine was strategically placed as well as carefully designed.

From this time on, the biblical authors portray Bethel with increasingly negative language. Soon after its construction, the Lord sent a prophet from Judah to speak words of judgment over the altar at Bethel. The bones of the priests of the high places who made offerings on the altar would be burned on it, and the altar itself would be split apart (1 Kings 13:1–3). But before these events took place in the days of Josiah (2 Kings 23:15–16), the altar at Bethel stood as a symbol of apostasy. The prophets associated Bethel with shame (Jer. 48:13), with wickedness (Hos. 10:15), and with unrestrained sin (Amos 4:4). That is why Bethel was a place that would meet God's fiery judgment (Amos 5:6). And so the Bible presents Bethel as a tale of two cities. It can be a place for true worship or a place of false worship, a city blessed or a city cursed, a place for finding divine direction or a place for meeting divine judgment.

Bethlehem

The mention of Bethlehem quickly calls to mind the cluster of New Testament stories that surround the birth of Jesus. We think of Mary and Joseph desperately searching for a suitable place to stay, of the shepherds in nearby fields, and of the murderous plans of King Herod. But Bethlehem has a long and deep relationship with the stories of the Old Testament as well. It is in those Old Testament stories that Bethlehem becomes a place associated with solutions.

The village of Bethlehem is located on the central ridge of the Judean hill country, 2,300 feet above sea level, just five miles south-southwest of Jerusalem. Its distinctive geography makes it an important player in the defense of Jerusalem. The Judean hill country is distinguished by its high mountain ridges that combine with narrow V-shaped valleys that discouraged invasion of the interior in general and of Jerusalem in particular. To approach Jerusalem from the south

meant use of the Ridge Route. Any diversion east or west from this route was a step in the direction of more difficult terrain. Bethlehem, therefore, made an important contribution to national security, for it stands on that road as a sentinel between Jerusalem and Hebron. That is why Rehoboam included it among the locations that he fortified when he set about shoring up the security of Jerusalem (2 Chron. 11:6).

But while easing the job of the soldier, eroded ridges and narrow valleys of the Judean hill country made life much more difficult for the farmer. The farmers near Bethlehem were forced to create their own acreage by building terraces on the hillsides, investing valuable time and energy in making farmland. Against such agricultural limitations, we can come to appreciate the value of the wide valleys that stretch out near Bethlehem, valleys that are atypical of the terrain we normally find in the hill country of Judea. Here the landscape opens into basins that combine with plentiful rainfall and rich soil to produce a substantial grain harvest. At least a portion of that wheat became the famous Bethlehem bread after which the village is named. In Hebrew the word *Bethlehem* means "house of bread."

The first contacts we have with Bethlehem in the books of the Old Testament are sad and disturbing. It was just outside Ephrath (Bethlehem) that tragedy struck the family of Jacob. His beloved wife Rachel was in the process of giving birth when complications set in and death took her from her husband's loving arms. Jacob buried her just outside of Bethlehem (Gen. 48:7). In Judges Bethlehem is mentioned numerous times in the closing chapters that describe Israelite society run amuck (Judg. 17–19).

But after the time of the judges, a new connotation is linked to Bethlehem; this village becomes a place where solutions are found. It all starts

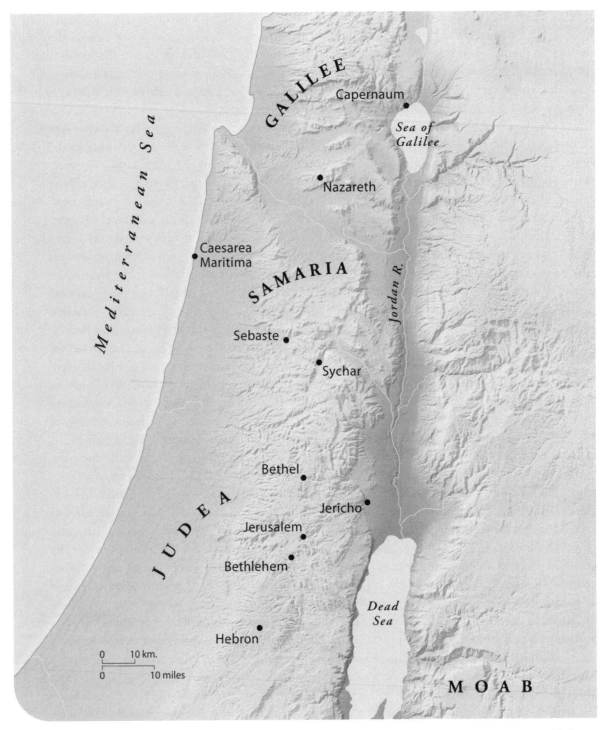

Bethlehem.

with the book of Ruth where we are introduced to Naomi, a woman whose life was in the process of going from bad to worse. Naomi, her husband, and their sons were living in what should have been grain-rich Bethlehem, when a severe famine struck the region, compromising Bethlehem's harvest and forcing Naomi and her family to migrate to Moab. While displaced from their home village, Naomi's family made the best of it, even finding wives for their sons. But within ten years, tragedy struck again as Naomi's husband and her two sons died. Grief-stricken and robbed of economic security, Naomi and her daughter-in-law Ruth returned to Bethlehem. With the famine at an end and the barley harvest in process, Bethlehem was buzzing with optimism, but it did not rub off on Naomi. She asked to be called Mara (Heb., "bitter") rather than Naomi (Heb., "pleasant"), for the Lord had made her life bitter with misfortune (Ruth 1:20–21). Her life was in need of solutions—solutions that would flow from the agricultural fields and threshing floors of Bethlehem. Here the Lord provided food for this impoverished family, a husband for Ruth, and a grandchild for Naomi. Combined, these changes restored family life and financial security to Naomi (Ruth 4:13–16).

However, Bethlehem had only started to deliver. During the darker days of King Saul, Israel needed new and effective leadership. A descendant of Naomi from Bethlehem would provide the solution (Ruth 4:17). The Lord sent Samuel to Bethlehem where he anointed David as Israel's new king (1 Sam. 16:1–13). And when the Philistines had taken over a critical access route to the interior of the kingdom, it was David who came from Bethlehem to defeat Goliath and restore security to Israel's western frontier (1 Sam. 17:12–54). This king from Bethlehem provided solutions for a flagging nation.

But the world faced even bigger problems than those that surfaced in the days of Ruth and David: it needed rescuing from the ruin of sin. And here Bethlehem again provides the solution. Micah announces that this Savior will be born in Bethlehem (Mic. 5:2). And the gospel writers join in turning our eyes to Bethlehem to see this solution arise in the birth of Jesus (Matt. 2:1, 5, 6, 8; Luke 2:4, 15; John 7:42). Thus Bethlehem lives in our Bible not just as a noteworthy agricultural village and military strongpoint, but as a place that provides solutions.

Boat (Ship)

Throughout its ancient history, Israel had never been known for its maritime prowess; it always paled in comparison to Phoenicia, its neighbor to the north whose domain was the high seas (Ezek. 27:4). Nevertheless, boats and ships find a place in the literature of God's people. Generally speaking, the Bible is aware of two types of watercraft, the larger ship and the smaller boat. Ancient examples of seaworthy ships include those ranging in size from forty to one hundred feet in length. With a few noted exceptions (Job 9:26; Isa. 18:1–2), the ships of the Bible were made of wooden planks, bent and shaped to form a shell into which wooden ribs were placed. Such a ship was powered and guided by oar, sail, and rudder. The large ships functioned in two ways. Some were designed for speed and making the nimble turns required in a naval battle (Isa. 33:21; Dan. 11:30, 40), while others were designed as cargo-friendly merchant ships (Prov. 31:14). A special class of the latter seems to be the Tarshish ship, which may have been used for transporting metals (Isa. 60:9; Jer. 10:9; Ezek. 27:12). These larger merchant ships also accommodated some paying passengers. For example, Jonah paid fare aboard a Tarshish ship (Jonah 1:3), and Paul booked passage on merchant ships during his long trips (Acts 20:13, 38; et al.). Paul's account of his experiences aboard an Alexandrian grain ship bound for Rome provides one of the most detailed and dramatic accounts of a shipwreck that we have from the ancient world (Acts 27).

The Bible also speaks of much smaller boats that ride the waves of inland lakes. Artwork from the biblical period, as well as the more recent discovery of the Ginosar boat buried in the mud of the Sea of Galilee, helps us develop a more accurate picture of such a boat. Made of wood, it was about twenty-seven feet in length and guided and directed by sail, oar, and rudder. This vessel was intimately linked to the fishing industry on the Sea of Galilee. Peter, Andrew, James, and John made their living on such a boat prior to their call to become Jesus' disciples (Matt. 4:18–22; Mark 1:16–20; Luke 5:2–11; John 1:35–42). This is also the kind of boat Jesus commandeered from time to time when he wished to escape the pressing crowds while moving from one segment of the lakeshore to another (Matt. 9:1; 14:13; 15:39; Mark 5:21; 6:32). And it is the kind of boat he used as a speaking platform when addressing large groups of people who had gathered on the amphitheater-like hillsides of the Sea of Galilee (Matt. 13:2; Mark 4:1).

The biblical authors sometimes used boats as symbols. For example, they used seagoing merchant ships as a symbol of wealth. That is

A model of a Canaanite merchant ship.

Z. Radovan/www.BibleLandPictures.com

the message behind Jacob's peculiar blessing of Zebulun, a tribe that would become a "haven for ships" (Gen. 49:13). The landlocked Zebulun would have no harbor of its own to host such ships but was close enough to the sea to benefit from maritime economy. Wealth is also the subtext in view when the trading fleet of King Solomon is described (1 Kings 9:26 – 28; 10:11, 22; 2 Chron. 9:21). As trading ships produce wealth, so wealth can produce arrogance; and when the Lord announces his judgment against the arrogant, he says that their ships that foster that arrogance will be destroyed (Isa. 2:12 – 17; Ezek. 27:1 – 9, 25 – 27).

The military advantage of a strong navy was owned by a number of nations in the ancient world, so the ship also became a symbol of warfare. In Balaam's final oracle, the enduring survival of Israel is contrasted with those who face the attack of the "ships … of Kittim" (Num. 24:24). Under God's hand, Jerusalem could enjoy security, which is artfully described as a place against which no galley or mighty ship will sail (Isa. 33:21); and even though Jerusalem is described as a warship unprepared to fight, it will still find success when God grants his protection (Isa. 33:23 – 24).

When the ire of God is kindled, however, his fierce anger can strike out as a literal or metaphorical storm against a ship. Like Solomon, King Jehoshaphat built a trading fleet to service his kingdom. God was angered by the alliance this king had made with King Ahaziah of Israel, and he let his anger be known by destroying the trading fleet that was the product of the alliance (2 Chron. 20:35 – 37). This experience may have given birth to the poetic extension of this event used to describe the fate of those who oppose the Lord and the establishment of his kingdom: "You destroyed them like ships of Tarshish shattered by an east wind" (Ps. 48:7). In the first

chapter of Jonah, this unwilling prophet finds his escape from his assigned mission thwarted by a divine storm. In contrast it is a sign of God's favor and an occasion for giving thanks when ships on the sea are blessed with survival during a terrible tempest. Then those on board can say, "He stilled the storm to a whisper; the waves of the sea were hushed" (Ps. 107:29).

Jesus' disciples knew about this kind of relief. On more than one occasion, they found themselves in a storm-battered boat. Given the connection between divine anger and such a storm, the disciples may well have concluded that their intended trip to the Gentile side of the lake, "the other side," lacked divine approval. But when Jesus stilled the storm to a whisper, it was occasion for them to give thanks and to know that the God who they thought was directing judgment against them was actually in the boat with them (Matt. 8:23 – 27; Mark 4:35 – 41; Luke 8:22 – 25).

Bread

To think of bread in the Bible's world was to think of food, a truth strongly underscored by the fact that the Hebrew word for "bread" (*lekhem*) doubles as the Hebrew word for food. That is because bread was the primary source of carbohydrates and protein for the people we meet in the Bible. It was consumed on a daily basis and in connection with every meal, whether the consumers were traveling or at home. If one was not eating a full course of daily bread, it was a sign that the pain of life and deep sighing had replaced eating (Job 3:24) or that subjugation had replaced freedom (Jer. 38:9).

Bread was made from flour that originated in the wheat or barley fields via a process that was part of the daily routine in Bible times. The flour was mixed with water, salt, and oil. The mixture was kneaded and formed by hand into flat or round loaves that were set aside to rise if yeast was added. Heat was applied to bake the bread in one of several ways. The bread might be made by making a fire on top of a flat stone. When the stone was fully heated, the coals and ashes were removed and the bread was placed on the stone to bake. Alternatively it might be made on a clay griddle, using a metal pan, or in an enclosed oven (Lev. 2:4 – 10). The end product varied in quality based on whether course or fine flour was used (Gen. 18:6; Lev. 2:1, 14 – 16) and whether the more desirable wheat or less desirable barley was the base grain (cf. 1 Kings 4:22; Judg. 7:13).

Social expectation and religious practice among God's people had an important connection to bread. When guests arrived at one's dwelling, social norms dictated that the host or hostess immediately provide the guests with bread (Gen. 14:18; 18:5 – 6; Luke 11:5 – 6). Such sharing of bread was an indication that a peaceful and trusting relationship had been formed. It was unthinkable that a person with whom bread was shared would turn against the giver (Ps. 41:9; Obad. 7). The irony between Jesus' offering Judas bread and Judas's subsequent act of betrayal should not be missed in the gospel account (John 13:18, 26 – 27).

And as Jesus reclaimed the disciples from fishing following his resurrection, we can appreciate the important message Jesus was sending when he had baked bread awaiting them on shore (John 21:9).

Various religious festivals and meals in both the Old and New Testaments employed bread. During Passover week, God's people were to remember the great deliverance from Egypt by eating bread baked without yeast (Ex. 12:17 – 20; Lev. 23:6; Deut. 16:3). Grain offerings brought to the Lord on various occasions could be presented in the form of baked bread as long as it was made with fine flour and contained no yeast (Lev. 2:4 – 13). And twelve loaves of bread were constantly to be found on a small table in the Lord's sanctuary, one loaf representing each tribe residing in the Lord's presence (Ex. 25:30; Lev. 24:5 – 8). In the New Testament as Jesus was bringing his earthly ministry to a close, he directed his disciples to prepare the Passover meal. The required bread that was on the table that night was redeployed in the New Testament meal that continues to be celebrated with bread today, the Lord's Supper (Mark 14:22; Luke 22:19).

The rhetorical role of bread in the Bible is found in both miracles and metaphors. Typically bread found its way to the dinner table via the grain fields; however, at times this staple was

A woman baking flatbread in the traditional way, on the bottom of a hot metal pan.
Z. Radovan/www.BibleLandPictures.com

provided in a miraculous way. In such instances, we are bound to search for the lesson in the miraculous provision of bread. While Israel was in the wilderness, a location unconducive to the growing of grain, the Lord said, "I will rain down bread from heaven for you" (Ex. 16:4). He did just that for decades in the form of manna. In this way he solicited Israel's trust and taught them that "man does not live on bread alone but on every word that comes from the mouth of the LORD" (Deut. 8:3). Jesus quoted this passage when Satan tempted him to provide miraculous bread for himself in the wilderness (Matt. 4:4). In a lesser-known account, Elisha multiplied twenty loaves of barley to miraculously serve a hundred men (2 Kings 4:42–44). This multiplication miracle affirmed that the message Elisha delivered had its origins with the Lord. And when Jesus multiplied bread in the feedings of the four thousand and the five thousand, he demonstrated not only his prophetic link to Moses and Elisha but also his divine heritage (Matt. 14:17–19; 15:33–34).

The common appearance of bread on the family table was also tapped as a metaphor in the Bible. As a staple food, bread was always around. In that light, the formula "bread of …" is employed to speak of qualities or conditions that persisted or that were characteristic of a person's situation. Examples include bread of tears (Ps. 80:5), bread of wickedness (Prov. 4:17), bread of idleness (Prov. 31:27), bread of adversity (Isa. 30:20), and bread of sincerity and truth (1 Cor. 5:8). As Jesus taught his followers how to compose a prayer, he used short petitions that nevertheless encompass a wide range of human needs. "Give us today our daily bread" (Matt. 6:11; cf. Luke 11:3) uses bread as a metaphor that requests God's assistance in providing all the basics needed for living. And finally, Jesus likens himself to bread

in the extended discourse of John 6. Like the manna provided in the wilderness by the heavenly Father, Jesus is "the bread that came down from heaven" (John 6:41, 50, 58), as well as the "bread of life" (6:35, 48, 51). This is a metaphor informed by the events in the wilderness and by the function of bread in biblical culture.

Bull (Calf)

The bull and bull calf were a common component of biblical culture in no small part because they were among the clean animals (Lev. 11:1–2). So long as the blood was properly drained, the butchering and eating of beef were without sanction (1 Sam. 14:32–34; 1 Kings 19:21). The fattened calf was reserved for a meal that marked

A bronze bull statuette discovered at Hazor, north of the Sea of Galilee.
Todd Bolen/www.BiblePlaces.com

a special occasion, such as the arrival of a noted guest, the return of a long-lost son, or a wedding celebration (Gen. 18:7–8; 1 Sam. 28:24; Matt. 22:4; Luke 15:23–30). However, when the fattened calf became part of the daily fare for the wealthy and powerful, Amos decried such meals as godless extravagance (Amos 6:4). Apart from providing meat for Israel's diet, bulls and oxen also loaned their strength for a variety of tasks. They were used to plow the agricultural fields, pull carts, and thresh harvested grain (Num. 7:3; Deut. 22:10; 25:4; 1 Kings 19:21; 1 Tim. 5:18). But the most frequent mention of bulls and calves in the Bible is in accounts of sacrificial offerings. These animals could be used for burnt offerings, sin offerings, and peace/fellowship offerings, so we find them sacrificed throughout the year as well as on festival days. When Solomon was confirmed as David's successor, a thousand bulls were sacrificed on one day (1 Chron. 29:21). But the blood of those bulls was only a placeholder for punishment earned by the rebellion of mortals. "Because it is impossible for the blood of bulls and goats to take away sins," Jesus shed his blood to redeem the world (Heb. 10:4).

During Old Testament times, bulls and bull calves often were associated with spiritual apostasy. They appear in reliefs and statues from a number of ancient cultures across the Fertile Crescent. Often these images were worshiped as idols, infused with a divine presence, or served as a pedestal on which an invisible deity stood. In Egypt a special bull calf was associated with Apis. In Canaan the bull image was associated with El and the bull calf with Baal, the son of El. The biblical authors cause us to recoil when they speak of God's people adopting the use of bulls or calves in a pagan way. For example, in Judges, we hear that Gideon's father had a sacred bull associated with a Baal altar in Ophrah (Judg. 6:25). While Moses was receiving the law of God on Mount Sinai, Aaron, in a desperate attempt to quell a rising revolt, cast a golden calf, built an altar in front of it, and announced the start of a festival for the Lord (Ex. 32:1–6). And when

Jeroboam I took control of the newly formed northern kingdom, he established a national religion that included worship centers at Bethel and Dan, each supplied with its own golden calf (1 Kings 12:28–30). We do not know enough about either of the latter two situations to say for sure whether the intentions were to encourage the people to worship the calf image itself or to provide a visible pedestal on which the invisible Lord might stand. In either case, the close association of the calf with paganism would result in the confused blending of biblical and pagan theology. Thus both uses of the bull calf were roundly criticized again and again by the biblical authors linking the bull calf to apostasy.

At other times, the bull appears in the Bible as a symbol associated with strength. In blessing the tribes of Ephraim and Manasseh, Moses said, "In majesty he is like a firstborn bull; his horns are the horns of a wild ox. With them he will gore the nations, even those at the ends of the earth" (Deut. 33:17). It seems likely that the same notion is communicated by the twelve bulls of the temple courtyard that stood beneath the sea of cast metal built by King Solomon's craftsmen (1 Kings 7:25). These strong animals facing the four cardinal compass headings represent the twelve tribes of Israel. Given the connection with power, the bull also becomes a symbol for political leaders or soldiers. The leadership in Egypt is likened to a "herd of bulls among the calves of the nations" (Ps. 68:30). As the Lord brings judgment against the nations that oppose him, their soldiers are likened to wild oxen, bull calves, and great bulls whose death will drench the land with their blood (Isa. 34:7). In his judgment speech directed at Babylon, Jeremiah calls for the divine victory with these words: "Kill all her young bulls; let them go down to the slaughter!" (Jer. 50:27). Egypt also is the target of Jeremiah's harsh language; he likens the mercenaries hired by Egypt to "fattened calves" who will turn and flee (46:21).

Finally, the calf is associated with two other qualities that also provide picture language for the biblical authors. The stubborn and undisciplined nature of the calf that insists on going its own reckless way is used to illustrate the attitude and behavior of God's people who at times were like an "unruly calf" (Jer. 31:18; cf. Hos. 4:16). And unbridled joy so aptly illustrated by the calf kicking up its heels is likened to the reaction of God's people when they experience the Lord's special healing: "And you will go out and leap like calves released from the stall" (Mal. 4:2).

C

Camel

The camel of the Bible is the single-humped dromedary with a light brown coat whose cantankerous bellowing still fills the air in Israel today. Its long legs fold beneath its sturdy body to allow for the boarding of passengers or loading of baggage. They then unfold to carry their cargo across relentless desert miles. The camel is particularly well adapted for such desert travel. When the sand begins to blow, its nostrils can close to narrow slits, and its long eyelashes prevent the blowing sand from reaching its deep-set eyes. Camel drivers prefer to feed and water their animals daily, but when crossing long stretches of waterless desert, the camel is the pack animal of choice, for it can go up to four days without taking on water. When it does replenish its water supply, the camel can drink upward of twenty-eight gallons at one time.

Because of the camel's ability to carry heavy loads, people have kept camels in their employ despite their ill tempers. While a donkey can be loaded with approximately one hundred pounds of freight, a single freight camel can carry five to six hundred pounds of cargo. In the Bible we see camels carrying people, such as Jacob's family (Gen. 31:17), and transporting heavy loads of spices, balm, and myrrh for the Ishmaelites, who added Joseph to their merchandise (Gen. 37:25). Camels also make an appearance in texts that speak about war (Judg. 6:5; 7:12). Given their lack of agility and the unstable ride they offer, camels were not used in the battle as fighting platforms but rather as the means to get to and from the battle. Such camels were bred for speed and were capable of trotting at ten miles per hour. Following David's victory over the Amalekites, four hundred young men fled the battle scene on this kind of camel (1 Sam. 30:17). Camel hair and skin were used in Bible times in a variety of ways, but camel meat was not used for food by the Israelites because camels were defined as unclean animals (Lev. 11:4; Deut. 14:7).

When a large herd of camels steps onto the scene in a Bible story, it is a symbol of great wealth or prestige. The late onset of sexual maturity in camels and their very long gestation period of eleven months dictate that a camel herd will grow at a cumbersome rate, making it much more difficult to raise a large herd of camels when compared to other domesticated animals of the biblical world. That is what made the camel such a wonderful gift (Gen. 32:15) and why those victorious in battle took them as prizes of war (1 Chron. 5:21; Jer. 49:29, 32). From Abraham (Gen. 12:16) to Job (Job 1:3) to the queen of Sheba (1 Kings 10:2), all those who make an appearance attended by a large herd of camels are thus defined as prosperous people.

The events that lie behind the account of Genesis 24 deserve special mention because of the rhetorical role the camel plays here. Formal mention of camels occurs eighteen times in this chapter, representing one-third of the total number of times camels are mentioned in the Old Testament. Abraham sent his servant to Aram Naharaim, his home region, to find a wife for his son Isaac. In the culture of this day, a marriage contract between two families was negotiated; this contract included a gift for the bride's family. When Rebekah's brother, Laban, got wind of the ten camels sent with Abraham's servant, each laden with "all kinds of good things" (Gen. 24:10), Laban became highly motivated to make a marriage contract with Abraham. These same camels that attracted the interest of Laban also played a role in revealing the character of Rebekah. As the servant of Abraham approached the well outside the city of Nahor, he asked the Lord to direct him to the young woman whom he had chosen for Isaac.

A camel carrying cargo. Freight camels are capable of carrying as much as six hundred pounds!
Library of Congress, LC-DIG-prokc-21852

It would be the one who volunteered to water his camels (vv. 14, 19–20). The exceptional nature of Rebekah's actions become apparent only when we become aware that each of these ten camels might drink upward of twenty-eight gallons of water. To water them all would require drawing water from the well and carrying it to the watering trough over a hundred times.

The account of Job's life also uses the camel in a rhetorical way. One of the very first things we learn about Job is that he had three thousand camels (Job 1:3), a fact that reveals the great prosperity he enjoyed. The trials of Job included the loss of those animals as Chaldean raiding parties swept down on those who were guarding the animals, killed them, and spirited away the camels (1:17). The camels make one final appearance in Job during the time of his restoration. At the close of Job's time of suffering, the Lord blessed Job with six thousand camels (42:12).

The camel was the largest of the domestic animals in the herds of those living in Jesus' day; he used their striking size in two metaphors. As Jesus delivered words of woe against the Pharisees, he said, "You strain out a gnat but swallow a camel" (Matt. 23:24). Strict Pharisees would strain their drinking water through a cloth so as not to consume a small, unclean creature like a gnat. Nevertheless, they neglected the larger matters of justice and mercy that amounted to swallowing a camel, a massive animal that was ritually unclean. And when a rich young man showed his reluctance to abandon his wealth in favor of God's kingdom, Jesus observed, "It is easier for a camel to go through the eye of a needle than for a rich man to enter the kingdom of God" (Matt. 19:24).

Capernaum

Many cities and villages received a visit from Jesus, but only one enjoyed the privilege of being called "his own town" (Matt. 9:1) — Capernaum, the city to which Jesus went when he went "home" (Mark 2:1). The ancient city of about twelve hundred people was located on the northwest shore of the Sea of Galilee. In this location Capernaum enjoyed a healthy economy fed by a diversity of local businesses. Because Capernaum was perched on the shore of the Sea of Galilee, the residents there could take advantage of all this inland body of water had to offer. Fishing, as well as the associated fish processing and boat-building enterprises, employed the time and energy of some living in this city. A volcanic past had left its deposit of basaltic boulders in this area. These were harvested and shaped for use in both the public and private buildings of Capernaum. And because such stone handled friction well, the people of this region became adept at transforming basalt into millstones for grinding wheat and large wheels for pressing olives, as well as door sockets, thresholds, and stairs. The volcanic past also provided the plain on the western shore of the Sea of Galilee with a rich soil that was first rate in producing an abundance of grain and fruit. And besides the fishing, basalt, and agricultural produce, we can include international commerce. Geography has conspired to make all the Promised Land an international crossroads linking Asia, Africa, and Europe. But where the Sea

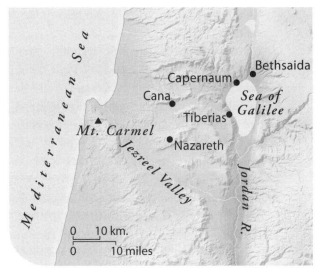

Capernaum.

of Galilee blocks and redirects international traffic along its western shores, cities like Capernaum also become players on an international stage.

Rhetorically, as the gospel writers present Capernaum to us, this city becomes intimately linked with the fulfillment of prophecy, the ministry of Jesus, and the international scope of Jesus' message. In the eighth century BC, Isaiah announced that the rising tide of Assyrian power would soon make its presence felt in the Promised Land. This potent empire would become the Lord's instrument for bringing judgment against his chosen people (Isa. 8; 2 Kings 15:29). The tribal territories of Zebulun and Naphtali would face particularly dark times as Galilee would be so overrun by Gentiles it would be called "Galilee of the Gentiles" (Isa. 9:1). But among those living in the dark shadow of death, there was a distant light. For those lands that had known the terrible consequences of the Assyrian invasion would also know the ministry of the Messiah (Isa. 9:1 – 2). Matthew notes that Jesus' move from Nazareth to Capernaum fulfills this prophecy and so links Jesus' residence there with the assurance that Jesus is the Messiah he claimed to be (Matt. 4:12–16).

Furthermore, Capernaum becomes closely linked to the words and actions of Jesus. While the gospel writers offer only a sample of all Jesus did in this city, it is clear that this city frequently heard Jesus speak and witnessed a large percentage of his miracles. The Gospels offer us but a partial list of those events. Here Jesus addressed the physical needs of Peter's mother-in-law as well as many others brought to him that day (Mark 1:29–34). He healed the royal official's son (John 4:46–54), the centurion's servant (Matt. 8:5–13; Luke 7:1–10), a man disabled (Mark 2:1–12), and a man possessed by an evil spirit (Mark 1:21–26; Luke 4:31–37). The last of these specifically occurred in the synagogue where Jesus customarily taught and where he gave the powerful discourse describing himself as the "bread of life" (John 6:58–59). Although Capernaum became intimately linked with the teaching and healing of Jesus (Luke 4:23), that did not mean everyone in Capernaum came to value this honor for what it was. Sadly, Capernaum found itself on a rather ignominious list. Jesus had performed more miracles in Korazin, Bethsaida, and Capernaum than in any other location, yet these privileged cities had failed to fully turn to Jesus as their Lord (Matt. 11:23–24; Luke 10:15).

Finally, Capernaum also can be associated with the international nature of Jesus' message

Caves form naturally throughout the mountains of Israel, like these in the Arbel cliffs.
© William D. Mounce

and his kingdom. Matthew calls attention to this fact with these rather unassuming words: "Leaving Nazareth, [Jesus] went and lived in Capernaum" (Matt. 4:13). Nazareth was a small agricultural village tucked quietly into a valley on the Nazareth ridge. This isolated hamlet was a place where everyone knew everyone else but whose residents remained unknown to the world at large. What Nazareth was not, Capernaum had become. This city was located only thirty miles from Nazareth, but in terms of culture it was a million miles away. Capernaum was located near the international highway and so within earshot of the traders moving across the world's stage on the international highway. As they moved their goods from one part of the world to the next, those traders also became the news broadcasters of their day. Consequently, when Jesus moved from Nazareth to Capernaum, he moved from obscurity to the limelight, assured that what he did and what he said would be given a larger audience as news about him spread with the merchandise traveling abroad. Thus Capernaum became not just a city rhetorically associated with the fulfillment of prophecy and with Jesus' ministry, but also with Jesus' intentions that the gospel might reach the far-flung corners of the world even before the miracle of Pentecost.

Cave

Natural caves punctuate the landscape of Palestine as well as the pages of our Bible. The geology of the hill country in Israel is ripe for their formation. The caves form within the layers of sedimentary limestone that can often be seen in the cross-sections of mountainsides. These layers of limestone have been tortured by folding, faulting, and twisting. The pressure exerted on the stone has been so great in places that cracks spread through the limestone layers compromising their structural integrity. Wind and rain combine with gravity to loosen those cracked stones; and when an entire layer collapses, a cave is born.

The caves that dot the Bible's landscape were put to use in a variety of ways by people living in Bible times. Even into the time of Jesus, caves like those discovered in Nazareth were used as homes. The capability of the cave to offer shelter was not lost on the shepherds either. When evening came, they would use natural caves located in the open country to keep their animals safe from predators and thieves. In that light, it is possible that Jesus was born in a cave. Luke notes that Jesus was placed in a manger, indicating that he was born where the animals were kept (Luke 2:7); and Christian writers like Justin Martyr have passed on the very early tradition that Jesus was born "in a certain cave near the village" (*Dialogue* 78).

Throughout both the Old and New Testaments, caves were also used as tombs. Noted biblical figures, such as Abraham and Sarah and Lazarus were buried in caves (Gen. 23:19; 25:9; John 11:38). In addition, natural caves were used by those who needed to hide from the enemies that pursued them (Judg. 6:2; 1 Sam. 22:1). Thieves hiding from justice also used them. Jeremiah seized upon this image when he criticized the people of his day for coming to worship at the temple while being indifferent about their lifestyle. The house of the Lord had begun to look like a robber's cave (Jer. 7:11). And finally, the Bible reports at least one instance where the privacy of a cave caused it to double as a restroom (1 Sam. 24:3).

When caves are mentioned in the Bible, they typically are mentioned in connection with the cultural categories just mentioned, but there are two instances that invite closer inspection. While in the culture of Bible times it was not unusual for a person to live in a cave, occupying a cave in the literature of the Bible carries the connation that things are not going so well. Lot and his daughters lived in a cave following a hasty retreat from Sodom. And once they were living in the cave, even more disturbing events follow (Gen. 19:30–38). The Amorite kings fleeing Joshua sought refuge in a cave (Josh. 10:16–17), as did the Israelites when threatened by Midianites or Philistines (Judg. 6:2; 1 Sam. 13:6). While fleeing from Saul, David regularly lived in a cave, whether at Adullam or En Gedi (1 Sam. 22:1; 24:1–3). And Obadiah used two caves to hide a hundred prophets of the Lord from the murdering hand of Jezebel (1 Kings 18:4). This theme continues in the New Testament and is listed as one of the indignities imposed on those who were persecuted for their faith (Heb. 11:38). And that is why, on the day of the Lord, the enemies of the Lord are pictured as seeking refuge from his justice-delivering hand by hiding in caves (Isa. 2:19–21; Rev. 6:15). So, in general, the literature of the Bible links living in a cave with a life that has been gravely disturbed by trouble.

Second, the connotation of hope becomes closely linked to a particular cave that finds frequent mention in Genesis. Abraham was a bedouin who moved seasonally with his herds to find the most desirable pastureland. The notion of purchasing a parcel of land remained out of view until his wife, Sarah, died and he needed to give her mortal remains a place to rest (Gen. 23:4). That is when he pressured Ephron the Hittite to sell a field that included a cave just outside of Kiriath Arbah (Hebron). This became an act necessitated by Sarah's death; but in the rhetorical flow of Genesis, this cave shows up again and again for a reason. God had promised Abram that he would grow to become a great nation; he further promised him that the long-awaited

Messiah would be born from this nation (Gen. 12:1–3). These two powerful promises were further linked by a third. Abram's family turned nation would come to possess Canaan (12:7). That promise loaned new importance to the purchase of the tomb from Ephron because it represented the first step in the fulfillment of that land promise. It is no wonder then that Abraham, Isaac, Rebekah, Jacob, and Leah would all join Sarah in that cave tomb (Gen. 25:9; 49:29–32). Located as it was on the main north-south road, this cave became not just a place for the family to come and remember their loved ones, but a place for recalling all the promises that God had made to their family. Thus the unpretentious cave of Machpelah became a hot spot on the map of the Genesis world, one to which the author of Genesis takes us regularly so that we too might recall the important connection of this cave to the core promises given to Abraham.

Cedar

Of all the trees mentioned in the Bible, none evokes the grandeur, the power, the beauty, and the utility of the cedar tree. This evergreen enjoys a commanding stature; because it can live for hundreds of years, it can grow to be hundreds of feet tall and achieve a circumference of thirty to forty feet. Early in its life this tree resembles a pyramid; but a mature tree has the profile of an elongated triangle with wide-spreading boughs that begin eight to ten feet above the ground.

Israel is a land without an in-country supply of construction-grade lumber, so its residents turned an envious eye north toward Lebanon where this timber giant grew, the finest of all trees, even of those in the garden of Eden (Ezek. 31:9). The harvested cedar lumber has many desirable qualities, including a pleasant red tone and a wonderful fragrance. The boards manufactured from this tree have a straight grain that is knot-free. And because the growth rings are so closely bound, the lumber naturally produces a very strong end product. For those who could afford them, boats and buildings made from cedar were of proven worth.

While the average people of the Old Testament would not have lived in a cedar dwelling or owned a boat made of cedar, they would have had contact with cedar via ritual practices mentioned in Leviticus and Numbers. The cleansing from infectious skin disease or cleaning of one's residence after a bout with mildew required the use of cedar (Lev. 14:4–6, 49–52), as did the ceremony involving the red heifer (Num. 19:6).

A giant cedar tree.
© Sybille Yates/www.BigStockPhoto.com

The most frequent mention of cedar in the Bible comes in those chapters that speak of David's palace, the temple in Jerusalem, and Solomon's Palace of the Forest of Lebanon. When David became king over all Israel, he accepted cedar logs and the building assistance offered by King Hiram of Tyre in order to construct his royal palace in Jerusalem (2 Sam. 5:11; 1 Chron. 14:1). After it was built, and noting the incongruity of his living in a cedar palace while the ark of the covenant resided in a tent, David sought to build a temple for the Lord (2 Sam. 7:2–7;

1 Chron. 17:1–6). But it was his son, Solomon, who enjoyed that honor. He called for cedar to be sent to Jerusalem for this purpose in spite of the great cost that would be incurred in felling the timber, floating it down the Mediterranean coastline, and bringing it inland to Jerusalem (1 Kings 5:6–14; 2 Chron. 2:1–16). When the building was complete, one would spy cedar no matter where they looked. Cedar planks and beams were employed in its roof, supporting structure, and decorative interior (1 Kings 6:9–10, 15–16). When the temple was complete, Solomon built a palace for himself, and because of the widespread use of cedar in it, including four rows of cedar columns, it earned the name the Palace of the Forest of Lebanon (1 Kings 7:1–7). There is so much cedar in these chapters of the Bible that we can nearly smell its fragrance on the pages, and that cedar is there for a reason. The repeated mention of this building material is clearly meant to distinguish these structures from all others, signifying their important role in advancing God's kingdom on earth.

The unique nature of the cedar also made it a prized ingredient in constructing metaphors. Cedar is used as a symbol of exquisite beauty in the Song of Songs. Here the young woman idealizes her lover who is "like Lebanon, choice as its cedars" (Song 5:15). Just a few verses later her brothers promise to prepare her for her wedding day by "enclose[ing] her with panels of cedar" (8:9).

Because cedar wood was so rare and costly, it was also used as a metaphor for prosperity and well-being. Balaam blessed Israel by likening the tents of God's people to "cedars beside the waters" (Num. 24:6). The prosperity of Jerusalem at the time of Solomon is expressed in this hyperbole: "The king made silver as common in Jerusalem as stones, and cedar as plentiful as sycamore-fig trees in the foothills" (1 Kings 10:27). The inspired poet and prophet celebrate the situation of the righteous one who "will grow like a cedar of Lebanon" (Ps. 92:12) and of Israel who "like a cedar of Lebanon … will send down his roots" and whose "fragrance [will be] like a cedar of Lebanon" (Hos. 14:5–6).

Furthermore, the cedar functions in metaphors that illustrate strength and power. The connection between royalty and cedar was so common in Jeremiah's day that he could ask the rhetorical question, "Does it make you a king to have more and more cedar?" (Jer. 22:15). The powerful leader, or one who thought himself so, might be linked to the massive cedar (Judg. 9:15). But although kings had demonstrated their power by harvesting this natural resource (2 Kings 19:23; Isa. 37:24), only the Lord had a voice that could break into pieces the cedars of Lebanon (Ps. 29:5). The proud and lofty so full of self-celebration were like the mighty cedar whose powerful frame was no match for the Lord (Isa. 2:12–13; Amos 2:9). The most extended use of this metaphor is the one in Ezekiel 31 that encourages the pharaoh of Egypt to find warning when recalling the fate of Assyria. Assyria had been like a cedar in Lebanon. Although this tree overshadowed the forest, towering above the rest of the vegetation with thick foliage, providing a resting place for

birds in its beautiful boughs, the Lord cut it down because it displayed pride and wickedness.

Chaff (Straw)

Chaff and straw are byproducts of the grain production that was fundamental to the well-being of those living in Bible times. When the grain was ready to be harvested, stalks of wheat or barley were brought up from the fields to the threshing floor where a variety of methods were used to break the bond between the kernel of grain and the rest of the plant. Once that step was taken, the resulting mixture was thrown aloft in a process called winnowing, which used the wind to carry off the lighter byproducts while the heavier kernels of grain fell back to the threshing floor where they could be gathered and stored for future use. The byproducts of the grain plant that blew downwind during the winnowing process drifted into three general categories. The larger and heavier stalks of the plant fell closest to the kernels of grain; this was the straw. Broken pieces of the grain stalks were lighter and so flew farther downwind. In Hebrew these are the *teven* (often translated "straw"). Finally, the husks that had surrounded the kernel of grain and the smallest surviving portions of the stalk flew the farthest downwind; this was the chaff.

The varying qualities of these byproducts earned them different roles in society. The dry straw was very easily ignited but was very quickly consumed. Consequently, it was not much good for sustaining a fire but functioned well as tinder used to get one started. The *teven* produced by the threshing process or by cutting up the straw after threshing was used in two different ways. It had some nutritional value and so could be used as food for the animals either on its own or mixed with barley (Gen. 24:25; Judg. 19:19;

1 Kings 4:28; Isa. 11:7; 65:25). The *teven* was also the product mixed into the clay during the process of making sundried mud bricks. As the clay hardened in the brick molds under the warming sun, it had a tendency to crack. Consequently, *teven* was added as a binder that helped keep the drying brick intact. This material is closely associated with the hardship of Israel while in Egypt. It is mentioned eight times in Exodus 5 when the Egyptians punish the Israelite slaves by requiring them to gather and produce their own straw for the brick-making process. Finally, the last of the byproducts, chaff, was so light and of so little value that it simply was allowed to blow away.

The poets and prophets of the Bible used these byproducts of the threshing process in a variety of metaphors. For example, some passages of Scripture play on the lack of strength and combustibility of these byproducts. The leviathan described in Job is so powerful that it regards sling stones as chaff and clubs as if they are straw (Job 41:28–29). The prayer of the psalmist is that the Lord's enemies might be driven from his life as chaff is driven before the wind (Ps. 83:13). And the prophecy of Nahum anticipates that the Assyrians will be consumed like the straw tinder used to start a cooking fire (NIV "stubble"; Nah. 1:10).

The lifelessness and general worthlessness of the chaff is also used to teach God's truth. Psalm 1 compares and contrasts the qualities and differing fates of the righteous and wicked persons. While the righteous person is portrayed as an ever-living tree that produces fruit, the wicked person is like the lifeless chaff that the wind blows away (Ps. 1:3–4). And in contrast to the Lord who is exalted and lifted up, capable of doing mighty things, those who oppose him can only "conceive chaff" and "give birth to straw" (Isa. 33:11). Not just people, but their ideology is

also compared to the threshing floor byproducts. The message delivered by the false prophets lacks substance and value; consequently, the Lord draws this comparison: "Let the one who has my word speak it faithfully. For what has straw to do with grain?" (Jer. 23:28). Hundreds of years later, Paul had put in place a very solid theological foundation for those living in Corinth. It was now up to them to build a solid wall on top of it. But if these Christians built a wall above that foundation of "straw" instead of something more substantial, the day of the Lord would reveal their shoddy building practices (1 Cor. 3:12).

Finally, straw and chaff are linked to divine judgment in both the Old and New Testaments.

The process of winnowing, which uses the wind to carry away the chaff while heavier kernels of grain fall back to the threshing floor.
© Richard Nowitz

The rebellion of Ephraim had invited God's anger into their lives. Hosea tells these rebels that they are destined to become like "the early dew that disappears, like chaff swirling from a threshing floor" (Hos. 13:3). Jeremiah addressed similar rebellion in his day. And God's message to his people was as clear as it was agricultural: "I will scatter you like chaff driven by the desert wind" (Jer. 13:24). It is this judgment imagery found in the Old Testament prophets that may inform the choice of images made by John the Baptist as he faced down the Pharisees and Sadducees who had come to be baptized by him. Their rebellion was akin to that of their fathers, a rebellion addressed by Hosea, Jeremiah, and others. So it is very natural for John to pick up the same imagery these Old Testament proph-

ets used when addressing it. One more powerful than John was already on the stage of the Promised Land: "His winnowing fork is in his hand, and he will clear his threshing floor, gathering his wheat into the barn and burning up the chaff with unquenchable fire" (Matt. 3:12).

Chair. *See* Seat.

Chariot

By the time the Bible's authors were making frequent mention of the chariot, it had evolved from a cumbersome cart into a light and sleek war machine. It had a wooden frame with wickerlike sides, a forward-reaching wooden beam to which

Assyrian King Ashurbanipal uses his chariot for sport — hunting lions.
Werner Forman Archive/British Museum, London

the horses could be yoked, wheels with spokes, and a rope floor to absorb bumps and steady the ride. While chariots were not made completely of metal, metal was used to strengthen key components. The design goal was to create a carriage that was both quick and agile, like the ones Nahum had in mind when he said, "The chariots storm through the streets, rushing back and forth through the squares. They look like flaming torches; they dart about like lightning" (Nah. 2:4).

The chariot was used in four primary ways. First, it was used for sport. Though the Old Testament does not mention it, ancient art pictures kings hunting wild game from a chariot. Second, during the New Testament era, chariot races had become very popular, with horse-racing venues, called hippodromes, popping up even in Israel. Third, the ancient chariot was a short version of the stretch limousine, the transportation of the rich and famous. When a chariot appeared on the roadway, it was likely that a king, commander, or official of some distinction was aboard (Jer. 17:25). But the most common use of the chariot in the Old Testament was for war. The typical chariot was drawn by at least two horses and carried three crew members: a driver who also wielded a spear, an archer, and a shield bearer. The chariot served as a mobile firing platform that carried the vital archers to the part of the battle where they were needed most. Once they let fly their hail of arrows, they could speed quickly to the next location that called for their services. And if the enemy began to retreat, the chariots could pursue the enemy soldiers, causing the sort of distress and confusion that prevented them from reorganizing for a return engagement.

In general the chariots mentioned in the Bible fall into two periods, one before and one after the days of King David. Before the days of King David, the chariot was not in the employ of God's people but rather was the dreaded weapon of the enemy. When it was deployed, it caused panic in Israel (1 Sam. 13:5 – 7). The chariots of the Canaanites and the Philistines presented such a threat that they prevented Israel from gaining a foothold on the plains and valleys of the Promised Land where these chariots were most effective (Josh. 17:16; Judg. 1:19; 1 Sam. 31:7). That changed with David, who was the first Israelite king to obtain chariots for his army (2 Sam. 8:4). Under Solomon the chariot became more commonplace. With the wealth he accumulated, David's son was able to build up his chariot corps and billet them at key locations, his so-called chariot cities (2 Chron. 1:14). As the chariot became a less threatening and more familiar sight in Israel, the psalmist urged his readers to keep things in perspective: "Some trust in chariots and some in horses, but we trust in the name of the LORD our God" (Ps. 20:7).

When chariots are driven onto the pages of our Bible, we do well to consider the rhetorical impression they bring with them. During the days of Moses, Joshua, and the judges, Israel's enemies were the ones with chariots. They brought terror to the stories in which they appear, for at this stage in their history, God's people simply had no reply for this horrifying weapon. Given those overtones, we will appreciate why divinely sponsored victories get particular attention when chariots are in the mix. Shortly after Moses had led Israel out of bondage in Egypt, the chariot corps of the pharaoh was kicking up dust on the horizon. The panicked people turned to Moses, who turned to the Red Sea with uplifted hands. God provided a water-free path for escape that became a water-filled trap for the Egyptians (Ex. 14). This moment was so powerful that it is recalled again and again as a symbol of God's presence and defending power (Deut. 11:4; Josh.

24:6 – 7; Ps. 76:6; Isa. 43:16 – 17). The other chariot battle told in great detail comes to us in Judges 4. Here Jabin king of Hazor, with his nine hundred iron chariots, faced off against Deborah and Barak. God called for the Israelite infantry gathered on Mount Tabor to do the unthinkable, leave the security of the high ground and make a frontal assault on the chariot corps advancing in the plain. In this battle the Lord disabled the chariots and again secured a victory where defeat seemed inevitable. Only when we appreciate how horrifying the chariots were can we appreciate how extraordinary deliverance was.

The chariot is not only the symbol of a great threat, but it is also the symbol of power, prestige, and wealth. When Joseph rose to power in Egypt, he was directed to ride through the crowds in a chariot (Gen. 41:43). Wanna-be leaders like Absalom and Adonijah secured a chariot in which to ride, hoping that this display of royalty might actually lead to the crown (2 Sam. 15:1; 1 Kings 1:5). Of course, the ability to own multiple chariots was an indication of extreme wealth. The author of Kings emphasizes the power and wealth of Solomon by observing that he had fourteen hundred chariots; and among his many business dealings, Solomon was involved in the international brokering of chariots (1 Kings 10:26, 29).

The Lord has his own fiery chariots (Ps. 68:17). Their appearance and function parallel many of the mortal chariot appearances noted above. Divine chariots showed up to give Elijah an honorary ride into eternity (2 Kings 2:11 – 12), to encourage Elisha (2 Kings 6:14 – 17), and to bring judgment on the nations that opposed the Lord (Zech. 6:1 – 8).

Finally, the invitation to join another person in his or her chariot seems to be a social signal that symbolizes trust. Ahab invites Ben-Hadad to join him in his chariot to negotiate the terms of a peace treaty following the defeat of this Aramean king (1 Kings 20:33 – 34). Jehu does something very similar when collecting support for his campaign against King Ahab (2 Kings 10:15 – 17). And in the New Testament, where chariots are rarely mentioned, we find the Ethiopian eunuch riding in a prestigious chariot as he reads the Scriptures. When he perceives Philip to have the answers he lacks, this important official invites Philip to join him in the chariot (Acts 8:28 – 31).

Cistern

A cistern is an underground water storage cavern designed and dug to capture and retain rainwater for future use. The extraordinary effort it took to acquire and maintain a suitable supply of freshwater in the Promised Land explains the great number of cisterns that have survived into the present from Bible times. Such cisterns are present among the archaeological ruins of small agricultural villages and palatial estates. In Bible times they were found in massive fortifications in the wilderness, as well as in the temple in Jerusalem. Cisterns like these became necessary in the Promised Land because it is a land with a very fragile freshwater supply. The water that meets one's daily needs was supplied when it rained (Deut. 11:11). And because it did not rain at all throughout the heart of the summer months, the rainwater that did fall had to be extracted from the water table via spring and well, or it had to be rescued from runoff by directing it into underground cisterns.

The digging and maintaining of a cistern was labor and time intensive. It began with the excavation phase of the project, which required a cavern that could hold enough water to meet the needs of those who would draw from it. This digging always left a hole that was broad on the bottom and narrow at the top; in profile the cistern often has the appearance of a bell or bottle. If the cistern was dug in porous limestone, water loss was mitigated by plastering the interior. A narrow, covered neck was established at the top of the cistern in order to limit the contamination of dust and dirt, to decrease the amount of water that was lost to evaporation, and to restrict the amount of sunlight hitting the water, so as to prevent the growth of algae. Channels were cut in the surface of the earth to direct the water from structures and surrounding terrain into the body of the cistern itself. And because this runoff water would also contain undesirable particles, small basins were built into those channels to slow the flow of water and allow

Cut-away view of a cistern from the site of Ashkelon.
www.HolyLandPhotos.org

particulate matter to settle out. As mentioned above, the establishing of this water resource was time and labor intensive. Consequently, it was a real blessing to take possession of a cistern someone else had dug (Deut. 6:11; NIV "well"). Once established, the cistern needed further investment of time and energy in order to maintain it. Each year when the water level in the cistern dropped, the sediment that collected in the bottom had to be removed; and if plastered, the interior had to be inspected and repaired to prevent leaks.

These water collection devices functioned in a variety of ways. First they provided water for the people who built them near their homes and for their livestock if they were built in the open country (2 Chron. 26:10). Because people gathered at cisterns to get water, they were also places to obtain information (1 Sam. 19:22). Although they were not designed as a place for people to live, those living in mortal fear of an approaching enemy might hide themselves in cisterns (1 Sam. 13:6). And because it was difficult to get out of a cistern, we also find cisterns functioning as prisons (Gen. 37:20; Jer. 38:6).

Rhetorically the cistern could become a symbol of hatred, wanton cruelty, and disrespect. Those imprisoned in dry cisterns were not at risk of drowning, nor were they likely to die from being pushed into this cavity. However, there was a very real risk that they would die slowly of starvation if left there (Jer. 38:9). So the cistern was a symbol of wanton cruelty when Joseph's envious brothers elected not to kill him outright but rather put him in a cistern (Gen. 37:20–24). And it was an indication of just how much the leadership in Jerusalem hated Jeremiah when they threw him into a cistern to die (Jer. 38:6–10). Disrespect is communicated not just when the living are put into cisterns but also when the dead are placed there. That was the message sent when Ishmael slaughtered seventy men and threw their bodies into a cistern near Mizpah (Jer. 41:7–9).

The cistern is also linked to security and sexual pleasure. When the Assyrian leader was trying to coax the ordinary citizens of Jerusalem into surrendering the city, he promised these Israelites a secure future with these words: "Make peace with me and come out to me. Then every one of you will eat from his own vine and fig tree and drink water from his own cistern" (2 Kings 18:31). The pleasure of extracting water from a cistern is employed in Proverbs where it is compared to the pleasures found in spending intimate time with one's own spouse. Hence, in the face of temptations to the contrary, we hear this encouragement: "Drink water from your own cistern" (Prov. 5:15).

Finally, a solid acquaintance with the ancient cistern is necessary to understand the simile used in Jeremiah that chastises God's people for their wandering ways. The most desirable form of water one can obtain is from a living spring. No excavation and little if any site development is necessary to take advantage of this groundwater. What is more, springwater is filtered water that always flows fresh. It was unthinkable that one would abandon a perfectly good spring for a poorly maintained cistern, but that is what God's people had done. In Jeremiah the Lord lays the facts on the table with this water-based language. "My people have committed two sins: They have forsaken me, the spring of living water, and have dug their own cisterns, broken cisterns that cannot hold water" (Jer. 2:13).

Cloud

Clouds form above our heads when invisible moisture in the atmosphere cools below the dew point. For five months of the year in Israel, this rarely if ever happens. During the summer season, the Promised Land is dominated by high pressure, making it one of the sunniest countries on earth. But with the winter months comes a change in the atmosphere signaled by cooler temperatures, welcome clouds, and the cloud-borne rain that sweeps moisture inland from the Mediterranean Sea. So when you see a cloud rising on the western horizon, you know that rain is on the way (Luke 12:54).

The Bible sees a greater reality behind this science. God is the one who directs the clouds to form and the rain to fall. "He makes clouds rise from the ends of the earth" (Ps. 135:7). "He covers the sky with clouds; he supplies the earth with rain" (147:8). The clouds are furthermore pictured as the chariot with which God charges across the sky (Pss. 18:9; 68:4; 104:3; Isa. 19:1). Undoubtedly, this image was designed to unseat the Canaanite imagery of their rain deity, Baal, who also is pictured as riding on the clouds of heaven.

The Bible authors not only know about natural clouds, but they are also aware of an important supernatural cloud. As soon as God's people took their first steps away from Pharaoh and into freedom, a pillar-shaped cloud led them. The infrequency with which God's people saw ordinary clouds surely made this cloud even more memorable, referenced again and again in the Old Testament. We first hear about the pillar of cloud in Exodus 13:21 but meet it again and again throughout the next forty years in the wilderness. This cloud covered Mount Sinai (Ex. 24:15) and filled the tabernacle (Ex. 40:35; Lev. 16:2). Once Joshua leads Israel into the Promised Land, we do not hear about this phenomenon again until Solomon dedicates the temple in Jerusalem. On that day, the priests had to withdraw from the building, for the glory of the Lord had filled his temple — the cloud was back (1 Kings 8:10–11; 2 Chron. 5:14). After this the supernatural cloud disappears again until the day of Jesus' transfiguration. As Jesus' face and clothing began to shine like the sun, a bright cloud enveloped both Jesus and the disciples with him

(Matt. 17:5; Mark 9:7; Luke 9:34–35). Thus the cloud that heralded the Messiah's coming participated in marking his arrival.

The appearance of this supernatural cloud signaled God's readiness to act as guide, protector, or communicator. Moses' prerogatives as Israel's leader did not extend to decisions about when to break camp, when to set up camp, or what route to follow between camps. God provided that guidance via the pillar-shaped cloud (Num. 9:15–23; Deut. 1:33). The cloud also was used as a shield or barrier against those with hostile intentions toward God's people (Ex. 14:19). And it participated in those moments when the Lord had an important message to share with his people (Ex. 19:9; Num. 11:25; Matt. 17:5).

The cloud, or pillar of smoke, leading the Israelites.
Scala/Art Resource, NY

Clouds are also associated with the end of the world. Daniel first reveals this in a vision in which he saw "one like a son of man, coming with the clouds of heaven" (Dan. 7:13). Jesus told both the disciples and the high priest in charge at his trial that he was the very person whom they would see "coming on the clouds of heaven" (Matt. 24:30; 26:64; Mark 13:26; 14:62; Luke 21:27). The apostle John saw Jesus coming on the clouds and sitting on a white cloud with a crown of gold on his head (Rev. 1:7; 14:14–16). It is ironic that he who would return on the clouds would be hidden by a cloud on the day of his ascension (Acts 1:9). But on the day of his return, those who are still alive will rise to meet their Lord among the clouds in the air (1 Thess. 4:17).

In addition to the natural and supernatural clouds associated with Bible events, we also find various characteristics or qualities of clouds employed in wordplay. The link between precipitation and clouds is exploited in two proverbs. The favorable disposition of a king is likened to the spring clouds that bring the moisture necessary to mature the grain fields (Prov. 16:15). But a man who boasts about giving gifts yet fails to deliver is like a cloud without rain (Prov. 25:14). False teachers are like that as well; so they are described as "clouds without rain, blown along by the wind" (Jude 12). The wispy and transitory nature of a cloud also finds its place in the Bible's poetry. Job bemoans the fragile nature of life and security, noting that both can vanish as quickly as a cloud (Job 7:9; 30:15). In contrast the Lord offers this simile destined to comfort the sinner: "I have swept away your offenses like a cloud" (Isa. 44:22). As thin and fragile as clouds appear to be, they also have the ability to conceal. When asking that the day of his birth be lost to everyone's recollection, Job prays that a cloud might settle over it (Job 3:5). When clouds become thick, they can completely block out the sky. The lament in Lamentations perceives the clouds to be so thick that God is covered by them "so that no prayer can get through" (Lam. 3:44). However, when the Lord is roused to help his people, the shade-giving quality of the cloud comes to Isaiah's mind. In a land of few trees, the passing of a cloud is welcome relief: "You silence the uproar of foreigners; as heat is reduced by the shadow of a cloud" (Isa. 25:5).

Coin

The people of the Bible had to purchase goods, obtain services, and pay taxes much as we do today. During the early days of the Old Testament, those wishing to do so had two choices. On the one hand, they could pay for goods, services, taxes, and tribute with products derived from the agricultural fields or pastures (2 Kings 3:4). On the other hand, purchasers could pay with an agreed upon weight of metal. When Abraham acquired a field from Ephron the Hittite, he weighed out "four hundred shekels of silver, according to the weight current among the merchants" (Gen. 23:16). The shekel in this instance and in all others in the Old Testament (with the possible exception of Neh. 5:15) is a unit of weight rather than a coin. However, by the seventh century BC, political leaders began to stamp coins as a way of facilitating commodity exchange and paying taxes. In that light, coins appear to have been used by the exiles returning from Babylon who wished to give an offering in support of the rebuilding of the temple in Jerusalem (Ezra 2:68–69; Neh. 7:70–72).

By the time Jesus was born and walked this earth, coins were a common and even confusing part of life in Israel. One would expect that Roman coins would circulate in this region because the Romans controlled it, so it is no surprise to find Roman coins like the copper quandrans and silver denarius mentioned in the Gospels (Matt. 5:26; 20:2). But Greek coins, such as the drachma, two-drachma, and four-drachma coins, were also in circulation (Matt. 17:24, 27; Luke 15:8), as well as one small Jewish coin of very limited value called the *lepton*, or widow's mite (Mark 12:42).

The complexity of the coinage in Jesus' day was further exacerbated by the fact that certain coins were required when making payment in certain locations. This of course necessitated the use of money changers who charged a fee for exchanging money. For example, the Tyrian shekel was the coin required when making payment for items in the temple markets, and so even more money changers set up shop in the temple complex (Matt. 21:12; Mark 11:15; John 2:14–15).

Coins make a rhetorical appearance in the Gospels in three different settings: in Jesus' discourses, as tools in opposition to Jesus, and in Jesus' parables. In the Sermon on the Mount, Jesus urges his followers to avoid the contentious-

A treasure of Tetra-Dracmas from the third century BC.

Z. Radovan/www.BibleLandPictures.com

ness and risk associated with legal trials. He tells his listeners to settle matters quickly and before the trial, lest they lose the last and the smallest coin they have (Matt. 5:26; Luke 12:59). As Jesus sent out the Twelve to announce the coming of God's kingdom, he urged them to take no gold, silver, or copper — the metals from which the circulating coins were minted (Matt. 10:9). Their focus was not to be on how many coins to take or how quickly their expense account was being drained; rather, it was to be on their mission of announcing the arrival of this world's eternal ruler. In both these instances, Jesus is reinforcing an attitude toward coins that sees them as tools to be used rather than an obsession to be pursued. He puts it bluntly: "You cannot serve both God and Money" (Matt. 6:24). As Jesus sat watching people putting money into the temple treasury, he saw the right attitude in action when an impoverished widow put in two small copper coins, all the money she had to live on (Mark 12:41–44).

Unlike the widow, there were those who intend to use coins to compromise Jesus' teaching or put him in harm's way. For example, while Jesus was in Capernaum, the collectors of the two-drachma tax approached Peter and wanted to know if Jesus was going to pay the temple tax (Ex. 30:13; 2 Chron. 24:9). The answer was not so easy. Jesus had made it clear to Peter and others that he had come to replace the temple (Matt. 12:6), yet there were those less well initiated into Jesus' kingdom who might be offended by his refusal to pay. So as not to confuse Peter or offend others, Jesus performed a miracle that produced a four-drachma coin with which to pay his and Peter's tax (Matt. 17:24–27).

A riskier moment involving coins unfolded in the crowded temple courts. Here, surrounded by Roman soldiers looking for Jewish worshipers who longed for the overthrow of their Roman overlords, the Pharisees and Herodians attempted to entrap Jesus with a question. Did he advocate payment of taxes to Caesar or not? A simple yes or no answer would have put him at great risk, so instead, Jesus asked for a denarius. Calling attention to the image of the Roman emperor stamped on the coin, he gave an answer that disarmed the dangerous question: "Give to Caesar what is Caesar's, and to God what is God's" (Matt. 22:21).

And then there was Judas. He provided the hate-filled Jewish leadership with access to Jesus at a time and place when an uprising was unlikely to be caused by Jesus' public arrest. The cost of the betrayal was thirty silver coins (Matt. 26:15; 27:3–5).

Jesus also used coins when teaching in his parables. In the parable of the unmerciful servant, coins are used as a symbol for the sin-debt owed by mortals as Jesus encourages us to forgive others as he has forgiven us (Matt. 18:35). Here a man finds himself faced by a debt too extraordinary to calculate, ten thousand talents. Yet the king forgives this debt. Inexplicably, this same man who has been forgiven the larger debt shakes down another servant who owes him a small debt, a hundred denarii. When the king learns of the lack of mercy shown by the man who has been shown mercy, he sends the unmerciful servant to jail until he pays back all he owes (18:23–35).

In the parable of the workers in the vineyard, money symbolizes the blessings meted out in various ways by the Lord. The landowner hires workers in the morning at the expected rate of one denarius for the day's work. At the close of the day, this generous man pays everyone a denarius, even those called to work at later times in the day. Jesus cautions against calling God unfair when he blesses others who appear to have invested less in God's kingdom (Matt. 20:1 – 16).

In the parable of the talents, money represents the gifts God gives his church to advance the kingdom. Like those who received the talents of money in the parable, the expectation is that these gifts will be well invested (Matt. 25:14 – 30).

And in the parable of the lost coin, the coin symbolizes the lost sinner who repents. The joy that fills heaven is like that of the poor woman who lost and then found one of her ten silver coins (Luke 15:8). These coins may well have been the dowry of this woman—money she counted on to sustain her should her marriage end prematurely in divorce or the death of her husband.

Cornerstone

When building anything, from a backyard shed to a suburban shopping mall, it is clear that certain architectural components of the structure are more important than others. These are the ones that play the key role in giving the building its symmetry and strength. In that light, two building stones from Bible times are viewed as more important than any of the others—the stone at the corner of the wall and the stone at the peak of the arch.

The cornerstone of a wall was, in part, selected because of its relative strength. It had to be able to carry the cumulative weight of all the stone courses rising above it. This stone also had to be the right shape. A plumb bob was used to make sure that a wall rose vertically, not leaning inward or outward; but it was the cornerstone that provided both a pleasing corner and a sighting tool to confirm that the wall was following a straight and true line. This kind of stone is mentioned in Zechariah. He encouraged those returning from the Babylonian exile to press on with the rebuild-

ing of the temple in Jerusalem and directed Zerubbabel, their leader, to quarry the mighty mountain until it became level ground, extracting an appropriate cornerstone for the foundation of the new temple (Zech. 4:7 – 9).

The other important building stone from Bible times is the keystone found at the peak of an arch. The arch rises above an intended opening, such as a door gate or window, redirecting the weight of the wall above the opening so that it does not collapse. The final stone to be added to the arch is the wedgelike stone or brick inserted at the very top of the arch. This stone is called the keystone.

While there is room for discussion on the topic, it seems that all of the structural stones we will discuss here are of the former variety, cornerstones (also called capstones in the NIV). That is because they are linked to the "corner" of the structure and/or its "foundation." By New Testament times the arch had become a more familiar architectural element than in Old Testament days, so some have understood certain passages discussed below to be images of the keystone rather than the cornerstone. In either case, we can say this for certain: the building stone mentioned in the metaphors below is a stone highly unique, highly prized, and critical to the success of a building project.

First, the biblical authors use the cornerstone as a metaphor in describing creation, human leaders, and the Messiah. After Job has had his chance to complain about the maladies that have befallen him, and his friends have had their opportunity to extrapolate the cause of Job's maladies, the Lord steps to the stage to demonstrate how limited mortals are in assessing the cause of their misfortunes or the benefits such misfortunes may eventually produce. The Lord directs one question after the next to Job, including this disabling rhetorical question about Job's knowledge regarding the fundamental principles at work when the world was created: "On what were [the earth's] footings set, or who laid its cornerstone?" (Job 38:6).

Second, the cornerstone can represent a human leader. In Psalm 118 the poet invites Israel to join in giving thanks for the deliverance of God's people from their foes. The king acknowledges that he was a most unlikely victor. He compares himself to a quarried stone that the builders examined and then rejected. But in the end and due to the intervention of a gracious and powerful God, this king was victorious. He became the most important stone in the building, the cornerstone (v. 22). In his prophecy against Egypt, Isaiah derides the leaders of that country. Though they are the perceived cornerstones of their nation, they have failed to give Egypt a solid foundation (Isa. 19:13). The cornerstone also appears in Jeremiah's denunciation of Babylon. When a mountain quarry fails to produce stones that might function at the corner of a wall, that quarry is considered to be of fading value. This is the legacy of Babylon: "No rock will be taken from you for a cornerstone, nor any stone for a foundation" (Jer. 51:26).

Third, the cornerstone can refer to the Messiah, Jesus. In contrast to the mortal leaders of

A Roman sarcophagus was used as the cornerstone for this building in Sepphoris, Galilee.

Todd Bolen/www.BiblePlaces.com

Judah who so often failed them, the Lord had plans for a better foundation: "See, I lay a stone in Zion, a tested stone, a precious cornerstone for a sure foundation" (Isa. 28:16). Zechariah also saw the coming of this cornerstone, adding that it would come from Judah (Zech. 10:4). And Jesus declared himself to be that building block. During the last week of his life, the chief priests and elders of the people questioned and attacked Jesus' claim to be vested with authority. After addressing these men with two parables that illustrated the error of their ways, Jesus took up the language of Psalm 118 and applied it to himself. These religious leaders had rejected Jesus just as a builder might reject a stone in the quarry. But this very stone that the builder rejected was the one the Lord had chosen to make his cornerstone (Matt. 21:42; Mark 12:10; Luke 20:17; Acts 4:11; 1 Peter 2:7). Consequently, this image is extended in Ephesians to portray the church as a building that rises from a certain foundation. Paul tells the Gentiles in Ephesus that they are no longer foreigners and aliens but citizens of God's kingdom. They are part of the church, a metaphorical building that is founded on the apostles and the prophets "with Christ Jesus himself as the chief cornerstone" (Eph. 2:20).

Cup

The cup of the biblical world looks less to us like a cup and more like a small bowl without handles. Cups of the average home were made from clay, but those used in wealthier homes or for more unique roles could be made of bronze, silver, or gold. The primary function of the cup was the same whether it was offered in a bedouin's tent or the palace of the Egyptian pharaoh (Gen. 40:11 – 13). It held the beverages commonly consumed during the day: water, milk, fruit juice, and wine.

But apart from this ordinary function, the cup also appears in some unique social settings.

Clay cup found at Susa, Persia.
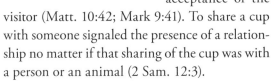
© www.Livius.org

To this day visitors to the Middle East are often taken aback by how quickly a cup is pressed into their hands by people whom they have just met; it is simply the way most social or business transactions begin. This modern tradition has roots that stretch deeply into Bible times where the offered cup was a sign of hospitality and illustrated the host's willing acceptance of the visitor (Matt. 10:42; Mark 9:41). To share a cup with someone signaled the presence of a relationship no matter if that sharing of the cup was with a person or an animal (2 Sam. 12:3).

The offering of a cup as a relational signal among mortals was also extended in the direction of the divine. The psalmist longs to show his thanks to the Lord and express his close relationship to him by pressing a cup into his hand. He sings of this desire: "I will lift up the cup of salvation and call on the name of the Lord" (Ps. 116:13). But this godly passion to connect with the Lord via the cup also expressed itself in ungodly ways when God's people filled up bowls and offered them to false gods (Isa. 65:11) or when they used cups to pour out libations to the demons (1 Cor. 10:21).

Another special use of the cup was in the practice of divination, using dark arts to discover hidden knowledge or to discern which path might lead to future success. We are surprised to learn that Joseph had such a cup (Gen. 44:5) and that he at least gave the appearance of using this cup for divination (v. 15). It is the role of Joseph's silver cup as a tool in revealing the true concern of Joseph's brothers for Benjamin, however, that captures the interest of the writer of Genesis. The apparent theft of Joseph's special cup was such a serious offense that it gave the brothers of Benjamin every reason to turn on their youngest brother and abandon him as they had abandoned Joseph years before. But the cup that purportedly provided access to deep secrets offered public knowledge that these men had changed.

Rhetorically the cup appears in the Bible to deliver either a very positive or a very negative message. The cup can signal divine favor, blessing, and forgiveness. That is particularly the case where the Lord is pictured as the host extending the cup of hospitality (Ps. 16:5), a cup that is not only filled but overflowing with blessing (23:5). The cup was also present at the Passover. In fact, if the later Jewish traditions represent the New

Testament reality, four different cups of wine were passed, a unique message associated with each. On the evening of Jesus' betrayal, he drew an Old Testament meal into the new era by taking the old Passover cup and speaking new words as it circulated around the table: "This cup is the new covenant in my blood, which is poured out for you" (Luke 22:20). As Paul wrote to the Corinthians about this New Testament meal, he said, "Is not the cup of thanksgiving for which we give thanks a participation in the blood of Christ?" (1 Cor 10:16). It is a cup that brings forgiveness and reminds the world that a new covenant rules the relationship between mortals and their Creator (1 Cor. 11:25).

The image of the cup that brings the wonderful news of blessing and forgiveness has a darker side. It also is used to portray the anger of the Lord and judgment against rebellion. The children of Israel were not immune from experiencing the cup of divine wrath. Jerusalem drained this cup down to the last dregs and so experienced the ruin, the destruction, famine, and sword that it brought (Isa. 51:17–19). Ezekiel also described the experience of Jerusalem in drinking this cup of wrath that brings scorn, derision, desolation, and sorrow (Ezek. 23:31–33).

But those forced to drink the cup of God's wrath most often are the nations who have become sworn enemies of the Lord and of his advancing kingdom. The nations who had so boldly opposed the Lord and his kingdom also received this cup: "Take from my hand this cup filled with the wine of my wrath and make all the nations to whom I send you drink it. When they drink it, they will stagger and go mad because of the sword I will send among them" (Jer. 25:15–16). This reality was lived out in the past and is anticipated in the future (Rev. 14:10).

The cup of God's wrath that represents the anger of God at rebellion and sin should never have fallen on his Son. Yet this request fell from Jesus' lips as he dropped to his knees in prayer: "My Father, if it is possible, may this cup be taken from me. Yet not as I will, but as you will" (Matt. 26:39). Jesus did drink the cup of divine wrath in our place so that we might truly enjoy the cup of our salvation.

D

Dan, City of

When the Bible speaks of Dan, it may be a reference to a son of Jacob, the tribe that descended from that son, or the city this tribe captured and made its own (Gen. 14:14; 30:6; 49:16). Here, as we focus on the city of Dan, we will see that this urban center has a very intimate relationship with Jacob's son and the tribe descended from him. Few places in the Promised Land offer the desirable living circumstances afforded by Dan. It is located at the southern base of Mount Hermon, approximately twenty-seven miles north of the Sea of Galilee. Here, for several reasons, Laish (the later Dan) became a large, fortified city even before the time of Abraham. First, it was rich in precious water, something that makes Dan most exceptional in a land that is so water impoverished. Near this city springs percolate up all along the base of Mount Hermon. This water quickly joins forces to form foaming, white-water streams that merge into the Nahr Leddan, a key tributary of the Jordan River. To the wealth of water, we can add the wonderfully rich and fertile soil that fills the pastures and agricultural fields around Dan. It is no wonder that the tribe of Dan called this "a land that lacks nothing whatever" (Judg. 18:10). Finally, Dan itself lies at a transportation hub. The massive flanks of

Mount Hermon redirect traffic around the base of this mountain so as to make Dan an important trade center and security gate at the northern tip of the Promised Land. The massive gates and walls of Dan guarded not just the residents of the city but the residents of the entire region. For those who lived in this land, "the snorting of the enemy's horses" in Dan and "neighing of their stallions" would cause the "whole land [to] tremble" (Jer. 8:16).

The biblical authors first mention this city at the time of Abram. When his nephew Lot was captured and spirited away by a city-state coalition, Abram put together a military coalition of his own and "went in pursuit as far as Dan," eventually rescuing Lot from the aggressors (Gen. 14:14). While the author of Genesis calls this city "Dan," it does not appear to have received that name until after it was taken over by the tribe of Dan. This tribe had tried and failed to secure a homeland in the region Joshua had assigned to it, so they moved north and took over the city of Leshem (or Laish), renaming it Dan after their forefather (Josh. 19:40–47; Judg. 1:34; 18:1). The next time Dan comes to center stage is following the death of Solomon. His united kingdom was divided into two separate entities, one of which was ruled by Solomon's son and the other by Jeroboam I. Jeroboam established Dan as his northern administrative center and erected a worship facility there staffed with priests who were not Levites and a calf image that was not the Lord (1 Kings 12:25–30). It continued to function as a royal cult site into and beyond the days of Jehu (2 Kings 10:29).

The rhetorical overtones and associations of Dan fall into three categories. First, Dan or, better, Laish, and its people are presented to us as innocents overridden by the ruthless tribe of Dan. This is a rather striking connotation, given the Lord's clear instructions that Canaanite cities like Laish and their inhabitants were to be totally wiped out. There was to be no intermarriage, no treaties, and no mercy shown—no exceptions (Deut. 7:1–6). This principle was clearly operative at the time of the judges, for this inspired author castigated the Israelite tribes who failed to fulfill this directive from the Lord (Judg. 1–2). That is what makes the description of Canaanite Dan so striking. This city is portrayed as vulnerable, unsuspecting, secure, and peaceful in the face of the Danites who made a violent attack on the city and burned it (Judg. 18:7–10, 27–28).

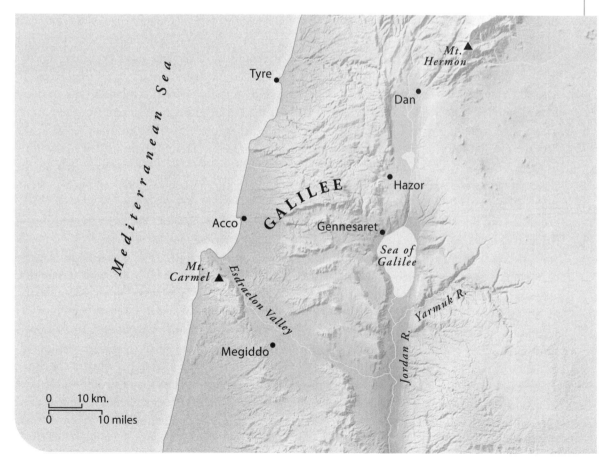

Dan.

Why did this inspired writer paint Canaanite Dan with such winsome language? This is clearly a bid to set the attitudes and actions of the Danites into a more negative frame. This incident, along with the others included in the final chapters of this book, is used to illustrate just how spiritually unkempt God's people had become during this period. And so rather than picture the taking of this Canaanite city in terms of Moses' directions in Deuteronomy, this attack against an innocent and unsuspecting people was designed to illustrate the degeneration in civility among God's people.

The second rhetorical setting in which we find Dan put to work is the formula "from Dan to Beersheba" (Judg. 20:1; 1 Sam. 3:20; 2 Sam. 3:10; 17:11; 24:2, 15; 1 Kings 4:25; 1 Chron. 21:2; 2 Chron. 30:5). This formula is a merism, a literary device by which two extremes are named with the intention of communicating the whole. The formula "from Dan to Beersheba" lists the northernmost and southernmost cities of the Promised Land. In doing so, the writer is not just drawing our attention to two cities but to all the land that lies between them. Thus "from Dan to Beersheba" is the equivalent of all the land of Israel.

This leaves the last and the most troubling connotation associated with Dan—spiritual apostasy. When the Lord made Jeroboam I king of his own portion of the Promised Land, his intentions were not to give Jeroboam a free hand in making public policy. He expected Jeroboam to honor him as he led God's people. So while at some level we can appreciate this king's need to stabilize and unite his new kingdom, we find the construction of the high place at Dan and the fostering of calf-associated worship to be what the prophets imply, rebellion and apostasy (Amos 8:14).

Dead Sea

The Dead Sea goes by a wide variety of names in the Bible, with the exception of "Dead Sea," which it acquired after the biblical period. It is called the Salt Sea (Gen. 14:3; Num. 34:3, 12; Josh. 12:3), the Sea of the Arabah (Deut. 3:17; Josh. 3:16; 2 Kings 14:25), the eastern sea (Ezek. 47:18; Joel 2:20; Zech. 14:8), and simply the sea (Ezek. 47:8; Matt. 21:21).

This inland lake, fifty-three miles long and ten miles wide, lies in a deep basin thousands of feet below the mountain ridges that surround it. From a distance, the Dead Sea is picturesque, even inviting, with its blue-green surface surrounded by gray-white mud flats that erupt with surreal and haunting geologic formations. But drawing closer, the lake takes on a more sinister feel, one that literally touches all the senses. To stand on the shore of this inland lake is to stand at the lowest place on the earth's surface, 1,300 feet below sea level. The pressure change in the descent to the lakeshore is clearly felt in the inner ear, while the rising temperature is felt on the skin. In the winter, lakeside temperatures can be comfortable, particularly in contrast to the cold and damp winter feel of Jerusalem. But in the summer, temperatures average 95°F and can reach an outrageous 125°F. Those high temperatures account for the high evaporation rate that leaves the lake basin bathed in a perpetual haze. On a summer day, up to one-half inch of water may evaporate from this closed basin. Furthermore, the pungent smell in the air, the incredible pain this water produces when it touches a small cut on your hand, and its impossible taste all betray this lake's high chemical content. The most dominant compound in the lake is salt. By contrast to the oceans of the world, which have a salt content of 3.5 percent, the Dead Sea has a salt content that approaches 33 percent. Thus the

Dead Sea is not only the lowest body of water on the earth's surface, but it is also the most chemical laden.

In the culture of the Bible, the Dead Sea functioned in two ways. As a dominating natural feature, it was often perceived as a political border. For example, this lake marked the eastern border of Canaan (Num. 34:3, 12), helped to mark the boundaries of Judah and Benjamin (Josh. 15:2, 5; 18:19), and was used to mark both real and anticipated restoration of Israel's borders (2 Kings 14:25; Ezek. 47:18). On the other hand, the salt and bitumen harvested from the lake were marketable commodities that produced an income for those willing to labor in the heat to obtain them. The salt was used regionally in a variety of applications, including preserving fish and seasoning food. Bitumen was sold to those who needed a waterproofing agent for their boats

and to the Egyptians who used it in the mummification process.

On the rhetorical side, the biblical authors import qualities of the Dead Sea into their messages. In the crescendo of his final chapter, Zechariah speaks of the coming day of the Lord. Among the various images he uses to describe the power and wonder of that day, he speaks of living water flowing outward from Jerusalem, half of which descends into the eastern sea (Zech. 14:8). This appears to be the same imagery at work in Ezekiel 47, but imagery that Ezekiel takes to new heights. In his fantastic tour of the new era, Ezekiel is brought to the entrance of the temple at Jerusalem. Water is pouring from that complex and descending in an ever-deepening torrent toward the Dead Sea (Ezek. 47:1–7). When the water arrives at the Salt Sea, an amazing thing happens: it changes this salty sea into

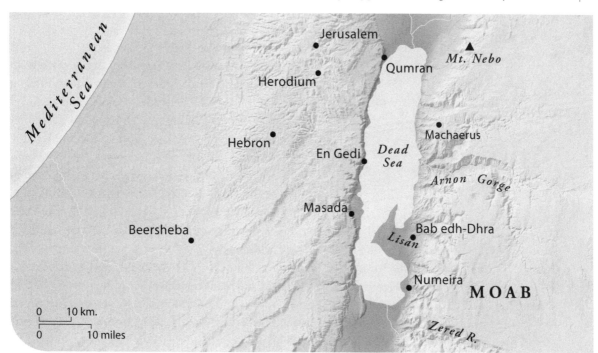

Dead Sea.

a freshwater lake. The body of water that was so chemical laden that it became known as the "Dead Sea" now swarms with living creatures. In fact, the number of fish is so great that fishermen spread their nets on the shoreline in anticipation of an extraordinary catch (Ezek. 47:7–10). Thus Ezekiel pictures the dramatic change of the new era by noting how the water from the new temple has the power to change this dead lake into a living sea.

On at least one occasion, Jesus also co-opted the Dead Sea into his teaching. During the last week of his life on earth, Jesus was crossing the

Fallow deer.
© Pawel Strykowski/www.BigStockPhoto.com

Mount of Olives, descending into the city of Jerusalem. As he walked this route, two landmarks came into view, the Herodium and the Dead Sea. The Herodium was a palace set on top of an artificially shaped mountain. When Herod the Great was looking for a building site for his palace-fortress that would double as a monumental tomb upon his death, he did not

find one high enough to suit his ego. Consequently, he picked a site and ordered that the soil and stone of a nearby mountain be moved to his building site. Herod had moved a mountain, an event that became a symbol for the pagan intrusion of a Roman-occupied Promised Land. Jesus said to his disciples that if they had faith and did not doubt, they too could move a mountain simply by saying, "Go throw yourself into the sea" (Matt. 21:21). Jewish tradition observes that the Dead Sea is the place for disposing of articles with a pagan connection (Mishnah, *Abodah Zarah* 3:3, 9). When we link the connotations of the Herodium and the Dead Sea, Jesus' point becomes clearer. People with wealth and power can move mountains. But in the kingdom of God, those with true faith can demand that the symbols of paganism be sent off to their proper place, and it will happen.

Deer

Today the wild deer has all but disappeared from the landscape of Israel. But particularly during the Old Testament era, this shy and graceful member of the animal kingdom lived among God's people in the Promised Land. These shy and skittish creatures preferred to remain secluded from the eyes of people and predators by living in forests and open woodlands. But when the ancients did glimpse the deer of their world, they were likely to see one of the three types known to inhabit this region: the red deer, the fallow deer, or the roe deer. The red deer is the tallest of the three, standing upward of five feet at the shoulder. The other two are much smaller and distinguished from one another primarily by the presence or absence of spots. The fallow deer is only about three feet tall, with thick, mooselike antlers. Its reddish-brown coat is punctuated by white spots that are sported not only by the fawns but by the mature animals as well. The mature roe deer is slightly smaller than the fallow deer, lacks the spots, and distinguishes itself by its solitary lifestyle, preferring to roam alone rather than in herds.

In Bible times deer were hunted for food. Deer are repeatedly listed among the animals that may appear on Israel's dinner table (Deut. 12:15, 22; 14:5; 15:22). There is no evidence that the deer was domesticated like the sheep and goat, but there is evidence from the ancient world that Assyrian kings established game reserves with managed deer herds. We are not sure if Solomon had such a reserve, but we do know that venison, together with beef and mutton, was on the list of meat required to feed his royal household each day (1 Kings 4:23).

The appearance and behavior of the deer is captured in a variety of metaphors in our Bible. The deer has a wonderful beauty that is enhanced by its sleek and graceful lines. The wife of one's youth is marked by the same qualities and so is compared to "a loving doe, a graceful deer" (Prov. 5:19).

Large predators also found the deer attractive, but in an entirely different way. So God created the deer with a remarkable ability to escape predators by bounding and leaping past obstacles that leave their pursuers frustrated and hungry. Isaiah promised that when the Messiah arrived, those who were disabled would experience his healing touch. Some of those who had been unable to walk well would "leap like a deer" (Isa. 35:6). We witness such miracles in the Gospels and Acts (Matt. 15:30; Luke 7:22; John 5:8–9; Acts 3:8).

Despite their ability to escape predators, members of the deer family are very cautious about exposing themselves, preferring to remain under the cover of the forest. When they do expose themselves, that exposure can be mitigated by taking up a position on high ground so that they can keep a sharp eye out for any approaching predators. High ground that affords the best view gives them greater confidence. Perhaps this is the image conveyed in the following passages. In two of these passages, it is David who is celebrating the heightened confidence he feels now that he has escaped his enemies. The Lord is the one who "makes my feet like the feet of a deer; he enables me to stand on the heights" (2 Sam. 22:34; Ps. 18:33). When closing his book, Habakkuk uses exactly this same language to celebrate the secure confidence he finds in his Sovereign Lord (Hab. 3:19).

There is, however, one threat faced by the deer that is unmitigated by their leaping ability, speed, or even retreat to higher ground. When drought or famine seizes the region, the lack of water and pasture create great hardship for deer. During such a time, deer wander from one dry streambed to the next in search of the vital drink of water their bodies demand. The psalmist likens his spiritual need to this physical need of the deer: "As the deer pants for streams of water, so my soul pants for you, O God. My soul thirsts for God, for the living God" (Ps. 42:1–2). And in the lament that bemoans the sorry state of Israel following the fall of the capital city, this inspired poet recalls the horrible moment when the Babylonians had broken through walls of Jerusalem. At that moment and although weakened by hunger, the royal family made a break for the Arabah, only to be overtaken and captured in the plains of Jericho (Jer. 52:6–8). For the inspired poet of Lamentations, this scene recalled deer that searched desperately for pasture during a famine but to no avail. Predators finally overtook and captured the weakened prey: "All the splendor has departed from the Daughter of Zion. Her princes are like deer that find no pasture; in weakness they have fled before the pursuer" (Lam. 1:6).

Dew

If you perceive dew to be a nuisance that delays the cutting of your lawn or an irritation that makes your morning jog more treacherous, a change in perception will be necessary to enter the thought world of the Bible where a heavy dewfall is always good news. The air around us typically contains moisture, but it largely remains invisible until the atmosphere is sufficiently cooled to the dew point. That is the temperature at which the invisible moisture in the air is compelled to show itself in the form of clouds, precipitation, or dew. Consequently, dew forms when moist air comes into contact with a collecting surface that is at or below the dew point.

This is exactly what happens in Israel almost every summer night. The Promised Land receives virtually no rainfall throughout the summer months, but that does not mean the atmosphere lacks water. The prevailing westerly winds of the summer season cause moisture-laden air masses, formed over the Mediterranean Sea, to penetrate deep into the Promised Land. When evening comes and the atmosphere cools, dew forms on plants, rocks, animals, and everything else. It is not unusual to awaken on a summer morning to find everything so covered with moisture that it appears as if it had rained. Far from an inconvenience, this heavy dew fall is a real blessing. When the spring rains stop falling, the summer crops are still maturing. The grapes, figs, pomegranates, and melons count on the dew as a principal source of moisture while

maturing during the summer months. Thus the summer dew means a successful harvest that contributes to a settled and secure life in this land (Deut. 33:28).

While the arrival of dew was critical to successful living in the Promised Land, it was also a controversial topic. In the Old Testament, both Baal and the Lord are said to be the source of this precious moisture. Old Testament authors often reveal words and actions of the Lord that resolve this ideological tension in his favor. The Lord calls himself the one who "rides on the heavens ... and on the clouds in his majesty"; he makes "the heavens drop dew" (Deut. 33:26, 28; cf. Prov. 3:20). He not only says it but also illustrates it in dramatic ways. When Ahab and Jezebel championed Baal, the Lord shut down both the rain and dew to demonstrate who really controlled this moisture (1 Kings 17:1). Later, when the returning exiles failed to prioritize the rebuilding of the temple, the heavens withheld their dew (Hag. 1:10); and when Israel got it right, the Lord reversed his judgment and allowed the heavens to "drop their dew" (Zech. 8:12).

But perhaps the most striking demonstration of the Lord's control of the dewfall occurs in Judges 6. This was a time when Israel was struggling to separate itself from the worship of Baal (Judg. 6:7–10). It had gotten so bad that Israelites had actually built altars for Baal in such places as Ophrah. When Gideon destroyed this worship site, he faced a hostile crowd who insisted that he be executed for dishonoring Baal in this way (6:25–31). Perhaps this best explains why Gideon subsequently asked for a miracle that required the unnatural manipulation of dewfall by the Lord. When Gideon held up a dry fleece surrounded by a threshing floor damp with dew, this visual sent a clear message to all (6:37–40);

the Lord and not Baal was the one who provided dew from the heavens and determined just where this precious gift would fall.

Dew also falls rhetorically in a variety of biblical texts where its various qualities are used as metaphors. Dew is generally associated with blessing. It is connected with the miraculous manna provided during Israel's time in the wilderness (Ex. 16:13–14; Num. 11:9). And we have seen what a remarkable blessing it is to have "God give you of heaven's dew" (Gen. 27:28). The very real blessing of dew makes it a fitting symbol for anything that is considered good and desirable. Moses asks that his words, words that come from the Lord, might descend on the people of God like life-giving dew (Deut. 32:2). In recalling the better days of his life, Job likens them to the tree whose branches are laden throughout the night with dew (Job 29:19). When people live in harmony with one another, the ensuing unity is "as if the dew of Hermon were falling on Mount Zion" (Ps. 133:3). A king's favor is like the "dew on the grass" (Prov. 19:12). And the restoration of Israel will occur when the Lord provides the necessary "dew of the morning" that will rouse his people from death (Isa. 26:19).

A second quality of dew is its pervasiveness; dew indiscriminately covers everything. When Hushai was providing Absalom with advice on how best to secure his position on David's throne after driving his father from it, Hushai urged Absalom to delay immediate military action against his fleeing father, gather a superior military force from throughout the kingdom, and then fall on David "as dew settles on the ground" (2 Sam. 17:12).

Finally, when tracing the mention of dew in Hosea, dew helps to define the evolving message of the book. Hosea first likens the flagging loyalty of Israel to dew. Just as the dew evaporates with warming rays of the morning sun, so the loyalty of Israel to their God had quickly vanished (Hos. 6:4). The evaporation of that loyalty led the Lord to impose judgment on them. Their loyalty had evaporated like dew, so the Lord would now make them disappear as quickly as the early dew (13:3). But for those who returned to the Lord and sought his favor, the Lord pictured his new relationship with Israel using an image that had only appeared with negative connotations earlier: "I will be like the dew to Israel; he will blossom like a lily" (14:5).

Dog

Many of us have enjoyed a very personal relationship with a dog, the family pet with which we have shared life, long walks, and even our bed. The biblical authors know of dogs but not as the companion animals that have enriched our lives. This is in no small part because the dog is one of the animals deemed "unclean" by the Lord's own definition (Lev. 11; Deut. 14:1–21). Although the dog is not formally mentioned in these lists, the only place it fits is among the unclean animals that are not fit for food or sacrifice. Far from being loving pets, dogs were to be shunned. This limits the contact the average Israelite would have with a dog and causes this animal to be perceived as a real pariah. The kindest acknowledgment of this beleaguered animal we find in the Bible is the faint praise in Ecclesiastes where a living dog is said to be better off than a dead lion (Eccl. 9:4).

Dogs of two types dominate the references in the Bible, working dogs that played a role in safeguarding the sheep (Job 30:1) and the wild to semiwild dogs that scavenge in packs, eating whatever carrion or discarded food they can find (Ex. 22:31). In the ancient Near East, two other types of dogs are known from ancient art and the archaeological record. Both Egyptian and Mesopotamian cultures employed dogs in hunting wild game. And Phoenicia joined the Egyptian and Mesopotamian cultures in linking the dog to worship centers that offered healing. Perhaps this has something to do with the perceived medicinal value of a dog licking a sore. But these latter uses of the dog are unknown or unreported by the Bible's authors.

Three specific traits or behaviors of the dog appear in biblical texts. Dogs have the rather disgusting habit of returning to their vomit. This

behavior is likened to the fool who shows an inclination to return to his folly (Prov. 26:11). Dogs are also very sensitive about their ears. That leads the inspired poet to make this comparison: "Like one who seizes a dog by the ears is a passer-by who meddles in a quarrel not his own" (Prov. 26:17). But the behavior of the wild dog most frequently noted by the Bible's authors is its propensity to lick blood from the dead or dying and to consume carrion. When a person is the object of this behavior, it is considered to be a sign of grave disrespect, because no one has stepped in to prevent this unclean animal from delivering this unseemly service. The disobe-

A working dog assists the shepherd tending the flock.

Todd Bolen/www.BiblePlaces.com

dience of kings can mean that they and their families will experience this indignity. Both the house of Jeroboam and Baasha are told that their remains will be consumed by dogs (1 Kings 14:11; 16:4). A bit later in Kings, Ahab and Jezebel conspire to execute the innocent Naboth and allow the dogs to lick up his blood. Consequently, the wanton disrespect experienced by Naboth would come home to roost on the day of their deaths, for dogs would lick up the blood of Ahab and devour the remains of Jezebel (1 Kings 21:19–24; 22:38; 2 Kings 9:10, 36). The Lord taps into this same behavior of the feral dogs when delivering a prophecy against his chosen people. He will send the "sword to kill and the dogs to drag away" (Jer. 15:3). Thus to be eaten or licked by this unclean animal is, in the Bible's perspective, to be abandoned by all who might otherwise care to save one from this indignity. In the story Jesus told about the rich man and Lazarus, the latter's pitiful condition is clearly marked by these words: "Even the dogs came and licked his sores" (Luke 16:21).

The inspired authors of the Bible also mention dogs in a variety of metaphors. The dog received so little respect as a creature that people perceived to be of low value are likened to dogs. This connotation is quietly present in the description of the three hundred soldiers of Gideon's army whom the Lord would use to rescue his people from oppression. These are the men who lapped "the water with their tongues like a dog" (Judg. 7:5). But this connotation is shouted during Goliath's thundering rebuke of the less experienced David and his weapons: "Am I a dog, that you come at me with sticks?" (1 Sam. 17:43). And in the New Testament, the sharp exchange between Jesus and the Canaanite woman is marked by the use of a dog as metaphor (Matt. 15:26–27; Mark 7:27–28). When this Gentile seeks help for her daughter from a Jewish Messiah, Jesus declares that the children's food is never tossed to the dogs. Although this woman is painted with this offensive image, she quickly responds by noting that even dogs like her get to eat the scraps from the table.

To be called a dog is one thing, but to be called a dead dog is to take matters yet another step. Nevertheless, that is what David did. After he had spared the life of Saul, he proclaimed himself to be nothing more than a "dead dog" surely unworthy of Saul's relentless pursuit (1 Sam. 24:14). Ironically, or perhaps quite intentionally, Saul's grandson Mephibosheth likened himself to a dead dog upon meeting David after David had been established as king of Israel (2 Sam. 9:8).

Isaiah appears to have the herding dog in mind when he directs criticism at Israel's spiritual watchmen who have failed to fulfill their responsibilities in protecting God's people. They are described as mute dogs that sound no warning, lazy dogs that prefer to sleep than work, yet demand that their insatiable appetite for food be addressed (Isa. 56:10–11).

Finally, the violent side of the feral dogs from Bible times becomes a symbol of enemies that bring harm. These are the violent men who threaten David and surround the Messiah in a menacing way (Pss. 22:16, 20; 59:6, 14). And in the New Testament, those who oppose Christ's gospel and his kingdom are likened to dogs (Phil. 3:2; Rev. 22:15).

Donkey

The unmistakable braying of the disturbed donkey was as common as it was unnerving in Bible times. This otherwise unassuming animal is mentioned more than 140 time in the Bible, as likely to be owned by the wealthy Job as a poor orphan (Job 1:3; 24:3). The donkey is smaller than the standard size horse and ranges in color from chocolate brown to dull gray. But no matter the color, the donkey almost always has a pair of narrow, dark stripes that run down the middle of its back and across its shoulders.

The donkey was such a common member of the Israelite household that it is mentioned in a number of their laws. If through negligence or malice one caused the death or injury of a donkey, the law required that the owner be compensated (Ex. 21:33–34; 22:10–13). An animal

Donkey carrying an Egyptian girl.
Copyright 1995-2011 Phoenix Data Systems

that was either straying or had fallen beneath its load was to be assisted immediately, even when that donkey belonged to an enemy (Ex. 23:4–5). And this hardworking animal in particular was to enjoy a day of rest on the Sabbath along with God's people (Ex. 23:12).

On the other days of the week, the donkey was employed in a variety of tasks. It plowed the fields (Deut. 22:10; Isa. 30:24), but this activity is rarely mentioned in contrast to the dozens of times we read about donkeys carrying people or goods on their backs (e.g., 2 Sam. 16:1–2). Although the donkey could carry only a fraction of the weight carried by a freight camel (about a hundred pounds compared to five hundred pounds), the sure-footed donkey bested the camel at walking the narrow, steep, and rocky trails that wound through the mountain interior of the Promised Land. And when it came time to graze, the donkey proved far less picky than a horse or camel, willing to eat lower quality forage that grew along the trails. In some cultures of the ancient Near East, the donkey was eaten and used for religious sacrifices, particularly the sacrifice that marked the confirming of a contract. But the donkey never found its way to the Israelite dinner table or altar, because it was an unclean animal. The one exception we see in the Bible is associated with the siege of Samaria when things had gotten so bad that people were willing to pay an exorbitant price for the head of a donkey (2 Kings 6:25).

A number of connotations are associated with the donkey in Bible texts. There was nothing special about owning a donkey, but owning large numbers of these animals was something special. The bedouin in particular measured their wealth via livestock, so we find the wealth of men like Abraham, Jacob, and Job defined in terms of the hundreds of donkeys they owned (Gen. 24:35;

30:43; Job 1:3; 42:12). An increase in this wealth could legitimately be achieved via gift, breeding, or divinely directed conquest (Gen. 32:13 – 15; Num. 31:32 – 35). And it is this connection between wealth and the donkey that explains the special mention of it in the Ten Commandments: "You shall not covet your neighbor's wife, or his manservant or maidservant, his ox or donkey, or anything that belongs to your neighbor" (Ex. 20:17).

Riding a donkey could be a symbol of wealth or prestige, particularly when each of your sons had one to ride (Judg. 10:4) or when the donkey had a distinctive appearance like the albino donkeys mentioned in the song of Deborah (Judg. 5:10). Riding a donkey can also signal that a trip is urgent. For example, Abigail rode quickly to assuage the anger of David and later did the same in response to the invitation to become his bride (1 Sam. 25:18 – 20, 42). And when her son died, the Shunammite rode as quickly as she could to seek the assistance of Elisha (2 Kings 4:22 – 24).

The use of the donkey in a metaphor is quite rare. In blessing his sons, Jacob called Issachar a "rawboned donkey," likely a reference to the animal's strength that would characterize this family and tribe (Gen. 49:14). God through the prophet Isaiah castigated the people of Isaiah's day for their rebellion with this image from everyday life: "The ox knows his master, the donkey his owner's manger, but Israel does not know, my people do not understand" (Isa. 1:3). Israel did not know nor acknowledge the Lord who had directed and fed them. When a donkey died, it was not likely to receive any kind of burial. That explains what Jeremiah meant when he said that King Jehoiakim would "have the burial of a donkey" (Jer. 22:19). And finally, the inspired writer of wisdom observes that the fool can only be controlled like an animal: "A whip for the horse, a halter for the donkey, and a rod for the backs of fools!" (Prov. 26:3).

There are two notable stories in the Bible in which the donkey plays a key role. In the first, Balaam has been hired by Moab to put a curse on the Israelites. His employer believed that Balaam had the ability to know the mind of God and to manipulate him through the practice of sympathetic magic. Even before Balaam had a chance to give it a try, the Lord appeared before him. But ironically it was not the gifted seer who saw the Lord; it was the donkey he was riding. Through a number of nonverbal and verbal exchanges with this animal, the simple donkey proved herself more adept and knowledgeable than Balaam (Num. 22:21 – 33).

The other account in which a donkey plays a prominent role is the day Jesus entered Jerusalem surrounded by thronging crowds who celebrated the coming of their King. Jesus had entered the city many times before, but he had not entered the city riding on a donkey (Matt. 21:2 – 9). This time he planned his entry carefully to fulfill what was said about the Messiah in Zechariah 9:9. He would come to his people "righteous and having salvation, gentle and riding on a donkey."

Dove

The word *dove* in our Bible can represent a variety of birds that we may know as doves or pigeons. These medium-sized birds are between eight and twelve inches in length, with plumage in a variety of pleasing tones. Today we still can see descendants of the Bible's doves in the soft blue-gray of the rock dove, the pale purple-pink of the turtle dove, or the ruddy brown pastels of the laughing dove. To live in Bible times was to be very familiar with these shy birds, some of which were migrants that used the Promised Land as a flyway while others were resident birds that remained in the Promised Land throughout the year.

The dove was domesticated very early in this region's history and so functioned in various ways in biblical culture. Rather than being caged, domesticated doves were kept close to home by creating nesting habitat for them. Wild doves roost on the ledges of rising terrain and in the small openings of rocky slopes. Domesticated birds were provided with artificial nesting sites called dovecotes or *columbaria*, which often consisted of nesting niches carved into a clay column or cave wall. Alternatively, the dovecote could be as simple as a few clay jars placed horizontally on the roof of a house.

The effort to make such a dovecote was easily justified for an animal that was both a source of food and approved for use in burnt offerings and sin offerings (Lev. 1:14; 5:7). Women who had given birth were to bring a lamb and a dove for sacrifice in connection with their purification rites, but when poverty prevented offering the lamb, a bird could be substituted for the lamb (Lev. 12:6–8). This is exactly what we see Mary doing following the birth of Jesus when she elects to offer two birds rather than a lamb and a bird (Luke 2:22–24). In this case and in many others, the poor were given the option of substituting a less costly dove for a more expensive animal, so the dove is linked to the worship of the poor in the land. During the days of the New Testament, there were upward of three hundred shops in Jerusalem that sold doves to pilgrims coming to worship at the temple. But the one dove market that felt Jesus' disapproval was located in the temple complex. He overturned the benches of those selling doves (Matt. 21:12; Mark 11:15), and he shouted at those who sold them, "Get these out of here! How dare you turn my Father's house into a market!" (John 2:16).

The habits and nature of the common dove were turned into a wonderful array of metaphors by the poets and prophets of the Bible. The tender beauty of this creature guaranteed that it would become a term of endearment. As the delight of the Lord, Israel is called his dove (Pss. 68:13; 74:19). In the Song of Songs, the beautiful yet timid young woman who is the object of desire is also called a dove (Song 2:14; 5:2; 6:9). Her eyes are further likened

Turtle dove.
© Nico Smit/www.BigStockPhoto.com

to those of a dove, perhaps because their color resembles the soft, pastel tones found in the feathers of this bird (1:15; 4:1).

The vocalization of the dove sounds to some like the bird is mourning. So the prophets speak of King Hezekiah moaning like a mourning dove as he looked to the heavens for healing and of others moaning like doves as they sought help and deliverance (Isa. 38:14; 59:11; Nah. 2:7). On the other hand, the cooing that was linked to mourning was also linked to romance, for the cooing of a dove signals that spring has arrived, a time when love is truly in the air (Song 2:12).

When danger threatens, the dove takes flight. The psalmist longs to exercise that ability in order to escape harm: "Oh, that I had the wings of a dove! I would fly away and be at rest" (Ps. 55:6). That flight may take the dove to the safety of its nest. In that vein, Isaiah likens the nations streaming toward Zion to doves that are winging their way homeward (Isa. 60:8). Alternatively, such flight might take the wild dove to a place of refuge in the clefts of the mountains. Jeremiah says that the residents of Moab will flee their towns ahead of the Babylonian invasion and dwell among the rocks just as a dove "makes its nest at the mouth of a cave" (Jer. 48:28).

The Lord looks at the migrating birds and notes how doves obey the divine direction of their instincts, observing the time of their migration, while the Israelites ignore the God-given requirements that are to direct their migrations through life. This rebellion would mean exile from the Promised Land; but when they returned, they would return from their exile like migrating doves (Hos. 11:11).

Finally, the dove is perceived as a bird of great vulnerability. This leads the Lord to compare Ephraim to a dove, so easily deceived and senseless in their sinning (Hos. 7:11). While this passage berates God's people for being like a dove, Jesus encourages his disciples to present themselves with the quiet vulnerability of a dove (Matt. 10:16).

In Christian art the dove has often been used to picture the presence of the Holy Spirit. This imagery is linked to the day of Jesus' baptism when the Spirit of God descended like a dove and lighted upon him (Matt. 3:16; Mark 1:10; Luke 3:22; John 1:32). Why, of all the creatures in our world, was the dove the form the Spirit chose to appear in? We would be remiss if we did not consider the possible connection between this choice

and the first dove we read about in the Bible. Noah sent a dove from the ark in an attempt to learn if the floodwaters had receded from the land (Gen. 8:8–12). This dove signaled the start of a new era in the world's history. Perhaps the appearance of the dove at Jesus' baptism helps signal the new era that was beginning in his life.

Dung (Manure)

We tend to be very discreet when talking about our bathroom habits and the product of our visits to the bathroom. It is a topic generally avoided in polite company, and we might expect it to be a topic avoided by the Bible's authors as well. But quite to the contrary, human and animal waste products are mentioned more often than we might expect in both literal and figurative contexts, though they often go unrecognized because our English translations have used more polite language that obscures their presence. While we honor the choice of those translators,

Woman with the drying manure she will use to build a fire.

we also acknowledge the unintended outcome of their decision, the softening of the rhetorical impact of those metaphors.

The Bible's mention of literal dung falls into two categories: human and animal waste. Given the unclean nature of human excrement, the Old Testament law directs that human waste be removed from populated areas and buried in a discreet spot (Deut. 23:13). The goal is obviously to diminish contact between people and the waste products produced by their bodies. Consequently, those instances where this norm is violated stand out starkly. The bellicose Assyrian commander who was threatening to put Jerusalem under a long siege predicted that things would get so bad that people would resort to eating their own excrement (Isa. 36:12). In his prophecy against Nineveh, the Lord promised this nation would be pelted with excrement (Nah. 3:6), something that humiliated the person on the receiving end as much as it was designed to humiliate a wanna-be deity like Baal (2 Kings 10:27).

Animal manure did not carry the same cultural stigma. It was useful for those who wished to build a fire or fertilize their fields. Wood was a very scarce commodity in the Promised Land and so was rarely used as fuel for a fire. Instead, the residents of this land would gather dry manure from the fields to use in making fires. Ezekiel recoiled from the Lord's directive to make a cooking fire using human excrement and was thankful that the Lord relented, allowing him to bake with the usual dry manure (Ezek. 4:12–15). To this day in the less-developed areas of Israel, we still find people gathering manure from the fields, mixing in salt, and forming flat, combustible pancakes used for cooking fires. The addition of salt allows the charcoal pancake to burn even more effectively than it would without the salt. When Jesus spoke about salt that had lost its saltiness being unfit for the manure pile, this is the cultural reality he had in view (Luke 14:35).

Apart from fuel for cooking, manure was also used to restore the fertility of agricultural fields and soil around fruit trees. Once the grain had been harvested, the shepherds were invited to bring their flocks into the agricultural fields to eat the leftovers and leave behind valuable fertilizer (Luke 2:8). But manure could also be gathered and mixed with straw to create compost that was dug in around grapevines (Luke 13:8). Even though this material disappears quickly from the surface (Job 20:7), it promises to improve the subsequent harvest.

Both human and animal waste appear in metaphors that fit into two categories, metaphors that liken dung to sin and metaphors that employ dung in judgment speeches. In the first instance, the uncleanness of human excrement is likened to the uncleanness of sin. The wise poet knows of those who are pure in their own eyes but who in reality "are not cleansed of their filth" (Prov. 30:12). And the divine poet gets very graphic in discussing the fall of Jerusalem, indicating that this city faced divine judgment because "her filthiness clung to her skirts" (Lam. 1:9). Nevertheless, Isaiah sees a time coming when the "LORD will wash away the filth of the women of Zion" (Isa. 4:4), a forgiveness that marks a new age. The same image appears in Zechariah where Joshua the high priest represents the nation of Israel. Here the Lord likens the removal of sin to the removal of this man's "filthy clothes" (Zech. 3:3–4).

Dung is also linked to metaphors associated with divine judgment. In these metaphors what typically happens to manure happens to those facing God's wrath. The composting of straw and manure as fertilizer is in view when Isaiah announces that Moab "will be trampled under him as straw is trampled down in the manure" (Isa. 25:10). The burning of dung as fuel is in view as the Lord announces his judgment on the ruling family of Jeroboam: "I will burn up the house of Jeroboam as one burns dung, until it is all gone" (1 Kings 14:10). And then there is a series of judgment speeches that declare that a person or nation will be made like dung. Sisera, Jabin, and Jezebel, for example, all became "like refuse on the ground" (2 Kings 9:37; Ps. 83:10). In a long list of woes, Isaiah sees God's own people struck down and lying like "refuse in the streets" (Isa. 5:25). And Jeremiah sees the same in store for the people of Judah whose dead bodies will cover the countryside and be untended by their families. Rather than receiving a dignified burial, the remains of these people will become fertilizer for next year's harvest, like manure on the ground (Jer. 8:2; 9:22; 16:4).

Dye

For most of the year in most places, the Promised Land is a pretty drab place. While beautiful in its own way, the natural landscape of Israel is generally quite bland, ranging in tone from light tan to dark brown, completely void of eye-popping colors. It is against this backdrop that we need to view the dye industry of the biblical world and the use of colored cloth as symbol and metaphor in the Bible.

The goal of the dyeing guild was to offer cloth in a variety of eye-catching colors, including red, purple, yellow, and blue. Minerals, plants, animals, and even insects were tapped for the pigments used in the dye. But the creatures that make the greatest mark in the world of dyeing are the shellfish called murex. These creatures, which live in the shallow coastal waters of the Mediterranean Sea, were harvested by the tens of thousands because of the vibrant purple liquid produced in their glands. Some of this liquid could be extracted by crushing the entire creature; but the very best of the indelible dye came from a small, stingy gland that offered its harvesters only one drop of dye per

Murex shells were crushed to make a vibrant purple dye.
Z. Radovan/www.BibleLandPictures.com

creature. It took somewhere in the neighborhood of twelve thousand shells to produce just 1.5 grams of dye. Given the labor involved, we can appreciate why the cloth that was colored by this purple dye was so precious and so costly. According to one ancient source, wool dyed purple was thirty times more expensive than an equal amount of wool that had not been dyed. This lucrative industry centered in places like Lydia's home, Thyatira, known for the wonderful purple cloth it produced (Acts 16:14); but pride of place went to the ancient Phoenicians who were the real experts in this art (2 Chron. 2:7, 14). The process and recipes for making dyed goods remains the unpublished secret of the craftspersons who made them. Nevertheless, we do find dye-making infrastructure in many communities along the eastern shore of the Mediterranean Sea where salt, heat, and sunlight were available to process the murex dye. The end product that went to market from these facilities included clothing, carriage seats, and hangings that adorned the royal gardens (Esth. 1:6; Prov. 31:21; Song 3:10).

We find in the Bible colorful dyed goods appearing in settings that suggest such vibrant goods were a symbol of distinction. Birth order was very important in Israel's culture because of important social connotations linked to it. When twins were born, the midwife had to be particularly careful to note which twin would receive the privileges of the firstborn. One way to mark this special child was with a scarlet thread that the midwife tied around the wrist of the firstborn (Gen. 38:28–30). There was also to be nothing mundane about the buildings and people associated with worship of the Lord. In that light, brightly dyed fabrics were used when constructing the tabernacle and the temple, and when dressing the clergy (Ex. 25:4; 26:1, 31, 37;

et al.). Garments that marked royalty were also dyed in bright colors, such as those worn by the Midianite kings and daughters of Saul (Judg. 8:26; 2 Sam. 1:24). And it was not just the royals but those whom the royals chose to honor who were dressed with such garments. The service of Mordecai and of Daniel was recognized by gifts that included brightly colored garments (Esth. 8:15; Dan. 5:7, 16, 29). And if political power or service did not earn one such a garment, then a person's wealth might well purchase one. A colorful purple garment was a signal that a person was very well-to-do. In Jesus' story about the rich man and Lazarus, we are not given the name of the wealthy aristocrat whose eternal outcome varied so dramatically from his poor counterpart, but we are told that he "dressed in purple and fine linen and lived in luxury every day" (Luke 16:19).

The dyeing process and the associated garments it produced are further used in several striking rhetorical settings in God's Word. These images and lessons become even more meaningful and unforgettable against the cultural background of the ancient dye industry. In the first chapter of Isaiah, the Lord strongly rebukes the rebellious nature of his chosen nation. Their behavior has been so outrageous that the Lord likens their sin to scarlet or crimson dye. We might well expect someone marked by this attention-getting, indelible dye to face the full weight of divine judgment. Yet this is the word of encouragement the Lord brings: "Though your sins are like scarlet, they shall be as white as snow; though they are red as crimson, they shall be like wool" (Isa. 1:18).

That forgiveness could be offered because another was dressed in a purple robe and because that one endured the derision associated with it. While Jesus was in Roman custody, the soldiers mocked his claim to be a king by dressing him in a red-purple robe, the symbol of privilege and royalty. Pilate put Jesus on display in this distinctively dyed robe, hoping that such humiliation might teach Jesus a lesson and satisfy the bloodlust of those calling for his death (Matt. 27:28; Mark 15:17, 20; John 19:2, 5). But this king was to follow a different path to royal recognition. And it was his death on the cross that resulted in the most extraordinary dyeing process mentioned in the Bible. John's look into life in heaven revealed a great multitude from every nation and people who had "washed their robes and made them white in the blood of the Lamb" (Rev. 7:14).

E

Eagle

Few images from the natural world have the power to captivate the observer's attention like the majestic soaring of an eagle. As many as six different species of eagle fly above the hills and valleys of the Promised Land, from the resident Bonelli's eagle to the migrating short-toed eagle. Yet there are only two literal references to eagles in the Bible; both warn the Israelites against considering the eagle as a source of food (Lev. 11:13; Deut. 14:12). The eagle typically hunts live prey, resorting to carrion only by necessity. But it is this latter practice that likely lands it on the list of unclean animals, detestable to the Israelites. Two other references to the eagle in the Old Testament are equally literal but at the same time other-worldly. These are the references to the living creatures that reside in the presence of the Lord; each have four faces, one of which is the face of an eagle (Ezek. 1:10; 10:14).

The remaining references to the eagle turn our attention to various habits and qualities of this raptor that are employed in metaphors. These are metaphors associated with the eagle's flight, nesting habits, and care of its young. To appreciate the fascination with the eagle's flight, we need to begin by recalling that people in Bible times had no experience with flight. The notion of humans flying seems quite banal to us, given the fact that three out of four Americans have flown in an airplane, most multiple times. But the notion of flight was thousands of years beyond those living in Bible times; hence

A female Bonelli's eagle.
© Jose B. Ruiz/www.naturepl.com

the flight of the eagle was even more captivating for the ancients, filling the people of Bible times with awe and wonder (Job 39:27; Prov. 30:19).

Three different dimensions of the eagle's flight are seized upon for use in metaphors, beginning with its ability to soar. With powerful sweeps of its wings, the eagle searches out rising currents of air that allow it to fix its wings and soar. In such thermals, the eagle can circle at altitude with apparent ease in contrast to other birds that must beat their wings to sustain flight. In a similar way, those who hope in the Lord can soar tirelessly through life. Their youthful energy will match that of the eagle in flight (Ps. 103:5): "They will soar on wings like eagles; they will run and not grow weary, they will walk and not be faint" (Isa. 40:31).

Second, flight allows the eagle to cover great distances in a relatively short amount of time. While earthbound travelers are left to circumnavigate, climb, or cross natural obstacles, migrating eagles can cross the thousands of miles between Africa and Europe in a direct line. The Israelite migration from bondage in Egypt to the base of Mount Sinai is likened to that of an eagle's migration: "You yourselves have seen what I did to Egypt, and how I carried you on eagles' wings and brought you to myself" (Ex. 19:4). In a reprise of this kind of escape, the woman of Revelation 12 is given the two wings of a great eagle to facilitate her escape (Rev. 12:14). In the world of metaphor, the transient nature of riches is also said to travel like an eagle: "Cast but a glance at riches, and they are gone, for they will surely sprout wings and fly off to the sky like an eagle" (Prov. 23:5).

The third characteristic of the eagle's flight noted by the biblical authors is its incredible diving speed. When hunting, the eagle can leave its lofty soaring perch and dive at speeds well over seventy-five miles per hour to attack its earthbound prey. When lamenting the shortness of mortal life, Job likened the speed of his passing days to the diving speed of an eagle (Job 9:26). Yet the most common use of this diving speed in metaphor is the celebration of military capability. When David lamented the loss of Saul and Jonathan, he called them "swifter than eagles" (2 Sam. 1:23). The same image celebrates the military prowess of Babylon in general (Jer. 4:13; Lam. 4:19; Dan. 7:4) and their king, Nebuchadnezzar, in particular (Jer. 49:22; Ezek. 17:3).

In addition to the flying characteristics of the eagle, the Bible also uses the nesting habits of the eagle in metaphors that speak about Edom. The young eagles are flightless and vulnerable for upward of twelve weeks after hatching. And since the parents are often gone hunting, they build their nests on high inaccessible rock outcroppings to prevent predators from attacking and killing the young birds. The Edomites did something similar, using the natural defenses of the high mountains of Edom to enhance their personal security. But the pride that joined that sense of security would be their downfall. The prophets liken the Edomites' living space to that of an eagle in their judgment speeches against this people: "'Though you soar like the eagle and make your nest among the stars, from there I will bring you down,' declares the LORD" (Obad. 4; see also Jer. 49:16).

Finally, the doting protection the eagle offers its young came to the mind of Moses as he longed to describe the loving protection the Lord had extended to the Israelites. At the close of his life, Moses composed a song that includes this powerful image. The Lord is like "an eagle that stirs up its nest and hovers over its young, that spreads its wings to catch them and carries them on its pinions" (Deut. 32:11).

Earring

The physical appearance of the earrings worn by those living in Bible times is quite similar to the earrings of today. Nevertheless, their distinctive function in Bible culture guarantees that figures of speech associated with the earring may be new to us. Although no earring mentioned in the Bible is ever described in detail, archaeological examples suggest that the earrings in Bible times varied as much in their size and design as they do today—everything from the simple hoop of gold to multifaceted jewelry that comes in an array of intricate geometric shapes. The primary metals for making such earrings were silver and gold, but when the Bible makes mention of an earring's composition, it always speaks of gold.

The earring functioned in a variety of ways. As today, it was a form of jewelry meant to enhance one's physical appearance, a decorative piece worn by men, women, boys, and girls alike. This use of earrings is alluded to in Hosea 2:13 but stated boldly by the lover in the Song of Songs who celebrates the way jewelry enhances the appearance of his beloved: "Your cheeks are beautiful with earrings, your neck with strings of jewels. We will make you earrings of gold, studded with silver" (Song 1:10–11).

Earrings were also employed as a form of currency. In the Old Testament period before precious metals were put into the form of coins, people needed

a practical way to carry precious metals on their person. The earring was one way of achieving that goal, and so the earring appears as a form of currency in a number of Bible stories. When the Israelites were getting ready to leave Egypt, they were not to leave empty-handed but were to ask for silver and gold that they could carry with them (Ex. 3:22). At least some of this portable wealth came to them in the form of earrings. Unfortunately, the Israelites used it for the wrong purpose while they were waiting at the base of Mount Sinai for Moses to return from his meeting with God. Impatient over Moses' delay on the mountain, the people confronted Aaron and demanded that he produce gods for them. In turn, Aaron demanded that the people remove the earrings from their ears, which he then cast into the golden calf. This unwholesome use of earrings was later countered by the wholesome gift of earrings that the people brought in support of the Lord's tabernacle (Ex. 35:22).

Another example of earrings being used as currency can be found in the book of Job. When

An intricate pair of gold earrings from around 400 BC.
Z. Radovan/www.BibleLandPictures.com

Job's brothers and sisters wished to give him a gift after he had gone through all his trials, they brought him a monetary gift in the form of gold rings (Job 42:11). The earring as a form of ancient currency also meant it would be sought as plunder by conquerors. The Lord's treasury grew following the defeat of Midian when the people brought an offering from the goods they plundered, a gift that included earrings (Num. 31:50). Following the defeat of the Ishmaelites, Gideon turned down the offer to start his own ruling dynasty and instead asked that each soldier give him one gold earring from the plunder they had taken (Judg. 8:24).

The earring that enhanced one's personal appearance and doubled as a form of currency also had a much darker side. In some cultures of the ancient Near East, the earring was worn as a talisman designed to ward off evil, perhaps driven by the mistaken notion that the earring would prevent evil spirits from entering one's body via the ear canal. It appears as if Jacob's family had drifted into this unwholesome use of earrings. So upon his return to Canaan, Jacob demanded that his family abandon the foreign gods that were among them "and the rings in their ears," which were buried under an oak at Shechem (Gen. 35:4).

It follows naturally that a piece of jewelry as ubiquitous as the earring would also find its way into the rhetorical language of the Bible. While the average person might walk about with a modest set of earrings riding above their shoulders, the very wealthy women of Zion walked along with outstretched necks, making their privileged status evident to all by their ostentatious earrings (Isa. 3:16). When those earrings became a symbol of pride-filled self-reliance, the Lord promised that he would snatch away all the symbols of wealth, including the earrings (vv. 18–19).

The close connection between the earring and currency leads to two other symbolic associations. The earring is likened to something that is extremely precious and to divine blessing. Constructive criticism is not always easily given or graciously accepted, but for the one wise enough to accept well-placed criticism and let it linger around his or her ears, it becomes like a precious earring: "Like an earring of gold or an ornament of fine gold is a wise man's rebuke to a listening ear" (Prov. 25:12). And in an allegory that laments the unfaithfulness of Jerusalem, the Lord marvels at the rebellion of his bride despite the fact that he has visited one blessing after the next on this city. In the language of the allegory, he has clothed her with an embroidered dress, put leather sandals on her feet, dressed her in costly linen garments, and put earrings in her ears (Ezek. 16:10–12).

Earthquake

Those who lived in the Promised Land were all too familiar with earthquakes. That is because they built their homes beside the longest and deepest geologic fault line on the surface of the earth, the so-called Afro-Arabian fault, which runs north and south through the Jordan River valley. Here two massive plates meet, the Arabian and African. As the Arabian plate attempts to slide past the African plate, it can get stuck. The forces moving the plate continue to direct pressure at the sticking point, storing up energy until the moment the plate breaks free. When the sticking plate slips, seismic shock waves radiate outward, causing the earth to shake violently. While a devastating quake strikes Israel only once every century on average, small tremors radiating from this fault line on a daily basis are a reminder that the next powerful earthquake may be but minutes away.

Two qualities of an earthquake are particularly noteworthy. First, it is unexpected. Whether the quake comes at dawn, midday, or midnight, moderns and ancients alike are destined to be caught off guard by its arrival. Second, powerful earthquakes can leave a mighty disaster in their wake, including a changed landscape, toppled structures, and the loss of life. As Ezekiel writes, "The mountains will be overturned, the cliffs will crumble and every wall will fall to the ground" (Ezek. 38:20). Builders of the ancient world did try to mitigate the harm caused by such tremors, putting wood beams between stone courses in order to absorb the pressure exerted on the building during a quake (1 Kings 6:36; 7:12; Ezra 6:4). But despite their efforts, we still find ample evidence in the archaeological record of collapsed walls and fallen pillars, victims of unexpected and powerful earthquakes.

The Bible only mentions one natural earthquake; it occurred in the eighth century BC during the reign of Uzziah, king of Judah. This quake must have been particularly devastating, living on in the minds of the people so that Amos could use it to date the time of his book. He wrote "two years before the earthquake" (Amos 1:1). Zechariah appears to mention the very same earthquake. In describing the "day of the Lord,"

An earthquake around AD 747 caused extensive damage to the buildings and road in Beth Shean.

he speaks of the Lord standing on the Mount of Olives and of that mountain ridge splitting in two in order to form a great east-west valley. This change in the natural landscape and the process by which it occurs will be so astounding that people will flee as they "fled from the earthquake in the days of Uzziah king of Judah" (Zech. 14:5).

The other earthquakes mentioned in the Bible are directly linked to the Lord. They may signal that a special revelation is about to be given, be a symbol of his anger at the flow of history, or stand as an exclamation point marking a significant moment in the history of the world's redemption. In the first case, the author of Exodus points us to that dramatic moment in time when God descended upon Mount Sinai to organize Israel as his covenant people. This special revelation of God was marked by an array of multisensory experiences, including a violent trembling of the mountain (Ex. 19:18). When discouraged Elijah was on the flanks of that same mountain, the Lord shook the mountain again. This time, however, the Lord disassociated himself with the trembling earth so that Elijah would hear a message different from the one God had spoken there before, one not characterized by the earthquake (1 Kings 19:11).

Jeremiah adds that an earthquake may be a symbol of the Lord's anger: "When he is angry, the earth trembles; the nations cannot endure his wrath" (Jer. 10:10). God clearly has a plan for history, a plan that allows for the success of his people and the unbridled spread of his message. When that plan is endangered by the presence of a foreign army in Israel or by his apostles being locked in prison, the Lord's anger might well translate into an earthquake that allows for history to resume the course the Lord had intended (Isa. 29:6; Ezek. 38:19; Acts 16:26).

Finally, the Lord also has used and will use earthquakes to mark significant moments in the history of this world's redemption. When Jesus surrendered his life on the cross, marking the moment in time when the full debt of sin had been paid, a tremendous earthquake shook Jerusalem, causing rocks to split apart (Matt. 27:51). Those who made fun of Jesus for claiming to be the Son of God were terrified by the earthquake but also got the message: "When the centurion and those with him who were guarding Jesus saw the earthquake and all that had happened, they were terrified, and exclaimed, 'Surely he was the Son of God!'" (Matt. 27:54). Only a short time later another violent earthquake struck Jerusalem, this time signaling that the Son of God who had died on the cross had now risen from the tomb (Matt. 28:2).

Jesus said that "earthquakes in various places" will be a reminder that the end is coming (Mark 13:8). The violent shaking of the earth will be part of the last days (Heb. 12:26–27). In Revelation a series of earthquakes is described, one following the next as time moves to its close (Rev. 6:12; 8:5; 11:13, 19). This series will culminate in the mother of all quakes: "No earthquake like it has ever occurred since man has been on earth, so tremendous was the quake" (16:18). The earth will shake this one final time to mark the moment when the kingdom of the world truly becomes the kingdom of our God.

Edom

The Edomites made a home on the narrow plateau that extends for 110 miles between the Zered River and the Gulf of Aqaba. Travel east off this plateau leads to the inhospitable Syrian Desert, while travel west leads to a 5000-foot freefall down the steep western slope of the mountains of Edom. Agriculture and herding were possible on this plateau, but lower rainfall totals made both a challenge. What really made Edom worth the high-altitude effort was the trade revenue extracted from merchants using the King's Highway, an international travel artery that stretched along the plateau of Edom from the Red Sea to Damascus.

The relationship between the Israelites and Edomites had many ups and downs throughout their mutual histories. The founding members of both societies were brothers, the Israelites descended from Jacob and the Edomites from Esau. When these two men parted company, Esau led his clan into the hill country of Edom (Gen. 36:9) to real estate that God had set aside for these descendants of Abraham (Deut. 2:2–6). Although Israelites and Edomites would live in separate spaces, their relationships were to be guided by mutual respect (Deut. 23:7). But despite the clear delineation of borders and a family link, these two nations were often at odds. The first sign of trouble was linked to Israel's entry into the Promised Land. After spending years in the wilderness, Israel was ready to move to the northeastern shore of the Dead Sea to start their conquest of Canaan. The shortest route between their wilderness camp and their destination lay through the land of Edom. But when Moses requested passage up the mountain passes and onto the King's Highway, his request was bluntly turned down twice despite his offer to pay for food and water the Israelites might consume while transiting Edomite land (Num. 20:14–21). As a result, Moses had to lead the Israelites on a lengthy detour that cost them many more weeks and many more lives. Despite this slight, Joshua

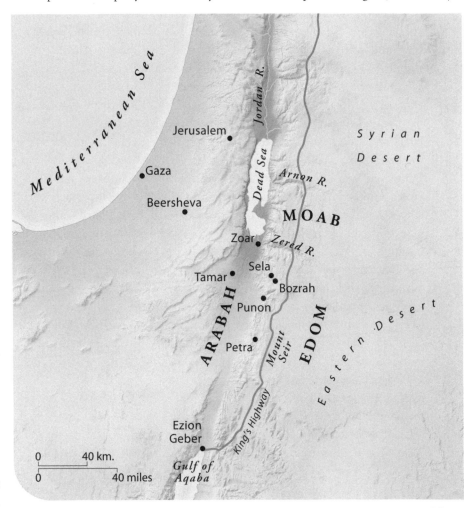

Edom.

was respectful of the land rights God had given the Edomites, drawing the tribal boundaries so Judah's borders would touch but not violate those of Edom (Josh. 15:1, 21). The next time we hear about Israel and Edom is the time of the united kingdom. David campaigned aggressively in this region, bringing it under his control and establishing garrisons there (2 Sam. 8:12–14; 1 Kings 11:15–16). He sang about Edom in this way: "Moab is my washbasin, upon Edom I toss my sandal" (Ps. 60:8). This dominance continued into the days of Solomon who enjoyed an alliance with Edom sealed by marriage contract and who used their country to build a seaport (1 Kings 9:26; 11:1). But in the days of the divided kingdom, Edom gained increasing autonomy (2 Kings 8:20, 22; 16:6).

The darkest days of the relationship between Israel and Edom occurred during the time of the Babylonian attack and capture of Jerusalem. Edom was in a unique position to understand God's purpose and plan for Israel, yet sensitivity to this plan was entirely absent during the Babylonian attack on Judah. When the Babylonian war machine pressed against the walls of Jerusalem and eventually deported its citizens, Edom not only failed to help but celebrated the misfortune of Israel, a fact recalled by the psalmist: "Remember, O Lord, what the Edomites did on the day Jerusalem fell. 'Tear it down,' they cried, 'tear it down to its foundations!'" (Ps. 137:7). They stood aloof as foreigners entered Jerusalem and carried away its plunder, even using this opportunity to join in the plundering themselves (Obad. 11–13). And when Israelite refugees fled toward Edom (Jer. 40:11–12), the Edomites cut down the fugitives and handed over the survivors (Obad. 14). This mistreatment of God's people is the likely motivation for the judgment speeches against Edom that pepper the pages of the Prophets. Jeremiah and

Ezekiel in particular deliver lengthy and scathing condemnations (Jer. 49:7–22; Ezek. 35:1–15).

While such speeches consume a portion of these books, the entire book of Obadiah is a judgment speech directed against Edom. Here the Lord employs the geography of the living space he gave Edom both to summarize the problem and outline his intended response. The high mountain ridge that the Edomites called home had given birth to a high-handed pride: "The pride of your heart has deceived you, you who live in the clefts of the rocks and make your home on the heights, you who say to yourself, 'Who can bring me down to the ground?'" (Obad. 3). The Edomites "stood aloof" while Jerusalem was plundered, they "looked down" on their misfortune, and "looked down" on their calamity (Obad. 11–13). God's response is clear as well as geographical: "Though you soar like the eagle and make your nest among the stars, from there I will bring you down" (Obad. 4).

Such passages artistically speak of the literal Edom, while other judgment passages appear to use Edom as a symbol for all nations and peoples who oppose the Lord; their end will be the same as the end faced by Edom (Isa. 34:5–15; Joel 3:19). Isaiah sees the coming Messiah covered in blood though victorious over all those who oppose him. "Who is this coming from Edom, from Bozrah, with his garments stained crimson?" (Isa. 63:1).

Egypt

As we wander through the pages of our Bible, Egypt is almost never out of sight. The biblical authors formally make reference to this country and its people more than 570 times, a place visited by biblical personalities as early as Abram and beyond Jesus. And although we still face certain challenges in synchronizing the history of Egypt with the Bible's history, we will see that the importance of Egypt to the rhetoric of the Bible is unquestioned.

Egypt is located at the northeastern tip of Africa, stretching south along the Nile River from the Mediterranean Sea to the first cataract at Aswan. While its size on a map impresses, the populated space is only about 5 percent of what we see there—the Nile valley and the Nile delta. The rest is desert. As the fifth-century Greek historian Herodotus said, Egypt is "the gift of the Nile," the fundamental building block of its existence and culture.

The Nile River fosters Egypt's survival in a number of ways. Water is essential to life, but rainfall is scarce throughout Egypt. Nevertheless, the powerful annual flooding of the Nile River mediates the absence of rain by saturating the agricultural fields with water that stands in these fields for months. The floodwaters bring with them a fresh coating of nutrient-rich sediment for growing wheat, barley, and flax. In a land of trackless desert, the river not only becomes a source of life, but it also becomes the transportation artery that connects its citizens. And when we join the treacherous set of six cataracts in the southern reaches of the Nile River with the desert that extends all around that river, we have the natural barriers that discourage foreign invasion and so enhance the security of those who live there. It is no wonder Egypt boasts both a long history and a long list of cultural achievements.

Egypt takes on a variety of faces in the Bible. Here we will focus on the major connotations that shape our reading of those texts: Egypt as refuge, Egypt as divine opponent, Egypt as political ally, and Egypt as political foe. For those living in the fragile ecosystem of the Promised Land, Egypt was a refuge. With a rainfall-dependent hydrology, the Promised Land was subject to frequent droughts and attending crop failures. Because Egypt enjoyed a river-based hydrology, the Nile offered its inhabitants a more certain life. During times of political or economic risk, the Lord used Egypt as a life raft to keep his

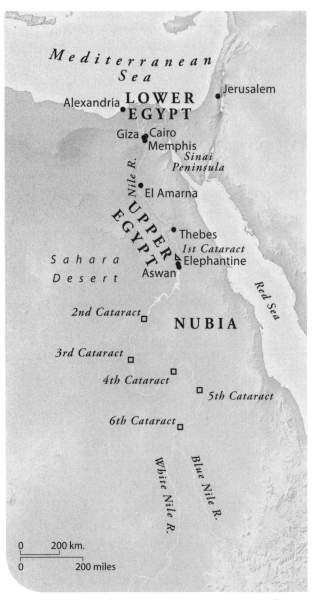

Egypt.

people and the hope linked to them alive. He sheltered Jacob's family here during a severe famine and sheltered Jesus here from the murderous hand of Herod (Gen. 39–50; Matt. 2:13–15). But there were also times when God's people either went to this refuge or longed for the certainty of this land when the Lord wanted them to live with the greater uncertainty that grows one's faith. Shortly after Abram was told that Canaan was the Promised Land, he left that land in the face of a famine. He left the uncertainty of Canaan for the security of Egypt only to find it fraught with danger to himself and his wife (Gen. 12:10–20). When the Lord used the vagaries of the wilderness to encourage Israel's trust, many complained and longed for a return to the more certain life in Egypt (Ex. 16:3; Num. 14:3–4; et al). And when the Lord used Jeremiah to direct the remnant of Judah to remain in the Promised Land, they seized Jeremiah and forced him to go with them to the place of refuge, Egypt (Jer. 42:4–43:7).

Aside from being a refuge, Egypt also comes to the pages of our Bible as a divine opponent, particularly in connection with the exodus events. At this time, the government of Egypt stood in square-shouldered opposition to promises God had made. The Lord had promised Abram that his family would become a great nation and that Canaan would be their homeland (Gen. 12:1–3; 15:18–21). But Egypt had enacted protocols designed to limit Israel's growth and blocked this nation's departure from Egypt (Ex. 1:6–22; 5:2; et al.). The divine response is one of the most dramatic we find in the entire Bible, a response that included devastating plagues and destructive waters (Ex. 7–11; 14). From this time forward, this divine victory over Egypt is intimately linked to the Lord's identity and is to be the motivation for Israel's obedience to the law. We find language like this from one end of the Old Testament to the other: "I am the Lord your God, who brought you out of Egypt to be your God. I am the Lord your God" (Num. 15:41; see also Deut. 5:6; Josh. 24:17; Judg. 2:12; 2 Kings 17:36; Ps. 81:10; Ezek. 20:9; Dan. 9:15; Hos. 13:4). This signature defeat of Egypt was also to motivate Israel's obedience to the law (Ex. 19:4–5; 20:2): "I am the Lord who brought you up out of Egypt to be your God; therefore be holy, because I am holy" (Lev. 11:45).

Years later, during the days of the united kingdom and early days of the divided kingdom, Egypt became a trading partner and political ally of God's people. Solomon married Pharaoh's daughter and exercised a lucrative trade partnership with Egypt (1 Kings 3:1; 9:16; 10:28–29). As the international stage became more threatening with the rise of Assyria and Babylon, the Lord urged Israel to trust him rather than Egypt. When they did not, the prophets spoke harshly about Egypt as ally (Isa. 31:1; Jer. 2:18; Lam. 5:6; Hos. 7:11).

In the end Egypt the ally became Egypt the aggressor once again. Shortly after the united kingdom divided, Shishak attacked Jerusalem and pillaged the treasury of the temple and the palace (1 Kings 14:25–26). Pharaoh Neco killed the last of Judah's reforming kings, Josiah, in a battle near Megiddo (2 Chron. 35:20–24). Egypt then became the king-maker in Israel, setting up Jehoiakim as a puppet ruler (2 Chron. 36:2–4). It was hostile and intrusive behavior like this that led the prophets to deliver harsh judgment speeches against Egypt (Isa. 19; Jer. 46; Ezek. 29) and that caused Egypt to become an exemplar of those powers that were hostile to the Lord (Ps. 68:31; Rev. 11:8).

Fig

The fig tree thrives in the kind of environment so prevalent in the Promised Land, rocky terrain covered with a thin layer of topsoil. In both its wild and domesticated forms, the fig tree is so common that it is one of the signature trees of Israel whose fruit is representative of the goodness of the land (Num. 13:23; Deut. 8:8). During the winter months, the fig tree has a ghostly appearance, with branches that resemble old, gray bones. But the changes in season are marked by the evolving appearance of this tree. The emergence of small leaves and the presence of early season figs signal the onset of spring (Hos. 9:10; Luke 21:29–30). The early spring leaves are unpretentious; but by late spring and early summer they become massive, with a span of more than twelve inches. As summer progresses those large leaves are shed to direct the energy of the tree toward producing the second set of fruit, the late season fig, which is harvested during August and September.

Both the fig leaves as well as the fig itself make their contribution in the life of the average Israelite. Shade is always a welcomed commodity in Israel however it is dispensed, and the large leaves of the fig tree are particularly suited for providing much-needed relief from the sun's rays. The fig itself is a fruit that is very high in sugar, making it both tasty and a great source of energy (Judg. 9:11). It was eaten fresh-picked from the tree; it was dried and stored in jars for consumption at a later time; and it was pressed

Sliced fig shows the juicy fruit common in the Middle East. Notice the large fig leaf.
© Fabienne Espagnol/www.BigStockPhoto.com

Fig   86

into cakes that were particularly suited for meals when traveling (2 Sam. 16:1–2).

Both the swallowing of the ripe fig and the falling of shriveled figs are used by the Bible's authors in similes. For example, Isaiah and Nahum speak of cities that are "ripe" for destruction. Isaiah announces that Samaria is like "a fig ripe before harvest—as soon as someone sees it and takes it in his hand, he swallows it" (Isa. 28:4). Nahum announces the falling of Nineveh with similar language: "All your fortresses are like fig trees with their first ripe fruit; when they are shaken, the figs fall into the mouth of the eater" (Nah. 3:12). If such ripe figs were not eaten, they would eventually shrivel up and fall from the tree. In a similar way, the divine authors say the starry hosts will fall from the heavens on the day of the Lord (Isa. 34:4; Rev. 6:13).

In addition to its role in such similes, the fig tree is also employed in symbolic language that speaks of security, judgment, and hypocrisy. The copious and dense foliage of the fig tree provides a welcome refuge from the sun. Thus to sit beneath a fig tree became a symbol of life that was secure and blessed. This was an apt description of life during the peaceful days Israel enjoyed under the rule of Solomon, when each person lived in safety "under his own vine and fig tree" (1 Kings 4:25). Years later, with Jerusalem under the risk of extended siege, the Assyrian commander offered the people in the city a return to those days (2 Kings 18:31). But this security would be reached in its ultimate form only when the Messiah walked the earth (Mic. 4:4): "'In that day each of you will invite his neighbor to sit under his vine and fig tree,' declares the LORD Almighty" (Zech. 3:10). Anticipation gave way to reality as Philip rushed to tell Nathanael about Jesus. It was important to Jesus that we notice where Nathanael was sit-

ting when this "true Israelite, in whom there is nothing false," heard the news (John 1:47). Jesus mentioned it twice: Nathaniel was sitting underneath a fig tree (John 1:48, 50).

The importance of the fig tree to the cultural well-being of those living in the Promised Land was so great that its removal became a symbol of divine judgment. If Israel failed to uphold its side of the covenant, the Lord might cause the fig trees to be cut down and/or consumed by an invading army (Jer. 5:17). Alternatively, the Lord might allow a plague of locusts or the ravages of famine to remove the fruit from those trees (Joel 1:7; Amos 4:9; Hag. 2:19).

And the fig tree itself became a symbol for the Jews living in Jesus' day who had failed to accept him as the Messiah. A fig tree that was planted and carefully tended was expected to bear fruit within a reasonable amount of time. This was so predictable that the idea found its way into this proverb: "He who tends a fig tree will eat its fruit, and he who looks after his master will be honored" (Prov. 27:18). But that was not the case with the fig tree in the parable told by Jesus. In this story, a man had planted a tree, tended it, and waited for three years, anticipating that it would produce fruit. His every inclination was to cut it down and use the space for something else. But the caretaker asked that it be given one more year of loving care before this drastic action was taken (Luke 13:6–9). In this case, the tree so representative of the Promised Land represented the people of the promise who lived in that land.

Finally, it was Jesus' frustration with the hypocrisy he saw in Jerusalem's religious leaders that led him to curse a fig tree on his way into this city. As he walked toward the city, he spied a fig tree boasting the leaves of early spring. By every expectation, this tree would also be filled with early season figs. But when Jesus arrived at the tree, not a single fig was to be found. The tree withered at his words of denunciation because it was a symbol of what he had seen all too often: people who had the outward appearance of spiritual vitality but who, upon closer inspection, failed to produce true fruit (Matt. 21:18–21).

Fish

Many kinds of fish swim through the biblical world, from the "great fish" that swallowed Jonah to the tiny sardines Jesus multiplied to make a meal for thousands. The fish we meet in the Bible come chiefly from the Nile River, the Mediterranean Sea, and the Sea of Galilee. The Nile River was home to over one hundred species of fish that thrived in its warm water. These fish were regularly placed on the dinner table (Num. 11:5). But in the Bible, we read more often about the dead and rotting fish that stunk up Egypt when the Lord turned the Nile water into "blood" (Ex. 7:18, 21; Ps. 105:29). The Mediterranean Sea along the Levant was a relatively poor fishery, but fishermen from Tyre cast their nets into the sea anyway (Ezek. 26:5, 14) and brought their catch to Jerusalem to sell in the fish market there (Neh. 13:16). It is the Sea of Galilee, however, that is the source for most of the fish we read about in the Bible. This inland lake contains more than eighteen species of fish; for our purposes, we

can divide them into three general categories of edible fish. Barbels are the bottom-feeding carp distinguished by the long barbs that extend from the corners of their mouths. These fish can reach twenty-four inches in length and weigh up to fifteen pounds. Second are the *musht* (Arabic for "comb"), fish distinguished by their large dorsal fins. The most popular member of this group is the so-called Saint Peter's fish, which can grow up to sixteen inches in length and weigh four pounds. Finally, the most prolific fish found in the Sea of Galilee is also the smallest, the sardine, with a long, slender body that averages only eight inches in length. From the day Noah departed from the ark, fish were approved for human consumption (Gen. 9:2–3). However, this general rule that defined fish as a legitimate source of protein was restricted by the dietary laws of Israel, which permitted the eating of sea creatures only if they had both scales and fins (Lev. 11:9–12; Deut. 14:9–10).

Tilapia, also known as St. Peter's fish, from the Sea of Galilee.
Z. Radovan/www.BibleLandPictures.com

Figurative and real fish are deployed in a variety of rhetorical contexts that I have grouped into four categories. First, the biblical authors play upon the great vulnerability of this creature; they are easily caught by hook or net and succumb quickly when pulled from the water. In this sense mortals can be as unsuspecting and vulnerable as fish "caught in a cruel net" when evil befalls them (Eccl. 9:12). Pulled up by hooks or caught in nets, Israel had become like "fish in the sea" ensnared by the powerful Babylonian war machine (Hab. 1:14 – 17).

Second, fish are mentioned in a variety of judgment speeches recorded by the Old Testament prophets. Here it is the remote living circumstances of the fish that are deployed rhetorically to show how very pervasive God's judgment will be, so pervasive that it will affect even the fish living in the sea. On the day of judgment, the fish will tremble in the presence of the Lord (Ezek. 38:20). The Lord declares, "I will sweep away both men and animals; I will sweep away the birds of the air and the fish of the sea" (Zeph. 1:3; see also Hos. 4:3).

Third, fish show up in a parable of Jesus that talks about the ultimate judgment of the world. This remarkable Rabbi frequently taught along the shore of the Sea of Galilee where the agricultural and fishing culture along the lake would have been in full view of his listeners. As he taught about the kingdom of God, he likened the judgment at the end of the age to fishermen who pulled their nets onto the shore. Because Jewish dietary law naturally divided their catch into fish fit for the dinner table and those that were not, "they sat down and collected the good fish in baskets, but threw the bad away" (Matt. 13:48). Jesus used this image to illustrate the contrasting fate of the wicked and the righteous at the end of time.

Finally, a number of Scripture passages begin with a small number of fish (or no fish at all) and then end with an uncountable number of fish. This is what we see in Ezekiel where this prophet of the Lord looks to a day when a river will exit the temple in Jerusalem, flow east, and enter the Dead Sea. In the current world, this inland lake is so chemically laden that no fish can inhabit it. But in the world Ezekiel sees, this most lifeless of all lakes will team with as many fish as the Mediterranean Sea (Ezek. 47:9 – 10).

The gospel writers mention fish in a set of stories that involve Jesus multiplying a small amount of food so that thousands could be fed. In both the feeding of the five thousand and the feeding of the four thousand, the disciples stared hopelessly at one another in the face of Jesus' direction to feed the masses. The best they could come up with were "five small barley loaves and two small fish" or "seven [loaves] and a few small fish" (John 6:9; Matt. 15:34). But Jesus was able to take these few sardines and feed thousands, demonstrating his divine power and origins. A similar multiplication of fish occurs in two Bible stories that are clearly meant to mirror one another in nature and purpose; one involves the calling of disciples and the other of recalling them to service. After Jesus used Peter's boat to speak to the people, he directed Peter to take the boat back out to fish. Despite Peter's protests, he did so and caught "such a large number of fish that their nets began to break" (Luke 5:6). When Peter and several of the other disciples went back to fishing following the resurrection, Jesus glimpsed Peter's boat on the same lake in the same circumstances, no fish aboard. At Jesus' direction, the disciples threw their nets in one more time and "were unable to haul the net in because of the large number of fish" (John 21:6).

Flower

Flowers enhance our lives in so many ways. They offer a splash of color to a drab day, sooth our emotions with their wonderful fragrance, and captivate us with their intricate designs. Based on the infrequency with which flowers are mentioned in the narrative portions of the Bible, we might well get the impression that the Promised Land was void of such wondrous flowers. The only time our attention is intentionally called to flowers is when Jesus himself makes mention of them in his discourse on worry. He encourages us to look carefully at the beauty of the wildflowers to learn a lesson about how ready God is to provide us with the clothing we need (Matt. 6:28; Luke 12:27).

Yet in reality Israel is a land blessed with a rich array of flowers. This small country entertains twenty-four hundred species of plants; many of these trees, shrubs, and smaller plants produce beautiful flowers. If you know where to look, you can find something blooming in Israel every month of the year, although the most

striking display occurs in the late winter to early spring when the wildflowers reach their zenith. From the white flower of the almond tree to the brilliant red-orange blossom of the pomegranate, from oleander to rhododendron, from anemone to cyclamen, crocus, and iris, the Promised Land is a land alive with flowers.

Some of these flowers are represented in the artwork of the tabernacle and temple. A lampstand provided light in the interior of the tabernacle; it was decorated with cups shaped like almond flowers (Ex. 25:31–36; 37:17–22). The cedar paneling that lined the walls of Solomon's temple included carved flowers (1 Kings 6:18,

A carpet of brightly colored flowers explodes on the landscape of Galilee during early spring.

29). The wooden doors that opened into the sanctuary were similarly decorated with carved flowers (1 Kings 6:32, 35). The pillars that stood guard at the entrance of the temple had capitals in the shape of lilies (7:22). And the large bronze sea, a water reservoir that stood in the courtyard of the temple near the altar, had a rim shaped like the lily blossom (7:26). The use of flowers in these important worship aids may simply be an example of "art for the sake of art." But the representation of the almond blossom may have a more important rhetorical role, recalling the white almond blossoms that appeared on Aaron's staff when the Lord used a miracle to confirm his status as the high priest of God's chosen people (Num. 17:1–13).

The artful use of flowers continues in the rhetorical design of the poets and prophets where the flower becomes a symbol of transience, restoration, and romance. The blossoms on the trees, shrubs, and flowers of the Promised Land last for only a segment of the plant's lifecycle. Consequently, they are a symbol of brevity or transience. Life is like that. The various seasons of life lead to that season when "the almond tree blossoms," the time in life when our hair turns white (Eccl. 12:5). Standing at the threshold of youth, it appears to take forever to grow up. But when we are grown up, we see that "man born of woman is of few days and full of trouble. He springs up like a flower and withers away" (Job 14:1–2). "As for man, his days are like grass, he flourishes like a flower of the field; the wind blows over it and it is gone, and its place remembers it no more" (Ps. 103:15–16). Wealth might appear to mitigate that notion, but not so, for the one with wealth will also pass away "like a wildflower." "For the sun rises with scorching heat and withers the plant; its blossom falls and its beauty is destroyed. In the same way,

the rich man will fade away even while he goes about his business" (James 1:10–11). What is true of mortals is also true of all they accomplish. In contrast to the Word of God, which endures forever, the best and most enduring of mortal accomplishments are "like the flowers of the field" that fall down flat (Isa. 40:6–8). This is particularly true of those bent on doing evil. In this case the godless city that appears to be successful is rather like a "fading flower" (28:1, 4). The ones who have rejected the law of the Lord will find that their "flowers blow away like dust" (5:24).

These somber images of the fading flower are balanced by more hopeful images that associate the spring flowers with restoration. Springtime is a time of hope, and the buds and blossoms of spring flowers embody that hope. In Isaiah the destruction of the nations opposed to the Lord will bring about an era when Zion is restored. Then "the wilderness will rejoice and blossom. Like the crocus, it will burst into bloom" (Isa. 35:1). And in calling for Israel to return from their wayward paths, the Lord speaks of what he is so anxious to do: "I will be like the dew to Israel; he will blossom like a lily" (Hos. 14:5).

Finally, the Song of Songs makes regular use of the sight and smell of flowers as it champions the beauty and intimacy of love. The place of budding trees and flowers creates an ambience conducive to love: "Let us go early to the vineyards to see if the vines have budded, if their blossoms have opened, and if the pomegranates are in bloom—there I will give you my love" (Song 7:12). The inspired poet describes the man's lips as "lilies dripping with myrrh" (5:13) and celebrates the appearance of the young woman with flattering images. She is a "lily among thorns" (2:2) whose waist is a "mound of wheat encircled by lilies" (7:2).

Flute

The flute or pipe is a very ancient musical instrument mentioned early in Genesis (4:21) and represented in the ancient art pieces of Egypt and Mesopotamia. The flute of the Bible is a wind instrument made either from a natural reed or fashioned into the appropriate shape from ivory, bronze, silver, or gold. It was composed of one round, hollow pipe or two such pipes that were attached parallel to one another. Holes were drilled along the length of the barrel so that when air was blown through the chamber to produce a tone, that tone could be varied when the musician altered his or her finger positions on the instrument.

The Bible associates the flute with three cultural settings. The first is prophecy. Saul met a group of the Lord's prophets who were returning from worship. As they walked together playing a variety of musical instruments, including the flute, the Spirit of the Lord filled them and they began to prophesy (1 Sam. 10:5).

The second cultural setting is that this instrument is connected to times of excited celebration. Its music filled the halls of the wealthy during their extravagant, though unwholesome, parties (Isa. 5:12). Its tones filled the air as Solomon was anointed king of Israel (1 Kings 1:40) and as pilgrims climbed the pathways to Jerusalem to worship at the temple (Isa. 30:29). The psalmist invites us to praise the Lord with strings

Two hollow pipes form the flute being played by this terra-cotta figurine.
Z. Radovan/www.BibleLandPictures.com

and flute as the Psalter is brought to its celebrative close (Ps. 150:4). Celebration is the connotation in view as Jesus mentions the flute in his critique of the generation of people who personally heard him speak. He compares them to the obstinate child who refuses to follow the lead of the other children playing in the marketplace no matter what kind of game they are playing: "We played the flute for you, and you did not dance; we sang a dirge, and you did not mourn" (Matt. 11:17).

The melody of the flute called people to celebrate, but it also could produce the sad tones that were appropriate during times of mourning. This is the third cultural setting. Job lamented the sorry state of his circumstances by suggesting that he was a flute that knew only one tone: "My harp is tuned to mourning, and my flute to the sound of wailing" (Job 30:31). Musicians who played somber music were hired to play sad music at the deathbed of the ruler's daughter who had come to Jesus for help. When Jesus came to the room where the body of the girl lay, he had to elbow his way past these flute players and put up with their derision just before he called this young girl back to the world of the living (Matt. 9:23).

Rhetorically the tone of the flute can signal that life is bad, life is good, or that life is moving from good to bad. The association of the flute with funerals and mourning led Jeremiah to use this imagery in the judgment speech he delivered against Moab: "My heart laments for Moab like a flute; it laments like a flute for the men of Kir Hareseth. The wealth they acquired is gone" (Jer. 48:36). Second, it shows up in Bible verses where life is portrayed as going well. When Job's associates tried to convince Job that evil people suffer, Job insisted the opposite was the case. He himself had seen the children of the wicked; their lives were as happy as any children he knew. "They sing to the music of tambourine and harp; they make merry to the sound of the flute" (Job 21:12).

The flute also finds its way onto the pages of our Bible when the inspired writers speak of a good life that is about to go bad. Isaiah warns the wealthy among his people that darker days are coming for them. That is because "they have harps and lyres at their banquets, tambourines and flutes and wine, but they have no regard for the deeds of the LORD, no respect for the work of his hands" (Isa. 5:12). Those flutes were about to go silent, as will the flutes that mark the celebration in "Babylon." The flute players will never again be heard in "Babylon" because the Lord's hand of judgment will silence them (cf. Rev. 18:22).

In addition to those cultural settings we find one instance in the Bible where the poorly played flute is used as a metaphor. Paul wrote to the church in Corinth concerning those who at times would "speak in a tongue." The flute was well known in the Greek cities as well as it

Massive stone walls fortified King Ahab's city of Dan.
Todd Bolen/www.BiblePlaces.com

was to those in Israel. They knew that a well-practiced artist could produce wonderful tones on this instrument. At the same time, they had also heard the flute being played in such a poor way that the listeners had no idea what tune was being played: "How will anyone know what tune is being played unless there is a distinction in the notes?" (1 Cor. 14:7). Paul likened the speaking in a tongue to poor flute playing: "So it is with you. Unless you speak intelligible words with your tongue, how will anyone know what you are saying?" (1 Cor. 14:9).

Fortress (Fortified City)

Fortresses and fortified cities were both a real and rhetorical part of the Bible's world. During the days of the Old Testament, established living centers fell into two general categories, villages that had minimal defensive protection and urban centers that were strategically fortified (Num. 13:19). In the case of fortified cities, builders could employ up to six layers of defense between attacker and defender. The innermost layer of protection was a stout building designed as a safe room for the king; it was called the citadel (1 Kings 16:18; 1 Chron. 11:7; Ps. 122:7). A defensive wall surrounded both this citadel and the principle buildings in the city. This wall, which might be twenty-five feet thick and over twenty-five feet high, bristled with towers and gatehouses that provided platforms for soldiers to use when defending the wall against those bent on attacking its integrity. To make it more difficult for attackers to get to the wall itself, a bank of earth (the glacis, or rampart) flowed downward from the wall. This very steep ramp could be covered with a layer of slick plaster to make the exposed journey to the base of the wall even more difficult. At the base of the glacis, a

second, lower wall line blocked access to the glacis. Finally, this lower wall was often surrounded by a dry moat (the fosse) located just outside of and below it, yet another obstacle that had to be crossed before encountering any of the other defensive components of the fortified city. Of course, every one of these layers of defense could be overcome. But by increasing the cost in lives and time spent, the design of the fortified city was to discourage a direct attack or lengthy siege.

Of course the purpose of these concentric layers of protection was first and foremost to protect the royal family and chief administrators of the state. But ordinary citizens who lived outside the wall knew just what to do when trouble appeared on the horizon. The cry would go up, "Let us flee to the fortified cities!" (Jer. 4:5). It was not only the capital city of the nation that was fortified, but also smaller outposts that controlled the primary routes to and from the capital city. Here soldiers were garrisoned to give early warning of an attack and to harass invaders as best they could, discouraging and delaying their advance (2 Chron. 17:2).

The oldest structure in the Promised Land is a fortified tower in ancient Jericho that is dated to more than five thousand years before the time of Abraham. It is not surprising that the Canaanites who opposed the arrival of the Israelites into the Promised Land had built fortified cities (Num. 13:28; Josh. 2:1). Once in the land and prior to the time of the Israelite monarchy, God's people appear to have lived primarily in open villages. When enemy combatants invaded their land, they would flee to natural defensive points like mountain clefts and caves (Judg. 6:2). But the advent of the monarchy in Israel brought increasing attention to fortification and to establishing a ring of fortified cities that guarded access to the capital (2 Sam. 5:9; 1 Kings 12:25; 15:17; 22:39;

2 Chron. 11:5–12), cities that in turn became the target of invading armies (2 Kings 18:13; 2 Chron. 12:4; Isa. 36:1; Jer. 34:7).

This all means that the first readers of the Bible were very familiar with the notion of a fortified city, its components, and their function. Consequently, the biblical authors could tap into this imagery and use it in a variety of rhetorical settings. Because the fortress system that surrounded the capital city was so fundamental to the nation's security, the loss of such cities became a symbol of that nation's total defeat. When the prophets speak of the fall of a nation, whether that be Phoenicia or Israel, they often characterize it by saying its fortresses have been lost (Isa. 23:11, 13, 14; 32:14; Jer. 49:27; Amos 1:4, 7, 10, 12, 14; 2:2; Nah. 3:12). No news was as unsettling to the nation's health as the news that "death has climbed in through our windows and has entered our fortresses" (Jer. 9:21).

Because the layers of protection could provide the residents with a sense of security and well-being, the fortress became a metaphor for the Lord. This image is particularly prevalent in the Psalms (Pss. 28:8; 31:2–3; 48:3; 59:9, 16–17; 62:2; 71:3; 91:2; 94:22; 144:2). "The Lord is my rock, my fortress and my deliverer; my God is my rock, in whom I take refuge. He is my shield and horn of my salvation, my stronghold" (Ps. 18:2). The inspired poet presents images of his God that literally tumble over one another, but the first and last images are of the Lord who offers the protection of a fortified city. There truly is nothing to fear when this premise is owned: "The Lord Almighty is with us; the God of Jacob is our fortress" (Ps. 46:7).

However, the fortress could become a symbol of Israel's pride and misplaced trust when this nation looked to its defensive works rather than to the Lord as its ultimate source of security (Jer. 5:17; Hos. 8:14; Amos 6:8). "Israel has forgotten his Maker and built palaces; Judah has fortified many towns. But I will send fire upon their cities that will consume their fortresses" (Hos. 8:14). David is the one who got it right; he both fortified his capital and still declared, "The Lord is my rock, my fortress and my deliverer" (2 Sam. 22:2).

The fortress appears in three other metaphors less frequent than those above. The Lord directs Jeremiah to confront his people with their sin. And lest Jeremiah think himself not up to the task, the Lord promises to make him a "fortified city" (Jer. 1:18). In two proverbs, the power that wealth brings is likened to a fortified city (Prov. 10:15; 18:11). Finally, one would do well to avoid personal conflicts, given this powerful image: "An offended brother is more unyielding than a fortified city, and disputes are like the barred gates of a citadel" (Prov. 18:19).

Foundation

Today most of us give very little thought to our home's foundation unless that foundation is giving us a problem. At such a time, we come to appreciate just how vital this unsung link between our living space and stable ground is. In Bible times people gave more thought to foundations because they were personally involved in the process of building and maintaining their own homes. Consequently, both real and rhetorical foundations are built into the message of the Bible.

The process of building a foundation wall in Bible times involved selecting an appropriate base, obtaining reliable building materials, and skillfully mating the two. Because a foundation is only as good as what lies beneath it, the first step is to identify a building site that offers a high-quality, natural base. Ideally that base will be level, stable, and well drained. In this regard bedrock offered the best natural base. But when bedrock was out of reach, the second option was to find a stable layer of soil on which to initiate the building process. In either case this typically involved digging a trench as deep as necessary to reach an appropriate base layer. While the trench was dug, the building materials had to be brought to the site. In the case of grand public buildings, the foundation stones might be harvested from a quarry (1 Kings 7:9–10); but in most cases locally collected fieldstone was the material of choice. The experienced eye of the builder would care-fully select and lay stones that fit well together, using the distinctive shape of each stone to inter-lock it with its neighbor. The goal was to build a foundation that was true to the line of the antici-pated wall, stabilized so as not to shift, and strong enough to avoid collapse under the weight of the upper courses. When finished the trench was backfilled with soil and rock, leaving most of the effort unseen though not unappreciated.

Although actual foundations are not men-tioned often by the biblical authors, the few places they are mentioned give us a good idea of the wide range of structures that required them,

Large stone blocks called ashlars provide a sturdy foundation for these retaining walls that sustain the Temple mount platform of first-century Jerusalem.

Danny Frese/www.BiblePlaces.com

including homes, defensive walls, towers, temples, altars, and prisons (1 Kings 5:17; Ezra 3:3, 10; 4:12; Luke 6:48–49; 14:28–29; Acts 16:26). At times a city's foundation is mentioned. This is likely a corporate reference to the various foundations, those of walls, towers, and gates, which gave the city defensible autonomy (Josh. 6:26; 1 Kings 16:34; Ps. 137:7; Lam. 4:11; Mic. 1:6).

The most frequent mention of foundations in the Bible is in rhetorical settings; and among the most common of these is mention of the "earth's foundations." In various texts, God is depicted as a builder who had laid the world's metaphorical foundations (Job 38:4; Ps. 104:5; Prov. 8:29; Isa. 48:13; 51:13, 16). "In the beginning you laid the foundations of the earth, and the heavens are the work of your hands" (Ps. 102:25). The notion of God as foundation layer suggests his ownership not just of the foundation but of all that rises above it. Only in cases of extreme disappointment with what was made would the builder physically express his anger at the foundation. But that is the image described when God unleashed his anger at rebellion: he burned the foundations of the earth, shook them, and laid them bare (Deut. 32:22; 2 Sam. 22:8, 16; Ps. 18:7, 15).

God is responsible not only for the physical foundation of the world but also for the ideological foundation that governs its daily existence. The psalmist says that "righteousness and justice are the foundation" of the Lord's throne (Pss. 89:14; 97:2). This base is embodied in the teaching of the prophets and the apostles but finds its culmination in the Messiah (Isa. 28:16; Rev. 21:14). The result is that the church itself is "built on the foundation of the apostles and prophets, with Christ Jesus himself as the chief cornerstone" (Eph. 2:20). This is the foundation that Paul so ardently worked to establish (1 Tim. 6:19; 2 Tim. 2:19). "By the grace God has given

me, I laid a foundation as an expert builder, and someone else is building on it. But each one should be careful how he builds. For no one can lay any foundation other than the one already laid, which is Jesus Christ" (1 Cor. 3:10–11).

How fitting it is that the most sustained imagery of building on a good foundation comes from Jesus himself. When he walked the earth, the foundation of which he himself had built, he challenged those who heard him to check the foundation on which they were building their lives. He did so using the image of two builders, one wise and one foolish. Jesus said, "He ... who ... hears my words and puts them into practice ... is like a man building a house, who dug down deep and laid the foundation on rock. When a flood came, the torrent struck that house but could not shake it, because it was well built. But the one who hears my words and does not put them into practice is like a man who built a house on the ground without a foundation. The moment the torrent struck that house, it collapsed and its destruction was complete" (Luke 6:47–49).

Fox

The sleek and solitary fox was seen much less frequently than other carnivores that inhabit the Bible lands; and in a corresponding way, it makes only rare appearances on the pages of the Bible. Two species of fox inhabit Israel and the northern Sinai, the red fox and the fennec fox. The mature red fox is about thirty-six inches in length, with a tail that comprises about one-third of that length. In contrast to the rusty red tones of its North American counterpart, this red fox sports a duskier coat. While the red fox prefers the hills and woodlands of Israel, the fennec fox is suited for life in the desert. It is the smallest member of the fox family, with mature males reaching just twenty-five inches in length, including their ten-inch tail. The pale-toned fennec fox is pressed into a nocturnal lifestyle even more so than the red fox of Israel due to the daytime heat of the Sinai. Although its distinctively large ears help dissipate its body heat, this fox still needs to stay out of the daytime sun, retreating to the cooler environs of its subterranean den. Despite these differences in appearance and habitat, both of these foxes have a similar diet. They are omnivores that will eat insects, small animals, and even fruit.

Red fox.
© Eric Isselée/www.BigStockPhoto.com

The Hebrew word for "fox" doubles as a term for the jackal. This means that Bible translators and interpreters who encounter this word must use other clues to determine which animal best fits a specific biblical passage. One place disagreement exists is over the type of animal mentioned in Judges 15. The Lord had planned to use Samson's strong feelings for a Philistine woman as an occasion for confronting the opponents of God's people. When Samson's Philistine bride was given to the friend who had attended him at his wedding, Samson caught three hundred foxes, tied them together in pairs, secured a burning torch to every pair's tails, and then set them free in the agricultural fields of the Philistines (Judg. 15:4–5). If these were in fact foxes, the bushy tails may well have combined with the animal's powerful desire to remain alone in order to bring about the havoc God had in mind for the Philistine economy.

While it is more difficult to discern a rhetorical element in this event, the fox clearly does become a rhetorical device in the four additional passages in which it occurs. Following the Babylonian siege and destruction of Jerusalem, the walls of this city were ruined. Nehemiah returned with a passion to restore those walls. But Tobiah the Ammonite mocked the Israelites' budding efforts to do so by employing the image of a fox. At times the diminutive red fox makes its den among the tumbled walls of a ruined city, so the fox and ruined wall were linked in reality. Because a fox weighs only about twenty pounds, a well-built wall would barely notice the passing of this animal. That is why Tobiah said, "What they are building—if even a fox climbed up on it, he would break down their wall of stones!" (Neh. 4:3).

Rather than the mature fox, it is fox pups we see in the Song of Songs. The foxes of Israel will eat the mature grapes, particularly those grown along the ground rather than on trellises. But it is the young foxes that run through those same vines while they are blooming, knock off the blossoms, and thus ruin the harvest. The intrusion of these unwelcome visitors is likened to the intrusions that interfere in the maturing relationship between the couple whose story is told in the Song. The young man asks that those intrusions be removed with this metaphor: "Catch for us the foxes, the little foxes that ruin the vineyards, our vineyards that are in bloom" (Song 2:15).

Jesus also mentions the fox in two metaphors. In the first, he is speaking about the great price that is paid by those who commit to being one of his disciples. Jesus had a town he called his own (Matt. 9:1), but he did not have a home of his own. This contrasts dramatically with the foxes, which did not have one but many holes. The fox would use one primary den to hole up during the daylight hours, but it would also make holes throughout its territory in which to cache its food supply; that way, if one food cache was compromised, others would remain intact. Jesus was calling his disciples to a life of trust that matched his own, one that appeared less secure: "Foxes have holes and birds of the air have nests, but the Son of Man has no place to lay his head" (Matt. 8:20).

Finally, Jesus called Herod Antipas a fox. Jesus was wandering from village to village in the territory governed by Herod Antipas when a group of Pharisees approached him with the warning that Herod was out to kill him. Jesus replied, "Go tell that fox, 'I will drive out demons and heal people today and tomorrow, and on the third day I will reach my goal'" (Luke 13:32). Ancient fables from Mesopotamia, Greece, and Rome all mention a trickster character that appeared as a fox. In these fables, the sly, crafty, and cunning qualities of the fox are championed. But it seems more likely that Jesus has a different aim in mind when using this metaphor in connection with Herod. By contrast to the lion, bear, and wolf, the fox was really a second-class predator in the Promised Land. Tapping into that reality, Jesus appears to be downgrading the risk posed by the second-rate position of Herod who answered to the Roman authorities over him. In the metaphor he is not like a lion or bear but more like a pesky fox whose intrusion needs to be managed not feared.

Frankincense

Today it is possible to buy a wide array of products designed to improve the fragrance of our person, our home, and even our vehicles. If we are going to place frankincense in a cultural category familiar to us, that category would be fragrance. Frankincense originates with a shrub-sized tree that has very specialized habitat demands; it grows only in the wild and only in special climate zones located in southwestern Arabia and Somalia. The Bible links this product with the ancient kingdom of Sheba (Isa. 60:6; Jer. 6:20). Harvesting of this aromatic begins when several inches of bark are stripped and the wood behind the bark is incised with a knife. In time, white droplets of sap will flow out of the incision, dry in the air, and crystallize into amber globs that are then scraped from the tree. In Bible times these globs were transported to markets around the world where the resin was ground into powder. Frankincense in this form could either be burned to produce the aromatic outcome desired or mixed with oil for application to one's skin. Given the limited habitat of the tree, the labor-intensive process of obtaining the resin, and the transportation costs to get this product to market, frankincense came with a very hefty price tag.

The related Greek and Hebrew words for frankincense are translated as "frankincense" or simply as "incense" in most Bible translations. In such Bible passages, we find this product primarily mentioned in connection with the worship rites of Israel. A very special blend of incense was made for use at the tabernacle or temple when the priests ground up various aromatics and mixed them according to set proportions (Ex. 30:34 – 38). The chief ingredient in the recipe was frankincense, and so the mixture itself also became known as "frankincense" (although the

NIV often translates with the word "incense"). The worship instructions guarantee that its aroma will completely permeate the worship area. Immediately before the curtain that separated the Holy Place from the Most Holy Place, there was a small altar for burning incense. Each day, twice a day, one of the priests entered the Holy Place to add more of the frankincense mixture to the altar so that this room would be filled throughout the day with a pleasing aroma (Ex. 30:7 – 8). The same mixture of aromatics was also placed between the loaves of bread on the golden table where the bread of the Presence was kept (Lev. 24:7). And each time a grain offering was presented and burned on the Great Altar, that offering was to include a small amount of frankincense (Lev. 2:1 – 2, 15 – 16; 6:15), which would result in "an aroma pleasing to the LORD" (Lev. 2:2) — that is, unless the offering was made by one who lacked a humble and contrite heart. In that case, "whoever burns memorial incense [is like] one who worships an idol" (Isa. 66:3).

Given that we are no longer asked to bring animals for sacrifice as part of our worship, it is easy to lose sight of the very practical role played by this frankincense mixture. Without it, the place of worship would have been filled with the varied and pungent odors of living, dead, and dying animals. No wonder the Lord directed that this cacophony of smells be replaced with the sweet aroma of frankincense burning in so many places.

The sweet smells of this aromatic are also part of the rhetoric of the Bible authors where

Frankincense provides a wonderful fragrance.
Todd Bolen/www.BiblePlaces.com

it serves as a symbol of economic well-being, sensual attractiveness, and royalty. When Isaiah scanned the horizon of life for an image that would adequately describe the well-being that will be known in the coming age of the Messiah, he selected this one: herds of camels covering the Promised Land, camels that had come from Sheba carrying gold and frankincense (Isa. 60:6). While variously interpreted, the image of so many camels so loaded clearly marks a time of economic well-being.

The powerful sensuality in the language of the Song of Songs makes use of frankincense in describing the features of the beautiful young woman who is the object of desire in this love poetry. Her breasts are likened to two fawns and then described as mounds of aromatics: "Until the day breaks and the shadows flee, I will go to the mountain of myrrh and to the hill of incense" (4:6). Just a few verses later, her enchanting aroma is again linked to "every kind of incense tree, with myrrh and aloes and all the finest spices" (v. 14).

Frankincense is also associated with royalty. Given the cost of the product, it is one way that the royal family might distinguish itself from the more common citizens: "Who is this coming up from the desert like a column of smoke, perfumed with myrrh and incense made from all the spices of the merchant? Look! It is Solomon's carriage" (Song 3:6). There is no missing this king by sight or smell. But another King's arrival was not so apparent. The magi from the east came to Jerusalem asking if anyone knew the whereabouts of the recently born King of the Jews. When they found Jesus, they bowed before him, worshiped him, and presented gifts fit for a king: "They opened their treasures and presented him with gifts of gold and of incense and of myrrh" (Matt. 2:11).

Furnace (Kiln)

The furnace mentioned in our Bibles is not a device for heating a building but rather an installation designed to obtain every last degree of heat from a fire and to direct that heat at an intended target. That target might be a crucible filled with ore. In this case the heat from the furnace melts the ore and allows the desired silver or gold to be separated from the dross. Alternately, the target of the heat could be bricks or pottery. The Babylonians in particular were known to harden bricks in furnaces to make the structures they built more durable. And all cultures of the ancient Near East had techniques for firing pottery with a furnace or kiln to turn the soft clay product into one that better stood up to the rigors of daily use.

The furnaces used to accomplish these tasks varied in size, shape, and composition to meet the intended application. At times the furnace was an enclosed kiln with a domed roof made of fire-hardened bricks, limestone, or clay. At other times the furnace was simply an open-air, stone-lined pit. But no matter its shape, the goal in every case was to support a fire stoked to high temperatures and to allow the heat from that fire to be directed at the intended target, whether a shelf filled with pottery or a crucible filled with ore.

Both heat and smoke are naturally associated with such a furnace. To fire clay vessels, a furnace had to produce and maintain a temperature nearing 1,850°F, while the melting of gold so that it would flow required temperatures well over 2,200°F. This kind of heat was produced by burning various products, including coal, which were coaxed to produce a high-temperature fire by blowing air into them, often by a bellows. This process guaranteed that a furnace would be known not just for the heat it produced but for its billowing smoke as well.

The Bible mentions a literal furnace in two

contexts. During the sixth plague against Egypt, Moses was directed to remove from a furnace soot that had cooled and toss it into the air. When he did so, festering boils broke out on both the people and their animals (Ex. 9:8, 10). In the second context, the furnace plays a more central role in the story (Dan. 3). King Nebuchadnezzar of Babylon had ordered all those living in his land to worship his recently built image of gold; those who refused were to be thrown into a large, heated kiln. Shadrach, Meshach, and Abednego declined the offer and so were summoned for execution. Before shoving them into the furnace, the king asked the telling question: "What god will be able to rescue you from my hand?" (Dan. 3:15). The answer came as the three faithful Israelites walked about in the superheated furnace and exited with flesh that was not singed, clothing that was not scorched, and hair that did not smell of smoke (Dan. 3:27).

The remaining mentions of the furnace in Scripture are in figurative language. In two instances the biblical authors call our attention to the smoke pouring from a working kiln. When Abraham looked down into the plain that used to house Sodom and Gomorrah, his view was obscured by dense smoke, "like smoke from a furnace" (Gen. 19:28). Years later, when Moses led the Israelites from their camp to meet the Lord

A mural depicting a typical pottery kiln.
Copyright 1995-2011 Phoenix Data Systems

at Mount Sinai, the mountain was covered with smoke as the Lord descended in fire upon it: "The smoke billowed up from it like smoke from a furnace" (Ex. 19:18).

In a number of passages, the biblical authors liken the way in which a heated furnace can refine metals to the way in which the Lord uses adversity to refine his children. The pain of the Egyptian oppression had left both physical and psychological scars on the Israelites. Yet by putting them into the "iron-smelting furnace," that is, Egypt, God had made his people who they needed to become before entering the Promised Land (Deut. 4:20; Jer. 11:4). In Proverbs the inspired poet likens the testing of God to the refining of silver and gold. The impure metal placed in the crucible is heated by means of a furnace to separate the slag from the highly desired pure metal: "The crucible for silver and the furnace for gold, but the LORD tests the heart" (Prov. 17:3; see also 27:21). This refinement is painful but effective: "See, I have refined you, though not as silver; I have tested you in the furnace of affliction" (Isa. 48:10).

The furnace that symbolizes the difficulties in life that improve the faithful can also be a symbol of God's judgment on those who reject him. Although the Lord's goal had been to refine Israel into precious metal, the process instead had produced dross: "Son of man, the house of Israel has become dross to me; all of them are the copper, tin, iron and lead left inside a furnace" (Ezek. 22:18). Consequently, the Lord was prepared to increase the temperature of the furnace and melt all the slag away: "I will gather you and I will blow on you with my fiery wrath, and you will be melted inside her. As silver is melted in a furnace, so you will be melted inside her" (vv. 21 – 22). The most mature form of this image is found in Jesus' own words that liken the experience to be found in hell to the experience one would find in a "fiery furnace" (Matt. 13:42, 50).

G

Garden

Several types of gardens are mentioned in the Bible: royal gardens, pagan worship gardens, industrial gardens, personal gardens, and cemetery gardens. While all these gardens contain plants and water, their design and level of sophistication differ markedly. Royal gardens are represented in all the major cultures of the ancient Near East. In every respect, these gardens were luxury parks designed for the enjoyment of the royal family. They contained large shade trees, meandering water channels, fountains, fragrant flowers, and fruit trees. Some kings even arranged for exotic animals and plants to be imported for their gardens. This is the kind of garden enjoyed by the Persian royal household at the time of Esther: "The garden had hangings of white and blue linen, fastened with cords of white linen and purple material to silver rings on marble pillars. There were couches of gold and silver on a mosaic pavement of porphyry, marble, mother-of-pearl and other costly stones" (Esth. 1:6). The fruit trees and other plants in such a garden would provide food for the royal family. But the primary function of the royal garden was to provide a place to escape the unrelenting heat of the day and the unrelenting challenges of life. It doubled as a place for both private reflection and lavish parties.

The second type of garden mentioned in the Bible is the one linked to the worship of pagan deities. This must have been a spiritual challenge for the people of Isaiah's day, because he mentions it on several occasions (Isa. 65:3; 66:17). "You will be ashamed because of the sacred oaks in which you have delighted; you will be disgraced because of the gardens that you have chosen" (1:29). Because they chose to visit such sacred gardens, they themselves would become "a garden without water" (1:30).

The third type of garden is illustrated by the famous garden of Gethsemane. The northern segment of the chalky ridge that lies just east of ancient Jerusalem was good for growing olive trees and was thus the site of an industrial olive grove. Jesus met frequently and privately with his disciples on this ridge. And what is more, it is the place where he struggled in prayer shortly before being arrested the week of his execution (John 18:1 – 2, 26).

The fourth type of garden was the one we may most likely think about when we hear the word *garden*. This was the personal garden where a family might grow their own vegetables. Typically such a garden was located as close to one's residence as was practical so as to limit unauthorized harvesting by thieves and animals. That was the goal of King Ahab who wanted the property of Naboth to grow vegetables because it was close to the palace (1 Kings 21:2). To plant such a personal garden signaled that you were settling into that location for the long haul. That is why Jeremiah encouraged the exiles in Babylon to "build houses and settle down; plant gardens and eat what they produce" (Jer. 29:5).

Finally, the Bible also knows of gardens that were linked to cemeteries. When King Manasseh died, he was buried "in his palace garden" (2 Kings 21:18). And King Jesus was not only crucified in a garden, but he was also buried in a new tomb located in that same garden (John 19:41).

Of course the garden of all gardens is the garden of Eden (Gen. 2). This very real space is carefully described by the author of Genesis to illustrate the parallels between it and the royal gardens of the ancient world. It had animals, trees, flowers, and copious amounts of water. The King who owned this garden customarily walked through it during the cool of the day (Gen. 3:8) and had brought Adam and Eve to live and

work in this wonderful spot. But the differences between the garden of Eden and a royal garden are equally striking. Adam and Eve did not just visit this garden when they needed to get away from life; this was where they lived all the time. The garden provided them with a place to live as well as a way of living. When sin entered the equation, the garden that symbolized their relationship to the King was also lost (Gen. 3:23–24). While some locations in the sin-ruined world were so attractive that they merited comparison with the garden of Eden (Gen. 13:10; Ezek. 28:13; 36:35; Joel 2:3), no place would be or could be its equal.

A second rhetorical use of the garden occurs in settings where restoration is the theme. The Lord called for Israel to abandon the abuses that had characterized their lifestyle during the time of Isaiah. When they did, they could anticipate a time of restoration. For then the Lord "will satisfy your needs in a sun-scorched land and will strengthen your frame. You will be like a well-

The royal garden of Assyrian King Ashurbanipal.

Todd Bolen/www.BiblePlaces.com

watered garden, like a spring whose waters never fail" (Isa. 58:11; cf. Jer. 31:12). Upon returning to the Promised Land, God's people thrived like a well-watered garden when they again planted gardens of their own (Amos 9:14).

The garden was a common motif in the love poetry of the ancient Near East; and so it shows up frequently in the Song of Songs. The young woman so enamored by the poet is described as a "garden locked up" (Song 4:12). She is celebrated for gardenlike beauty and compelling fragrance (4:15–16). "My lover has gone down to his gar-den, to the beds of spices, to browse in the gardens and to gather lilies" (6:2).

Gate (of a City)

The most commonly mentioned gate in the Bible is the defensive gate of a fortified city. The design and placement of this gate required special care because it had two conflicting missions to achieve—it both granted access and denied access. The gates proper were thick wooden doors whose vulnerability to ax, battering ram, and fire was mitigated by overlaying them with a metal

This impressive mud-brick gate guarded the city of Laish (Dan) at the time of Abraham.

like bronze. But by the time of the Israelite monarchy, the gate had developed into much more than a wooden doorway. The gate was perceived as a larger complex, consisting of a ramp, towers, courtyard, and gatehouse. The ramp both narrowed the approach to the city and exposed the vulnerable right side of attacking soldiers (the side opposite from which the shield was carried). At the end of this ramp stood the first or outer gate, which typically was flanked by two defensive towers. Just beyond this outer gate, one entered a large, open plaza that filled the space between the outer gate and the main, inner gate. This inner gate was built into a four-walled fort called a gatehouse, which stood watch over entry into the city proper.

The primary role of such a gate complex was protection, offering security without eliminating access (Deut. 3:5; 2 Chron. 8:5). When the gates of the city were closed and locked in the face of an enemy attack, they posed quite an obstacle to the approaching soldiers. If such soldiers were successful in reaching either the outer or inner gates, the towers and gatehouse provided an aerial platform that the defending soldiers could use to rain down grief on the attackers. And if the attackers were successful in getting up the ramp and through the outer gate, the courtyard, and the inner gate, their problems had just begun, for now they had to negotiate the dangerous passage through the gatehouse. This narrow passageway was flanked by rooms filled with soldiers. From the relative safety of those chambers, the defending soldiers had the chance to skewer those attempting to squeeze through the gatehouse into the city.

When the enemy was nowhere in sight, the gate complex still formed a bottleneck, slowing the flow of traffic in and out of the city. As people slowed and even stopped near the gate, it became a social center that played a number of roles. When the elders, the king, or one of the

prophets were about business that required their contact with many citizens, they might well conduct that business in the city gate (2 Sam. 18:24; 19:8; 1 Kings 22:10; Job 29:7–8; Prov. 31:23; Jer. 17:19–20). Legal cases involving property transactions, marriage, and even murder were heard in the city gate (Gen. 23:17–18; Deut. 22:15; 25:7; Josh. 20:4; Ruth 4:1, 11). Sellers and buyers could meet one another in the market set up at the gate (2 Kings 7:1; Isa. 60:11). And there is evidence both in the archaeological record as well as the Bible that the gate was home to certain illicit worship practices (2 Kings 23:8).

On the rhetorical side of things, the city gate came to represent strength (Ps. 48:12; Isa. 60:18). For example, Moses celebrated the strength of Asher, promising this tribe, "The bolts of your gates will be iron and bronze, and your strength will equal your days" (Deut. 33:25).

The city gate became so intimately linked with those in the city that it became a symbol for the entire city and its inhabitants. That is clearly the message in Psalm 87 where the inspired poet writes, "The LORD loves the gates of Zion" (v. 2)—not the structure but the people behind it. Consequently, the fortunes of those living behind the city gates are often described in terms of what happens to the gate itself. In certain instances, great harm had come to those gates and the citizens of the city. That is particularly the case when the gates were burned with fire (Neh. 2:3, 17; Jer. 17:27), "battered to pieces" (Isa. 24:12), or abandoned (Lam. 1:4; 5:14). A powerful message was being sent when one of the Lord's own warriors tore the gate of a city out of its sockets and carried it off to a distant hill (Judg. 16:3) and when the Lord promised that foreign "kings will come and set up their thrones in the entrance of the gates of Jerusalem" (Jer. 1:15). At such times of distress, the city gates were personified as mourning or wailing for those who had come into harm's way (Isa. 3:26; 14:31). On the other hand, the rebuilding of a gate that was ruined symbolized a time of restoration and renewal. This is particularly the focus in Nehemiah. After surveying the damage to Jerusalem and finding every gate severely damaged, Nehemiah's strategic restoration of the walls and gates became a symbol of the restoration of normalcy in the city itself (Neh. 2–3).

As the gate provided entry into the city, so a metaphorical gate provided entry into a new season of life. The expression "gates of death" is frequently used in poetic texts to describe one's arrival at the last stage of life (Job 17:16; 38:17; Ps. 107:18; Isa. 38:10). The heartrending plea of the psalmist evokes this image: "O LORD, see how my enemies persecute me! Have mercy and lift me up from the gates of death" (Ps. 9:13).

Because the days in which cities had gates were a time of danger, those gates were closed and locked at dusk (Josh. 2:5). But the coming of the Messiah spelled the arrival of a new era, a time of universal peace. The cry goes out: "Lift up your heads, O you gates; be lifted up, you ancient doors, that the King of glory may come in!" (Ps. 24:7). Upon his arrival, things will change in Zion: "Your gates will always stand open, they will never be shut, day or night" (Isa. 60:11). In the New Jerusalem, "on no day will its gates ever be shut, for there will be no night there" (Rev. 21:25).

Gazelle

The gazelle is a member of the antelope family and a native of the Promised Land. When the Bible mentions the gazelle, its authors are likely referring either to the mountain gazelle or the dorcas gazelle. Both are very similar in appearance but differ in their habitat preference. The gazelle is a small mammal just over three feet in length, standing two and a half feet at the shoulder, and weighing thirty-five to seventy-five pounds. The mountain gazelle is generally brown with a dark, narrow flank band that separates its brown sides from its white underbelly. The large, dark eyes of the gazelle look even larger because of the white band that frames its eyes and extends to its nose. The dorcas gazelle differs from its cousin by having a lighter upper coat of sandy red tones. The male and female of both species have horns, although the horns

Mountain gazelle.
© Hanne & Jens Eriksen/www.naturepl.com

of the male, which grow up to twelve inches in length, are two to three times longer than those of the female. In either case the horns initially curve outward and then gently inward, so that when viewed from the front, the horns form a heart shape that is open at the top.

The difference in color between the mountain gazelle and the dorcas gazelle signals different habitat preferences for these two species. The mountain gazelle is found more frequently in the northern portions of Israel where it roams the hills, grasslands, and lightly wooded fields in search of the greenery that is its steady diet. In contrast the lighter-toned dorcas gazelle prefers the drier landscapes of the Negev where it goes in search of small patches of grass and the leaves of the acacia tree.

The gazelle has two distinguishing qualities—beauty and speed. When we look closely at the features of this animal, we can appreciate why ancient Near Eastern poets celebrated the beauty of this animal. It has big dark eyes, a long neck, and slender legs, all of which combine to give it a most pleasing appearance. It may well be the most beautiful animal of the biblical world. This beauty is coupled with remarkable speed. The gazelle favors the company of its herd where many watchful eyes and listening ears identify the presence of predators long before they become a threat. But if danger comes too close, the herd breaks into a darting array of brown streaks, an inbred strategy designed to confuse the predator, which often pauses, not knowing which animal to pursue. As the predator pauses, the gazelles turn on their afterburners. When gazelles are serious about accelerating away from trouble, they can quickly reach fifty miles per hour, a speed they can sustain for about one hundred yards.

In the six places the Bible mentions a literal gazelle, it always associates this animal with food. In the dietary laws listed in Deuteronomy, we find that the gazelle is repeatedly listed as an example of a clean animal the Israelites could eat without reservation (Deut. 12:15, 22; 14:5; 15:22). The only other place the gazelle is literally mentioned is on a list of animals required to feed those in Solomon's employ when he was king of Israel (1 Kings 4:23).

When the biblical authors use the gazelle in a figure of speech, it is the animal's speed and beauty that come to the foreground. Although no mortal was literally as fast as the gazelle, those who were fleet of foot could be compared to this animal. The Gadites, who had joined David during that difficult period in his life when he was relentlessly pursued by Saul, are said to be "as swift as gazelles in the mountains" (1 Chron. 12:8). However, this highly desirable quality did not work out so well for Asahel. After Saul had died, his army, led by Abner, lived on to fight another day. When Joab and the army of David bested Abner in combat, Joab's brother went in relentless pursuit of the fleeing Abner. Asahel was fast, "as fleet-footed as a wild gazelle" (2 Sam. 2:18), but his speed only put him in harm's way more quickly. The youthful Asahel died when he caught up with the more experienced warrior Abner. This speed burst is also in view as the inspired poet of Proverbs speaks about getting out of an unfortunate agreement one might have struck with a neighbor. In this circumstance the poet encourages the humble pressing of one's case that will culminate in freeing "yourself, like a gazelle from the hand of the hunter" (Prov. 6:5). And in his judgment speech against Babylon, Isaiah declares that Babylon would flee like a frightened gazelle from the lands they had conquered (Isa. 13:14).

Seven of the sixteen instances where a gazelle is mentioned in the Bible occur in the Song of

Songs. In two instances the gazelles are called to be witnesses of what is being said (Song 2:7; 3:5). It is possible that the oversized eyes and ears of the gazelle are in view, making this animal an apt witness of what is done and said. In two other instances the adorable fawns of the gazelle are mentioned as the lover describes the immature but beautiful breasts of his beloved: "Your two breasts are like two fawns, like twin fawns of the gazelle that browse among the lilies" (4:5; cf. 7:3). And on three occasions the young woman likens her beloved to a gazelle (2:9, 17; 8:14). Here the athleticism and strength of the male love interest in this poem make him comparable to the gazelle, which sports those same qualities.

Goat

Because of its valuable contributions to daily living, the domestic goat joins the sheep as the animal most likely to be raised by a family during Bible times. Goats produced the milk they drank, provided the tent in which they lived, helped preserve their pastures, and were offered as sacrifices for their sins.

Although the goat was listed among the clean animals (Deut. 14:4), goats were eaten less frequently than sheep because the meat of mature goats is less desirable. Where the goat earned its keep was in milk production. The average goat could produce twice the amount of milk when compared with the average ewe, milk that was

Sheep and goats in the Judean wilderness.
Z. Radovan/www.BibleLandPictures.com

also higher in nutritional value (supplying more protein and fat).

Second, the goat was important in providing shelter from the elements. The soft wool of sheep was the material of choice for weaving clothing, but goat hair produced the best tents. Goat hair woven to form a tent sheet would swell when it became wet, making the shelter water resistant; and it would shrink when it dried, allowing air to circulate through the material and ventilate the living space. Consequently, the goat hair tent became the dwelling of choice for the Israelites when they were on the move. This also explains why goat hair was used in the composition of the tent that covered the tabernacle proper (Ex. 26:7).

Third, the goat made an important contribution toward maintaining the health of the pastures that fed the flocks, pastures that were subject to overgrazing if sheep were left to eat at their own pace. Sheep are prone to linger in one location, but goats move regularly as they eat. When goats and sheep are mingled in one flock, the sheep follow the lead of the goats and keep moving. This prevents overgrazing and thus preserves the health of the pastures vital to both.

Finally, the most common appearance of the goat on the pages of the Bible is in connection with various sacrifices the Lord asked of his people (Gen. 15:9; Ex. 12:5; Lev. 1:10; 3:12; 4:23; et al.). In these cases the goat joined other animals that stood as placeholders. The shedding of their blood as punishment for the sins of a mortal did not provide forgiveness, but rather anticipated the adequate punishment for sin that was finally achieved in the sacrificial death of Jesus (Heb. 9:11–14; 10:1–5).

The goat was so fundamental to life in Bible times that it became a metaphor and symbol in the language of the Bible. The following examples illustrate that the connotations associated with the goat can be both positive and negative. In the Song of Songs, the inspired poet is thoroughly captivated by the beauty of the young woman who is the love interest in this poem. Her hair is like "a flock of goats descending from Mount Gilead" (Song 4:1; 6:5). Only when we appreciate the great value of the goat to this culture can we come to appreciate how much of a compliment this is. The poet in Proverbs encourages the reader to find greater security in life by giving attention to the condition of one's flock. The resulting security is defined in terms of a ready milk supply provided by the goats (Prov. 27:27). The goat as leader is also a positive metaphor that circulates through a number of Bible passages. Jeremiah encourages the Israelites who are leaving Babylon to leave their captivity like the goats that lead the flock (Jer. 50:8). The stately stride of this leadership (Prov. 30:29–31) helps us appreciate why the Greeks and particularly Alexander the Great are described in Daniel with the imagery of a charging goat that uses its nimble feet and powerful push to take control of the ancient world (Dan. 8:5, 8, 21).

These positive connotations associated with the goat live in company with the negative connotations we also encounter in our Bible reading. The goat is often pictured as a carrier of sin and its consequences. This connotation was firmly set in the minds of ancient Israelites, given the imagery used on the annual Day of Atonement, a sacred day on which the priests and people were cleansed of their sins (Lev. 23:26–32). On that day the high priest led two goats into the presence of the Lord where lots were cast; one goat was selected for immediate sacrifice, and the other became the scapegoat (Lev. 16:7–10). The high priest would place both hands on the head of the scapegoat and symbolically transfer the sins of the people onto that animal by confessing those sins over that animal. With the sin and consequences now linked to the scapegoat, this animal was driven far into the wilderness away from God's people (Lev. 16:20–22).

This negative image of the goat as a sin carrier driven away from the people to die in the wilderness may explain why Jesus used the goat to illustrate the fate of the lost in speaking about the end times. When the Son of Man comes in his glory, the people will be gathered to him. Jesus describes this gathered group as a mixed flock containing both "sheep and goats." Such a mixed flock was the norm in the Promised Land, but from time to time the shepherd would separate the sheep from the goats. Jesus uses that image here, putting the sheep on his right and the goats on his left, "as a shepherd separates the sheep from the goats" (Matt. 25:32–33). While the sheep in this illustration represent the Lord's redeemed, the goat that had for so long been associated with the scapegoat now represents those to whom sin will cling forever, those consigned to an eternal separation from Jesus.

Grain (Wheat, Barley)

Wheat and barley were the primary types of grain present in the biblical world, and so they are naturally the grains mentioned most often in the Bible. Wheat is the more desirable of the two but is more difficult to grow since it is fussier about soil quality and climate. On the other hand, barley is more adaptable to poor growing conditions but is a coarser grain more likely to be consumed by the poor, used as food for animals, or consumed as a last resort (Judg. 7:13; 1 Kings 4:28; Ezek. 4:9; John 6:9).

Because grain was a staple food during Bible times, every family did what they could to grow their own. The wheat and barley were both planted when the early rains of autumn softened the soil for plowing and planting. Then everyone anxiously monitored the conditions during the growing season, which would determine the quality of the spring harvest (barley in March–April and wheat in May–June). The success or failure of the seasonal grain harvest is mentioned in numerous Bible stories but is particularly important to the events concerning Joseph (Gen. 37–50) and Naomi (Ruth). To appreciate the mention of grain in all such stories requires us to place ourselves in the cultural circumstances of those whose very existence was connected to their grain supply: "We and our sons and daughters are numerous; in order for us to eat and stay alive, we must get grain" (Neh. 5:2).

In the culture of Bible times, we find grain functioning as food, as an offering, and as a form of currency. The critical protein and carbohydrates required to remain healthy were acquired by eating the grain raw (Deut. 23:25; Matt. 12:1), roasted (1 Sam. 17:17; 2 Sam. 17:28), or transformed into baked goods (2 Kings 4:42). Such products were not merely associated with every meal, they were the chief component of that meal. The Lord also asked his people to present the product of the grain fields before him as an offering. For example, the grain offering, described in Leviticus 2, was to accompany other offerings presented before the Lord, including the burnt offering, sin offering, and fellowship offering. Additionally, the first sheaf of harvested barley was brought to the priests and presented before the Lord as a wave offering (Lev. 23:9–14). Seven weeks later, during the Feast of Weeks (Pentecost), the initial harvest from the wheat fields was offered to express thanksgiving for the harvest (Lev. 23:15–21; Num. 28:26–30). Finally, beyond its food value and use in worship rites, grain also doubled as a form of currency. A given amount of grain was the equivalent of a day's wage (Rev. 6:6). Grain was used to pay taxes and tribute (1 Sam. 8:15; 1 Kings 4:28; 2 Chron. 27:5). And surplus grain was exported by grain-producing nations as well as traded for services or other commodities (1 Kings 5:11; 2 Chron. 2:10, 15; Isa. 23:3).

The rhetorical use of grain by the biblical authors naturally follows these realities. The Promised Land was special for many reasons, not least of which was its ability to produce grain. The Lord whetted the appetite of Israel for this special land by telling them it was "a land with wheat and barley" (Deut. 8:8). This was the Lord's own land. He superintended the soil and climatic conditions so that it could produce an abundance of this vital product. As the

psalmist says, "You care for the land and water it; you enrich it abundantly. The streams of God are filled with water to provide the people with grain, for so you have ordained it" (Ps. 65:9). The land of Israel was a land whose "valleys are mantled with grain" (65:13).

But the presence of this incredible bounty was conditioned on the covenant loyalty of Israel. When they paid attention to the laws and followed them, the Lord would flood the people with ample grain, but when they failed, so did the grain harvest (Deut. 7:12–13; 11:13–15; 28:17–18). Given this theological foundation, the prophets are very quick to point out the link between Israel's disobedience and the resulting loss of the grain harvest. At those times they will

A ripening wheat field promised one more year of life for those who anticipated the harvest.

"sow wheat but reap thorns," bearing the shame of their harvest (Jer. 12:13). "They sow the wind and reap the whirlwind. The stalk has no head; it will produce no flour. Were it to yield grain, foreigners would swallow it up" (Hos. 8:7).

But a gracious God always looked for signs of repentance. And when that repentance signaled a new stage of life in his people, restoration of the grain harvest followed: "He who goes out weeping, carrying seed to sow, will return with songs of joy, carrying sheaves with him" (Ps. 126:6). When the Lord again provides grain, the mood of his people will lighten as they rejoice in the bounty he provides (Jer. 31:12; Joel 2:19). In fact, they themselves will flourish like the grain growing in their fields (Hos. 14:7). When God's people are tracking well, their joy over the Lord exceeds the joy over their grain fields. As the psalmist sings, "You have filled my heart with greater joy than when their grain and new wine abound" (Ps. 4:7).

Grain is such a precious commodity that it also is used as a symbol for the redeemed. In the parable of the sower, the seeds that are sown represent different kinds of people who have encountered the life-saving message of the gospel. In particular the seed that falls into the good soil are those who hear the word and accept it. They in turn produce a crop that is "thirty, sixty or even a hundred times what was sown" (Mark 4:20).

That is saying something in a culture where a good year's harvest is fivefold what was planted. And in the parable of the weeds, believers are represented by the wheat that is allowed to grow in the fields with the weeds until the harvest. At that time the wheat will be gathered and brought into the Lord's own barn (Matt. 13:30).

Grape (Grapevine)

The grapevine is a signature plant of the Promised Land whose production demanded a significant amount of time and energy from the residents of that land. When Moses directed a reconnaissance team to bring back evidence of the agricultural capability of the Promised Land, those men returned with a huge cluster of grapes suspended on a pole carried by two men (Num. 13:23). It is no wonder that the grapevine is listed among the plants that characterized the goodness of this land (Deut. 8:8). And we can appreciate why settled life is one characterized by living peacefully under one's own vine and fig tree (1 Kings 4:25).

Grapes were eaten or processed in various ways, and provision was made so that even the poor without land of their own would have access to this product. Grapes were eaten fresh off the vine. They were also spread out to dry in the sun in order to produce raisins, which

White grapes in Galilee.

might, in turn, be pressed into cakes. The raisins and raisin cakes were particularly valued as travel food, given the energy provided by their high sugar content. Additionally, some grapes were boiled down into a jellylike substance called *dibs* or stomped and processed to make wine. Grapes and grape products were a staple food in Bible times. That is why the Lord directed those with grapevines to leave grapes that fell to the ground and to ignore those missed during the initial picking so that the poor of the land might have access to this important food item as well (Lev. 19:10; Deut. 24:21).

The road to a successful grape harvest was a long one. First, an appropriate growing environment had to be created on a sloping hillside. This meant building a terrace, wall, and watchtower. Since grapes were not grown from seeds but from cuttings, healthy stock had to be acquired and planted; then followed years of cultivation and pruning in advance of the first usable grapes produced. It is easy to see that grapevines required the most attention of any plant grown by God's people in the Promised Land.

Rhetorically, grapes sprout in many Bible passages, including those that liken Israel to a grape or grapevine. The Lord compared finding Israel to finding "grapes in the desert" (Hos. 9:10). Yet these promising grapes often turned sour: "I had planted you like a choice vine of sound and reliable stock. How then did you turn against me into a corrupt, wild vine?" (Jer. 2:21). The Lord looked ever so carefully among the leaves of his precious vine for good grapes, but again and again was disappointed at finding only bad (Isa. 5:2). It is against this backdrop of lackluster grapevines that we may best read the extended metaphor of John 15. In contrast to the failures of Israel as a grapevine, Jesus declares himself "the true vine" (John 15:1). The ability of God's people, the branches, to produce good fruit is now located in their connection to Jesus, the Vine: "I am the vine; you are the branches. If a man remains in me and I in him, he will bear much fruit" (John 15:5).

Judgment against both Israel and the nations is also linked to the grapevine. When Israel failed to live up to the covenant God had made with them, the consequences were expressed among their grapevines and through images associated with their grapevines. God had promised that negative consequences would attend Israel's rebellion; among those were the loss of the critical grape harvest (Deut. 28:39), a reality experienced during the time of the prophets (Isa. 32:10; Jer. 8:13). The grapevines would not only be lost, they also would serve as images of what would happen to God's people during those difficult days. Israel would be stripped like a gleaned grapevine (Jer. 6:9). The rebellion of the nations was also met with divine judgment illustrated by images from the vineyard. The reality behind the following images was well known in Bible times; but here it describes the fate of the nations: "For, before the harvest, when the blossom is gone and the flower becomes a ripening grape, he will cut off the shoots with pruning knives, and cut down and take away the spreading branches" (Isa. 18:5). Edom would be "stripped bare" of its grapes, and the nations will be trampled underfoot as one treads grapes while making wine (cf. Jer. 49:9–10; Joel 3:13).

Two metaphors and one adage round out the rhetorical use of grapes and grapevines by the biblical authors. In the song of Moses that participates in closing the book of Deuteronomy, Moses describes the enemies of God's people as connected to the vine of Sodom and Gomorrah. Moses cautions against attraction to their mind-set and lifestyle by saying, "Their grapes are filled with poison and their clusters with bitterness" (Deut. 32:32). Grapes appear in a markedly different metaphor in the love poem of the Song of Songs. Given the connotations and value of a cluster of grapes, we may appreciate why this poet likens the breasts of the beloved young woman to "clusters of the vine" (Song 7:7–8). Finally, on two occasions, the prophets mention an adage apparently quoted by those wishing to explain the reason for their misfortune: "The fathers have eaten sour grapes, and the children's teeth are set on edge" (Jer. 31:29; Ezek. 18:2). In both instances, the prophets correct this misperception, in effect saying, those who eat sour grapes will have their own teeth set on edge. Each person suffering should not look to their parents' failures but to their own for a potential cause of their suffering.

Grass

The grass of the Bible's world is not associated with a lawn, golf course, or athletic field. The grass mentioned in the Bible is the spreading green carpet that grows naturally over the ridges and down the valleys of the rural countryside. Although such a scene is filled with dozens of plant species and hundreds of thousands of individual plants, they are all but lost in the pervasive sea of green that the biblical authors call "grass."

Where one would find such a field of grass depends on the time of year. During the wet winter season of Israel, grass is everywhere. Grass fills the ridges, covers the otherwise dry slopes of the wilderness, and even pokes out of clay rooftops where seeds scattered by the wind or by birds gain a tentative foothold. God is the one who provides the necessary rain, so he is responsible for creating this seasonal flourish of green (Deut. 11:14–15; Ps. 147:8). But the late-spring desert

winds are waiting. At the close of the winter season, sirocco winds rage in off the desert for three to four days at a time, elevating the temperature and causing the relative humidity to plummet. The first to wither are the lonely seedlings that have sprouted in the clay roofs (2 Kings 19:26); then the lush green fields turn yellow-brown while the green slopes of the wilderness quickly fade. As summer settles in, herdsmen must move their animals north to the wetter parts of the country and search out the northern side of rising terrain where heat and evaporation take less of a toll on grassy fields. In the desert, grass can now be found growing only in the sheltered wadi bottoms where roots can still reach the groundwater (1 Kings 18:5). But even wise herdsmen fear the drought that seizes the land when the winter rains fail. No rain means no grasslands, no pasture, and a season of suffering for wild and domestic animals alike (Jer. 12:4–5; 14:5).

The Bible mentions two practical roles that a field of grass might play. In a land full of uncomfortable rocky outcroppings, a green grassy field was a wonderful place to sit. The thousands who had gathered to hear Jesus speak and who were about to receive a miraculous meal were invited to sit down because "there was plenty of grass in that place" (John 6:10). But most often people were not sitting in a grassy field; they were using the grass of that field to feed their animals. Oxen, donkeys, cattle, mules, horses, sheep, and goats all required the nutrients found in these plants. Such open fields were their pastureland.

While we expect to see animals eating grass, seeing a person doing so is shocking. This unexpected sight of a mortal grazing like an animal signaled great humiliation. When pride mixed with power in King Nebuchadnezzar's heart, he was driven from his palace into the pasturelands where he ate grass with the cattle (Dan. 4:25, 32–33).

Elsewhere in the Bible we find a lush field of grass used in positive metaphors. When looking across the rolling carpet of a green field, any attempt to differentiate, much less count, the individual blades of grass is impossible. What a blessing it is, if your descendants become "like the grass of the earth" or "spring up like grass in a meadow" (Job 5:25; Isa. 44:4). The flourishing, grassy field of the winter season is also likened to people or cities that are blessed. People flourish like grass when the rain and dew of God's Word falls on them (Deut. 32:2), and Jerusalem would flourish like grass under the restoring touch of the Lord (Isa. 66:14).

But as the season changes, so does the appearance of the grasslands; the short-lived grass that is here today and gone tomorrow becomes a metaphor for the brevity of life and the comparative insignificance of mortals. In contrast to the eternal God, mortals are like "the new grass of the morning—though in the morning it springs up new, by evening it is dry and withered" (Ps. 90:5–6). "All men are like grass, and all their glory is like the flowers of the field. The grass withers and the flowers fall, because the breath of the LORD blows on them. Surely the people are grass. The grass withers and the flowers fall, but the word of our God stands forever" (Isa. 40:6–8).

The short-lived grass also illustrates the fate of the wicked. The psalmist has known the pain that evildoers can stir in the believer's life. But this

Grass covers the slopes during the wet winter season in Israel.

inspired poet takes heart in the fact that they will soon be gone, "for like the grass they will soon wither, like green plants they will soon die away" (Ps. 37:2). And for the enemies of Zion so bent on causing the ruin of Jerusalem, this prayer ascends from the mouths of those walking up to the temple for worship: "May all who hate Zion be turned back in shame. May they be like grass on the roof, which withers before it can grow" (Ps. 129:5–6).

Jesus turns our eyes to the hillside carpeted with fine greenery for one last lesson. Well aware of how debilitating unchecked worry can become in the lives of people whose days are filled with uncertainty, Jesus turns the eyes of his listeners to the lilies of the field that have poked their colorful heads through the green tapestry: "If that is how God clothes the grass of the field, which is here today and tomorrow is thrown into the fire, will he not much more clothe you, O you of little faith?" (Matt. 6:30).

Grave (Tomb)

The presence of sin in the world assures the ongoing occurrence of death and the need for graves. With death even more certain than taxes, we find that ancients and moderns alike plan for that inevitable day by identifying a final resting place. During Bible times this planning was particularly important because the day of one's death was also the day of one's burial (Deut. 21:22–23). Consequently, travel plans late in life were limited to assure that one died in proximity to the family tomb (2 Sam. 19:37).

The design and appearance of biblical graves depends on the era and on the socioeconomic status of the deceased. Archaeology from Bible times suggests a variety of options. Some may have found their final rest in a simple stone-lined pit that was covered with slabs of rock. Others were buried in an underground chamber that extended laterally at the bottom of a ten-foot entrance shaft. Still others might be buried in a cave or a rock-hewn chamber. But in virtually all cases, no matter the design of the grave, burial took place outside the bounds of the city, village, or town so as to prevent the ritual contamination inherent in contact with a dead body or grave (Num. 19:11–16). The one striking exception to this rule is the city of Jerusalem, which contained the royal tombs of David's family (1 Kings 2:10; Neh. 3:16).

An ornately decorated grave at Bet-Guvrin, formerly the biblical Judean city of Maresha.

Literal tombs could take on rhetorical importance. A bedouin family would not be particularly concerned about land ownership, given their itinerant movement from place to place. But for the family of Abraham, the land promise given by God changed that. Land was linked to faith; consequently, Abraham purchased a cave near Hebron not only to provide a resting place for Sarah, but also to begin the land ownership that would culminate during the time of Joshua (Gen. 23:3–20; Josh. 14–21). Even when this special family was living in Egypt, Jacob insisted that he be buried in that same grave (Gen. 50:5). The tomb of Rachel marked with a pillar (Gen. 35:19–20) and the tomb of Joseph at Shechem (Josh. 24:32) functioned in a similar way; they were not just a grave but also a place to remember the destiny that linked this land, this family, and the rescue from sin.

Overtones of honor or dishonor also were linked to the deceased in regard to grave location and what people did at the gravesite. Being buried in the family tomb was considered honorable (see, e.g., Judg. 8:32; 2 Sam. 2:32; 21:14; 2 Kings 9:28; 2 Chron. 16:14; 35:24), so special mention is made of those dishonored by their failure to find their final rest either in the family tomb or in the tombs reserved for the kings (1 Kings 13:22; 2 Chron. 21:20; 24:25; 28:27). Apparently, executed criminals were buried in a distinct location that caused the dishonor of their crimes to linger; in contrast it was a special honor for a nonfamily member to be buried in the family tomb. Hence we have Isaiah's words about Jesus that contrast his criminal status with this burial honor; "He was assigned a grave with the wicked, and with the rich in his death" (Isa. 53:9; see Matt. 27:59–60). The actions and demeanor of those who visit the tomb also communicate honor or dishonor. Honor is shown by

those who come to mourn, to weep, to see to the preparation of the body, to refurbish or redecorate the grave (2 Sam. 3:32; Job 21:32; Luke 11:47–48; 24:1; John 11:31, 35). However, it is a sign of great dishonor when those who come to the grave are there to throw the bones from it (Isa. 14:19; Jer. 8:1).

The grave also appears in a wide range of attention-grabbing metaphors. Because of the close connection between death and the grave, the grave can be used as a metaphor for death. This is particularly prevalent in Old Testament poetry where death is described as reaching the grave, coming to the grave, being carried to the grave, or being destined for the grave (Job 3:22; 5:26; 17:1; 21:32; Pss. 49:14; 88:5). The war machines of Babylon that would descend upon Jerusalem brought death with them—their quivers are likened to "an open grave" (Jer. 5:16). The Babylonians would eventually carry God's people into an extended exile. Because the grave is synonymous with absence, the tomb also became a symbol of this exile. We find this symbol in the restoration language where dry bones reassemble, are clothed with flesh, and breathe again (Ezek. 37:1–10): "O my people, I am going to open your graves and bring you up from them; I will bring you back to the land of Israel" (v. 12). Harsh and cruel words are a potent weapon in the hand of those wishing to bring harm. The psalmist suggests that the mouth that forms deceitful words can bring about the "death" of one's reputation: "Their throat is an open grave; with their tongue they speak deceit" (Ps. 5:9; cf. Rom. 3:13). Jesus also used the grave as a metaphor when leveling harsh criticism at the Pharisees. These individuals took pride in doing more than was necessary to remain ritually pure. But their life and example were more harmful than helpful to those seeking righteousness. Consequently, Jesus compared them to "unmarked graves, which men walk over without knowing it" (Luke 11:44) and to "whitewashed tombs, which look beautiful on the outside but on the inside are full of dead men's bones and everything unclean" (Matt. 23:27).

Of course no tomb deserves greater mention than the tomb of Jesus. The fact that Jesus was placed in a tomb does not separate him from the rest of us; but his empty tomb does just that: "Why do you look for the living among the dead? He is not here; he has risen!" (Luke 24:5–6).

H

Hail

Hail is an icy form of precipitation associated with severe thunderstorms. It forms when water droplets are seized by the powerful updrafts of tall, mature thunderstorms and swept above the freezing level. Complimentary downdrafts recirculate the now-frozen water droplets through the warmer portion of the storm where they receive a fresh coating of moisture. Once again the frozen droplets are propelled above the freezing level in a cycle that repeats again and gain. Eventually the growing pellets of ice become so large that they are too heavy to remain within the cloud's circulating winds and are expelled ahead of the storm, falling to the ground as hail.

In the average year, hail falls on the coastal plain of Israel four to five times. Eighty-eight percent of hail events occur from December through March. The hailstones that fall during these months are typically quite small, on average little more than one-eighth of an inch in diameter. In contrast, hail almost never occurs from May to October; yet the severest thunderstorms that have the potential to produce the largest hail are those that occur in late spring. For example, in April 2006 a severe thunderstorm produced hailstones that were the size of Ping-Pong balls.

Israel is a land that desperately longs for precipitation. While rain and snow are more than welcome, hail is not. That is because it brings only a small amount of moisture and couples that meager moisture with the ability to harm fruit trees and field crops. The small hail that falls from December through March typically does little harm. But damaging spring hail storms that occur when the grain is ripening and the fruit trees are blooming can decimate the produce from that growing season (Hag. 2:17).

When hail falls in the Bible, it is never a benign event; God is using it as a divine weapon designed to coerce behavior or destroy an enemy (Isa. 30:30; Ezek. 38:22; Rev. 8:7; 16:21). The psalmist describes God's deliverance through the elements of nature in Psalm 18: "Out of the brightness of his presence clouds advanced, with hailstones and bolts of lightning" (v. 12). Two other biblical accounts give us dramatic examples of this meteorological warfare. When Pharaoh refused to let Israel leave Egypt despite the Lord's direct command for him to do so, Egypt felt the pain of a number of plagues. One of those was a miraculous hailstorm that started and ended at Moses' command (Ex. 9:13–35). This plague, designed to break down the pride of Egypt, devastated the flax and barley harvest, stripped every tree, and took the lives of both animals and people who had failed to take shelter. Years later a divine hailstorm struck again, this time in the Promised Land. Five city-states led by the king of Jerusalem made a bold attempt to push Joshua and the army of Israel from Canaan (Josh. 10:1 – 15). But these kings had not just taken on Joshua; they had taken on the Lord who had promised Israel that Canaan would be theirs. God threw the coalition troops into confusion and then dogged their retreat with an intense hailstorm. More died from the battering hailstones than from the swipe of Israelite swords (Josh. 10:11).

The psalmists often turn rhetorically to the hailstorm of the exodus to solicit trust from God's people and encourage their praise. Psalm 78 revisits the plagues on Egypt, not to gloat, but as a call to trust the powerful loyalty that God had shown Israel in the past. The hailstorm that destroyed their vines and cattle illustrates God's passion for his people (vv. 47 – 48). In other instances the psalmists call for Israel to give thanks to the Lord and praise him for all his mighty works of the past. A reprise of the hailstorm used against Egypt can be found in Psalm 105:32 – 33.

While rain and snow are welcome forms of precipitation in Israel, hail is not.
©Sergio Azzini/www.BigStockPhoto.com

The fact that God controls this meteorological phenomenon helps define his otherness. When the inspired poets wish to make the point, all it takes are a few well-placed questions, the answers to which are all too obvious: "Have you entered the storehouses of the snow or seen the storehouses of the hail, which I reserve for times of trouble, for days of war and battle?" (Job 38:22 – 23). "He hurls down his hail like pebbles. Who can withstand his icy blast?" (Ps. 147:17).

In all the cases presented so far, hail is mentioned as a real phenomenon. That leaves just two instances in the Bible where hail is used as a metaphor. As divine warrior, God had quite literally deployed hail against his mortal opponents. When he directed Assyria to turn its weapons upon Samaria, the capital of the northern kingdom, he likened the Assyrian military to "a hailstorm and a destructive wind" that would throw this city forcefully to the ground (Isa. 28:2). Perhaps this is also the way we should understand the reference to hail in Ezekiel where the Lord is pushing back against the message of the false prophets who claimed that Jerusalem would be spared a full destruction by Babylon. The Lord likened this message to a flimsy, whitewashed wall that would be swept away by hailstones.

Apparently hail is used in these verses to allude to Babylon (Ezek. 13:11, 13).

Harp

The harp appears in a wide array of settings. It is as likely to be played in the home of a shepherd as in the royal court. It accompanied the singing in Solomon's temple and at this moment accompanies the singing in heaven. The harp of Bible times is a stringed instrument, rectangular in shape and easily held in one's arms. It can be played while standing, walking, or sitting. The strings of this instrument are stretched between a crossbar and wooden sound box that are joined to one another by upright arms rising from either side of the sound box. Distinct musical tones are produced by fixing the four to eight strings of the harp under varying degrees of tension and changing that tension with the application of light finger pressure. When the strings are plucked with the finger or with a plectrum, the vibration is amplified by the hollow sound box producing a sustained tone. The Bible gives examples of this instrument being played both solo (1 Sam. 19:9) and as part of an ensemble (Isa. 5:12; Dan. 3:7).

The harp appears in a wide variety of settings, almost all of which carry the connotation of joy and celebration. Laban lamented the fact that Jacob had left his household so quickly and without celebration: "Why didn't you tell me, so I could send you away with joy and singing to the music of tambourines and harps?" (Gen. 31:27). National celebrations also made use of the harp. For example, it was played during processions following a military victory (2 Chron. 20:28). When the rebuilding of Jerusalem's wall was complete, the dedication of this public works project included the joyful music of the harp (Neh. 12:27); and when the ark of the covenant was moved to Jerusalem by David or into the temple by Solomon, the harp was played (2 Sam. 6:5; 2 Chron. 5:12). The light and happy tones of the harp could not help but lift one's spirits, even when an evil spirit was in the room. When Saul was tormented by an evil spirit, he called for a harp player because the music soothed him (1 Sam. 16:16, 18, 23). Prophets and teachers of wisdom also valued the harp as a musical instrument that could help set the mood for the words they were about to speak (2 Kings 3:15–16; 1 Chron. 25:1). "I will turn my ear to a proverb; with the harp I will expound my riddle" (Ps. 49:4). The music of the harp became so intermeshed with the worship life of Israel at the temple that a group of musicians dedicated themselves to practicing and providing harp music in support of worship (1 Chron. 15:16, 21, 28; 16:5; 2 Chron. 29:25).

The link between worship and the harp is nowhere clearer than in the Psalms where playing the harp or the call to play this instrument becomes the equivalent of worship or the call to worship (Pss. 43:4; 57:8; 71:22; 81:2; 92:3; 108:2; 149:3; 150:3). "Praise the LORD with the harp; make music to him on the ten-stringed lyre" (33:2). "Shout for joy to the LORD, all the earth, burst into jubilant song with music; make music to the LORD with the harp, with the harp and the sound of singing" (98:4–5). "Sing to the LORD with thanksgiving; make music to our God on the harp" (147:7).

But at times the positive connotations and harmonious tones associated with the harp in the Psalter turn sour and face prophetic criticism. That is the case when the harp is played at the parties of those who have no regard for the deeds of the Lord (Isa. 5:12). In cases like this the joyful music is out of place given the judgment about to fall. Amos warns those who strum on their harps like David and improvise on musical instruments that their carefree days are about to come to a close (Amos 6:5). The same criticism that falls upon the spiritually complacent also falls upon those whose worship is perfunctory. The Lord says, "Away with the noise of your songs! I will not listen to the music of your harps" (5:23).

When harps stop playing, it is a signal that life is not all it could or should be. When the Israelites were exiled to Babylon, their captors asked them to sing joyful songs about Zion accompanied by their harps. But the exiles had no heart for it. "By the rivers of Babylon we sat and wept when we remembered Zion. There on the poplars we hung our harps" (Ps. 137:1–2). Other musicians would follow this lead, terminating their music in the face of national catastrophes. Judgment speeches against Babylon, Assyria, Tyre, apocalyptic "Babylon," and the world in general all include this somber news. The joyful music of the harp would cease when the Lord visited his punishment on their rebellion (Isa. 14:11; Ezek. 26:13; Rev. 18:22). "The gaiety of the tambourines is stilled, the noise of the revelers has stopped, the joyful harp is silent" (Isa. 24:8).

Yet as the tones of the harp are stilled among the Lord's enemies, the sound of other harps continues to produce wonderful melodies. These are the harpists playing in the heavenly Jerusalem who accompany the songs in praise of the Lamb (Rev. 14:2). John saw the saints in glory who were victorious in their fight against the beast: "They held harps given them by God and sang the song of Moses the servant of God and the song of the Lamb" (Rev. 15:2–3).

Hebron

Hebron is located twenty miles southwest of Jerusalem on the central ridge of the mountains that run north and south through the heart of the Promised Land. The higher elevation of the Hebron hills improves their ability to extract moisture from the eastward flowing air masses, giving this region annual rainfall totals that exceed most other places in the hill country. The life-giving rain falls on rich, basin farmland around Hebron, causing grapes, grain, olives, and almonds to

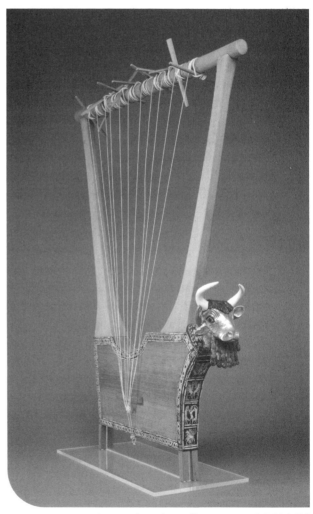

An ancient harp from around 2600 BC was found at Ur of Chaldea.

abound. No wonder the reconnaissance team sent into the Promised Land by Moses brought a sample of the produce from Hebron to illustrate the capability of this land (Num. 13:22–23). Hebron was also a transportation hub. Here the central Ridge Route that served as the primary north-south road through the hill country intersected secondary roads leading south into the Negev. This made Hebron a trading center where bedouins and farmers could meet to exchange pastoral and agricultural goods. When Jerusalem became the capital of all Israel, Hebron further assumed the role of guardian. The north-south roadway that carried commodities was also the roadway that could carry an invading army; consequently, Rehoboam included Hebron among the cities he fortified in defense of Jerusalem (2 Chron. 11:5–10). All of these factors combined to make Hebron a unique and highly desirable city offering practical and strategic advantages to those who lived there.

Hebron is mentioned frequently in the Old Testament from the time of Abraham to the time of the divided kingdom. Throughout this time assorted connotations evolved and mixed with one another to shape the rhetorical overtones linked to this city. Hebron is associated with the memorial altar established here by Abram. When Abram and Lot parted company, the Lord assured Abram that all the promises he had received were intact (Gen. 13:14–17). Abram's family would come to own this land and would live in it as a great nation. In response Abram built a memorial altar at Hebron (13:18). Thus this location became not just a stop on the seasonal migration route of Abram's family, but a place to worship, to recall the promises that lifted this family above all others, and to reflect on their vital role in God's rescue plan.

In time Hebron took on an additional role, the host of Abraham's family tomb. As a bedouin, Abraham had pitched his tents and grazed his animals on public land. But when Sarah died, the need for a tomb on family-owned property came to the fore. The lengthy report on the negotiation for this property assures the reader of Genesis that this property was unquestionably family owned, the first field of the Promised Land officially in the proper hands (Gen. 23:2–20). As the bodies of Abraham, Isaac, Rebekah, Jacob, and Leah joined Sarah's body here (25:9; 35:27–29; 49:29–32), this tomb combined with the memorial altar built by Abraham to make Hebron a sacred reserve. In that light we dare not miss its mention and rhetorical role in Numbers 13. The reconnaissance team sent by Moses to explore Canaan visited Hebron (Num. 13:22). Given the link between this location and Israel's divinely directed destiny, this place should have inspired their hopes and animated their desire to be in this land. But when the ten gave their report, it was not the memorial but the size of the people at Hebron that dominated their perspective and their discouraging report (the descendants of Anak, Num. 13:22; cf. 13:28, 33). In striking contrast, King Herod the Great raised a monumental building here centuries later, the Macpelah or Haram el-Khalil, to carry the memories linked to this location forward into the first century.

When Joshua finally led all of Israel into the Promised Land and divided it among the families, certain cities among all the tribes were reserved for the clergy, the so-called Levitical cities. From such cities, the Levites had the opportunity to teach, to encourage healthy worship habits, and to lead by example. Hebron was one of those cities (Josh. 21:11–13). This connotation associated with Hebron may explain why the Lord chose Hebron as David's first

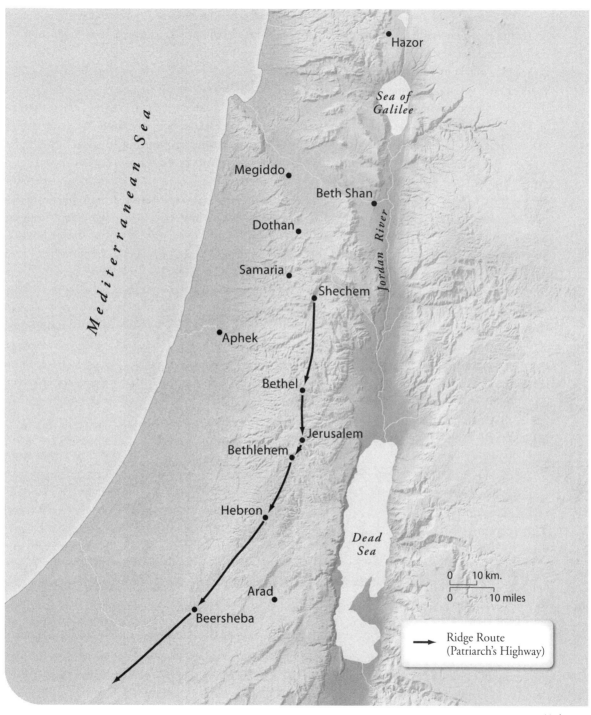

Hebron.

capital. When David assumed the title of king following the death of Saul, the northern portion of Israel sought to maintain its autonomy under the family of Saul. For more than seven years, a civil war raged; and during that time, the Lord directed David to make his capital at Hebron (2 Sam. 2:1–4). As we have seen, Hebron was a highly desirable location for many reasons. But given the Lord's passion to have his new king be one whose heart was in the right place, we can appreciate how a Levitical city would have supported David's spiritual health in this trying time.

Even after the civil war came to an end and David established Jerusalem as the capital of his reunited kingdom, the connection between Hebron and royal legitimacy continued. This connotation drew the attention of David's son Absalom when he sought to win the country away from his father. As Absalom's conspiracy matured, he headed for Hebron ostensibly to worship but in reality to enact a coup d'état: "As soon as you hear the sound of the trumpets, then say, 'Absalom is king in Hebron'" (2 Sam. 15:10). We cannot appreciate the spirit of his rebellion, but we can appreciate how the royal connotations associated with Hebron played a rhetorical role in his coup.

Helmet

The basic function of the helmet has remained the same throughout the ages. Whether a bike helmet or the helmet of a medieval knight, its purpose is to protect the face, neck, and head from injury. During Bible times this protective headgear was donned by soldiers called into battle.

The shape and design of such protective helmets, made of leather, metal, or a combination of the two, varies from one historical period to the next and from one culture to the next. For example, the Assyrian soldiers wore conical metal helmets. Depictions of Philistine warriors show them wearing helmets of uncertain composition that sport an elaborate crest. And Roman soldiers wore metal helmets that included an aft-facing shelf to protect the neck and hinged side pieces that hung down like drooping ears to protect against blows directed at the sides of the head.

Re-enactor displays a Roman helmet.
Jay King

When the biblical authors mention a helmet, it is more likely that they are thinking of the helmet worn by a foreign soldier than the helmet worn by an Israelite soldier. In fact, the two related Hebrew words for helmet are not native to this language but reflect vocabulary borrowed from other cultures. While an Israelite monarch might have a helmet (1 Sam. 17:38), the ordinary foot soldier of Israel went without until late in the monarchy. The first mention of helmets being provided for ordinary soldiers appears late in the monarchy when we hear of Uzziah's "well-trained army," which is provided with body armor and helmets (2 Chron. 26:14). Thus, from the Israelite perspective, the people most likely to be putting on a helmet are foreign soldiers (1 Sam. 17:5; Jer. 46:4; Ezek. 23:24; 38:5).

A bronze helmet is mentioned twice in the story of David and Goliath, playing a different but related rhetorical role in each of the two verses. Among the impressive array of armor worn by the Philistine champion, we find mention of a bronze helmet (1 Sam. 17:5). Assuming this was the traditional helmet depicted in ancient reliefs, it would have added even more height to this giant of a man, making his appearance all the more menacing. The only other person mentioned in this story who owns a helmet is Saul, so it is he whom we would expect to engage with Goliath. When fear and lack of faith caused Saul to demur, he tried to pass his helmet off to David (1 Sam. 17:38). Ironically, not even Saul's helmet would find its way into David's fight with Goliath; David would go into battle armed with his faith and a shepherd's sling. He would look neither like the helmet-wearing Goliath nor the trembling Saul; instead, he would look like the confident man who had the kind of heart Israel's leader needed. Thus, while Goliath and Saul are set apart by owning a helmet, David is set apart by his lack of a helmet.

In two poetic passages (Pss. 60:7; 108:8), Ephraim is called God's helmet. Here the psalmist mentions two tribal territories, likening Judah to God's scepter and Ephraim to his helmet. This rather peculiar statement may best be decoded geographically. The capital of David and Solomon's united kingdom was Jerusalem of Judah. Therefore it is appropriate that Judah should be associated with the symbol of the legitimate ruler, the scepter. For the most part, Judah enjoyed a high degree of security because the mountains of Judah resisted enemy invasion from the east, west, and south. However, the one geographical vulnerability of Judah in general and Jerusalem in particular lay to the north where the topography eases access to this otherwise inaccessible region. Perhaps this is why Ephraim, which lies to the north of Judah, superintending the northern access routes via the Benjamin plateau, is described as a protecting helmet.

In one instance, it is not mortals but God himself who puts on a helmet like a warrior getting ready for battle. The early portion of Isaiah 59 bemoans the sorry state of the world. Hands stained by blood, tongues that mutter wicked things, lies, and a lack of justice dominate the landscape. In a world thickly clouded by sin and its consequences, hope for rescue could not rise from within. Consequently, the Lord metaphorically dressed as a warrior to reclaim his rightful possession: "He put on righteousness as his breastplate, and the helmet of salvation on his head" (v. 17).

This image is clearly informing the two final appearances of "helmet" in the New Testament. As the letter to the Ephesians comes to its close, Paul realizes that the presence of the gospel among these Christians will provoke a counterattack waged by the Devil, the rulers, the authorities, and the spiritual forces of evil in the heavenly realms (Eph. 6:12). Consequently, the Christians reading this letter need to prepare for the fight by putting on armor as God did in Isaiah 59:17. This includes the special helmet the Lord had donned, "the helmet of salvation" (Eph. 6:17). Paul summons this image one more time in his first letter to the Thessalonians. The return of Jesus will be like a thief in the night, but his coming is not to surprise Christians. Like their compatriots in Ephesus, the Christians in Thessalonica are to live dressed for battle, "putting on faith and love as a breastplate, and the hope of salvation as a helmet" (1 Thess. 5:8).

Honey

Honey was the sweetener and the sweet treat of choice during Bible times, a term that describes two different but related products. On the one hand, the term *honey* points to the honey derived from wild beehives or the beekeeper's apiary. In several Bible passages, wild honey is clearly implied, because it is harvested from the carcass of a dead animal, the forest floor, or among the rocks (Judg. 14:8; 1 Sam. 14:25; Ps. 81:16). Until recently it was presumed that beekeeping was not part of early Israelite culture, appearing only in Greek and Roman periods. But in 2007 a large apiary was discovered at Tel Rehov, Israel, with upward of one hundred beehives that hosted as many as a million bees. This archaeological find that dates to the time of the united monarchy suggests that the collection of both wild and domestic honey may have been more common during the Old Testament than was formerly thought to be the case. The second product, which also goes by the name honey, is *dibs*. It is produced when grapes, dates, or figs are mashed and boiled down into a paste or thick syrup, which like bee honey might be spread on bread. Unless the context dictates otherwise, either product may be in view when the biblical authors speak of honey.

Both types of honey were highly prized and celebrated as food: "Eat honey, my son, for it

Beehives found at Tel Rehov provided its ancient residents with a supply of honey.
Hebrew University photo by Amihai Mazar

is good; honey from the comb is sweet to your taste" (Prov. 24:13). The high sugar content of honey provided a jolt of energy for those wearied by travel or a fight. Wild honey "brightened the eyes" of Jonathan during a battle with the Philistines, and *dibs* was welcomed by David during his harried flight from Absalom (1 Sam. 14:27; 2 Sam. 17:29). Honey was such a desirable product that it was presented as a gift to win the support and assistance of distinguished persons (Gen. 43:11; 1 Kings 14:3). And it was exported from the Promised Land to places like Tyre (Ezek. 27:17). But honey was not to be used in connection with the grain offering (Lev. 2:11); this prohibition may be related to the inclusion of honey in pagan rituals, rituals that ensnared God's people during Ezekiel's day (Ezek. 16:19).

The most common rhetorical use of honey is in the descriptor of the Promised Land, which essentially became another name for Canaan, the land "flowing with milk and honey" (Ex. 3:8, 17; 13:5; et al.). Of the twenty times the word *honey* appears in the Pentateuch, fifteen are within the confines of this formula. As the Israelites spent much of this time in a trackless wilderness, the description certainly provided an inviting picture of the Promised Land. But it may also be a descriptor that honors the distinct differences between the northern and southern sections of Canaan. Because the north receives more rain, there is considerably more vegetation that provides flowers for the bees to use in making honey. In contrast the south receives considerably less rain, and so we find agriculture giving way to the pastoral life and the goat's milk that was a staple in the Israelite diet. Thus the diverse nature of the Promised Land is captured in this expression by naming two important commodities associated with its northern and southern subregions.

Because honey was a food that brought wonderful pleasure to the palate, it became a metaphor for those things that were highly pleasing. For example, God's Word is likened to honey. The ordinances of God are "sweeter than honey, than honey from the comb" (Ps. 19:10). "How sweet are your words to my taste, sweeter than honey to my mouth!" (119:103). In a lesser but similar way, the kind words of the wise are like honey: "Pleasant words are a honeycomb, sweet to the soul and healing to the bones" (Prov. 16:24). And in the love poetry of the Song of Songs, the enchanted groom awaits every word that comes from the mouth of his bride: "Your lips drop sweetness as the honeycomb, my bride; milk and honey are under your tongue" (Song 4:11).

Honey is a wonderful treat; but as with all sweets, too much of a good thing can lead to a bad experience: "If you find honey, eat just enough—too much of it, and you will vomit" (Prov. 25:16). This reality is transferred into a lesson on humility later in the same chapter: "It is not good to eat too much honey, nor is it honorable to seek one's own honor" (25:27).

The eating of wild honey taken directly from the hives scattered about the countryside became a symbol for a more rustic kind of living. When King Ahaz refused to ask Isaiah for a sign that confirmed Isaiah's prophecy concerning Jerusalem's deliverance from the Syro-Ephraimite alliance, he was given one anyway. The prophecy spoke of the birth of Immanuel, a child soon to be born into the royal court of Ahaz as well as a title for the Messiah himself (Isa. 7:14). The Immanuel of Isaiah's day would eat curds and honey because the Assyrians would devastate the land and disrupt the agriculture cycle, forcing even the royal family into a simpler way of living (7:15, 20–25). That same lifestyle is used to characterize John the Baptist whose diet consisted of locusts and wild honey (Matt. 3:4; Mark 1:6). This simple diet set him apart from the priestly aristocracy. Although John was a priest, his diet helped to distance him and his message from the abuses promulgated by those who lived in the upper city of Jerusalem and enjoyed a more lavish diet.

Horeb. *See* Mount Sinai.

Horn. *See* Ram's Horn.

House

No one picture fits all the possibilities of the biblical use of the word *house*. A house could be a goat-hair tent perched on a hill (Gen. 27:15) or a building in downtown Damascus on Straight Street (Acts 9:11). It could be the lavish dwelling

A goat-hair tent provided shelter for many family members.
Library of Congress, LC-DIG-ppmsca-02749

of a tax collector (Luke 19:5) or the hovel of an impoverished widow (2 Kings 4:2). It could be a royal palace (2 Sam. 11:27; Esth. 4:13) or the home of a prostitute (Josh. 2:1). Houses from the biblical world varied markedly from one another depending on the period of history in which they were built, the socioeconomic status of the owner, and the region that provided the raw materials from which the house was built. At base the house was a place of shelter for the extended family, a place to keep one's animals and store one's food. It was where the family might gather for the evening meal and then retire to sleep the night away.

By extension, the term *house* is also used to describe a localized place on earth where God might be worshiped. For Jacob, this became a nondescript, overnight stopping place just outside of Luz where his sleep was disturbed by a remarkable dream. Upon awaking in this rural setting, he declared, "How awesome is this place! This is none other than the house of God" (Gen. 28:17). Jacob subsequently renamed the place Bethel, literally "house of God" in Hebrew. Although it is true that even the highest heavens are unable to contain him (1 Kings 8:27), God was willing to allow a number of earthbound structures to be called the house of God or the house of the Lord. This was true of the tent sanctuary erected at Shiloh, the temple built by Solomon in Jerusalem, and its successor building raised during the days of Ezra (1 Sam. 1:7; 1 Kings 8:43; Ezra 1:5; Jer. 7:2; Hag. 1:2–4, 8). Although the later temple complex in Jerusalem was enhanced by Herod the Great, Jesus still referred to it as his "Father's house" (Luke 2:49; John 2:16). The temple in Jerusalem was visited again and again by God's people who celebrated along the way and encouraged one another with these words: "Let us go to the house of the Lord" (Ps. 122:1).

A house could also be a group of people who were related to one another by blood. This "house" could be the extended family members who worked cooperatively and lived together in a household compound (Mark 3:25). A house could also be an entire tribe of ancient Israel, such as the "house of Levi" or the "house of Judah" (Ex. 2:1; 2 Sam. 2:4). Additionally, the term was used to name those who were descended from Jacob, the so-called house of Jacob or house of Israel (Ex. 19:3; Ruth 4:11; Ps. 115:9).

In a narrower sense, *house* in the Old Testament was another term for dynasty. The war between "the house of Saul and the house of David" helped settle who would rule all of Israel following the death of Saul (2 Sam. 3:1). When the united kingdom divided, the northern kingdom enjoyed continuity in its leadership under the dynasty of David, but the southern kingdom limped along under a variety of dynasties, including the "house of Jeroboam," the "house of Ahab," and the "house of Jehu" (1 Kings 13:34; 2 Kings 8:27; Hos. 1:4). This understanding of the word *house*, as well as the notion of house as God's temple, are needed to understand the exchange between David and the Lord in 2 Samuel 7:5–16. David longs to build a house for the Lord (a temple), but instead the Lord promises David that he will receive a "house." His dynasty will continue and eventually produce a messianic king who will rule an eternal kingdom.

The term *house* was also used as a metaphor for life, the human body, and heaven itself. In Proverbs a house is closely linked to a way of living. Its readers are urged to flee the house of the adulteress (Prov. 2:18; 7:27) and instead linger at the house built by wisdom (9:1). To follow this sage advice is to build a sturdy house, a lifestyle linked to successful living: "By wisdom a house is built, and through understanding it is established" (24:3). When Jesus encourages his listeners to check the foundation on which they are building their lives, he tells the parable of the wise and foolish builders. In this parable the two different homes are being built on two very different foundations; one will collapse in the face of life's challenges, while the other will endure (Matt. 7:24–27; Luke 6:47–49).

House is also used as a metaphor for the body. The aging process has its impact on the body, poetically described as the time "when the keepers of the house tremble" (Eccl. 12:3). Another use of the metaphor for the mortal body occurs when Jesus describes what happens when an evil spirit has come out of a person: "It says, 'I will return to the house I left.' When it arrives, it finds the house unoccupied, swept clean and put in order" (Matt. 12:44).

As Jesus comforted the disciples in the hours before his death, he evoked the image of the family house to which a room was added each time a son was married to accommodate the bride and her husband. Jesus was about to depart, but his plan was to travel ahead and do some building: "In my Father's house are many rooms; if it were not so, I would have told you. I am going there to prepare a place for you" (John 14:2). That means we can join the psalmist in saying, "I will dwell in the house of the Lord forever" (Ps. 23:6).

Hyssop

The hyssop plant mentioned a dozen times in the Bible is most likely Syrian hyssop (*Origanum syriacum*). Syrian hyssop can easily get lost among all the other plants that grow on the brush-covered Judean hillsides. Compared to other more colorful plants, its appearance is less than inspiring. Hyssop is characterized by a set of bleak, woody stems that extend two feet above the base of the plant. Only in the summer months is there a flourish of small white flowers that break the monotony of its gray stems and dull green leaves. The habitat of Syrian hyssop is portrayed in the Jewish maxim "If a flame catches the cedars, what will the hyssop do that is in the rock?" (*Moed Katan* 25b). Home for hyssop is any of the dry, rocky outcroppings found throughout the Promised Land.

Hyssop was used in a variety of ways in Bible times. When food needed cooking or the body needed warming, the thin woody branches of the hyssop plant made very good kindling. Ground hyssop was also added to food. Today one can still buy a spice in the markets of Jerusalem called *za'atar*; this is a mixture of powdered hyssop leaves, sesame seeds, ground sumac fruit, salt, and pepper. But in the Bible, hyssop is mentioned most often as a tool with which to sprinkle liquids during various rituals. The stiff branches gave this tool rigidity, and the leaves provided a collecting surface for the liquid, which could be shaken in whatever direction one desired.

The first mention of using hyssop for sprinkling is in the description of the first Passover. Through a series of plagues, the Lord punished Egypt for their refusal to let the Israelites leave their land. The last and final plague was the most devastating; every firstborn son in Egypt would die. The Israelites were protected from this plague by the blood of the Passover lamb, which was applied to the door frames of their homes by using "a bunch of hyssop" (Ex. 12:22).

Passover was only the first of many instances in which the hyssop plant was associated with cleansing. When the Israelites left Egypt and received the Law at Mount Sinai, Moses sprinkled the cleansing blood of a young bull on the people (Ex. 24:8). The writer to the Hebrews observes that this was done by using the branches of the hyssop (Heb. 9:19). The Law that the people heard that day included other rituals that connected hyssop to cleansing.

Those who had recovered from an infectious skin disease were to undergo inspection by the priest and ceremonial cleansing before they returned to the camp. Blood from a sacrificed bird mixed with fresh water was to be sprinkled on this person as part of the cleansing rites that used the hyssop plant (Lev. 14:4–6). A similar rite was used to cleanse a house after it was over its mildew problems (14:49–52). Finally, the "water of cleansing" was used in a ceremony to restore an individual who had come into contact with a corpse. This special water was made outside the camp when a red heifer was burned up and mixed with the ashes of cedar wood, hyssop, and scarlet wool (Num. 19:6). Through rites like these, hyssop became associated with ritual cleansing.

A hyssop plant with its white blossoms.
Copyright 1995-2011 Phoenix Data Systems

Both the size of the plant and its connection to ritual purity play a rhetorical role in three passages of Scripture. The extraordinary wisdom given to Solomon allowed him to speak with authority on most topics, including the plant communities of the biblical world: "He described plant life, from the cedar of Lebanon to the hyssop that grows out of walls" (1 Kings 4:33). In this botanical merism, the inspired author names the largest tree of the region and one of the smaller plants, the hyssop. By naming the cedar and hyssop in this formula, the biblical author was saying that Solomon's knowledge extended to every plant of every size.

As hyssop was used in various ceremonies linked to cleansing, this plant became closely linked to the idea of purity. As David felt the sting of guilt associated with the sin of adultery, he poured out his confession before the Lord in Psalm 51. The familiar words take on new meaning when we see the relationship between hyssop and ritual cleansing: "Cleanse me with hyssop, and I will be clean; wash me, and I will be whiter than snow" (Ps. 51:7).

In a related way, the connection between hyssop and Passover may best explain why John alone mentions the use of the hyssop plant at Golgotha. From the start this gospel writer had shown an interest in linking Jesus with the sacrifice of the Passover lamb. In the very first chapter, this gospel quotes John the Baptist who calls Jesus the Lamb of God who takes away the sin of the world (John 1:29). And as John speaks of Jesus' death, he links the time of the crucifixion with the time the Passover lambs were sacrificed (19:14). Given this rhetorical inclination of the gospel, it is not surprising to find that the hyssop plant that painted blood on the doors in Egypt makes an appearance at Golgotha: "A jar of wine vinegar was there, so they soaked a sponge in it, put the sponge on a stalk of the hyssop plant, and lifted it to Jesus' lips" (19:29).

I

Ibex (Wild Goat)

Today's visitors to Israel are assured of seeing an ibex in one of two locations. Ibex can be seen in the hunting scenes depicted in ancient rock carvings, and they are present in many of the national parks thanks to a conservation program that aggressively worked to restore this threatened species. The program was so successful that today the largest herd of ibex in the world resides in Israel under the watchful eyes of the National Parks Authority who have made the ibex the symbol of the national park system.

The ibex resembles the domestic goat in size and color. Mature animals weigh between 55 and 150 pounds; on average they are thirty inches tall at the shoulder with a body that extends for four feet. The coat of the ibex changes from the light gray displayed in summer to a darker brown during the winter season, all the while retaining a white underbelly. What really distinguish the ibex from their domestic counterparts are the horns they sport. Males have massive horns that grow throughout their lifetimes. They sweep in a semicircular curve over their backs, achieving a total length of fifty inches. The horns of the female are less impressive at twelve inches.

The habitat of the ibex takes those who seek them into some of the most rugged and uninhabited landscapes of the Promised Land. Herds of ten or so animals live together in the desert where their light-colored coats reflect the afternoon sun, allowing them to remain active throughout the day. Their habitat of choice is the sheer slopes of the mountains. It is truly a marvel to watch these natural athletes as they lightly dance across unstable scree fields and make death-defying leaps from one small ledge to the next. The Hebrew name for this animal grows from the verb that means to climb, a fitting name for one of nature's most efficient mountaineers.

Unlike other desert dwellers, the ibex has to find water and food every day. This means they must leave the security of their rock ledges to find the small pools of water that collect here and there in their desert home. These wild goats are true ruminants that browse among the small patches of grass they can find and nibble at the leaves of acacia trees sprinkled throughout the wilderness. When necessary, these agile climbers will actually climb up into trees to snatch leaves unclaimed by others.

Predators that wish to feast on the ibex face a variety of challenges. When these wild goats are not in search of water or food, they retreat to the near-vertical slopes where the color of their coats allows them to all but disappear against the mountainside. If an ibex is spotted by a predator, the predator can be assured that the keen eyesight of the ibex has already given its presence away long before it could become a threat.

In the Bible the ibex is almost as hard to spot as it is in the wild. This is due to the variety of names Bible translators have given this animal: ibex, wild goat, mountain goat, and graceful deer. The first mention of the ibex is in the dietary laws given in the Torah. There the ibex is listed among the clean animals available for the Israelites' to eat (Deut. 14:5). This may explain why David held up in a place called the Crags of the Wild Goats (1 Sam. 24:2). At this time in David's life, he had already been identified as the king who would replace Saul. The current king of Israel was so threatened by this news that he aggressively sought to end David's life. Consequently, David fled to the wilderness to hide from Saul. The Crags of the Wild Goats (the region around modern En Gedi) provided David with two things he needed to survive in this hiding place—springs of water and a large herd of ibex that he could hunt for food.

It also seems likely that an ibex appears on the pages of our Bible during the harrowing test Abraham faced in Genesis 22. Here Abraham showed his absolute trust in the Lord by demonstrating his willingness to sacrifice his son Isaac at God's direction. Before Abraham could plunge the knife into Isaac, God ended the test. At that moment Abraham looked up and saw a ram caught by its horns in a bush, which he sacrificed in place of Isaac (Gen. 22:13). Given the immense size of a male ibex's horns and its propensity to eat leaves from bushes, the animal described in this story may well be an ibex.

The biblical authors mention the ibex rhetorically in three additional passages. Psalm 104 is a hymn of praise that celebrates the wonder of the created world. Among the sights that inspire awe and praise is the sight of the ibex touring its natural habitat: "The high mountains belong to the wild goats" (Ps. 104:18). Mature female ibex give birth to one or two kids each year. To give her young the best chance at survival, she gives birth in the isolated crevices of her high mountain home well out of anyone's sight but the Lord's. As God quieted Job's search for the reason for his suffering, he asked Job a series of revealing questions, including this one: "Do you know when the mountain goats give birth?" (Job 39:1). Finally, the poetry of Proverbs also mentions the female ibex. Her warm, soft eyes and long, graceful legs are a thing of beauty. Thus this beautiful animal becomes a metaphor for the wife of one's youth (Prov. 5:19; NIV translates with "graceful deer").

Incense

In the ancient Near Eastern world, incense was widely used among many of the cultures that had contact with the Israelites. Although it was not a product unique to God's people, it was a product that was to find unique applications among them. Incense is a product derived from a variety of plants, each of which has highly aromatic qualities. Dried portions of these plants are

Sweeping horns mark the male ibex.
© Odelia Cohen/www.BigStockPhoto.com

ground and then mixed together to produce the desired end product. Depending on the nature of the mixture, incense could be added to wine as a spice, applied to the skin or ingested as a medicine, used to prepare the body of a loved one for burial, or employed as a perfume that covered more pungent body odor. The earliest mention in the Bible suggests that ordinary Israelites owned incense for their personal use, because they were invited to include such incense in the offering they brought in support of the tabernacle's construction (Ex. 25:6; 35:8, 28).

The incense used in the worship life of God's people was to be distinct from the incense they used in their everyday lives. The recipe for this special mixture is found in Exodus 30:34–36. It was to be mixed by a designated "perfumer" who was not to deviate in any way from the prescribed recipe (Ex. 37:29). And what is more, no one was ever to use this particular mixture in everyday applications; it was "holy to the LORD," reserved for use in his sanctuary (30:37–38). This incense appears in a variety of worship settings. Every morning and evening the priest was to replenish the incense that constantly burned on the incense altar in the tabernacle or temple (30:6–8). In the same room, incense

A specially formulated incense was burned on the altar of incense in the Israelite Tabernacle.

Todd Bolen/www.BiblePlaces.com

was to be spread along each row of the bread of the Presence, which sat on a special table in the Holy Place (Lev. 24:7). And each time a grain offering was presented, this offering was to include some of this special incense mixture (2:1–2, 15–16; 6:15). Thus the air surrounding the sanctuary of the Lord would constantly be filled with sweet-smelling smoke. This smoke played a practical role in the life of those who came to worship there: it masked the pungent odors associated with the slaughter of many animals, and it also drove away insects that otherwise would have been a constant source of irritation.

Rhetorically the burning of incense before the Lord became a symbol associated with Aaron and his family, those priests who served as the chief intermediaries between Israel and their Lord. This privilege marked the uniqueness of this family (Num. 4:16; 1 Sam. 2:28; 1 Chron. 6:49). When the sons of Aaron abused this privilege (Lev. 10:1) or when certain Levites agitated for the right to make this offering themselves (Num. 16:1–30), people died as the Lord reaffirmed the special connection between the high priest and this incense.

The smoke rising from the incense censor is also a symbol of protection. On the Day of

Atonement when the high priest of Israel entered the innermost part of the sanctuary, this sacred smoke offered a special kind of concealment so that the priest would not die before sprinkling blood on the atonement cover (Lev. 16:11–14). The smoke from Aaron's censor served a similar role following the rebellion of Korah, Dathan, and Abiram. When the Israelite community grumbled against Moses and Aaron following the death of those associated with the Levite rebellion, the Lord caused a plague to break out among the people. At that moment Aaron seized a censor filled with burning incense and stood between the living and the dead to stop the spread of the plague (Num. 16:46–48). The smoke became a wall of protection.

Additionally, the offering of incense became a symbol that marked obedience to the Lord or rebellion against him. If incense was being offered at the sanctuary by the right people on a regular basis, this was a sign that God's leaders and God's people were living in harmony with him (1 Kings 9:25; 2 Chron. 13:11). But the inappropriate offering of incense was a symbol of rebellion. Examples include the offering of incense at a high place (1 Kings 3:3; 22:43), the offering of incense by someone other than the priest (2 Chron. 26:16–19), or the more frequent offering of incense to a pagan deity (Isa. 27:9; 65:3; Jer. 44:15–19; Ezek. 8:10–11; Hos. 2:13; 11:2).

The biblical authors use incense as a metaphor for the counsel of a wise friend and for the prayer of believers. The wonderful fragrance of incense had the power to lift one's spirits; the inspired poet likens that lift to the one provided by the words of a true friend: "Perfume and incense bring joy to the heart, and the pleasantness of one's friend springs from his earnest counsel" (Prov. 27:9). In other settings the rising incense smoke is likened to the rising prayers of the believers. With uplifted eyes, the psalmist pleads, "May my prayer be set before you like incense" (Ps. 141:2). For the beleaguered saints whose lives were meeting trouble at every turn, the book of Revelation offers assurance linking incense smoke to prayer (Rev. 5:8; 8:3–4). In each image, the censor producing the smoke is in the presence of God himself in heaven. This assures the troubled saints that their prayers have made it into the presence of God even when their circumstances may suggest otherwise.

Inn

While traveling on business or a family vacation, the hotel or motel that provides our overnight lodging is a welcome sight. As people traveled from one place to the other during Bible times, they too needed a temporary home away from home, a need that was met in a variety of ways.

Although they lacked many of the amenities we might associate with a modern hotel, such as a whirlpool, workout room, shower, and beds, inns operated during the latter portion of the Old Testament era and into the New Testament. We lack detailed descriptions of these commercial establishments, but Jeremiah appears to have such a place in mind when he longs to travel to a place far removed from the Lord's rebellious people: "Oh, that I had in the desert a lodging place for travelers, so that I might leave my people and go away from them" (Jer. 9:2). And Luke most certainly is speaking about a commercial establishment when he mentions the inn in the story of the good Samaritan (Luke 10:34).

Despite the presence of inns in both the Old and New Testament world, we rarely hear of people spending the night in commercial inns. Instead, travelers were likely to make camp for the evening in the open country. This is what Joseph's brothers were doing when they discovered that the money used to buy grain had mysteriously returned to their sacks (Gen. 42:27; 43:21), what Moses and his family did when they stopped for the night (Ex. 4:24), and what the Israelites did after crossing the Jordan River (Josh. 4:3, 8). Smaller groups could expect local residents to extend hospitality. Such travelers would linger near a tent compound (Gen. 18:2) or wait at the city gate (Judg. 19:15) for someone to offer them a place to stay for the night. Job defended his righteousness by saying, "No stranger had to spend the night in the street, for my door was always open to the traveler" (Job 31:32). Still today we are encouraged to show hospitality: "Do not forget to entertain strangers, for by so doing some people have entertained angels without knowing it" (Heb. 13:2).

Because inns are mentioned infrequently in the Bible, their presence in a text invites closer scrutiny. The commercial inn that appears in the parable of the good Samaritan plays a quiet but important rhetorical role in this narrative. An expert in the law sought to test Jesus' orthodoxy by asking him how one came to inherit eternal life. This eventually led to the question regarding the identity of the "neighbor" to whom kindness was owed (Luke 10:29). Jesus answered that question by telling the story of a Jewish man who is robbed and beaten on the Jerusalem-Jericho road. The most unlikely aid-giver of those passing by is the Samaritan. Yet he is the one who tends the Jewish man's injuries, places him on his

Sketch of an inn — a commercial installation designed to accommodate the needs of caravans and other long-distance travelers.

own donkey, and takes him to a commercial inn. The good Samaritan makes Jesus' point about a neighbor being anyone in need long before he takes the injured Jewish man to the inn and pays for his stay. But this last detail, which includes payment not only for one night but for as many nights as necessary for the man to recover, brings this story to its climax (Luke 10:34–35).

Perhaps the most famous mention of an inn is the one associated with the birth of Jesus in Bethlehem. English translations often represent that moment in this way: "She wrapped him in cloths and placed him in a manger, because there was no room for them in the inn" (Luke 2:7). But is this well-known translation the best translation? I think not. At the practical level, a commercial inn located in the village of Bethlehem does not make much economic sense. Bethlehem was not located along a major roadway, and therefore it isn't likely that an inn in that village would have enough guests to make a profit. And what is more, commercial inns were typically located a full day's travel away from major cities. At a mere five miles outside of Jerusalem, Bethlehem would hardly meet this criterion. The language evidence also appears to point us in a different direction. When we look at the vocabulary used in the gospel of Luke, we find that this inspired author uses the undisputed Greek word for traveler's inn (*pandochion*) in the story of the good Samaritan (Luke 10:34). But the word used in Luke 2:7 (*kataluma*) is also used by Luke to describe the guest room where Jesus would celebrate his final Passover (22:11). While it is possible that *kataluma* could be understood as "inn," Luke appears to be using it as the word for a "guest room" located in a private home.

Rhetorically this introduces a new and disturbing element into the Christmas story. Joseph and Mary were traveling to Bethlehem because Joseph had to register in "his own town" (Luke 2:3). Assuming that Joseph had family here and given what we know of the ancient hospitality code, we would presume that Joseph would have sought lodging for himself and Mary in the home of a relative. But upon Joseph and Mary's arrival, the family members would not make this room available, perhaps because of the questions that lingered around Mary's pregnancy. Thus Luke's statement about there being no room in the guest room suggests yet another indignity that challenged Joseph and Mary that night.

J

Jericho (Old Testament)

Jericho is a splash of green in an otherwise barren landscape. This oasis in the Judean wilderness is located on the west side of the Jordan River approximately ten miles northwest of the spot where the Jordan enters the Dead Sea. The culture and fame of this city were shaped by its supply of freshwater, its proximity to minerals in the Dead Sea basin, and particularly by its ability to superintend east-west traffic. A very powerful spring that today still gushes at a rate of twelve hundred gallons per minute gave life to Jericho.

This amount of water would change life anywhere, but it particularly changed the character of this wilderness-bound city. The ample supply of water not only hydrated its residents, but it also made the production of food possible. Water combined with the tropical climate of Jericho to turn the desert into a food basket full of produce, including fruit, grain, and dates. In fact, conditions were so desirable for growing date palms that the city also went by the name City of Palms (Deut. 34:3; Judg. 1:16; 3:13; 2 Chron. 28:15).

Jericho's proximity to the Dead Sea opened another avenue of revenue for those living there. The Dead Sea basin naturally yielded both salt and bitumen, products the residents of Jericho were eager to harvest and sell to others. But perhaps the most important advantage owned by Old Testament Jericho was its ability to superintend traffic, making it a key eastern gateway into Canaan. Those traveling westward from the

mountains of Moab found the easiest descent path into the Jordan Valley to be a ridge that sloped into the valley opposite Jericho. At the bottom of the valley, travelers could cross the Jordan at one of the best natural fords in the region. And once on the west side of the river, travelers could continue their journey into the interior of Canaan via a number of roadways that radiated from Jericho. Thus the natural pathways leading to and away from Jericho made it a gateway for superintending traffic.

This last quality of Jericho is the one that brought it into direct confrontation with God's people and his plan for them. At about ten acres, the Old Testament city of Jericho was not a particularly large fort, but if Israel's army was to keep the travel doorway open to the land east of the Jordan where many Israelite families were setting up their homes (Num. 32), this particular fortification could not be left in hostile hands. Consequently, the Lord promised Joshua that this city would be fully delivered into his hands (Josh. 6:2), a promise fulfilled when the walls of the city collapsed.

The biblical authors mention Jericho in several rhetorical ways. Prior to the fall of Jericho, this city is mentioned frequently in Numbers and Joshua as a way of orienting the reader to the location of the Israelite camp; for example, "The Israelites traveled to the plains of Moab and camped along the Jordan across from Jericho" (Num. 22:1; cf. 26:63; 31:12; Josh. 3:16; 4:19; 5:10, 13). Jericho was around more than five thousand years before Abraham was born, making it a landmark of supreme importance. Because everyone knew where this city was on their mental map of the land, these biblical authors used it to orient their readers. By their doing so, the constant refrain increases the tension of the plot, reminding readers that a fortress

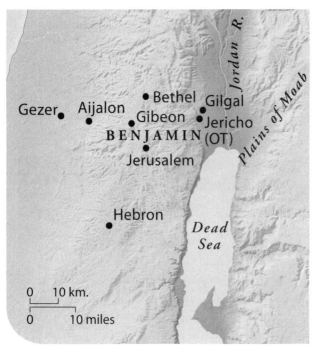

Jericho.

blocks the path to the Promised Land, a problem that begs for resolution that will not come until Joshua 6.

After the walls of this city had fallen, Jericho became synonymous with this divinely sponsored miracle. This is also something the biblical authors exploit. On the one hand, it is used to explain why the Amorite and Canaanite population finally got off the sidelines and into the game. After the Lord had dried up the Jordan River, allowing the Israelites to cross into Canaan on dry ground, the Amorite and Canaanite population west of the Jordan had lost all courage to fight and mustered no organized resistance to Israel's invasion (Josh. 5:1). That changed with the defeat of Jericho; it is one of the events that catalyzed the king of Jerusalem to organize a military response involving multiple city-states (10:1). On the other hand, for Joshua and the Israelites, the miraculous defeat of Jericho became a symbol of all the Lord could do for them (8:2; 10:28–30). If doubt threatened to rob the Israelites of confidence, they could say to one another, "Remember Jericho!" This call went out not only for Old Testament believers, but goes out for New Testament believers as well (Heb. 11:30).

And faith is just what God asked of Israel with regard to the notion of refortifying this critical site. Once Jericho had been defeated, common sense would dictate that the new owners would refortify and occupy this key location so that they could control who could or could not travel east and west along this strategic roadway. But in a further call to faith, God asked Israel to leave Jericho unfortified. Perhaps "asked" is too soft a term, for Joshua said, "Cursed before the Lord is the man who undertakes to rebuild this city, Jericho: 'At the cost of his firstborn son will he lay its foundations; at the cost of his youngest

will he set up its gates' " (Josh. 6:26). It seems that Israel honored this command of the Lord, trusting that he would be the guardian of this eastern portal — that is, until the time of wicked King Ahab. The godlessness of this leader is characterized in many ways. One of the most unique is that he allowed Hiel of Bethel to refortify Jericho — rebuilding that cost Hiel the life of his sons (1 Kings 16:34).

Jerusalem

For the biblical authors, there is no more important city in the Promised Land than Jerusalem. It is mentioned by name nearly eight hundred times and alluded to by other appellations in hundreds of other passages. This critical city is located approximately sixteen miles west of the north shore of the Dead Sea. It lies in the mountains of Judah on this region's border with the Judean wilderness.

For all of its deserved fame, Jerusalem is not a particularly desirable living space. Growing food is difficult. Although the city proper at 2,500 feet above sea level receives sufficient rain to grow grain, the steep slopes and narrow valleys that make up and surround Jerusalem provide very few tillable acres for growing grain unless one takes on the monumental task of making usable farmland by building terraces. Water is also a problem. Two springs offered water to the residents of the Old Testament city; but combined these two springs would barely support a city of modest size. When the city grew beyond those limits, significant public works projects were required to create tunnels, reservoirs, and even aqueducts that transported water to the city from many miles away. Furthermore, this city with relatively poor water and food potential is also isolated from international trade. Jerusalem is located miles from the nearest seaport and international trade route.

But despite these negatives, Jerusalem enjoyed one important advantage in Bible times: it boasted a high degree of security. The city itself was nestled deep in the Judean highlands, requiring attackers from the coast to negotiate a narrow and difficult passage before arriving at the city. And if foreign armies chose to make that risky approach, they were confronted by a city built on high ridges and surrounded by narrow, deeply cut valleys on three sides. With only the more vulnerable northern approach to defend, Jerusalem was a very secure city.

The fame of Jerusalem grew through major moments in the history of Israel. Prior to the time of King David, there was no Jerusalem but a city called Jebus occupied by the Jebusites. The city was assigned to the tribe of Benjamin (Josh. 18:28) but was not secured as a possession of God's chosen people until the time of David who defeated this city and made it the capital of his recently reunited kingdom (Judg. 1:21; 19:10; 2 Sam. 5:6–10). David was responsive to his calling as the leader of God's people who were custodians of the divine promises that meant rescue for the world. Consequently, he set about making Jerusalem not just his political capital, but the chief religious center of Israel as well. He did this by bringing the ark of the covenant to Jerusalem (2 Sam. 6) and by expressing his desire to build a permanent temple here for the Lord (7:1–7). But this privilege was reserved for Solomon, David's son. He is the one who built the temple at Jerusalem that would be visited again and again on the high religious festivals by the families responsible for tending the precious promises of God (Deut. 16:16–17; 1 Kings 6). In the end, it was not mere political gamesmanship that brought about this uniting of God's

promises and this city; it was the plan of God who had chosen this city and put his name on it (1 Kings 11:36; 14:21). For that reason the psalmist encourages all to "pray for the peace of Jerusalem" (Ps. 122:6) so that this city might fulfill its divine assignment.

But when Israel displayed contempt rather than fidelity to the plan of God, the Lord allowed Jerusalem to feel the pain of siege and destruction as the Babylonians burned, smashed, and pillaged their way through this holy city (2 Kings 25). After God's people had spent seventy years in exile in Babylon, God invited a remnant to return and rebuild a less imposing place, but one that more piously participated in awaiting the Messiah's arrival. The city that Ezra and Nehemiah rebuilt got a further architectural upgrade under the supervision of Herod the Great. Jesus taught in the streets and throughout the temple complex of this renovated city that would be the setting for history's most remarkable events. Jesus said that "he must go to Jerusalem" (Matt. 16:21) to suffer and die and so that "everything that is written by the prophets about the Son of Man will be fulfilled" (Luke 18:31).

Rhetorically, the biblical authors recognize that Jerusalem, like other capital cities, was a potent symbol of the state. That is why massive public buildings were erected in this city, why foreign dignitaries came to Jerusalem, and why foreign armies attacked it. Jeroboam recognized the importance of this symbol and therefore attempted to separate the citizens of his newly minted northern kingdom from Jerusalem by establishing an alternative capital city and rival sanctuaries (1 Kings 12:12–30).

In many passages, Jerusalem is really not the physical buildings and walls of the city itself but the people who live there. For example, Scriptures that speak of the angel sent to "destroy

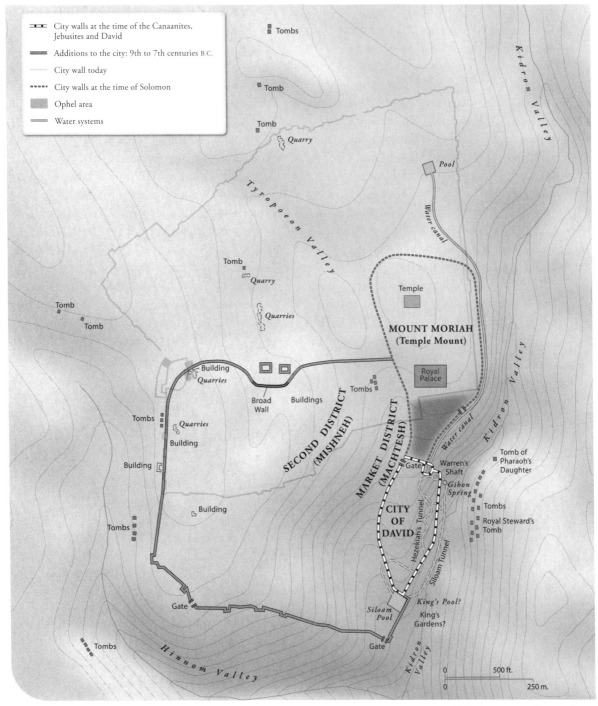

Legend:
- City walls at the time of the Canaanites, Jebusites and David
- Additions to the city: 9th to 7th centuries B.C.
- City wall today
- City walls at the time of Solomon
- Ophel area
- Water systems

Tombs

Tomb

Tomb

Quarry

Kidron Valley

Pool

Water canal

Tyropoeon Valley

Tomb

Quarry

Quarries

Temple

**MOUNT MORIAH
(Temple Mount)**

Tomb

Tomb

Building

Quarries

Broad
Wall

Buildings

Tombs

**Royal
Palace**

Kidron Valley

Tombs

Quarries

Building

**SECOND DISTRICT
(MISHNEH)**

Building

Water canal

Building

MARKET DISTRICT (MACHTESH)

Gate

Warren's
Shaft

*Gihon
Spring*

Tomb of
Pharaoh's
Daughter

**CITY
OF
DAVID**

Hezekiah's Tunnel

Siloam Tunnel

Tombs

Royal Steward's
Tomb

Tombs

Gate

*Siloam
Pool*

King's Pool?

King's
Gardens?

Gate

Hinnom Valley

Kidron Valley

Tombs

0   500 ft.
0   250 m.

Old Testament Jerusalem.

Jerusalem" (1 Chron. 21:15) or the carrying of "all Jerusalem" (2 Kings 24:14) into exile are not speaking of the destruction or deportation of buildings and walls but of the people who lived within them. The same is true for passages that call its citizens to attentiveness: "Awake, awake! Rise up, O Jerusalem" (Isa. 51:17); that call for repentance: "O Jerusalem, wash the evil from your heart and be saved" (Jer. 4:14); or that recall its past performance: "O Jerusalem, Jerusalem, you who kill the prophets and stone those sent to you" (Matt. 23:37). But in many passages the fate and fortune of city and citizenry are linked; both would face harm when those living in the city failed the Lord (2 Kings 21:12–13; Jer. 26:18; Mic. 3:12). But promises of restoration and blessing also extended to both city and citizens (Ps. 132:13–16; Jer. 33:10–11; Zech. 1:16; 8:3).

Finally, the earthly Jerusalem is a symbol for the heavenly counterpart that will be occupied at the end of time (Heb. 12:22; Rev. 3:12; 21:10). Like its earthly counterpart, the heavenly Jerusalem will enjoy the presence of the Lord, yet without the threat of his punishing hand (Isa. 24:23; Jer. 3:17). The sound of weeping and crying will no longer be heard in this city (Isa. 65:18–19). God will be with his people in a city freed from tears, death, crying, and pain (Rev. 21:2–4). Like its earthly counterpart, the heavenly Jerusalem will also see nations advancing toward it; however, their goal is not to attack but to join Israel in the worship of the Lord (Ps. 102:21–22; Isa. 66:20; Jer. 3:17; Zech. 8:22). "Many nations will come and say, 'Come, let us go up to the mountain of the LORD, to the house of the God of Jacob. He will teach us his ways, so that we may walk in his paths.' The law will go out from Zion, the word of the LORD from Jerusalem" (Mic. 4:2).

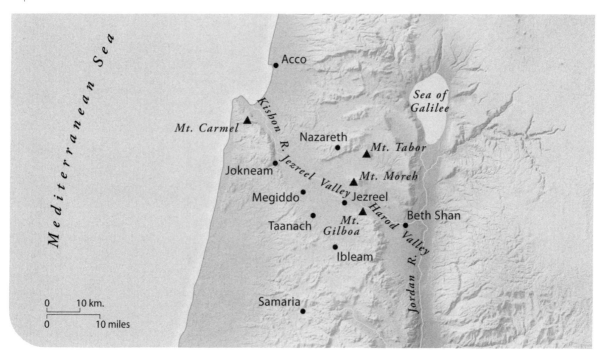

Jezreel Valley.

Jezreel Valley

The Jezreel Valley is a large east-west valley system that cuts through the northern portion of the Promised Land, dividing the mountains of Galilee from the mountains of Samaria. Viewed from above, the Jezreel Valley resembles a large arrowhead and shaft whose tip points at the Mediterranean Sea and whose trailing shaft (also called the Harod Valley) reaches eastward to the Jordan Valley. Each of the arrowhead's three sides is approximately twenty miles in length, while the shaft extending from the eastern side of the arrowhead is eleven miles in length.

In contrast to other valleys of the Promised Land, which are typically narrow and difficult to travel, the Jezreel Valley is distinguished by its breadth, low elevation, and lack of contour. The level nature of the terrain is set in stark contrast to the mountains and ridges that surround it — Mount Carmel, Mount Gilboa, Mount Tabor, and the Nazareth ridge. This valley is also distinguished by the richness of its topsoil and abundant rainfall that is redistributed around the valley by the Kishon River and held in its many springs. In fact, there are times when the valley is sodden by too much water. Following a dramatic downpour, the valley drains slowly, leaving farm fields flooded and forcing travelers to find drier footing on the mountain slopes.

The great value of the Jezreel Valley is associated with agriculture and transportation. In a land where adequate topsoil for growing grain is often measured in inches, here the depth of the topsoil is measured in hundreds of feet. This rich bed of alluvial soil was ideal for growing the grain on which those living in Bible times depended. Nevertheless, this valley's greatest contribution to the culture of those living in the land had to do with transportation rather than agriculture. East-west travel through the Promised Land could be a real problem because of blockage by multiple north-south mountain ridgelines. The Jezreel Valley provided a way through the mountains. An east-west crossing of this valley is defined by elevation changes in hundreds rather than thousands of feet. Consequently, the international highway that linked the cultures of Asia, Africa, and Europe passed through the heart of this valley, giving birth to cities that counted their life spans in millennia, cities like Megiddo, Jezreel, and Beth Shan. And given the critical nature of this valley, it witnessed many battles superintended by great generals like King David, Thutmose III, Alexander the Great, and Napoleon.

When the biblical authors mention the Jezreel Valley, the twin connotations of desirability and risk are always in view. This is aptly exemplified in the language of Manasseh and Ephraim as these tribes received their allotments in the Promised Land. They saw the desirability of expanding their control into the rich Jezreel Valley but expressed concern over the Canaanites who held this land and favored use of the dreaded "iron chariots" (Josh. 17:16).

In the memory of God's people, this valley is linked to both outstanding examples of faith and horrible examples of failure. The great examples of faith come early. During the days of Deborah and Barak, Canaanites and iron chariots filled this valley as the Israelite militia gathered on the safer slopes of Mount Tabor. When God called for his people to abandon the safety of those slopes, charge onto the floor of the Jezreel Valley, and engage the Canaanites on terrain that favored their chariots, the Lord rewarded their obedience with a stunning victory (Judg. 4:1 – 16). Just a few pages later, the Bible's authors present the story of Gideon. This time it was thousands of Midianites, Amalekites, and other eastern peoples who were encamped in the Jezreel Valley (Judg. 6:33). Gideon had gathered a sizable fighting force to repulse them. But at the Lord's direction, Gideon faithfully reduced that number to a mere three hundred soldiers so that this valley again might witness a victory marked with God's unmistakable signature (7:1–8).

This trajectory of faithfulness, which could and should have been sustained, was not. During the final days of King Saul, the Philistines targeted this critical valley (1 Sam. 29:11). Sadly, Saul's faith had all but expired, and so his efforts to hold this critical real estate were all in vain. He took his own life as he watched the last corners of this valley fall to the Philistines. And in the end, he left David with the nearly unthinkable task of reuniting a kingdom divided not only by politics but broken into noncontiguous pieces by the Philistines (1 Sam. 31:7). David rose to the challenge, and the Jezreel Valley became one of the districts under Solomon's control (1 Kings 4:12). But that good news is briefly told and quickly forgotten in light of King Josiah's death. Josiah was the last of Judah's reforming kings, the last hope for reining in the apostasy that would bring about exile. Tragically, his vital role came to an end when he chose to play a role in international politics that God had not intended him to play. Egyptian forces marched north, bent on assisting the flagging Assyrian military in a battle with the Babylonians. Although Egypt's fight was not with Israel, Josiah engaged the Egyptian military in this valley near Megiddo and paid for it with his life (2 Kings 23:29–30).

Thus the Jezreel Valley is linked with striking examples of faith and unfortunate failings. The final mention of this valley, in Hosea, appears to encompass both. Hosea is directed to name his son Jezreel as a warning of the coming massacre that will occur in this valley in combination with an Assyrian invasion, an invasion that would bring an end to Israel's northern kingdom (Hos. 1:4). But the Jezreel Valley shows up again, this time in a phrase that speaks of hope. Hosea foresees a time when there will be restoration, a time when one leader will come up out of the land, "for great will be the day of Jezreel" (v. 11).

Jordan River

The upper Jordan River is that segment of the perennial stream that comes to life at the base of Mount Hermon, fed by the melting snow from its summit and from the copious springs percolating from its base. The clear and fast-moving headwaters of the upper Jordan join forces and enter the Sea of Galilee on its northern shore. The lower Jordan River begins when this water leaves the southern end of the Sea of Galilee, meandering back and forth through the rift valley, cutting a channel that is twice as long as it would be if the river were to travel directly between the Sea of Galilee and the Dead Sea.

A variety of characteristics mark the lower Jordan River as unique. First, it is very low in elevation. Exiting the Sea of Galilee at nearly 700 feet below sea level, it does nothing but descend from there to the Dead Sea at 1,300 feet below sea level. The river's name may well reflect this reality; the Jordan is the "descender." Its low elevation is put to work in a geographical merism in which the psalmist mentions the lowest and highest elevations in the Promised Land to make the point that he will remember the Lord no matter where he might be, "from the land of the Jordan [to] the heights of Hermon" (Ps. 42:6). In addition to being low in elevation, the ancient river was swift, turbulent, and muddy. Nineteenth-century explorers report running twenty-seven significant white-water rapids between the Sea of Galilee and the Dead Sea; such turbulence churned the river into a muddy brown color. For someone who came from a land of clear-running streams, it took some convincing to use this river for a cleansing bath. The leprosy-bound Naaman nearly missed his opportunity for healing when he hesitated to follow the prophet's directions and bathe in this murky water (2 Kings 5:10–12).

The river played a rather limited role in day-to-day living of those in Bible times. One might presume that in a water-starved land, the Jordan would be an important water resource. But for most of its course, the low elevation and increasing chemical content limited its value as a source of freshwater. Furthermore, its contribution to agriculture was also limited due to the poor quality of the soil that lay immediately adjacent to the river channel. Rivers of the ancient world were used as transportation arteries; not so the Jordan, for the river was not navigable due to the white-water rapids. And the plain along the Jordan was filled with dangers for ancient travelers. In the northern portions of the valley, large predators threatened to attack even the wary (Jer. 12:5; 49:19; 50:44), while summer temperatures in the southern part of the valley, easily exceeding 100°F, increased the risk of dehydration.

The biblical authors mention the Jordan River in a number of different settings. Given the prominent nature of this natural feature, it could be used as a landmark to orient readers to the location of events being described (Gen. 50:10–11; Num. 22:1; 26:3, 63; Deut. 1:1, 5). That same prominence caused the Jordan River to be used as a boundary marker. In the Torah, the inspired author identifies the eastern border of the Promised Land as the Jordan River (Num. 34:1–12). Again and again in Deuteronomy, we are led to anticipate

The lower Jordan River was muddy and turbulent in Bible times.

www.HolyLandPhotos.org

the crossing of the Jordan by the Israelites, a crossing that would mark their entrance into the Promised Land (Deut. 6:1; 11:8, 11, 31; 12:10; 31:13; 32:47). Subsequently, the Jordan River was used to mark the boundary division between various tribes (Josh. 13:23, 27; 14:3; 15:5; 16:1, 7; et al.).

Bible readers would do well to pay attention to those moments when they see people crossing the lower Jordan, for two reasons. First, it was a risky venture. In the absence of bridges, those wishing to cross the river had to wade, a task that brought the traveler into contact with muddy banks and swirling currents. Because of the murky nature of the water, one had to carefully search for secure footing even at natural fords. Second, the direction of crossing carried important connotations. The story of Joshua's crossing of the Jordan River from east to west is described in great detail, marked by its miraculous nature and the erection of a memorial to recall the event (Josh. 3–4). This event imbues a crossing from east to west with a very positive connotation, because it marks the entry of Israel into the Promised Land. Others who cross the Jordan in the same direction find their lives entering a time of hope, promise, and new

beginnings (Gen. 32:10; 2 Sam. 19:39; 2 Kings 2:13–14). In contrast we often find that those who cross the Jordan from west to east are entering a period in their lives that is more turbulent and less certain (Gen. 13:10–11; 1 Sam. 13:7; 2 Sam. 2:8, 29; 17:22; 1 Kings 17:3, 5).

It was not just crossing the river but also baptisms associated with the Jordan River that signaled the start of a new era. The gospel writers note that John the Baptist was using the Jordan River to baptize those who had come out to him (Matt. 3:6; Mark 1:5). Presuming that Bethany beyond the Jordan (John 1:28) lies opposite the city of Jericho, we dare not miss this important collocation of events. The first Elijah divided the Jordan River opposite Jericho, crossed the Jordan on dry ground, and then was quickly carried to heaven in a whirlwind (2 Kings 2:5–12). The *new* Elijah — that is, John the Baptist (Matt. 11:14), came onto the stage of the Promised Land exactly where the earlier Elijah had left this world. And it was this new Elijah who baptized the greatest of all the prophets and the one who fulfilled the promises the earlier prophets had made. John baptized Jesus in the Jordan (Matt. 3:13) and so marked the start of Jesus' public ministry.

K

Key

Locks were placed on doors and gates of the biblical world to prevent access to all except those authorized to enter; and those authorized to enter gained access via a key, which in turn became a symbol of their authority. A literal key is in view in two of the nine instances where the biblical

authors mention a key; both are in the Old Testament. During that period of time, lock and key were primarily made of wood. In profile, the key looked something like a very large toothbrush — ten to twenty inches in length — with the last several inches of the tip bent up at a slight angle. The tip had perpendicular wooden teeth protruding from the end. The door or gate itself was held in the locked position by a horizontal wooden plank that prevented the door from being opened unless one slid this plank to the side. With the door closed and this plank in the locked position, a mechanism located on the inside of the door allowed wooden pins mounted perpendicular to the plank to fall into place and prevent the plank from sliding. The one wishing to unlock the door from the outside had to push the large key through a fist-sized opening cut in the door to get at the locking mechanism on the inside. The key was then positioned so that the teeth in the key would engage the pins in the lock, pushing them up and out of the way so that the plank could be pushed aside, hence unlocking the door.

This kind of key known from archaeology is never described in the Old Testament but is mentioned in two passages. In the first, the key is used by the servants of King Eglon to open his private chamber. The Israelite judge Ehud had visited the Moabite king Eglon and had ended his visit by killing the king who had been oppressing God's people. The long wait for the king led his servants to presume he was using the bathroom, so they delayed entering the room until they were too embarrassed to delay any longer. The key was brought, and the door to this private room was opened (Judg. 3:25). The second literal key mentioned in the Old Testament is the one used by Levites who had been given the special assignment of protecting access to the temple precincts in Jerusalem. They were responsible for the key that allowed that area to be opened each morning (1 Chron. 9:27).

In the majority of instances in which the biblical authors mention a key, it is being used

A late Roman Period house key made from iron.
Z. Radovan/www.BibleLandPictures.com

figuratively; to possess a key symbolizes one's authority, and to receive a key acknowledges that one has been given new authority. In the first instance, the key symbolizes authority. Speaking of Jerusalem, Isaiah laments that the "key to the house of David," which controls access to the palace and king rests in the hands of a non-Israelite (Isa. 22:15–22). This literal key not only opened locks but symbolized the authority of a very important member of the royal court. Isaiah says the day is coming when that authority will be repositioned: "I will place on [Eliakim's] shoulder the key to the house of David; what he opens no one can shut, and what he shuts no one can open" (v. 22). Isaiah looks forward to a time when the authority inherent in the key will again rest on the shoulder of an Israelite. In a similar way, John speaks of the glorified Christ as the one who ultimately will hold this "key of David" and exert all the authority associated with it in an eternal kingdom (Rev. 3:7). This authority includes power over death. Because Jesus alone had defeated death, he could declare, "I hold the keys of death and Hades" (Rev. 1:18).

When one gives the metaphorical key of authority to another, it is a way of acknowledging the recipient's fitness to wield such authority. As a student of Jesus, Peter had been listening carefully to what his Teacher had been saying. At the critical moment when Jesus asked all of his special students to answer the question, "Who do you say I am?" (Matt. 16:15), it was Peter who clearly identified Jesus as the long-promised Messiah. Jesus praised that answer, acknowledging that such sophistication merited special honor: "I will give you the keys of the kingdom of heaven" (16:19). Peter had more to learn before Jesus turned him loose as an independent teacher. But Peter showed by this answer that he was well on the road to receiving full authority as a teacher of God's truth.

The Lord gives another type of key to heavenly beings. It again represents authority, this time to control the freedom of Satan and the demons to enter the world of mortals. "The key to the shaft of the Abyss" allows a divine agent called a "star" to release the inhabitants and ideology of the Abyss on the world (Rev. 9:1). The same key is also mentioned later in Revelation in the hands of an angel who will employ it to restrict Satan for a period of one thousand years (Rev. 20:1).

Finally, the key can be the fundamental insights that open the door to knowledge of the truth. The Pharisees and teachers of the law believed they held this key firmly in their hands. Yet Jesus attacked this premise head-on when he said to them, "Woe to you experts in the law, because you have taken away the key to knowledge. You yourselves have not entered, and you have hindered those who were entering" (Luke 11:52).

Kiln. *See* Furnace.

Knife

The biblical knife is a tool of varying size and composition designed to hold a sharp edge for cutting. The earliest knives were made from flint, and later knives were made from various metals, but the use of copper, bronze, and iron knives never eliminated the presence of the tradi-tional flint knife, a tool that was both less expensive and held its cutting edge in superior fashion. When manufacturing the flint knife, the craftsman dealt a carefully calculated angled blow at a cone of flint, causing a triangular piece of the rock to flake off. When done properly, the resulting triangle of stone had a very sharp edge on one side yet remained thick enough on the opposite edge to give the cutting tool structural integrity. Later various metals were melted and cast to form a knife that was from six to ten inches in total length. At times the knife and handle were cast as one piece, while at other times a tang was cast for insertion into a wooden handle. In contrast to the flint knife, the cast knife might have a cutting edge on both sides.

The traditional flint knife appears in two contexts where the rite of circumcision was performed after this important rite had been neglected for a time. As Moses headed for Egypt on his mission to lead God's people out of that land, the Lord suddenly and unexpectedly met Moses on the way with the intention of killing him because he had failed to circumcise his son. Zipporah, Moses' wife, quickly took a flint knife and performed the neglected rite (Ex. 4:25). In the second instance, Joshua was preparing to lead Israel into the war that would win the Promised Land for Israel. Prior to the engagement, God ordered Joshua to make flint knives and circumcise all the Israelites who had not been circumcised during their decades in the wilderness (Josh. 5:2–3).

Apart from circumcision, the knife functioned in three other ways. First, it was used to slaughter animals destined either for the dinner table or for ritual sacrifice. Second, when the grapevines needed pruning, the vinedresser used a pruning knife that likely had a curved blade, to trim back the vines. And a third type of knife, the penknife, which was smaller than the others, was used by a scribe to cut and trim a reed pen so that it would distribute ink in a uniform and pleasing way on the page. This kind of pen is mentioned just once in the Bible. The Lord had directed Jeremiah to deliver a message to the people of Israel by writing it on a scroll. The message on this scroll, which was a call for repentance, was read not only at the temple but also in the palace before King Jehoiakim. Rather than repent, this king of Israel began to cut it apart with a scribe's knife and burn it segment by segment in the fire (Jer. 36:23).

Ironically, the knife that was traditionally used to slaughter animals is never formally mentioned in the context of butchering animals. Its first appearance is in Genesis 22 in the narrative that relates the harrowing test of Abraham. As he and his son trudged on toward the place of sacrifice, it was Abraham who carried the butchering knife (v. 6) and raised it to slay his son Isaac (v. 10). The second appearance of such a knife is among the disturbing stories that close the book of Judges. After the concubine of a Levite was abused and murdered by the men of Gibeah, this man cut up his concubine's body and sent the parts into all the areas of Israel to call attention to the crime and solicit a punitive response (Judg. 19:29 – 30). In both cases the use or threatened use of the butchering knife on people plays a rhetorical role in heightening the intensity of the narrative.

Pruning knives are mentioned in Isaiah's judgment speech against Cush. Typically the grape vines were pruned on a schedule—before the plant went dormant in the fall to remove branches that were not productive, and after the grapes set to direct as much of the plant's energy at the maturing fruit as possible. God promises that his act of judgment against Cush will resemble those carefully scheduled uses of the pruning knife: "He will cut off the shoots with pruning knives, and cut down and take away the spreading branches" that represent the vitality of Cush (Isa. 18:5).

Two proverbs refer to a knife. The first takes us to the royal dining hall where a king has set the meal before his guests. Typically the invitation to dine also came with an agenda; those who indulge in the meal might well expect to give the king what he would request of them. The more one ate the larger the request might be. In that light the proverb urges diners to exhibit self-control, using this hyperbolic language: "When you sit to dine with a ruler, note well what is before you, and put a knife to your throat if you are given to gluttony" (Prov. 23:1 – 2). The second comes in a series of proverbs that identify four evil behaviors. The fourth of those speaks of the abusive oppression of the poor with this colorful language: "[There are] those whose teeth

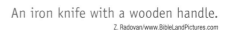

An iron knife with a wooden handle.
Z. Radovan/www.BibleLandPictures.com

are swords and whose jaws are set with knives to devour the poor from the earth, the needy from among mankind" (30:14). Once again, the language is meant to be arresting as we find the tool that was used to butcher animals turned upon fellow human beings in this imagery.

L

Lamb

During the lambing season, thousands of new lambs were born in ancient Israel. Given the importance of the lamb to this culture, it was a time of great celebration. Following a gestation period of five months, ewes gave birth to either a single lamb or twins. In time such lambs would mature and provide their owners with wool for clothing (Prov. 27:26). But some of these lambs were selected for immediate use on the dinner table (Amos 6:4). Meat was not eaten every day by the average Israelite, but when it was served, the most desirable dish a family could have for dinner was the tasty, tender meat of the lamb. Nevertheless, the lamb appeared on the altar of God much more often than the dinner table. By all accounts, it was the most frequently used animal in this form of worship, mentioned over eighty times in the books of Exodus, Leviticus, and Numbers where God defines the way he is to be worshiped. Once a lamb was eight days old, it was eligible to be used as a sacrifice (Lev. 22:27). From the eighth day on, it might be used for the daily sacrifices offered on behalf of the nation (Ex. 29:38–41), as a personal offering (Lev. 4:32), or to commemorate a king's coronation (1 Chron. 29:21–22). And there was one special festival to which the lamb became intimately attached, the festival of Passover (Ex. 12:3–5).

In cultures where the use of money was rare, bartering goods replaced paying for goods with cash. The lamb became a key product in these exchanges. Lambs were given as a gift during a treaty ceremony (Gen. 21:28–30), regarded as wages (30:32–33), used in international trade (Ezek. 27:21), taken as the spoils of war (1 Sam. 15:9), and paid as tribute by a vassal state (2 Kings 3:4; Isa. 16:1). Thus the family that was truly blessed by the Lord was one whose bank account was filled with a ready supply of "cash"—that is, one whose flocks were producing an abundance of healthy lambs (Deut. 28:4; 32:14).

The appearance of this animal, its demeanor, and its use in the sacrificial system combined to shape the connotations linked with the lamb, beginning with its image as an innocent substitute. This young animal, without defect, whose blood was shed before the altar became the symbolic substitute for the one seeking to divert the anger of God from themselves to their animal. Of course an animal, no matter how innocent in appearance, could never be an adequate substitute for a human being (Heb. 10:4). Nevertheless, the lamb became a placeholder awaiting the ultimate sacrifice of the innocent Christ.

Second, the lamb became a symbol of Israel's dedication to the Lord, of their full surrender to him. This notion of surrender was replayed daily during the morning and late afternoon segments of the whole burnt offering. At these times a male lamb without defect was offered to symbolize Israel's total commitment to the Lord (Lev. 1:10; Num. 28:3–4). To appreciate the image of surrender, we need to see why such an animal was considered so valuable. By all accounts the defect-free male lamb was exactly the animal you wanted to keep and use as breeding stock in order to replicate its genetic heritage throughout your herd. Surrender of this precious animal to the Lord was evidence of Israel's willingness to offer the best and illustrated their willingness to trust the Lord to superintend the health of their flock.

Finally, the lamb carried with it the connotation of vulnerability. Mature sheep have very limited defensive skills in the face of large predators, the lambs even less. Consequently, Jeremiah likened himself to a vulnerable lamb destined for slaughter in the face of those who sought to harm him (Jer. 11:19). Jesus told the disciples that he was sending them out like defenseless lambs among wolves (Luke 10:3). Yet their dangerous work would usher in an age of great peace, one in which the lamb and the wolf would live peacefully beside one another (Isa. 11:6; 65:25).

These connotations further become figures of speech in the Bible where the lamb is used as a metaphor for God's enemies, God's people, and Christ. Isaiah foretold the outcome for the nations that resisted the rule of the Lord: "The sword of the LORD is bathed in blood, it is covered with fat—the blood of lambs and goats" (Isa. 34:6). On the other hand, when the lamb is used as a metaphor for God's people, that vulnerability is overshadowed by the tender care and protection offered by the shepherd: "He tends his flock like a shepherd: He gathers the lambs in his arms and carries them close to his heart; he gently leads those that have young" (Isa. 40:11). In that light Jesus urged Peter, his surrogate shepherd, to feed his lambs (John 21:15).

The lamb is also a metaphor for the Messiah. Isaiah predicted that this ultimate substitute for sin would be compliant in the face of his unthinkable mission; "He was led like a lamb to the slaughter" (Isa. 53:7). When John the Baptist saw Jesus approaching him, the image

Biblical authors portray the lamb as the innocent substitute for sin.

of the Passover lamb so overwhelmed him that he exclaimed, "Look, the Lamb of God, who takes away the sin of the world!" (John 1:29). This truth was echoed by Paul (1 Cor. 5:7) and by Peter who links our redemption to "the precious blood of Christ, a lamb without blemish or defect" (1 Peter 1:19). The great crescendo of this imagery comes in the book of Revelation where Jesus is referred to as the Lamb twenty-seven times. He is the Lamb who was slain (Rev. 5:6), whose blood cleanses the saints (7:14), who will become the shepherd of his people (7:17), and who rules from his eternal throne (22:3).

Lamp

When the sun was not shining or in places where the sun did not shine, oil lamps allowed people in Bible times to carry on with their routine tasks. Lamps were such a common feature of daily life that the absence of lamplight was used as a sign

that the rhythm of normal living had ceased (Jer. 25:10; Rev. 18:23).

The lamp was a fired ceramic container, the appearance of which evolved as the centuries rolled by. It began as a shallow, open bowl of modest size with a low rim. One to four places on that rim were pinched into narrow Vs to hold wicks. By the time of the New Testament and under the influence of Greek and Roman design, the lamp had become a round or slipper-shaped container that was enclosed. A small, round opening at the top of the lamp allowed the oil to be replenished, and an enclosed spout replaced the pinched rim as a way of holding the wick in place.

No matter the shape, the lamps of the Old and New Testaments functioned in the same way. The body of the lamp contained the olive oil used as fuel; its size was conditioned upon the amount of oil needed to keep the lamp burning for a designated amount of time. The typical household lamp was built to hold sufficient oil to burn throughout

An oil lamp with pinched edges to hold the wick in place.

Todd Bolen/www.BiblePlaces.com

the night. A twisted cord of flax was used as a wick that would absorb the oil and deliver it to the top of the wick where ignition of the oil occurred. The wick itself was also consumed during the burning, so from time to time it had to be pulled out to keep the lamp lit and burning.

The oil lamps that are so commonly unearthed in archaeological investigations in Israel are much less common in the Bible. Real household lamps are mentioned only twice. The guest room built for Elisha in Shunem was furnished with an oil lamp (2 Kings 4:10), and many lamps provided light in the room used by Paul when he was speaking in Troas (Acts 20:8).

The majority of times we encounter lamps in the Bible, they are being used as symbols or metaphors. If a lamp was to burn for an extended period of time, additional oil had to be added and the wick maintained. Thus a burning lamp was associated with thoughtful attentiveness. In part the wife of Proverbs 31 demonstrates her noble character by maintaining in her home a lamp that burned all night (Prov. 31:18). The five wise virgins in Jesus' parable about the end times brought extra oil for their lamps and so were prepared to meet the bridegroom (Matt. 25:1 – 8). Similarly, the servants awaiting the return of their master from a wedding banquet are attentive to their lamps so they are burning when he arrives (Luke 12:35). An illuminated lamp is not just a symbol of attentiveness but also the symbol of an intense search. When the Lord searches Jerusalem to root out the complacent, he says that the search will be conducted with lamps (Zeph. 1:12). And in the parable of the lost coin, the intensity of the woman's search is also marked by the lighting of a lamp (Luke 15:8).

The great cultural value of the lamp makes it a likely metaphor for the Lord and his Word, for good deeds, for David and Jesus, and for life itself. David praised his God by saying, "You are my lamp, O Lord; the Lord turns my darkness into light" (2 Sam. 22:29; cf. Job 29:3). And the inspired poet declared, "Your word is a lamp to my feet and a light for my path" (Ps. 119:105). God's commands are a lamp (Prov. 6:23) that allow us to put a light in all the dark corners of our lives so that we might inspect who we really are (Prov. 20:27). Those who know God's Word and particularly the truth about Jesus are urged never to put that "lamp … under a bowl" but instead to allow that illuminating news to shine for all to see (Mark 4:21 – 22). In this way John the Baptist was a lamp to his generation of listeners (John 5:35).

When the life-giving words of Jesus changed the hearts of his listeners, they would change the way in which they behaved. Jesus compared the good deeds that follow faith to the light of a lamp. He encouraged his disciples to become a light for the world, reminding them, "Neither do people light a lamp and put it under a bowl. Instead they put it on its stand, and it gives light to everyone in the house" (Matt. 5:15).

In a striking parallel, both David and Jesus are called lamps. When David was nearly struck down in a battle with the Philistines, his men swore that they would never again allow David to be put in harm's way, so that "the lamp of Israel will not be extinguished" (2 Sam. 21:17). The image of the lamp became a metaphor for David's continuing dynasty. Even when members of this dynastic family did a poor job of leading God's people, the Lord promised that he would honor his promise to David, the lamp, in that he would always have a lamp burning before him in Jerusalem (1 Kings 11:36; 15:4; 2 Kings 8:19). This promise was to last into eternity (2 Chron. 21:7). So it is no surprise to see that David's greatest descendant, Jesus, is also described as a lamp; the New Jerusalem will bask in his light:

"The city does not need the sun or the moon to shine on it, for the glory of God gives it light, and the Lamb is its lamp" (Rev. 21:23).

In contrast to this enduring lamp, those who oppose the Lord with their life will find the lamp, which is their own life, snuffed out: "The light of the righteous shines brightly, but the lamp of the wicked is snuffed out" (Prov. 13:9; cf. 20:20; 24:20).

Linen

Wool was the textile of choice for defeating the cold in Bible times, but nothing compared to linen when one wanted soft, breathable fabric. Linen is derived from the four-feet-tall, annual plant known as flax. Processing began as the mature plant was pulled up by its roots to assure that the stem and long fibers within it would remain intact. After initial drying, the plant was soaked in water for at least three to four weeks so that the woody interior of the plant might begin to rot. The plant was then dried again before being subjected to crushing blows designed to sever the bond between the core of the plant and the outer flax fibers. As the plant began to fall apart, it was pulled through combs of varying sizes to strip the less desirable portions of the plant away from the valuable flax fibers.

People in Bible times used the yarn and thread made from the flax fibers in many ways. The aggressive beating of the flax plant meant that some fibers would be broken. These shorter fibers were twisted together to produce the wicks used in oil lamps. The longer fibers were twisted into threads that were combined on a loom to produce soft, comfortable linen cloth. This cloth varied in tone from light brown to golden brown, but it could be bleached into a brilliant white or dyed in a wide array of colors. This high quality cloth was used by the keepers of the Dead Sea Scrolls, who stored

A field of flax.
© Jostein Hauge/www.BigStockPhoto.com

their precious documents in linen wrappings. The prized Egyptian linen made a bed even more inviting (Prov. 7:16). But the most frequent mention of linen in the Bible likely coincides with its most frequent use, the manufacture of fine clothing.

When the biblical authors mention that someone is wearing linen, it distinguishes that person; linen clothing was a high-end product associated with the well-to-do. In judgment speeches against Tyre and "Babylon," linen helps define the wealth of those facing condemnation (Ezek. 27:7, 16; Rev. 18:12, 16). Samson was not a wealthy man, but he made a wealthy man's wager, offering linen garments to his thirty wedding companions if they could solve his riddle (Judg. 14:12 – 13). And in Jesus' story about the rich man and poor Lazarus, the economic distance between the two is emphasized by noting that the wealthy man "dressed in purple and fine linen" on a daily basis (Luke 16:19).

The connection between fine linen clothing and wealth naturally led the royals of the ancient world to dress in linen garments and to recognize those whom they wished to honor with linen as well. When Joseph rose to power in Egypt, Pharaoh "dressed him in robes of fine linen" (Gen. 41:42); and when the Persian king chose to honor Mordecai, this Jewish man left the king's presence dressed in "a purple robe of fine linen" (Esth. 8:15).

Given the unique nature of the Lord, it is fitting that his residence on earth as well as those who serve him there would be adorned with this special cloth. For that reason, linen is mentioned more often in Exodus than in any other book of the Bible. Here the Israelites are encouraged to make an offering of the linen that they had taken with them from Egypt so that various components of the tent sanctuary and its courtyard could be made of fine linen. Because those men who served there as priests were to be distinguished from others in society, their garments, such as their tunics, turbans, ephods, breastplates, sashes, and even undergarments, were made from linen (Ex. 28:4, 5, 6, 8, 15, 29, 42).

While the angels do not have physical bodies in need of clothing, those who appear to mortals often do so wearing linen garments that shine radiantly (Ezek. 9:2, 3, 11; 10:2, 6, 7; Dan. 10:5; 12:6 – 7; Rev. 15:6; 19:14).

In each instance above, the person who is being distinguished from others is being distinguished at least in part by his or her appearance in a linen garment. Jesus had suffered so many indignities on the day of his death, it is no wonder his friends longed to restore some dignity in his interment by burying him in a linen shroud (Matt. 27:59; Mark 15:46; Luke 23:53; John 19:40).

Linen garments also serve as a metaphor for piety, Israel, and righteousness. Immediately after the inspired author of 1 Samuel characterizes the wicked sons of Eli, he champions the piety of Samuel by noting that he is wearing a linen ephod (1 Sam. 2:18). Not long after, David appears in a linen ephod. Although he is not a Levite like Samuel, David dons the dress of a pious Levite when bringing the ark of the covenant to Jerusalem (2 Sam. 6:14). Thus the pious Samuel and pious David are linked in this book through their attire.

A linen belt was a very precious possession, just as Israel was a very precious possession of the Lord; however, when God's people worshiped other gods, they made themselves worthless. In that light Jeremiah was directed to purchase a linen belt and wear it for a time. This time of enjoyment would end when the Lord directed his prophet to remove his expensive belt, hide it in the crevice of a rock, and leave it there until it was ruined and useless (Jer. 13:1 – 11). In this way the Lord illustrated how his precious Israel had fallen into ruin.

Finally, a linen garment also was used to symbolize the righteousness of Christ's church, the bride who is given special clothing for her wedding day in Revelation 19:8: "'Fine linen, bright and clean, was given her to wear.' (Fine linen stands for the righteous acts of the saints.)"

Lion

The lion of the Bible is the large, buff-brown cat that typically comes to mind when people hear the word. Second only to the tiger in size, the lion can grow to be ten feet in length and weigh between 400 and 550 pounds, making it the largest predator in the biblical world. In contrast to other predators, the lion is built for strength rather than speed. To be sure, the lighter lioness can quickly accelerate to forty miles an hour, but this burst of speed is sustainable for only a short distance. Consequently, lions tend to hunt with other members of their pride, using the cover of darkness to stalk within striking range where their substantial strength can be unleashed on their unsuspecting prey.

Wild lions were a real threat to travelers in ancient Israel.
© Nilanjan Bhattacharya/www.BigStockPhoto.com

While we correctly associate lions with Africa, they were also quite common in the Promised Land throughout the biblical period. The Old Testament authors mention the lion frequently, using eight different Hebrew words to discriminate between lions of different gender and age. In the process of doing so, they display personal knowledge of the lion's habitat and habits (Job 38:39–40; Prov. 19:12; 20:2; 30:30; Amos 3:12). So while our experience with lions may be limited to online pictures or visits to the zoo, people of the biblical world traveling in the open country between villages were well aware that they shared the countryside with lion prides.

Encounters with lions did happen and did not end well for those who had the experience. This perception aided Joseph's brothers who wished to cover up their actions by showing their father Joseph's bloody garment. Upon seeing it, Jacob immediately came to the conclusion that Joseph had been killed by a wild animal (Gen. 37:33). Consequently, those who survive an encounter with a lion or who, in fact, take the life of the lion have a story worth hearing. So it was with Samson, David, and Daniel (Judg. 14:5–7; 1 Sam. 17:34–37; Dan. 6:7–27). Nevertheless, most encounters with lions did not have happy endings, particularly when God elected to use lion attacks to make a point. When the prophet of Judah failed to follow the instructions he was given and when those settled in Samaria by the Assyrians failed to worship the Lord, he used fatal lion attacks to display his displeasure (1 Kings 13:24–28; 2 Kings 17:25–26).

More often than not when we encounter a lion in the pages of the Bible, it is in a figure of speech that taps into the characteristics of the lion or a mortal's experience with one. In the positive figures of speech that mention a lion, it is the boldness, strength, and independence of this great cat that come to the foreground. The most sustained use of this image is found within a trajectory that reaches from Genesis to Revelation, linking the lion to the tribe of Judah. In Jacob's blessing of Judah, we hear him say; "You are a lion's cub, O Judah; you return from the prey, my son. Like a lion he crouches and lies down, like a lioness—who dares to rouse him?" (Gen. 49:9). This messianic verse links Judah and the coming King of Judah to the lion. Perhaps that is why Solomon designed a throne platform for himself that included twelve lions (1 Kings 10:19–20). In a lament that marks the close of the southern kingdom, Ezekiel uses the lion in an extended metaphor to refer to the final kings ruling the house of Judah (Ezek. 19:1–9). That poetry does not end the story on a positive note, but neither is it truly the end of the story. For the Messiah did come and succeed where mortals had failed. As John exclaims, "See, the Lion of the tribe of Judah, the Root of David, has triumphed" (Rev. 5:5).

The courageous lion is also used to describe individuals like Saul and Jonathan (2 Sam. 1:23), the tribes of Gad and Dan (Deut. 33:20, 22), and all the people of Israel (Num. 23:24; 24:9; Mic. 5:8). Finally, the Lord himself is portrayed as a lion coming out of the Jordan's thicket to chase away Edom and Babylon (Jer. 49:19; 50:44). When he roars to those in exile, it is his indication to his people that it is safe to return to the Promised Land (Hos. 11:10).

On the other hand, negative images of the lion also abound as the biblical authors use the horror of a lion attack to convey the risk and deep pain we may encounter in life. In this case the lion may be an unnamed person as it is so often in the Psalms, someone who is tearing and ripping, catching the helpless, crouching in cover, and roaring (Pss. 7:2; 10:9; 17:12; 22:13, 21; 35:17; 57:4). Ironically, those responsible for such abuse can be members of the Judean royal family who are attacking their subjects (Ezek. 22:25; Zeph. 3:3). When God's people are feeling such pain, they may even point to the Lord as being the lion who is stalking them, dragging them from the path, and mangling them (Job 10:16; Lam. 3:10–11). The lionlike attack that comes against God's people is also linked to nations like Assyria and Babylon (Isa. 5:29; Jer. 2:15; 4:7; 25:38; Nah. 2:11–13). And at least once an inspired author pictures the role of the Devil in our lives with lion imagery: "Be self-controlled and alert. Your enemy the devil prowls around like a roaring lion looking for someone to devour" (1 Peter 5:8).

Given the dangers presented by both the real and metaphorical lions pictured in the Bible, we can appreciate the comforting images of an era when lions are either absent (Isa. 35:9) or take on a completely different character. In the era to come, the lion will reside peacefully with the calf and eat straw like the ox (11:6–7; 65:25).

Locust

Up to eleven different Hebrew words are used in the Old Testament when referring to the locust. While it is unclear if this wide range of vocabulary is being used to differentiate between species of locusts or to discriminate between stages of the locust's lifecycle, this wide-ranging vocabulary certainly indicates that those living in Bible times were very familiar with this insect.

Several species are known to intrude into the Promised Land, but the one most likely in view by the biblical authors is the desert locust (*Schistocerca gregaria*). The female of this species lays its eggs four inches beneath the soil to await the moist conditions that will mean plenty of food for the hatching hoppers. With food available, the hoppers change both color and behavior. They turn from green to yellow and black in color; and they exchange their solitary life for swarming, forming masses that cover the ground. An abundance of foliage triggers a similar reaction in the adult desert locust, causing them to change in color from brown to yellow. Taking to the wind, the winged adults can cover more than one hundred miles in a day to arrive at prime feeding locations.

Various characteristics of the locust are mentioned in the Bible, starting with the swarming behavior that can result in there being 100 million locusts in one square mile. They advance like a well-organized army on the move (Joel 2:8). And because each member of this army can con-

sume its own weight in food each day, land that once resembled the "garden of Eden" can quickly become a "desert waste" (2:3). The beating wings of this horde can sound like "crackling fire" (2:5) as they blot out the sunlight by their vast numbers (2:2, 10). The waves of destruction that lap at the vulnerable landscape are aptly expressed in these words of Joel: "What the locust swarm has left the great locusts have eaten; what the great locusts have left the young locusts have eaten; what the young locusts have left other locusts have eaten" (Joel 1:4).

When real locusts appear on the pages of the Bible, they are sent by the Lord to address human rebellion and urge mortals to repent. The first example is the locust plague that befalls Egypt (Ex. 10:1–20). The Lord had already ravaged the fields and fruit trees of Egypt with a violent hailstorm. But when this failed to elicit the proper response from Pharaoh, the Lord used a powerful east wind to carry an unprecedented locust swarm off the desert and into the developed areas, denuding the landscape, filling homes, and destroying the agricultural fields and pastureland of this proud

A desert locust.
Adrian Pingston/Wikimedia Commons

nation. This locust plague became a signature event recalled by Israel's poets (Pss. 78:46; 105:34).

The locust was also linked intimately to the theology of Israel via the covenant stipulations in Deuteronomy. If God's people rebelled against the Lord, they could expect God to make his displeasure known in many ways, including the invasion of locusts (Deut. 28:38, 42; 1 Kings 8:37). Unfortunately, both the days of Joel and Amos witnessed such a punitive invasion of locusts. Joel not only gives us a vivid picture of how this swarm of locusts looked and the destruction the locusts caused but also leverages this horrific invasion into a call for God's people to repent (Joel 1:10–14). A later invasion of locusts during the time of Amos is also linked to divine displeasure. Even the less desirable food for the locusts, the trees, faced destruction during this plague: "'Many times I struck your gardens and vineyards, I struck them with blight and mildew. Locusts devoured your fig and olive trees, yet you have not returned to me,' declares the LORD" (Amos 4:9; cf. 7:1).

While locusts often would eat the food grown by Israel, Israel also used the locust as food. Fifty percent of a dried locust is composed of valuable protein; and God listed it among the clean creatures that might be eaten by the Israelites, particularly during their time in the wilderness (Lev. 11:22). The gospel writers mention that John the Baptist also ate locusts when he was in the wilderness (Matt. 3:4; Mark 1:6). This simple diet not only provided necessary protein for John, but it further distinguished him and his message from the corrupt priestly aristocracy whose tables were filled with the finest food.

Figurative use of the locust in the Bible leans on the swarming behavior of this insect, its small size, and the transitory nature of its visits. Along with many other ancient Near Eastern writers, the biblical authors often compare the size of an invading army to the uncountable number of individuals in a swarm of invading locusts (Judg. 6:5; 7:12; Jer. 46:23; 51:14). Always implied if not directly mentioned is the army's ability to destroy: "Your plunder, O nations, is harvested as by young locusts; like a swarm of locusts men pounce on it" (Isa. 33:4). While swarms are massive, individual locusts, particularly in their early stages of development, are quite small. This leads certain members of the Israelite reconnaissance team to liken themselves to locusts when comparing themselves to the residents of Canaan (Num. 13:33; NIV "grasshoppers"). And when describing his weakened state, the psalmist likens himself to this inconsequential insect that is so easily shaken off one's clothing (Ps. 109:23). When the food supply in an area has been depleted, the locusts move on. Nahum uses this picture to describe the way Nineveh will be despoiled by merchants and leaders alike who will strip the land of its wealth and then leave an impoverished land in their wake (Nah. 3:16–17).

Loom

The loom is a tool used by weavers to interlace individual threads to create the cloth destined to become a tent, bed covering, or piece of clothing. During the biblical period, two types of loom were in use, the horizontal loom and the vertical loom. The horizontal loom, sometimes called the *ground loom*, was the older and more portable of the two. It consisted of two straight, wooden limbs about three feet in length. The warp threads (those that ran left-to-right before the seated weaver) were tied to these two limbs and held taut when the two branches of the wooden frame were staked to the ground at its four corners. The vertical loom accomplished a similar goal but in a different plane. The frame of the vertical loom consisted of a horizontal beam held aloft by two vertical posts. The threads of the warp (the vertical threads) were tied to the horizontal beam and allowed to dangle toward the ground. They were held taut by clay loom weights tied to the end of each warp thread.

The process of weaving on either type of loom was the same. Horizontal threads, the *woof*, had to pass in and out of the warp threads to create a solid piece of cloth. To aid in this

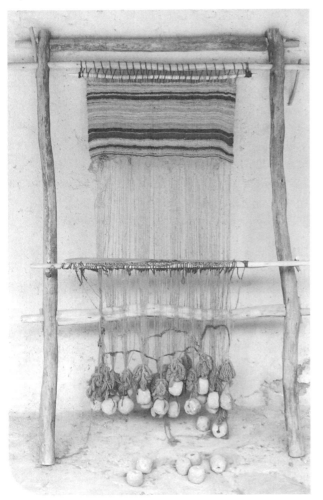

A vertical loom.
Todd Bolen/www.BiblePlaces.com

process, the weaver tied the woof thread to a slender bone needle called the *shuttle* that pulled the woof thread in and out through the warp threads. When one circuit of the shuttle was complete, the weaver would use a pin (another piece of wood aligned with the woof access) to push the woof threads up into the previous row, tightening the weave. The process of interlacing the woof through so many warp threads could be very time consuming. This led to various innovations designed to speed up that part of the process; among them was the addition of the heddle rod. The heddle rod was a flat piece of wood that was woven in and out between the threads of the warp. When the weaver adjusted the angle of the heddle rod, the threads of the warp separated, creating a gap called the *shed*. Now, rather than having to weave the shuttle through every single thread individually, the weaver could simply push the shuttle through the open shed. A change in orientation of the heddle rod separated the threads in the opposing direction, allowing the shuttle to return just as quickly on the reverse pass.

The biblical authors mention the loom most frequently in metaphors, but a real loom appears in the story of Samson and Delilah. The Philistine rulers had had enough of Samson and the troubles he had brought to them. Their goal was to use his feelings for Delilah to bring an end to that trouble. So on more than one occasion, she begged Samson to reveal the secret of his strength and how he might be subdued. During the third round of this drama, Samson said, "If you weave the seven braids of my head into the fabric on the loom and tighten it with the pin, I'll become as weak as any other man" (Judg. 16:13). With Samson's head in her lap, Delilah likely used a horizontal loom to weave his hair like woof threads into the warp on the loom, tightening his hair with the pin after each pass. But when she tested the truthfulness of Samson's words, he "awoke from his sleep and pulled up the pin and the loom, with the fabric" (v. 14).

The remaining biblical appearances of the loom are in metaphors. As Job struggled with the painful challenges he was facing, he lamented how quickly the days were passing. For all intents and purposes, it seemed as if his life would end before his life would see improvement. Drawing on the image of the speeding weaver's shuttle, Job said, "My days are swifter than a weaver's shuttle, and they come to an end without hope" (Job 7:6).

Hezekiah also had the image of a loom in mind when serious illness appeared to be cutting his life short. He compared his life to a piece of cloth that God had been carefully weaving on a loom. Just as a weaver would cut the threads of the warp that bind the cloth to the crossbar of the loom, so God had cut him off from the loom, making an end of him (Isa. 38:12).

The heddle rod is likened to a spear in the story of David and Goliath. Here the author of 1 Samuel describes the appearance of Goliath in great detail to shape our impression of this mighty warrior and to help us appreciate the faith-filled boldness David displayed in fighting him. This is where we meet the curious metaphor "his spear shaft was like a weaver's rod" (1 Sam. 17:7; for a similar use of this same metaphor, see 2 Sam. 21:19; 1 Chron. 11:23; 20:5). The heddle is an important part of the loom, but its size does not impress; so the point of comparison would seem to be its appearance. The heddle had a leather thong or leash that allowed the weaver to manipulate it more easily. Perhaps Goliath also had a leather leash on his spear that reminded the biblical authors of the leash on the heddle. Wrapping the leash around the spear and using the leash when throwing the spear would cause the weapon to rotate and its flight path to be stabilized. The net result was a more accurate throw with greater range. Thus the point of the metaphor is to impress the reader with the nature of this weapon. By describing Goliath's spear in this way, the author of 1 Samuel was helping the reader picture a weapon whose range and accuracy posed a great risk to anyone who stepped onto the field of battle.

M

Manger

Left on their own, donkeys and oxen would eat throughout the day at the time and place of their own choosing. But as work animals, their day was filled with responsibilities that precluded leisurely and unscheduled dining. A complete meal was reserved until evening when the work was done and these animals were tucked into a secure location for the night. Only then would the owner bring these hard workers their well-deserved food, placing it in a manger. Such feed boxes were very simple containers made from limestone or compacted mud and clay. They were either round or rectangular in shape with a hollowed out interior where the food was placed. Of all the places in the ancient world we might look for decoration, this was not it. The ordinary manger was utilitarian, unremarkable, and unadorned.

In the Bible, mangers are generally mentioned in connection with the feeding of donkeys and oxen, working-class animals who earned their keep in agricultural and travel settings. The oxen were used to plow farm fields and thresh the harvested grain; donkeys might also be used to plow but were particularly used to transport people and goods (Deut. 22:10; 25:4; 2 Sam. 16:1–2; Isa. 30:24). For them to have the energy necessary to carry out these assigned tasks, their owners had to provide them with nutrient-rich food at the close of the work day so that they could obtain the strength needed to accomplish the tasks awaiting them when the sun rose again. The food placed in the manger met that need. Of course, it took effort to fill the manger with food each day for hungry draft animals, but one proverb illustrates the value of investing that time: "Where there are no oxen, the manger is empty, but from the strength of an ox comes an abundant harvest" (Prov. 14:4). If there were no oxen, there would be no need to fill the manger with food; but without the contribution made by the family oxen, the amount of grain harvested would diminish.

One would expect domesticated oxen to remain near such a manger, but not so wild oxen.

A stone manger found at Megiddo.
© William D. Mounce

This reality is mentioned in the closing chapters of Job where a set of rhetorical questions illustrates the serious limits faced by Job and all mortals when compared to their God. The Lord asks, "Will the wild ox consent to serve you? Will he stay by your manger at night?" (Job 39:9). If the raw power of the wild ox could be harnessed, the farm family of Bible times would quite literally reap the benefits. But no matter how desirable the premise, wild oxen defy domestication and want nothing to do with a feeding trough. There are many places where mortal limits become evident; one of the closest was the manger, the overnight feeding station for the family work animals.

Isaiah mentions the donkey's love for its manger in a metaphor that criticizes Israel's lack of respect for the Lord. No one needs to point a hungry donkey in the direction of its feed box; this animal knows just where to go when the workday is done. In the metaphor, God's people are contrasted with such a donkey. Despite the Lord's reoccurring blessing of Israel, they failed to celebrate the source of that blessing: "The ox knows his master, the donkey his owner's manger, but Israel does not know, my people do not understand" (Isa. 1:3).

Finally, the manger plays an important rhetorical role in the Christmas story, shaping our expectations of the child laid in it. Mary knew that the child in her womb was destined to be a special king. During the angel Gabriel's visit to Mary, this messenger of God not only described the special nature of her pregnancy but also observed that her son would sit on "the throne of his father David" and that he would "reign over the house of Jacob forever" (Luke 1:32–33). This announcement created a set of expectations, not least of which was that her child would enjoy an appropriate birthing room, if not in a palace, at least in a nicely furnished home. One chapter later when Luke gets around to recounting the actual birth of Jesus, most of the details surrounding that birth are discreetly kept out of public view. One detail, however, is not just mentioned, but emphasized. Jesus was placed in a manger, a fact mentioned three times in the otherwise spartan account of Jesus' birth (Luke 2:7, 12, 16). What is more, the shepherds were told, "This will be a sign to you: You will find a baby wrapped in cloths and lying in a manger" (2:12). For Luke a "sign" was always an event or image that carried special meaning. So what is the special meaning we are to attach to the child in the manger? We may have become so accustomed to the image of the baby in the manger that the incongruity does not strike us as it should. No baby, much less a baby destined to be a king, much less a baby destined to rule an eternal kingdom, would be found in a manger. Consequently, this unremarkable baby bed says something remarkable about this infant King. He would not rule the world with the arrogance evident in Emperor Augustus or Herod the Great. This was a different kind of king. And long before we hear Jesus say it, the humble baby bed sends the message: "The Son of Man did not come to be served, but to serve, and to give his life as a ransom for many" (Matt. 20:28).

Manna

The need for the special food called manna became apparent within weeks of Israel's departure from Egypt. God had led his people deep into the Sinai where the provisions they had brought with them from Egypt had given out and where the meager two inches of annual rainfall precluded any hope of growing grain to make new bread. Overwhelmed by hunger pangs, they complained to Moses and Aaron, even longing for the life of bondage in Egypt that at least included food (Ex. 16:3). In part God met their nutritional needs with manna.

Various attempts have been made to link this manna with a naturally occurring substance in the Sinai region, but all prove unsatisfying. Some have suggested that manna is the equivalent of a white secretion produced by aphids on the tamarisk tree or the secretion from one of a variety of plants that grow in the Sinai, such as the hammada plant. But the quantity of resin produced, the limited number of places these plants grow, and the limited season the secretions are available make these candidates suspect. The very detailed description of manna we find in the Bible may well be given to illustrate its other-worldliness. It arrived daily, appearing after the morning dewfall evaporated. What was left behind is likened to frosty flakes or an off-white resin (Ex. 16:14, 31; Num. 11:7). It appeared each morning except for the Sabbath (Ex. 16:4–5, 25–26), starting on the very day the Lord said it would and ending forty years later when the Israelites crossed the Jordan into Canaan (Ex. 16:35; Josh. 5:12). On the mornings it materialized, each family was able to gather enough so that every member had two quarts (Ex. 16:16). It was then ground with a hand mill or crushed using a mortar so that it could be cooked or baked into cakes (Num. 11:8). Its taste is variously described, likened to wafers made with honey (Ex. 16:31) and to olive oil (Num. 11:8). When all this information is compiled, we come to the intended conclusion that no natural substance matches this description, a fact supported by the name the Israelites gave to this special food (Ex. 16:14, 31). They called it "manna," Hebrew for "What is it?"

This special food had three interrelated roles to play in the life of God's people. First, it provided them with the carbohydrates and protein necessary to sustain life in a place where the survival of so many without miraculous intervention was out of the question. Second, a portion of this manna was to be saved and placed in or near the ark of the covenant (Ex. 16:32–34; Heb. 9:4) to remind future generations of God's great compas-

sion in preserving his people with this special food (Neh. 9:19–20). But the one role that rises above the rest is its role in testing Israel (Ex. 16:4; Deut. 8:16). Any manna that the people kept overnight, with the exception of the manna collected for the Sabbath, would rot by the next morning (Ex. 16:19–20). In this way God tested Israel's faith to see if they would count on his promise to provide manna the following day. Bread was critical to their diet and survival, but one thing was even more fundamental in life than that; consequently, manna was given "to teach … that man does not live on bread alone but on every word that comes from the mouth of the LORD" (Deut. 8:3).

The subsequent references to manna in the Bible all illustrate that God's people failed this

The Israelites gather manna in the wilderness.

test on a regular basis, making it necessary for Jesus to fulfill this component of the law and to replace that manna with something more precious. Even after the manna had stopped, the manna preserved in the sanctuary was to remind Israel of the Lord's ability and willingness to provide. But as the psalmist reviews the health of Israel's faith, it is clear that even this physical reminder of God's miraculous provision becomes another miracle in a long list of miracles experienced by Israel that God's people had forgotten (Ps. 78:24).

Satan had been successful in limiting the effectiveness of Israel by tempting them to doubt God's goodness and so directed a similar temptation at Jesus in a bid to derail his mission on earth (Matt. 4:1 – 11). As Jesus spent his forty days in the wilderness without bread, the Tempter urged Jesus to take the ever-prevalent stones and turn them into a meal for himself. Quoting Deuteronomy 6:16, Jesus recalled that obedience and faith are better than bread. Jesus overwhelmed temptation and the Tempter with Scripture, succeeding in this test that Israel had so often failed.

The next time Jesus mentioned manna was shortly after he had fed more than five thousand people by miraculously multiplying just a small amount of bread. Those who benefited saw a new Moses in this man Jesus. They declared their willingness to make him their leader if only he would perform this miracle again and again, providing them with food on a daily basis just as Moses had done (John 6:15, 30 – 31). These people, too, were on the verge of failing the "manna test" because they had failed to see that a new and better "bread" stood before them. The problem with the old manna was that people who ate it got hungry again and eventually died. Jesus declared himself to be a new kind of bread that

had come down from heaven. Those who link themselves to this manna will never go hungry and never die (John 6:35 – 58; Rev. 2:17).

Manure. *See* Dung.

Megiddo

The ancient city of Megiddo is located on the southwestern edge of the Jezreel Valley at a very strategic point along the international highway. This thirty-five-acre site saw nearly continuous settlement throughout the period of the Old Testament, alternately occupied by Canaanites, Egyptians, Israelites, and Assyrians from 3500 to 350 BC.

This long history of occupation was promoted both by the natural resources available nearby and by its strategic location. Megiddo has access to two springs that provided its early residents with all the water they needed, and it lies adjacent to some of the best farmland in the region, the fertile Jezreel Valley. But the importance of the city is best defined by its strategic location. The Promised Land itself hosted the international highway because it offered a friendly route of travel between the Mediterranean Sea and the hostile Syrian Desert. As this highway stretched north along the coastal plain of Israel, it ran into the ridge of Mount Carmel, which blocked easy passage to the north and east. The most level and shortest route through this mountain blockade traced a valley between Aruna and Megiddo. This Aruna-Megiddo valley road wound down through a valley that in places compressed international commerce into a pathway only a few yards wide before allowing it to exit into the Jezreel Valley just south of Megiddo. If the land of Israel was the critical land bridge between continents, then the pass near Megiddo became the narrowest portion of that bridge, allowing its owner to tax the trade goods and stem the movement of armies. Perhaps no greater testimony to the importance of this city can be found in the ancient record than the one offered by Thutmose III, a fifteenth-century BC ruler of Egypt. When the then Canaanite city of Megiddo was ready to fall to a seven-month Egyptian siege, Thutmose directed his commanders to capture and fortify the city as best as they could, because, in his words, Megiddo had the value of one thousand cities.

Eventually Megiddo did fall back into Canaanite hands and was defeated by Joshua (Josh. 12:21). When it came time to divide up the Jezreel Valley among the tribes of Israel, the valley itself was split among three tribes. Perhaps this was to prevent any one tribe from reaping all the benefits of this critical real estate. But the plum city, Megiddo, was assigned to that portion of Manasseh that settled west of the Jordan River (Josh. 17:11). Yet despite its critical value and in what was a clear sign of the times, we learn that Manasseh was not able to drive out its Canaanite residents (Judg. 1:27). In fact, it was not until the time of Solomon that Megiddo resided firmly in Israelite hands. The strength of this ruler is illustrated by the fact that he not only held Megiddo but turned it into a fortified administrative center (1 Kings 4:12; 9:15).

To appreciate two other references to Megiddo by the biblical authors, we place ourselves at Megiddo to see the dramatic miracles and victories that were in sight from this ancient city. In the days of Deborah and Barak, the Israelite infantry had gathered on Mount Tabor, facing off against a Canaanite chariot corps gathered in the valley below. God asked the unthinkable, an infantry charge off the rising terrain into the plain to engage the Canaanite chariots. Their faith was rewarded with a miraculous victory "by the waters of Megiddo" (Judg. 5:19). A miraculous victory also was in store for the Israelites who followed Gideon into battle against the Midianites. After reducing the Israelite fighters to a ridiculously small number, the Lord used hundreds to defeat uncountable thousands, a victory that again occurred just down the valley from Megiddo (Judg. 7). A third miraculous victory is connected with Mount Carmel and the valley floor just north of Megiddo. During the reign of Ahab and Jezebel, Baal worship had virtually replaced worship of the Lord in the northern kingdom. Elijah summoned the prophets of Baal to a contest on Mount Carmel in which God miraculously sent fire to consume Elijah's sacrifice. Elijah then had the prophets of Baal slaughtered in the valley just north of Megiddo (1 Kings 18). Consequently, the valley around Megiddo was filled with the memories of divinely sponsored victories.

These memories likely played a role in a fateful decision made by King Josiah of Judah. During his reign, the world was changing. The Assyrian Empire that had so dominated the world stage was reeling and about to fall to the rising Babylonians. In 609 BC Pharaoh Neco II of Egypt set out to prop up the faltering Assyrian army in what would become the Assyrians' last battle with Babylon. This meant that the Egyptian army would travel the international highway north through the region under Josiah's control. We do not know why Josiah elected to block the Egyptian advance, but we do know where he chose to do so: at Megiddo. This was the one place a smaller army could hope to waylay a larger army; and what is more, it was a place where the Lord had so often given Israel unexpected victories. But this time Josiah's agenda was not aligned with the Lord's; his efforts failed,

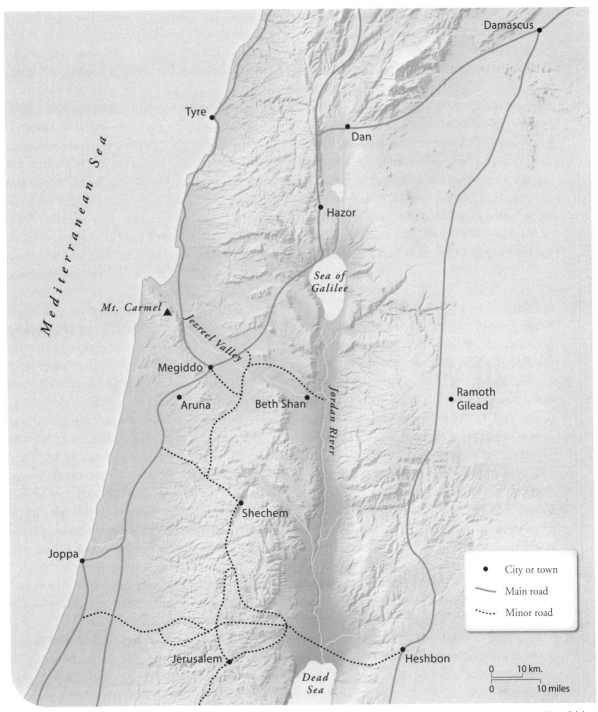

Megiddo.

and his life was ended in the attempt (2 Kings 23:29–30; 2 Chron. 35:20–24).

Megiddo also makes an appearance in Revelation 16:16. John tells us that the battle for control of creation that began in the garden of Eden would end at a place called "Armageddon." This place name is composed of the Hebrew word for hill or mountain and the city name, Megiddo. Whether this place is mentioned by John to signal the literal location of that last battle or as a symbolic name meant to capture the importance of the battle, one thing is clear. The battle associated with the "hill of Megiddo" will finally and decisively end this world's struggle and mark the Lord as final victor.

Milk

When female mammals become pregnant and give birth, their bodies are stimulated to produce the milk that will nourish their young. So it was that the cows, camels, sheep, and goats that lived among the Israelites brought milk into their culture (Deut. 32:14). But of all the animals found in herd or flock, the goat outdistanced the others as a provider of milk (Prov. 27:27). Bred once each year, the does (female goats) of the Israelite flocks were capable of producing an average of three quarts of milk per day for ten months so long as they were milked every day. While the cow could produce more milk on a daily basis, it required more pasture to do so and was less amenable to grazing on steep slopes. And in contrast to the ewe, the doe produced twice as much milk, milk that had higher protein and fat content than that offered by the ewe.

So it was that goat's milk became a staple in the Israelite diet, finding its way onto a list of products considered fundamental to the survival of all mortals (Sir. 39:26). Milk was drunk when it was fresh; but without refrigeration, it had to

be processed if it was to last. Thus a portion of the family's milk was placed into a skin that was hung and then swung to churn the milk. This led to the production of longer-lasting milk products, such as cheese, butter, and yogurt.

As milk was regularly drunk by the family, it further became a symbol linked to hospitality, Israel's cultural distinction, and the Promised Land. As potential guests approached a bedouin tent, their fear of rejection or bodily harm was quickly allayed when the host began a welcoming ritual that included an offer of milk. Abraham hurried to greet the three strangers who were lingering near his tent, offering them food to eat and milk to drink as a symbol that they were welcome (Gen. 18:8). As the defeated Sisera fled the pursuing Israelite army, he, too, came to a tent seeking protection. When he asked for water, Jael brought out a skin of milk (Judg. 4:19; 5:25). Sisera presumed that her offer spelled security; but this symbol of welcome quickly gave way to an unwelcomed blow to the head.

A curious statement found three times in the Torah places a unique dietary restriction on Israel (Ex. 23:19; 34:26; Deut. 14:21). They were permitted to eat young goats, and they were allowed to drink milk, but they were not to boil a young goat in the milk of its mother. Interpreters have tried to explain this restriction in a number of ways. The more persuasive links this meal to the Canaanite culture. Because the Lord wanted Israel to recall its special mission by living a culturally distinct lifestyle, a kid cooked in its mother's milk was off the menu.

Milk also appears in the frequently mentioned formula used to describe the Promised Land, "a land flowing with milk and honey" (Ex. 3:8; 3:17; 13:5; 33:3; et al.). As the Israelites spent years in a trackless wilderness, the description certainly provided an inviting picture of the Promised

Land. But it may also be a descriptor that honors the distinct differences between the northern and southern sections of Canaan. Because the north receives more rain, there is considerably more vegetation that provides flowers for the bees to use in making honey. In contrast the south receives considerably less rain, so we find agriculture giving way to the pastoral life and the goat's milk that was a staple in the Israelite diet. Thus the diverse nature of the Promised Land is captured in this expression by naming two important commodities associated with its subregions.

Goats produce higher quality milk at twice the rate of the average ewe.

Philippe Lissac/Godong/www.panos.co.uk

Milk also appears in a variety of metaphors. For example, it is associated with the handsome and healthy appearance of a person, an appearance that makes a person winsome and desirable. The messianic warrior king is described in Jacob's blessing of Judah as one whose "teeth [are] whiter than milk" (Gen. 49:12). The much desired bride of the Song of Songs has milk "under [her] tongue" (Song 4:11), while her beloved has striking eyes that are "washed in milk" (5:12). The princes of the thriving city of Jerusalem are described as "brighter than snow and whiter than milk" (Lam. 4:7). But as the city lies in ruin, so does the appearance of those same princes who are now "blacker than soot" (4:8).

Another metaphor for milk is blessing and abundance. Job recalled a time before the start of his suffering when his path was drenched in milk—that is, God's favor (Job 29:6; NIV "cream"). The prophets anticipate a day when milk will not just be present in the Promised Land but when "the hills will flow with milk" (Joel 3:18). Isaiah, in particular, takes that one step further, announcing that God's people will "drink the milk of nations" (Isa. 60:16).

As milk nourishes the body, so God's Word nourishes the soul. Milk is thus used as a metaphor for God's Word: "Come, all you who are thirsty, come to the waters; and you who have no money, come, buy and eat! Come, buy wine and milk without money and without cost" (Isa. 55:1). Peter taps into the same image, urging us to "crave pure spiritual milk" (1 Peter 2:2). Milk can also stand for that portion of God's Word that is easier to digest, the basic teachings. In that light the New Testament writers urge God's people to start with milk as do infants but then move into a more substantial diet of biblical teaching (1 Cor. 3:2; Heb. 5:12–13).

Mill (Millstone)

Bread was a staple in the diet of Bible times, and millstones were needed to turn coarse kernels of grain into finely ground flour that could be baked into that bread. This tool that allowed the operator to apply crushing force to the grain had to be made from a wear-resistant, hard stone like basalt (Job 41:24). Because of the passion to design a more efficient tool for grinding grain, the basalt mill took on a variety of forms throughout Bible times.

The hand mill of the Old Testament period is called the saddle quern. It consisted of two stones: a base called the saddle and a top stone called the rider (Deut. 24:6). The saddle was eighteen to thirty inches in length and approximately ten to fifteen inches in width. The upper surface of the saddle was recessed slightly inward so that the smaller, four-pound rider might nest into it. The operator of this mill would put a small portion of grain on the surface of the saddle. Then kneeling in front of this stone with one hand on either side of the loaf-shaped rider, the operator could push the rider back and forth on the saddle, grinding the grain between the two stones.

By New Testament times, there was an alternative to the saddle quern mill—the round hand mill. It consisted of two circular stones both eighteen to twenty-four inches in diameter, a stationary base and a rotating top stone. The upper stone nested into the lower stone, but this time the grinding was done with a rotating motion rather than a back-and-forth motion. This mill was typically operated by two persons (Matt. 24:41). Both would hold on to the wooden handle located on the perimeter of the upper stone.

Women grinding grain using a traditional handmill called a saddle quern.
Library of Congress, LC-matpc-06019/www.LifeintheHolyLand.com

A hole cut in the center of the top stone allowed grain to trickle into the space between the two stones. The operators would join forces to rotate the upper stone over the stationary lower stone to grind the grain.

New Testament culture also witnessed the use of a larger grain mill called the donkey mill. This round mill also had two parts. The substantial base of this mill narrowed to form a cone-shaped top. The upper portion of the mill had an hourglass shape. It was hollowed in the middle so that it could rest on top of and rotate around the cone of the base. The operator would pour grain in the open top of the mill and then rotate the upper portion of the mill to grind the grain. This was the largest of the mills described so far and was often turned by an animal, hence, its name, the donkey mill.

When decoding the rhetorical use of a grinding mill in the Bible, it is necessary to get the correct image in mind and then link that image to the appropriate cultural connotation. For example, certain New Testament passages have the large, heavy stones of the donkey mill in view. Jesus was particularly concerned about the most vulnerable members of his kingdom, children and those who were new to the faith. In several passages, he offers this dire warning: "If anyone causes one of these little ones who believe in me to sin, it would be better for him to have a large millstone [lit., "donkey's millstone"] hung around his neck and to be drowned in the depths of the sea" (Matt. 18:6; cf. Mark 9:42; Luke 17:2). This same kind of donkey millstone was thrown into the sea by an angel in John's vision.

The steady hum of the millstone became synonymous with the quiet regularity of everyday life. Because flour was ground every day to make one's daily bread, no one was to accept a millstone, even the upper part of a millstone, as collateral for a debt lest the life of the debtor be severely disrupted (Deut. 24:6). But something even worse was in store for rebellious Israel. When God allowed the Babylonians to overrun the Promised Land, any semblance of normalcy would cease: "I will banish from them the sounds of joy and gladness … the sound of millstones and the light of the lamp" (Jer. 25:10). The same image describes the disruption that will strike "Babylon": "The sound of a millstone will never be heard in you again" (Rev. 18:22). And it is the image of two women grinding grain at a round mill that will signal just how ordinary the day will be when the Son of Man returns (Matt. 24:41).

The more elite members of society did not operate a hand mill themselves but used slaves and servants to do that work. Thus operating a grinding mill can also carry the connotation of humble servitude. When Moses described the breadth of the plague against the firstborn in Egypt, he used a merism that named the top and bottom persons in society to rhetorically include all in the pronouncement: "Every firstborn son in Egypt will die, from the firstborn son of Pharaoh, who sits on the throne, to the firstborn son of the slave girl, who is at her hand mill" (Ex. 11:5). When the Philistines wished to humiliate the weakened Samson, they put him to work grinding with a mill (Judg. 16:21). In Isaiah's

judgment speech against Babylon, the tender and delicate "daughter of the Babylonians" is told to "take millstones and grind flour" as a symbol of her humiliation (Isa. 47:1–2), a humiliation that also would be known in Israel when "young men [were forced to] toil at the millstones" (Lam. 5:13). And it may not have been just the fact that a woman dealt Abimelech a lethal blow but that she did so using an upper millstone that so embarrassed him that he called for his armor-bearer to kill him on the spot (Judg. 9:53–54).

Mount Carmel

Mount Carmel is actually an extended mountain ridge that angles across the Promised Land from northwest to southeast for thirty-one miles, interrupting the connection between the coastal plain and the Jezreel Valley. Running parallel to the Mediterranean Sea for twenty miles, it finally dips its toe into the sea as the promontory many have come to call Mount Carmel.

Two qualities mark Mount Carmel as unique in the region, its elevation and its lush greenery. The highest portion of the Carmel ridge achieves an elevation of 1,790 feet above sea level. That height coupled with the very dense brush that filled its slopes in antiquity made it impractical for ancient travelers to climb up and over this natural obstacle. In a land where most of the topography favors north-south travel, Mount Carmel becomes a significant barrier to it. Consequently, travelers on the international highway were forced to seek out natural chalk valleys that bisected this mountain. Those easier passages are marked by prominent cities like Jokneam, Megiddo, and Taanach.

Although the name Carmel has been variously interpreted, all interpretations link this name to the mountain's lush greenery. The gardenlike appearance of the mountain slopes is related to its elevation and proximity to the sea. As moist air masses move northeast across this rising terrain, they are lifted and cooled, and therefore deposit above-average amounts of precipitation on the mountain's flanks. While other locations near Mount Carmel receive twenty inches of annual precipitation, Mount Carmel itself is virtually assured of thirty-two inches of rain. And because the higher slopes of Mount Carmel cool more efficiently at night, the moist sea air that blankets Mount Carmel condenses to form dew on as many as 250 nights each year, adding even more moisture to its fertile slopes.

Given the prominence of this landmark, it is not surprising that we see it used as a border in Bible times. Joshua told the tribe of Asher that their southwestern border would touch Mount Carmel (Josh. 19:26). Later the Assyrian king, Shalmaneser III, met with King Jehu of Israel to receive tribute from this Israelite king at Mount Carmel. An Assyrian campaign summary from the time of Shalmaneser strongly implies that Mount Carmel was serving as the border between Phoenicia and Israel at the time.

The elevation of Mount Carmel also helped mark it as sacred ground. Before the Israelites entered the land under the command of Joshua, the Egyptians knew it as "holy headland," rising terrain that came to sponsor an altar dedicated to the Lord (1 Kings 18:30). During the days of Ahab and Jezebel, this altar lay in ruins in no small part because the royal family had made the worship of Baal the state religion. Apparently it was during this time that the water rich heights of Mount Carmel became closely associ-

An aerial view of Mount Carmel and the surrounding area.

ated with the rain deity, Baal. Thus when Elijah challenged the prophets of Baal to a contest that would establish whether the Lord or Baal deserved Israel's worship, he did not select a neutral site for this contest but Mount Carmel (1 Kings 18:19–20). If Baal could be defeated on this, his home field, then the true weakness of this so-called deity would be evident to all. Following Baal's failure, Elijah descended from Mount Carmel to kill the pagan prophets, only to climb the mountain again (18:42). Here Elijah saw the fire that fell from heaven replaced by falling raindrops that further validated the Lord's right to this holy headland. In the days ahead, Elijah's successor, Elisha, frequented its flanks to maintain the connection between the Lord and this important mountain (2 Kings 2:25; 4:25).

When the biblical authors mention Mount Carmel in figurative passages, they refer to its elevation and lush beauty. In his judgment speech destined for Egyptian ears, Jeremiah foretells the coming of the great Babylonian king Nebuchadnezzar. This warrior is described as one "who is like Tabor among the mountains, like Carmel by the sea" (Jer. 46:18). Amos also employs the elevation of Mount Carmel, but in a geographical merism. The judgment of the Lord against Israel will induce many to flee, but Amos indicates that there is no place high or low enough to put them out of God's reach: "Though they hide themselves on the top of Carmel … [or] at the bottom of the sea" the Lord's hand will reach them (Amos 9:3).

The enduring beauty of Mount Carmel is used by the man wishing to capture in poetic verse the beauty of his beloved: "Your head crowns you like Mount Carmel" (Song 7:5). Even if other parts of the Promised Land might show the effects of a drought, the plants of Mount Carmel endured. It was unthinkable that they should wither; consequently, when the prophets spoke of unthinkable judgments that would befall people on earth, the unthinkable nature of those judgments was characterized by a Mount Carmel whose trees had dropped their leaves (Isa. 33:9) and whose foliage had withered (Amos 1:2; Nah. 1:4). But as judgment is pictured with a withered landscape, so restoration is pictured by the splendor of Mount Carmel's natural greenery (Isa. 35:2): "But I will bring Israel back to his own pasture and he will graze on Carmel and Bashan" (Jer. 50:19).

Mount of Olives

The Mount of Olives is the north-south mountain ridge that rises along the eastern edge of Jerusalem. The crest of this substantial, two-mile ridge is several hundred feet higher than the hills on which Jerusalem is built. It never was enclosed within the walled portion of Jerusalem, yet it has always been considered part of the city and has played a frequent role in its history. During Bible times this ridge was filled with olive trees, thus its name. The garden of Gethsemane was an industrial olive grove on the northern portion of this ridge that included a facility for pressing the oil from harvested olives. Gethsemane means "oil press."

When Jesus was visiting Jerusalem, he often retired to the Mount of Olives to teach his disciples privately or to spend the night (Luke 21:37; John 8:1). He even had a favorite place, an "olive grove," that doubled as a classroom (John 18:1–2). For a Galilean like Jesus who was accustomed to life in the open countryside, we can appreciate how the quiet privacy of such a location was inviting after spending time in the crowded and noisy sectors of Jerusalem.

Many churches and holy sites now dot the Mount of Olives because of the many Bible events that took place there. Two connotations associated with the Mount of Olives inform the way we hear those stories that are linked to this ridge. The first connotation is the connection between the Mount of Olives and escape into the Judean wilderness, which lays only a short walk east from the Mount of Olives. The Judean wilderness is a difficult place to live but a great place to hide from those wishing to harm you. We see it playing that role in the life of King David when his son attempted to take over the throne of Israel. Absalom had organized and executed a plan to seize his father's throne. The conspiracy against David was so strong that he elected to flee his capital; in doing so, he made the arduous climb up the Mount of Olives weeping all the way (2 Sam. 15:30). His eastward journey took him over this ridge and into the wilderness, replaying a scene from earlier days when David had used this very wilderness to hide from the ruthless pursuit of Saul. With this in view, consider the struggle of Jesus on the Mount of Olives. Following his meal in the upper room, he led the disciples onto the flanks of the Mount of Olives where he struggled with the next step in his Father's plan (Matt. 26:30, 38–39). Clearly part of this struggle was related to his location. Like David, Jesus could have used the Mount of

Modern tombs now cover the southern slopes of the Mount of Olives.

Olives as a springboard for escape. Just another forty-five minutes of walking up and over the summit put him into the Judean wilderness and out of harm's way. The Mount of Olives offered a route of escape as it had for David, but Jesus knew our salvation lay down a westward walk to the cross, not an eastward walk into the wilderness.

The second connotation associated with the Mount of Olives links this space with the coming of the Lord to judge the world and assume the role as its rightful leader. This message is clearly sent in Zechariah 14:4 and evidenced by the hundreds of graves that line the Mount of Olives today. Four events from Jesus' life gain new depth when viewed against this connotation. On the Sunday of Jesus' triumphal entry, he rode a donkey over the Mount of Olives toward Jerusalem (Matt. 21:1; Mark 11:1; Luke 19:29, 37). The excited and hopeful response of the crowd that met him on the way was generated by the connection between what Jesus was doing and where he was doing it. Jesus was doing what the long-promised King was to do — riding into Jerusalem on a donkey (Zech. 9:9). Were the dramatic events described in Zechariah 14:4 and taking place on the Mount of Olives coming to pass?

Second, the Mount of Olives also hosted Jesus' great discourse on the end of the age (Matt. 24 – 25; particularly 24:3). As they walked up this ridge, the disciples called Jesus' attention to the magnificent buildings of Jerusalem (24:1). Jesus used this opening to discuss both the coming fall of Jerusalem and the last days of this world's history. Given Zechariah's prophecy, which connects the end times and the Mount of Olives, we can again appreciate how the setting played a role in amplifying the message.

The third event from Jesus' life that finds new depth of meaning here is his arrest on the Mount of Olives. Judas knew the spot Jesus frequented, so under cover of darkness, he led those hostile to Jesus' cause to the very spot (John 18:2 – 3). Zechariah had prophesied that the Messiah would come here to end opposition to him and begin the judgment of the world, but in an ironic reversal, the opposition to Jesus finds success here and the process of judging Jesus begins.

The final event associated with Jesus' life, his ascension into heaven, also takes place on the Mount of Olives. Following his resurrection, Jesus led the disciples to the mount one last time (Acts 1:12). After he had disappeared from their sight, two angels explained the next step, one that builds a bridge to Zechariah's prophecy: "This same Jesus, who has been taken from you into heaven, will come back in the same way you have seen him go into heaven" (Acts 1:11). And he will come back as the conquering King in the same place from which his followers saw him ascend.

Mount Sinai (Horeb)

There is little doubt that whether the biblical authors speak of "Mount Sinai" or "Horeb" they are referring to the same location. Debate continues as to the exact peak and even the exact region in which to look for this special peak. But a convincing line of evidence that makes use of Israel's travel itinerary (Num. 33:1 – 36) places Mount Sinai in the southern reaches of the Sinai Peninsula. Furthermore, if early Christian tradition has it right, we can be more precise than that. The fourth-century monastery of St. Catherine's was built at the base of 7,482-foot Jebel Musa, declaring it to be the Mount Sinai of the Bible. Here and throughout the southern Sinai, red granite peaks rise frequently and dramatically from the valley floors, many reaching elevations topping 8,000 feet. But their grand beauty is enjoyed by very few, even today, because the peaks of the southern Sinai and the valleys that bisect them enjoy little vegetation due to annual rainfall totals that struggle to reach one inch.

After freeing the Israelites from their harsh life in Egypt, the Lord did not lead them directly to the Promised Land but brought them to Mount Sinai. Here he presented the covenant that was to define their attitudes and their behavior, as well as their relationship with him (Ex. 24:16; 31:18; 34:2–4, 29, 32). When the Lord came down on Mount Sinai (Ex. 19:11), this impres-

sive mountain hosted an unforgettable multisensory experience that included thunder, lightning, a thick cloud, trumpet blasts, smoke, fire, and an earthquake (19:16–19; 24:16–17). God told Moses to put limits in place so that no one might try to climb or even touch this mountain (19:12), but one wonders if anyone would have had the inclination to do so.

The Lord may have chosen to use this setting for the giving of the law for two reasons. First, the dominating peaks of this region put mortals in

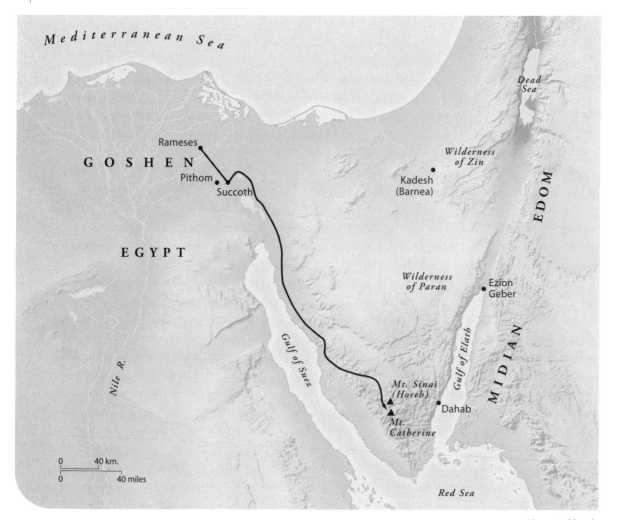

Mount Sinai.

their place. On the Nile Delta, the highest things on the horizon were all made by mortals, permitting, even encouraging, mortals to think more of themselves than they ought; but here in the southern Sinai, people are appropriately humbled by the magnificent terrain shaped by the hand of God. Here humans are inclined to feel as small as they are, with attitudes perfectly positioned to receive a message from God. In addition to that, the southern Sinai also facilitated understanding of a mortal's total dependence on the Lord. A lack of rain and other natural resources forced Israel to turn to God for survival. The few miracles mentioned in Exodus and Numbers must only be examples of the divine intervention necessary to sustain God's people in this place for nearly one year. Thus God may have selected Mount Sinai for this special moment in Israel's history because it provided a physical context that shaped a receptive audience for what he had to say.

When subsequent mention of Mount Sinai (Horeb) is made by the biblical authors, it serves to validate the instruction given on this mountain, recall the unique role of Israel, and distinguish the uniqueness of the Lord. The directives of the Law may have been written in human language and delivered to Israel by a human hand, but their origins were strictly divine. From time to time this critical fact is recalled by punctuating the Law itself with references to Mount Sinai: "The LORD our God made a covenant with us at Horeb" (Deut. 5:2; cf. Lev. 7:38; 25:1; 26:46; 27:34; Num. 28:6; Deut. 4:10, 15; 18:16). In the final chapter of the Old Testament, we read this encouragement: "Remember the law of my servant Moses, the decrees and laws I gave him at Horeb for all Israel" (Mal. 4:4). And in the New Testament, Paul makes the mountain nearly synonymous with the covenant itself (Gal. 4:24–25).

This mountain not only helps validate the directives God gave there, but it also helps to distinguish Israel as a unique people. Unlike any other nation on earth, "the LORD spoke to you face to face out of the fire on the mountain" (Deut. 5:4). Thus the experience of Israel on Mount Sinai is listed among those moments in Israel's history that mark them as God's special people with a special calling from the Lord (Neh. 9:13; Acts 7:38). At one point in Elijah's life, he was not feeling very special. Discouraged, he traveled all the way from the Promised Land to "Horeb, the mountain of God" (1 Kings 19:8). And on the flanks of the mountain where Israel had its mission defined, God redefined Elijah's role and reanimated his passion for that mission.

Finally, the events occurring on Mount Sinai also translated into a title that served to mark the Lord as unique among competing deities. In poetic verse the Lord is called "the One of Sinai" (Judg. 5:5; Ps. 68:8). Many deities clamored for Israel's attention, but only "the One" had made his presence known at Mount Sinai. In the image presented by the inspired poet, the building of the temple in Jerusalem gave this unique God the opportunity to move from one mountain to the next. The same God who had manifested his presence at Mount Sinai moved from that peak to the sanctuary on Mount Zion (Ps. 68:17).

Mountain

Specific mountains like Mount Sinai and Mount Zion are mentioned or alluded to by the biblical authors because these mountains were the site of key events or important buildings. Here the focus is not on specific mountains, but on the mountainous terrain of the Promised Land. For those living in this special land, mountains were never out of sight, because a spine of mountains stretches north and south through the heart of Canaan. From Lower Galilee to Judah, this central mountain zone steadily increases in altitude from 1,500 feet to well over 3,300 feet above sea level. And as the mountains get higher, they also press closer to one another, forming the narrow V-shaped valleys so characteristic of the Judean highlands.

This change in topography brings a necessary change in culture as well. Traveling from north to south in this zone of the Promised Land, we find the growing of grain becoming more difficult and international commerce fading. Yet the same terrain that discourages international trade was also a protective shield that made invasion of the interior more difficult. The psalmist turns that reality into this comforting message: "As the mountains surround Jerusalem, so the LORD surrounds his people both now and forevermore" (Ps. 125:2).

Those living among these mountains used them in a variety of ways. When Joshua was dividing up the Promised Land among God's people, mountain ridges served as natural boundaries between tribal allotments (Josh. 15:8–9; 18:13–16). High mountain ridges also provided viewing platforms for lookout posts that doubled as signaling stations (Isa. 13:2; 18:3; 40:9). And if a foreign army advanced inland and threatened the cities, those who made their homes in those cities would flee into the clefts of rising terrain to seek refuge from the attack (Judg. 6:2; Jer.

Mountainous terrain runs north and south through the heart of Israel.

© John A. Beck

16:16; Lam. 4:19; Ezek. 7:16; 34:6; Matt. 24:16; Mark 13:14; Luke 21:21; 23:30; Heb. 11:38). The enemy invasions that caused such flight were often precipitated by Israel's assimilation into pagan culture that included the worship of false gods at mountain shrines (Deut. 12:2; Isa. 57:7; 65:7; Jer. 3:23; Ezek. 18:6, 11, 15; 22:9; Hos. 4:13).

But God had given the mountains to Israel for a different purpose; they were to provide a variety of blessings for his chosen people. Precious metals might be obtained from those mountainsides, and building stones could be quarried from their slopes (Job 28:9). Those same highlands provided habitat for the game the Israelites might hunt and eat (1 Sam. 26:20; Ps. 76:4). The green pastures fed by the rainfall would, in turn, feed the sheep and goats (Ezek. 34:13 – 14; Matt. 18:12). And farmers would grow grain, grapes, and olives on their terraced slopes (Ps. 72:3, 16; Jer. 31:5; Joel 3:18; Amos 9:13). Finally, the less frequented higher elevations provided individuals with a quiet place that was suitable for mourning, meditation, praying, and private instruction (Judg. 11:37 – 38; Matt. 14:23; 15:29; Mark 6:46; John 6:15).

The biblical authors also call attention to three qualities of the mountains again and again in their writings: their massive size, their endurance, and their role in blocking travel. "Big" is of course a relative term; and in the culture of Bible times, the biggest things one could point out were the mountains. They are first mentioned in Genesis where they give scale to the depth of the floodwaters (Gen. 7:19 – 20; 8:4 – 5). The massive size of the mountains is also brought before the eyes of Bible readers in a bid to help us appreciate the power of our God who can weigh these mountain as well as cause them to shake, tremble, crumble, skip, and melt like wax (Pss.

18:7; 97:5; 114:4; Isa. 5:25; 40:12; 64:3; Mic. 1:4). Therefore we do not need to fear even if "the mountains fall into the heart of the sea" (Ps. 46:2), for our God is bigger than the splash that would cause.

In addition to noting the massive size of the mountains, the Bible also observes their enduring nature. The majority of the central mountain zone in the Promised Land is composed of hard limestone that erodes at a rate of one centimeter every thousand years. So while slow and steady erosion did occur, people did not observe changes in the mountains within their lifetime, suggesting that the mountains endure forever. By contrast the Lord is even older than those mountains (Ps. 90:2), as is the divine wisdom that shaped them (Prov. 8:25). The love and righteousness of God on which we so desperately depend are even more enduring than that hard limestone (Ps. 36:6). He promises, "Though the mountains be shaken and the hills be removed, yet my unfailing love for you will not be shaken nor my covenant of peace be removed" (Isa. 54:10). And while earthly kingdoms will come and go, there is one kingdom that will both destroy and outlast them all—the eternal kingdom of God. In Daniel's vision that kingdom is pictured as a great rock; it "struck the statue [and] became a huge mountain and filled the whole earth" (Dan. 2:35; see vv. 44 – 45).

Mountains in Bible times also presented significant obstructions to travel. In the hill country of the Promised Land, it was rare that the best route between two places was a direct route. Rising terrain often caused one to detour many miles while traveling. But when the Lord decides to make it easier for his anointed ones to accomplish their assigned mission, the mountains that block a more direct route are leveled or removed (Isa. 40:4; 45:2; 49:11; Zech. 4:7; Luke 3:5).

Mountain Goat. *See* Ibex.

Myrrh

Myrrh is not native to the Promised Land but had to be imported from either southern Arabia or eastern Africa where various shrubs of the genus *Commiphora* grow. The woody shrubs of this genus have short, stiff, thorny branches. The shrubs naturally exude a gummy resin, and by incising the branches, the amount of resin available for commercial harvest can be increased. When the resin dries, it is reddish brown in color and very bitter to the taste. Nevertheless, it gives off a strong but pleasant scent that has variously been described as earthy, woody, and balsamic. The dried resin is either ground for use in incense burners or diluted to make oil. In either case, the processed commodity was very valuable, carried by traders, and distributed throughout the ancient Near East (Gen. 37:25; Rev. 18:13).

Myrrh is either ground for use in incense burners or diluted to make oil.

Todd Bolen/www.BiblePlaces.com

Myrrh was used in a variety of ways. In a world without deodorant and air fresheners, myrrh was burned by the well-to-do to improve the scent of a room or worn as a personal fragrance to cover body odor. When Esther and the other harem women went through a rigorous beauty regimen before being presented to the Persian king Xerxes, they were treated with oil of myrrh for six months so that their skin would be permeated with the smell of the exotic scent (Esth. 2:12). But there is more to myrrh than first meets the nose; various cultures also discovered the antiseptic nature of this product and applied it to wounds and sores. For those living in Egypt, myrrh even had a role to play after death, used as one of the ingredients in the embalming process. The Israelites had a very special use for myrrh. They anointed individuals and ordinary objects with a special oil containing myrrh to mark them as set aside for special service to the Lord (Ex. 30:23).

The role of myrrh as a symbol of sensual stimulation is the one we find most often when reading the Bible. The adulteress included the mention of her bed being perfumed with myrrh and other spices in her intoxicating invitation to young men (Prov. 7:17). But this illicit use of myrrh stands in contrast to the wholesome imagery used elsewhere. Psalm 45 is a wedding song composed and used in connection with the marriage of a king. As this king rides to the wedding ceremony, he is smartly dressed with his sword at his side. He not only looks great; he also smells great, poised for the delights of his wedding day: "All your robes are fragrant with myrrh" (Ps. 45:8). Given the connection of myrrh to marriage delights, we are not surprised to find it used more often in the Song of Songs than in any other Bible book. Here the young bride-to-be wears a sachet of myrrh between her breasts, which she likens to her beloved (Song 1:13); her breasts themselves are likened to a "mountain of myrrh" and "hill of incense" (4:6). She is further pictured as a garden that includes myrrh (4:14; 5:1) and as one whose hands drip with myrrh (5:5). The pleasant scent of myrrh and all the sensual overtones that go with it are also linked to the man in the Song who is "perfumed with myrrh" (3:6) and whose "lips are like lilies dripping with myrrh" (5:13).

This expensive product also plays a literary role in two familiar Bible stories. In the first, myrrh appears shortly after we meet Joseph who finds himself in a most perilous situation; the jealousy of his brothers had matured into a hate-filled plan to murder the upstart brother and his dreams of lording it over them. But when a caravan of traders passed nearby, they changed the course of their plan and Joseph's fate. Joseph was sold to the traders and added to the products they carried, which included "spices, balm, and myrrh" (Gen. 37:25). Pound for pound, that precious myrrh was much more valuable than the slave Joseph had become. This apparently incidental mention of myrrh takes on new depth when it occurs again in Joseph's story. Fearing the worst but hoping for the best, Jacob agreed to send Benjamin to Egypt as his sons again sought grain from the Egyptian official who seemed so curious about them. To influence the goodwill of that official, Jacob sent along some of the best products of the land and a special import as well, myrrh (Gen. 43:11). At the second mention of myrrh, the attentive reader is struck by how dramatically Joseph's fortunes had been reversed. The young man who had become a commodity like myrrh and was transported with the myrrh to Egypt had now become so influential that his favor was being curried by a special gift of myrrh.

Finally, we see myrrh appearing both at the opening and close of Jesus' life. Myrrh was more precious per ounce than gold, and the magi who came to honor the newborn King of the Jews brought gifts of both (Matt. 2:11). On the day of Jesus' death, he was honored once again with myrrh. Joseph of Arimathea and Nicodemus secured Jesus' body after his crucifixion and did what they could in this difficult time to honor one who had been so dishonored in the hours before. They prepared his body for burial with a "mixture of myrrh and aloes" (John 19:39).

N

Nazareth

The village of Nazareth was tucked into a small valley on the prominent Nazareth ridge in the region of Lower Galilee. Every town or city has distinctive qualities, and first-century Nazareth was no exception. This small village was char-acterized by its size, insignificance, and Jewish nationalism. Nazareth was a small village by anyone's standards, with a population of no more than three hundred residents. Although this village existed during Old Testament times, it is unmentioned there, just as it is unmentioned by the Jewish historian Josephus and by the Jewish traditional writings. The smallness of Nazareth joined with its isolation to make it an insignificant place; but those same qualities also made it a haven for those who wished to isolate themselves from contemporary culture. The Romans and the Jewish leaders who supported their presence in Israel wanted the Promised Land to become more integrated with the ideology and culture of the larger Roman world. This was offensive to Jews who heeded God's call for them to be unique among the nations, so they sought escape from the process of hellenization in places like Nazareth.

As we trace mention of Nazareth in the New Testament, we find it to be a place that shaped Jesus and that Jesus sought to shape. Although Jesus was born in Bethlehem, he would grow up in Nazareth, the village of Mary and Joseph, which is even called their "own town" (Luke 1:26; 2:4, 39). Where you grow up says something about who you are, and that was certainly true of Jesus. We are permitted only a fleeting glimpse of Jesus' life in Nazareth, the time when "Jesus grew in wisdom and stature, and in favor with God and men" (Luke 2:52). But it is enough for us to get the impression that Jesus' understanding of the world and himself, his social skills, and his early perspective on life were honed by the culture of Nazareth.

Matthew observes that Jesus' presence in Nazareth fulfills the prophecy that said, "He will be called a Nazarene" (Matt. 2:23). Exactly which prophecy Matthew has in mind remains a bit of a puzzle. He may be thinking of Isaiah 11:1, which speaks of the coming Messiah as a shoot (Heb., *ntsr*), or he may be playing on the insignificance of this village, which informs the way Jesus fulfills Isaiah 53:3, the prophecy that says the coming Messiah will often face public humiliation and be despised. In either case, there is no doubt that Nazareth created something of a public relations challenge for Jesus. Nathanael, who was from a nearby village, wondered aloud upon hearing that Jesus was from Nazareth: "Nazareth! Can anything good come from there?" (John 1:46). So while some like Matthew celebrated the relationship between Jesus and this village, others disparaged it, including the Romans. When Jesus was crucified, they put a notice above Jesus' head that mockingly stressed the disconnection between his claims and his roots in Nazareth. It read:

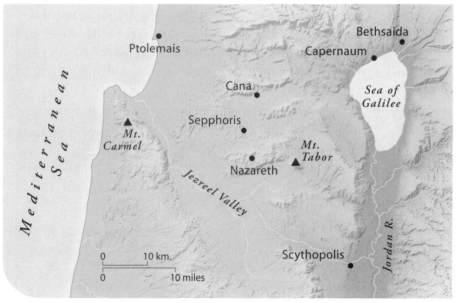

Nazareth.

"JESUS OF NAZARETH, THE KING OF THE JEWS" (John 19:19).

Eventually Jesus made the very important move from Nazareth to Capernaum, a move that also fulfilled Old Testament prophecy (Matt. 4:13 – 16). Yet even after Jesus made this strategic move from the isolation of Nazareth to the public thoroughfare of Capernaum, his identity was still linked with Nazareth. He is often referred to as "Jesus of Nazareth" as a way of distinguishing him from other men who also had been given the name Jesus. Philip, Peter, and Paul all call him Jesus of Nazareth (John 1:45; Acts 2:22; 3:6; 10:38; 26:9). The crowds of faithful followers know him by that name (Matt. 21:11; Mark 10:47; Luke 18:37; 24:19). Even Jesus' mortal opponents and evil spirits refer to him as Jesus of Nazareth (Matt. 26:71; Mark 1:24; Luke 4:34; John 18:5, 7; Acts 6:14).

Clearly Nazareth helped shape the person and reputation of Jesus, but Nazareth was also a village that Jesus sought to shape by his teaching. For all the wonderful advantages of small village life that Nazareth had to offer, it carried with it one liability that becomes apparent when Jesus returned to Nazareth to speak in the synagogue there (Luke 4:14 – 30). Upon entering the synagogue on the Sabbath, Jesus was given the privilege of reading from Isaiah; and as a rabbi, he was invited to offer interpretation of the text as well. After he had read the beautiful words of Isaiah 61:1 – 2, which speak of the Messiah's work on earth, he delivered this ground-shaking interpretation: "Today this scripture is fulfilled in your hearing" (Luke 4:21). At first everyone celebrated this announcement. Imagine the welling pride of those in despised Nazareth; finally this insufferable village would receive some praise, because none other than the Messiah himself had grown up there. But within moments, this adulation turned to outrage as Jesus touched on the fact that Gentiles would be part of his kingdom (4:24 – 27). Jesus had dared put his finger on the very part of Nazareth's culture he wished to change; this Jewish community saw no room for Gentiles in a future kingdom. Sadly, instead of expanding their vision of God's kingdom, they rejected Jesus' message and attempted to use the local landscape to execute him (4:28 – 30).

Net (Trap)

The nets mentioned in the Bible fit into two general categories, hunting nets and fishing nets. The hunting nets were primarily designed to capture deer and birds. One type of hunting net was carefully camouflaged and placed over a deep pit. When an unsuspecting deer walked over the pit, the net collapsed under the animal's weight, entangling its legs while confining it in the pit. A second type of hunting net was set up vertically and laid out in a sweeping half circle where natural cover allowed it to be camouflaged and where natural features limited potential escape routes. In this case hunters would rush a herd of deer, directing them to flee in the direction of this improvised corral. When a panicked deer dashed into the net, the mesh collapsed and entangled it, preventing its escape. A third type of hunting net was directed primarily at fowl. In this case the net was either thrown from hiding or collapsed over the unsuspecting birds by well-hidden hunters. Two principles guided the laying and deploying of all such nets. First, the net had to be carefully hidden. As the proverb states, "How useless to spread a net in full view of all the birds!" (Prov. 1:17). Second, the net had to effectively entangle the legs or wings of the prey so that it could not use its natural escape skills (Ps. 57:6; Prov. 29:5).

Fishing nets for trolling the inland waters of the Promised Land are also mentioned in the Bible; and they, too, are of more than one type. The cast net was used to fish in the shallows near shore (Mark 1:16). It was a round net some twenty to twenty-five feet in diameter with weights tied around the perimeter. The fisherman would swing this net over his head to unfurl the net to its full diameter; he would then throw the net over the suspected location of the fish that would be trapped beneath it. A second type of net was the dragnet (Ezek. 47:10; Hab. 1:15). This net was also used along the shoreline but harvested fish from a much larger area. One end of this hundred-yard-long dragnet was pulled perpendicular to the shoreline by a boat.

Galilee fishermen using a dragnet.
Library of Congress, LC-matpc-05687/www.LifeintheHolyLand.com

Floats on the top line of the net and weights on the bottom line of the net kept it oriented vertically as it was pulled through the water. One team of fisherman remained on shore and walked up the beach as the boat proceeded parallel to the shore with the net held taut between the two. Eventually the boat would turn back toward the shore, pulling the arcing net and the captured fish to shore. A third type of fishing net was used in the deeper water of the lake; that was the trammel net (Luke 5:1 – 11). Like the dragnet, the trammel net was a long net held vertically by floats and weights, but this net was deployed in a full circle by the crew of the fishing boat. Once this aquatic corral was in place, a fisherman would move to the center of the corral and create a disturbance that would panic the fish into fleeing away from him and toward entanglement in the net.

While real nets are mentioned by the biblical writers, metaphorical nets appear more frequently. The ungodly are said to lay such nets in the path of the innocent to bring them harm. The net itself might be made of flattery, economic exploitation, legal manipulation, or slander (Pss. 10:9; 140:5; Prov. 29:5; Hos. 5:1). But the result is always the same—the innocent are put into desperate circumstances leading to statements like this: "They spread a net for my feet—I was bowed down in distress" (Ps. 57:6). So it is that mortals are faced with a walk through life beset by unexpected abuses just "as fish are caught in a cruel net, or birds are taken in a snare" (Eccl. 9:12). Yet at times, God sees to it that the wicked are caught in the net they have laid for the innocent (Pss. 9:15; 35:7 – 8; 57:6; 141:10).

The net can also represent divinely sponsored misfortune that befalls those in need of correction. Hosea criticized the fickle nature of Israel, comparing this people to a senseless dove that would be caught: "When they go, I will throw my net over them; I will pull them down like birds of the air" (Hos. 7:12). Years later the destruction, famine, and sword that would descend upon Jerusalem left the sons of Jerusalem "like antelope caught in a net" (Isa. 51:20; cf. Lam. 1:13). Among the royal art pieces of Mesopotamia, we have a relief depicting war captives entangled in a net. This metaphor is also used by the Lord as he describes the nature of the exile that would be faced by princes and people alike (Ezek. 17:20; 19:8; Hab. 1:15 – 17). "I will spread my net for him, and he will be caught in my snare; I will bring him to Babylonia" (Ezek. 12:13).

Because of Jesus' proximity to the Sea of Galilee and because a number of his disciples were fishermen, fishing nets of various types are common in the Gospels. In fact, Simon Peter and Andrew were fishing with cast nets along this inland lake when Jesus called them to become "fishers of men" (Matt. 4:19). Their response was immediate: "At once they left their nets and followed him" (v. 20). For them the nets were not merely a way to pass idle time, but represented economic stability, which was not replaced by what Jesus was offering. Thus the surrender of this tool illustrates a powerful faith commitment.

Jesus also used the net as a metaphor for the kingdom of heaven (Matt. 13:47). It is likened to the deep-water trammel net let down into the lake to catch all kinds of fish. While this parable acknowledges that a time is coming when there will be a separation of the good and bad fish, the mission of the disciples was not to separate but to gather from the world in the same way a fishing net indiscriminately gathers from the sea. This message was clearly reinforced by the disciples' memory of two parallel miracles associated with the calling and recalling of the disciples to ministry. In each case we observe a net inexplicably bursting with all kinds of fish (Luke 5:2 – 7; John 21:5 – 8).

O

Oil (Olive Oil)

Olive oil was a signature product of the Promised Land (Deut. 8:8). To obtain this precious oil, the olive harvest underwent multiple pressings. During the first press, which produced the best oil, the olives were placed in a concave, circular basin. An upright stone wheel that was custom fit to roll around within the concave basin of the press crushed the olives into a gooey pulp. This pulp was then placed in baskets that sat above a receptacle collecting the precious virgin olive oil. Subsequent pressings made use of a beam press. The olive-filled baskets drained of the virgin oil were now placed beneath a heavy wooden beam anchored to a wall, yet capable of moving in the vertical plane. With weights added to the far end of the beam and the beam itself acting like a lever, this press exerted a powerful force on the baskets, causing more oil to flow from the crushed olives, which was collected in a basin located alongside the press.

The oil obtained from these pressings was used in both ordinary and sacred ways. It is no exaggeration to say that the people of the Bible came into contact with oil every day. It was a staple in the kitchen used in the preparation of food (Prov. 21:20), as likely to be found in a military outpost as it was in the poorest of homes (1 Kings 17:12–16; 2 Chron. 11:11). When evening came or when the dark corner of a room required searching, an olive oil lamp provided the needed illumination. Wise was the one who kept extra oil at the ready, particularly for special occasions (Matt. 25:3–10). Olive oil was also mixed with sweet-smelling ingredients to produce body lotions worn on a daily basis by virtually everyone (Eccl. 9:8; Song 1:3, NIV "perfume"; Amos 6:6, NIV "lotions"). With bathwater in short supply and dry air threatening the vitality of the skin, this special oil masked body odors and kept the skin moist and supple. In the latter regard, Jesus urged those who were fasting to keep using this oil so as not to call unneeded attention to themselves (Matt. 6:17). Olive oil was further used to soothe the wounds of the injured (Isa. 1:6; Luke 10:34) as well as treat leather shields so they would not crack when dry (2 Sam. 1:21; Isa. 21:5). When a special guest arrived, protocol required that this guest be honored with the anointing of oil, a blessing mentioned in David's famous psalm (Ps. 23:5) and a courtesy a host failed to extend to Jesus (Luke 7:46). Given the widespread and fundamental roles oil played, we can appreciate why such oil assumes the essential nature of currency. It could be used to pay one's debts (2 Kings 4:1–7), pay tribute to an anticipated ally (Hos. 12:1), hire foreign craftsmen, and purchase imported lumber (1 Kings 5:11; Ezra 3:7).

Oil also played an important role in Israel's sacred life. We encounter oil again and again in Exodus and Leviticus where it becomes an intimate part of the worship life in Israel, particularly in connection with the grain offering (Lev. 2:1–7). Fine oil that produced little smoke provided illumination in God's sanctuary (Ex. 27:20), and oil made from a special recipe was used to anoint both components of the sanctuary and the clergy who served there (30:22–33). This oil, which appears in so many corners of Israel's worship life, clearly has a link to the Promised Land so well known for its olive oil. And perhaps that is the point. The olive oil used in worship served as a link to the land that further recalled all the promises God had linked to the land.

The symbolic and metaphorical use of oil by the biblical authors naturally follows. The Lord is the one who provided the necessary circumstances for the olives to mature and ripen on the tree (Ps. 104:14–15). Thus an abundance of oil was symbolic of divine favor and blessing (Deut. 7:13; 11:14). Recalling better times in his life, Job described them as a time when "the rock poured out for me streams of olive oil" (Job 29:6). Both Jeremiah and Joel link a time of spiritual restoration with a time when the holding basins will overflow with oil (Jer. 31:12; Joel 2:19, 24). Thus the season of the Lord's favor is marked by the "oil of joy" or the "oil of gladness" (Ps. 45:7; Isa. 61:3; Heb. 1:9). In contrast the displeasure of the Lord at Israel's apostasy was marked by a divinely sponsored shortage of this vital oil. Even before they were established in the Promised Land, God warned that indifference to his covenant would lead to empty oil jars and lamps that lacked fuel (Deut. 28:40, 51; Joel 1:10; Hag. 1:11). "You will plant but not harvest; you will press olives but not use the oil on yourselves" (Mic. 6:15).

Oil also appears as a metaphor for spoken language and one's reputation. The psalmist welcomes correction that comes from a righteous man; it is like "oil on my head" (Ps.

141:5). But not all speech is as beneficial as it may sound. Other inspired poets hold up the hand of caution, for those who speak to us do not always have our best interests in mind. A companion feigning loyalty is one whose "words are more soothing than oil, yet they are drawn swords" (Ps. 55:21). The same warning attends the words of the adulteress: her "speech is smoother than oil" (Prov. 5:3). For a man to keep a good reputation, he must decline her words and other invitations to sin. Every effort must be made to maintain a good name, for that good name is more precious than the finest oil (Eccl. 7:1; NIV "perfume").

Owl

The eagle owl, the scops owl, and the little owl are the most common owls of Israel today. The eagle owl, or great owl, is the largest member of the owl family in the region, standing thirty inches tall with a wingspan of up to seventy-nine inches. This bird is marked not only by its size but also by its two upright ear tufts and haunting

Reconstrucion of a beam press at Tel Hazor. This type of press was widely used to obtain precious olive oil.

www.HolyLandPhotos.org

orange eyes. The scops owl, or desert owl, is only eight inches long, has a more slender body, and much shorter ear tufts. The little owl has no ear tufts at all and a plump, round face. It is slightly larger than the scops owl and is the most likely of the three to be seen during the daylight hours.

These owls and others that reside in the Promised Land have a number of common traits. Owls are seen less frequently by people because they prefer to live in remote areas and because their preferred time of activity is at night when most humans are asleep. During the daylight hours they are difficult to spot because of the plumage they sport. Dressed in dusky plumage sporting tones of gray to brown often broken with white spots or streaks, owls blend into the

A little owl.
© Graham Taylor/www.BigStockPhoto.com

trees, rocks, and ruins where they roost during the daylight hours. In fact, people are more likely to hear an owl than see one. All the owls vocalize and may be distinguished from one another by the combinations of hoots or whistles that comprise their twilight communication.

Bible translations and Bible scholars have struggled in their bid to identify the owls mentioned in the Old Testament. Up to eight Hebrew words have been linked to the owl, but the NIV translators mention only six: the horned owl, screech owl, little owl, great owl, white owl, and desert owl. It is difficult to link a specific owl with a specific Hebrew word, because biblical references to the owl are few and offer limited clues regarding appearance or vocalization that would be most helpful in making the identification certain. So while the specific type of owl the biblical author may have in view in any one passage will remain a matter for discussion, the fact that an owl of some kind is being mentioned in such passages seems certain.

A list of owls including the six types mentioned above is found in the larger list of animals defined by the Lord as unclean and so unfit for the diet of the Israelites (Lev. 11:16–18; Deut. 14:15–17). The Israelites themselves were not permitted to eat meat from which the blood had not been properly drained (Deut. 12:16). And because the owl was a bird of prey that ate meat with blood in it, the eating of an owl would mean that the person eating it would be participating in the diet of the owl. Thus the owl was placed on the list of prohibited food.

The biblical authors use the owl in two types of metaphor. The first is linked to the haunting call of the owl. Micah describes the horrible judgments that would fall upon Samaria and Jerusalem because those cities had abandoned their faithful walk with the Lord. Far from being a distant reporter of these events, Micah speaks of the distress it has brought to his life: "Because of this I will weep and wail; I will go about barefoot and naked. I will howl like a jackal and moan like an owl" (Mic. 1:8).

All of the other instances where the owl is used as a metaphor play on this bird's desire to live in isolation from mortals. In two cases the Lord's inspired poets describe themselves as isolated owls. Difficult days are always made easier by the kind touch and comforting words of others, while isolation only adds to the burden. As Job suffered through multiple challenges in his life, he described himself as a "companion of owls" (Job 30:29) — that is, someone who spends time alone. And severe affliction lead the psalmist to say, "I am like a desert owl, like an owl among the ruins" (Ps. 102:6).

Owls also appear in the judgment speeches of the prophets. God often used nations to correct the erring attitudes and behavior of his people. When such nations rebelled against the Lord,

they would feel the weight of God's judgment, judgment that would find their cities abandoned to the owls. Of Assyria we are told, "The desert owl and the screech owl will roost on her columns. Their calls will echo through the windows" (Zeph. 2:14). The same message was given to Babylon: "There the owl will dwell. It will never again be inhabited or lived in from generation to generation" (Jer. 50:39; cf. Isa. 13:21; 14:23). The most sustained use of this metaphor is reserved for Edom. In the highlands where the Edomites had built their nests and preyed upon others from the heights like the eagle (Obad. 4), divine judgment promised that the metaphorical eagle would be replaced by the owl. "The desert owl and screech owl will possess it; the great owl and the raven will nest there" (Isa. 34:11). "She will become a haunt for jackals, a home for owls" (v. 13). "The owl will nest there and lay eggs, she will hatch them, and care for her young under the shadow of her wings" (v. 15).

P

Palm Tree

The palm trees of the Bible are date palms, trees that have much to offer those living near them. Their deep, water-seeking root systems support long, slender trunks that culminate in circles of fanlike fronds that shade the fruit maturing beneath them. A full-grown date palm takes twenty years to mature and can be more than ninety feet tall, including the circle of fronds, which itself can be from seven to ten feet in diameter. Those living in Bible times found a use for

nearly every component of the tree. The fruit, which matures at the close of the summer, was eaten fresh or dried and pressed into cakes. It was also mashed and boiled down into an edible paste called *dibs*, which was spread on bread. And some in the ancient Near East used the harvested fruit to make liqueur or wine. Apart from the fruit, the palm fronds were used as roofing material while fibers from the tree were woven to make mats, baskets, ropes, sandals, and other household items.

Important locations in the ancient world could be marked either by a great number of palm trees or by the presence of a singular, prominent tree. As the Israelites traveled south through the forbidding Sinai wilderness, they came upon an oasis distinguished both by the number of springs and the presence of seventy palm trees (Ex. 15:27; Num. 33:9). Such a cluster of palms was a welcome sight in this dry land, promising copious water and much-needed shade. The city of Jericho was distinguished by the groves of date palms that grew in its environs and the commercial harvest of dates that occurred there. This city was known by a second and perhaps earlier name, "City of Palms" (Deut. 34:3; Judg. 1:16; 3:13; 2 Chron. 28:15). In contrast a single prominent palm, which came to be called the Palm of Deborah, marked a location between Ramah and Bethel where Deborah typically sat to resolve disputes (Judg. 4:5).

In the culture of Bible times, the palm tree was a symbol of both fertility and freedom. Because the palm tree is the premier tree of the wilderness oasis, it is naturally associated with water and survival. This, in addition to its copious clusters

A date palm.
Copyright 1995-2011 Phoenix Data Systems

of fruit, made it an ancient symbol of blessing and fertility. Because its fruit is harvested at the close of summer, marking the end of the harvest season, it came to play an important role in the Feast of Tabernacles (*Sukkot*), which the Israelites celebrated in the fall of the year. God directed his people to gather palm fronds along with the branches from other trees to make temporary shelters in which they could live during the festival (Lev. 23:40; Neh. 8:15). The shelters recalled the temporary housing used by the Israelites during their stay in the wilderness; and the palm branches, linked to agricultural fertility, reminded God's people to give thanks for the bounty of that season's harvest. The overtones of blessing and fertility also saw the palm included in the artwork of both Solomon's and Ezekiel's temples (1 Kings 6:29, 32, 35; 2 Chron. 3:5; Ezek. 40:22, 26, 31, 34, 37; 41:18, 20, 25, 26). The date palm was conspicuously incorporated into the walls, doors, and gates because it was a symbol of the fertility, bounty, and blessings that God regularly brought into the lives of his people.

Second, the palm tree became a symbol of Jewish victory and freedom. We see this connotation come to life during the time between the Old and New Testaments when palm branches attend Simon's victorious entry into Jerusalem and liberation of the temple (1 Macc. 13:51; 2 Macc. 10:7). This symbolic association is further confirmed in a backhanded way by the Roman emperor Vespasian. He commemorated his AD 70 victory over Jerusalem by minting a coin known as the JUDAEA CAPTA coin. On one side of that coin, we find a Roman soldier standing tall over a humbled and grieving Jewish woman. Between the two is a palm tree, the symbol of Jewish freedom; it was incorporated into the design of the coin to mock the Jewish quest for political freedom.

The palm tree as a symbol of Jewish freedom and independence may be the best explanation for the action of the crowds on the Sunday of Jesus' triumphal entry (Palm Sunday). As Jesus made his way down the Mount of Olives, the crowds excitedly shouted, "Blessed is the King of Israel!" while waving palm branches (John 12:13). John is the only one to specifically mention this detail. One wonders if that had something to do with the palm branches he saw being waved in another celebration, the one in heaven. Thousands from every nation stood before the Lamb of God to celebrate the victorious salvation he had brought to them: "They were wearing white robes and were holding palm branches in their hands" (Rev. 7:9).

Finally, the palm tree is used metaphorically. The tall, slender elegance of the young woman in the Song of Songs is likened to the palm tree (Song 7:7–8). This young woman is unnamed, but other young women who displayed similar beauty are given the name Tamar, the Hebrew word for the date palm (Gen. 38:6; 2 Sam. 13:1;

14:27). In another figure of speech, the psalmist contrasts the situation of the righteous and the wicked by likening the wicked to the short-lived and the righteous to the enduring, upright palm (Ps. 92:7, 12). The tall palm tree is also contrasted to the sagging reed in two judgment speeches, one directed against Israel and the other against Egypt. In both cases the comparison is part of a merism designed to indicate that everyone in these two societies will experience God's anger: "So the LORD will cut off from Israel head and tail, both palm branch and reed in a single day" (Isa. 9:14; cf. 19:15).

Pasture (Pastureland)

Every family needed access to a pasture, because this was the most efficient way to meet the daily nutritional needs of the sheep, goats, camels, and donkeys under their care. A pasture is natural grassland, whether in a valley, on the slope of a hill, or in the wilderness where low-growing grasses flourish without the aid of human cultivation. The amount of vegetation and the quality of the vegetation offered by a pasture varied considerably based on the quality of the soil, the amount of local rainfall, and the rate of evaporation. "Desert pastures" were of lower quality (Jer. 9:10) while "well-watered" (Ezek. 45:15), "fertile pasturelands" (Mic. 7:14) were prized. But even good pastures can go bad. When the rain stopped and a drought gripped the land, the pastures needed to meet the nutritional needs of the family animals withered (Gen. 47:4; 1 Kings 18:5–6; Jer. 14:6; Joel 1:19–20). Pastureland could also be ruined by an invasion of locusts or an invasion of soldiers (Joel 1:18). And even high-quality pastures could be ruined if animals were allowed to overgraze them. The ancients knew from personal experience that a given amount of pastureland was able to support only a certain number of animals (Gen. 13:6). What is more, if those animals are allowed to graze too long in one location, they could damage the roots of the plants, permanently damaging this otherwise renewable resource (Ezek. 34:18).

Land ownership and grazing rights played a role in defining where one could pasture the family animals. On the one hand, the Lord maintained the ultimate ownership of the land (Lev. 25:23); he saw to its distribution among the tribes, clans, and families of Israel. But on the other hand, it became necessary for those given parcels of this land to work out the boundaries between urban space, farmland, and pastureland. The most detailed mention of this division occurs when the biblical authors are describing the Levitical cities. Unlike the other tribes, the Levites did not receive a continuous parcel of land but forty-eight cities scattered throughout the other tribes, so that the clergy might live and teach among all Israel. Approximately one thousand acres of land around each Levitical city was cut away from the surrounding tribal land and given to the Levites (Num. 35:2–5). What is striking is the frequency with which this detail is mentioned, fifty-three

The quality of natural pastureland varied considerably in Israel but was necessary to sustain the family animals.

times in Joshua 21 and forty-two times in 1 Chronicles 6. If nothing else, this further demonstrates how important the need was to establish farming and grazing rights for every family in Israel so that their food supply would not be put at risk by a larger and more powerful entity.

It naturally follows that the pasture would become a symbol for the ability to sustain; loss meant economic ruin, while restoration of pasturelands symbolized hope. The nations that plotted the destruction of Israel said, "Let us take possession of the pasturelands of God" (Ps. 83:12). In response the Lord promised that both Edom and Babylon would face ruin—ruin that was symbolized by the destruction of their pasturelands (Jer. 49:20; 50:45). In contrast the restoration of Israel and its continued viability as God's people was symbolized by continuing access to pastureland. Isaiah prophesied, "The poorest of the poor will find pasture" (Isa. 14:30). Pastureland would be available on "every barren hill" (Isa. 49:9). Pastureland once empty during the exile would again be filled with animals and their shepherds (Jer. 33:12 – 13). The Lord promised, "I will bring Israel back to his own pasture and he will graze on Carmel and Bashan," two locations that enjoy abundant rainfall and rich pastures (Jer. 50:19). "I will bring them together like sheep in a pen, like a flock in its pasture" (Mic. 2:12).

Pastureland is also mentioned in the judgment speeches of the prophets as they addressed urban centers. What was once open pastureland had been claimed for urban development, the building of citadels, homes, and markets. But Jerusalem, Rabbah, and Ashkelon were told that their prized urban centers would be so devastated and decimated that they would again become pastureland (Isa. 32:14; Ezek. 25:5; Zeph. 2:7).

The biblical authors also employ the image of pasture as a figure of speech. When God's people are being pictured as sheep, the luxuriant green pastures become a metaphor for the basic needs of life that are addressed by the attentive shepherd: "The LORD is my shepherd, I shall not be in want. He makes me lie down in green pastures" (Ps. 23:1 – 2). The psalmist encourages the "flock" to place their full confidence in the shepherd: "Trust in the LORD and do good; dwell in the land and enjoy safe pasture" (Ps. 37:3). Jesus was well versed in this Old Testament imagery, so in speaking of himself as the Good Shepherd, he promised that all who followed him would "find pasture" (John 10:9).

In one instance the Lord himself is likened to Israel's "true pasture" (Jer. 50:7), but in three others this term becomes a metaphor for the Promised Land. Although the Lord allowed destruction of this "pasture" (25:36), he promised that he would gather the remnant of his flock "out of all the countries where I have driven them and will bring them back to their pasture, where they will be fruitful and increase in number" (Jer. 23:3; cf. Ezek. 34:14).

Pig

The type of pig most familiar to those living in the Promised Land was the wild boar. Weighing between 150 and 300 pounds, wild boars stand approximately three feet tall at the shoulders and are four feet in length. They are covered with short, stiff hair that is gray to brown in tone. In many of these animals, a distinct ridge of this hair stands at attention down the middle of the neck and back. Their threatening appearance is further heightened by a pair of tusks, lower canine teeth four to eight inches in length, which protrude from their mouths with sweeping, upward curves. Wild boars prefer the company of the herd, wandering the countryside and gathering food as they go. They will eat just about anything they come across, including nuts, grain, insects, small mammals, and refuse. Given the difficulty they have in shedding heat, they prefer the forests but will gladly raid the vulnerable vines of open agricultural fields if given the chance (Ps. 80:13).

Sows can bear up to twelve piglets at a time.

Pigs are widely raised and consumed today in many cultures, but not in Israel. Because pork is high in protein, pigs can provide high-quality nutrition. Nevertheless, the purity laws of the Israelites prohibited pork from being served at the dinner table and sacrificed on the altar. While certain health considerations may lie behind this prohibition, it seems more likely that it was designed to further distinguish God's people from their neighbors. Evidence from Canaanite, Philistine, Egyptian, Greek, and Roman culture indicates that these societies raised pigs and included pork in their diet and in their worship rites. In this regard, Isaiah rages against Israelites who have sold out to this kind of worship, people who "eat the flesh of pigs," or who "present pig's blood" in their worship (Isa. 65:4; 66:3, 17). When the Syrian king Antiochus Epiphanes sought to extinguish the distinctiveness of Jewish culture, he used the eating of pork as a loy-

A wild boar.
© Eric Isselée/www.BigStockPhoto.com

alty test to determine whether a Jew had actually surrendered to Greek culture (2 Macc. 6:18; 7:1; 4 Macc. 5:2, 6; 6:15). And when he wished to desecrate the altar in Jerusalem so that it could no longer be used for worship (2 Macc. 6:1–6), he sacrificed a pig on it.

The disdain for this animal is clearly evident in every mention of the pig in the Bible. When choosing a fitting simile to contrast something desirable with something repugnant, the inspired author brought together a gold ring and a pig's snout: "Like a gold ring in a pig's snout is a beautiful woman who shows no discretion" (Prov. 11:22). Jesus often spoke about the broad, inclusive sweep of his kingdom. Yet he cautioned his disciples to use discretion in choosing when and with whom to share the gospel: "Do not throw your pearls to pigs. If you do, they may trample them under their feet, and then turn and tear you to pieces" (Matt. 7:6). Here Jesus was making reference to the eating technique of wild boars—tearing at and overturning the soil with their snouts and feet—as well as to the serious injuries that can result when wild boars charge, slashing their victims with their tusks. Peter also used a pig as a metaphor. He likened false teachers to a "sow that is washed [and] goes back to her wallowing in the mud" (2 Peter 2:22). Because pigs do not have sweat glands, they need to remain in shaded areas or wallow in the mud to remain cool. Just as pigs naturally returned to their wallowing, so false teachers are unchanged by their contact with the gospel.

Pigs appear in two familiar gospel lessons, both of which involved a trip to the Decapolis where pigs were being raised. The Decapolis cities were built as Roman administrative centers and showplaces of Greco-Roman culture. As such, these large and ornate cities invited the locals to sample and then join the cultural world they represented. In the parable of the lost son, a young man left home to pursue life apart from the supervision and direction of his loving father. He went to a "distant country" (Luke 15:13), perhaps only as far away as the Decapolis, where wild living was a way of life. Here there was no prohibition on pork; so when this young man had squandered all he had, he found work tending pigs. Life became so grievously difficult that even the pig food looked attractive to this hungry young man (vv. 15–16). In this story the pigs not only illustrate the depth of his fall, but also the depth of his father's love, as evidenced in the restoration that occurs when he returns home.

On another occasion, Jesus invited his disciples to join him in a trip "to the other side" of the Sea of Galilee, the Gentile-filled Decapolis (Mark 4:35). After meeting a man possessed by many demons, Jesus performed an exorcism, allowing the fallen spirits to enter a herd of pigs grazing on a hillside. These possessed pigs immediately ran down the hillside into the water and were drowned (5:11–13). Again the presence of the pigs adds a taste of Decapolis realism to the narrative. And if later Jewish association of pigs with Roman soldiers was operative here, Jesus was also illustrating what would happen when pagan Roman culture met the real King of this world.

Plow

The plow was arguably the most important agricultural tool owned by a family, a labor-saving replacement for the hoe. Made from a durable hardwood such as oak, the plow consisted of a yoke to which the draft animals could be harnessed and a three-foot handle(s) that reached to the waist of the driver. Between the two was the business end of the plow, a wooden beam three to four inches in diameter and approximately twenty inches in length. Located between the yoke and handle, it was oriented so that it lay parallel to the soil and so that it could be tipped at a slight angle by the driver to engage the soil. This beam typically terminated in a sharpened bronze or iron plow point.

The function of this tool was not to turn over the soil as modern plows do, but merely to loosen the top three to four inches of soil. The first pass of the plow prepared the soil for the scattering of the seed. A second pass of the plow at a right angle to the first pass covered the scattered seed with soil. Nested in this loosened soil, the seed had access to moisture and enjoyed a growing medium conducive to sprouting.

The rhetorical use of the plow in the Bible presumes that the reader can picture the plow and the way it was typically used. At times the images used by the biblical author cohere with the expected norm, but more often than not, they diverge to create the desired impact on the reader. Ideally, every family had their own plow and draft animals to plow their fields. Samson mentioned the inappropriate use of someone else's plow and animal to point out the inappropriate way the answer to his riddle was discovered: "If you had not plowed with my heifer, you would not have solved my riddle" (Judg. 14:18). Samuel also pointed to a deviation from the norm when Israel was clucking about the advantages of having their own king. In response, Samuel told them that the sons they had hoped would work their own fields would be spirited away by the king to plow his fields (1 Sam. 8:12). Given the importance of this equipment, one would never think of intentionally destroying it. But the commitment of Elisha to his prophetic training becomes clear when we see him slaughter his draft animals and burn up his plow (1 Kings 19:21).

There is one place and only one place that we expect to see a plow at work: in a grain field. This expectation contributes to the arresting nature of the following images. Recalling the oppression faced in earlier days, the psalmist says, "Plowmen have plowed my back and made their furrows long" (Ps. 129:3). The prophet Amos asks, "Do horses run on the rocky crags? Does one plow there with oxen?" (Amos 6:12). That was unthinkable, just as unthinkable as Israel's perversion of justice. All such injustice had its price. Micah anticipates a time of payment and pictures it this way, "Zion will be plowed like a field" (Mic. 3:12).

Plowing of the grain fields was done within a critical window of time in October and November. This is when the early rains softened the sun-baked soil of summer, making it tillable. It was so critical to get the plowing done within

A wooden plow with a metal plow point.

Kim Guess/www.BiblePlaces.com

this window of time that God makes special mention of it in the Sabbath day legislation: "Even during the plowing season and harvest you must rest" (Ex. 34:21). Only something as disruptive as a famine would cause the plow to sit idle for an entire year (Gen. 45:6). Against this backdrop, we can more deeply appreciate the image of the sluggard, one who "does not plow in season; so at harvest time he looks but finds nothing" (Prov. 20:4). Between the harvesting of grain in the late spring and the season of plowing in late fall came the dry summer months when the farmer was not in the field. The productivity and bounty of the anticipated kingdom of God are captured in this image: "The days are coming … when the reaper will be overtaken by the plowman" (Amos 9:13).

As the metal plow point was driven through hard soil and into stones, it would become dull and require maintenance. In the best of worlds, you would repair the tool yourself or take it to someone nearby who could help you with the task. Certainly no one wanted a tool as important as the plow held hostage by one's avowed enemy. But that is exactly what happened in King's Saul's time. We read, "Not a blacksmith could be found in the whole land of Israel, because the Philistines had said, 'Otherwise the Hebrews will make swords or spears!' So all Israel went down to the Philistines to have their plowshares, mattocks, axes and sickles sharpened…. So on the day of the battle not a soldier with Saul and Jonathan had a sword or spear in his hand" (1 Sam. 13:19–20, 22). Sharpening was part of the expected maintenance, but no one dreamed of reshaping this valuable tool into a weapon. Nevertheless, the prophet Joel urges the nations facing a war with the Lord to do just that: "Beat your plowshares into swords" (Joel 3:10; for the reverse image that anticipates peace, see Isa. 2:4; Mic. 4:3).

The use of the plow required that its operator attend very carefully to the task. Looking back while plowing could lead to striking a large stone and damaging the plow point or plowing an area already finished. Looking back might also break the plow driver's concentration, causing him to take the necessary weight off the plow and causing the plow to run on top of rather than through the soil. Jesus made use of this image when speaking about the commitment he asked his followers to make. Those who were plowing a field had to concentrate on the task at hand and not look back. In a similar way, Jesus said that those who put their hand to the plow and look back are not fit for the kingdom of God, because they are failing to make that kingdom a real priority in their lives (Luke 9:62).

Pomegranate

Pomegranate may refer either to the tree or to the fruit that grows on this tree. While the pomegranate tree is adaptable to a wide variety of soil types and climates, it prefers the temperate climate offered by locations around the Mediterranean Sea, including the Promised Land where it could be included in the family's orchard (Song 4:12–13). It is a deciduous tree that sports dark green leaves guarded by sharp thorns. Typically this rounded tree is no more than sixteen feet high, but larger trees with a span of thirty feet are known; such a large tree was so distinctive it could be used as a landmark (1 Sam. 14:2). During the springtime the pomegranate tree produces bell-shaped, crimson flowers whose brightness and fine scent summon the attention of all nearby. Six to seven months after flowering, the fruit ripens and is ready for harvest. The ripe pomegranate is also crimson in color, ranging in size from three to five inches in diameter.

The symmetrical fruit is further marked by a distinctive calyx, which tradition says provided Solomon with the model for the shape of his royal crown. When the pomegranate's tough rind is split apart, one finds multiple compartments filled with a jellylike pulp and lined with row upon row of seeds, upward of six hundred seeds per pomegranate. The weight of the seeds accounts for more than half the weight of the fruit.

The pomegranate was used in various ways. The rind was employed in the tanning process and used medicinally to treat various illnesses. But it was the pulp and seeds that were most in demand. At the close of the summer season when the last rainfall was but a distant memory, the refreshing taste of the pulp and seeds was a welcome treat. Once split open, the fruit could be eaten fresh or pressed to obtain pomegranate juice that was drunk immediately or fermented to make wine. The pomegranate also found its way into the artistic expression of ancient Near Eastern cultures. The aesthetically appealing shape of the fruit was copied when designing household items such as vases and tables. But more often the archaeological record reveals religious artifacts in which the design of the pomegranate has been incorporated. Given the large number of seeds it produced, the pomegranate became a fertility symbol and so found its way into the religious images of the Canaanites, Edomites, and Philistines.

Pomegranate fruit.
© Leonid Nyshko/www.BigStockPhoto.com

Those who wrote the Bible and their first readers were very familiar with this tree and its fruit. In the description of the Promised Land, it is listed as one of the seven signature commodities (Deut. 8:8); and when the reconnaissance team sent out by Moses returned with a representative sample of the land's bounty, one of the three products they brought back to display were pomegranates (Num. 13:23). Ironically, it was not the pomegranates of Canaan but those of Egypt that the Israelites longed for when times grew difficult in the wilderness (Num. 20:5). Once God's people entered the Promised Land, pomegranates became a regular part of their diet, but like the other foods of the land, their presence was linked to the people's covenant faithfulness. When obedience to the law disappeared, so did the pomegranates, whether to divinely sponsored locusts, plagues, or drought (Joel 1:12; Hag. 2:19).

Pomegranates also appear in the metaphoric language of the Song of Songs. In this lengthy poem, the poet celebrates the ruddy symmetry of the young woman's temples: "Your temples behind your veil are like the halves of a pomegranate" (Song 4:3; 6:7). And the young woman likens her breasts to this shapely fruit, a plant from which fine fruit juice and wine were produced (8:2).

Artistic representations of the pomegranate are also common to the worship life of ancient

Israel. The robe the high priest wore beneath the ephod had "pomegranates of blue, purple and scarlet yarn around the hem" (Ex. 28:33). Between those pomegranates were gold bells that may well have reflected the bell-like shape of the pomegranate flower.

The architecture of Solomon's temple also featured representations of pomegranates. Two large pillars flanked the main entrance of the temple itself, and the capitals of each of those massive pillars were encircled with two rows of pomegranates (1 Kings 7:18, 20, 42; 2 Chron. 3:16; 4:13; Jer. 52:22 – 23). These are mentioned so often and in such detail that we are led to believe that these four hundred pomegranates were more than merely art for the sake of art. The search for their symbolic value leads us to two possible options. The large number of seeds in the pomegranate was a symbol of fertility the Lord gave to the Promised Land. Thus it may be that the use of the pomegranates on the garments of the high priest and on the pillars of the temple were meant to recall the important link between God's people and the fertile land they occupied. Alternately, these pomegranates may be a symbol of righteousness linked to the Law. Later Jewish tradition sees the pomegranate and its six hundred plus seeds as a representation of the six hundred thirteen traditional laws of the Torah. This is why Torah scrolls often have handles shaped like pomegranates. If this later tradition reflects symbolism present earlier in Israel's history, the pomegranates would be a reminder of God's Law and of the call to righteous living.

Q

Quiver

The quiver is a portable container for arrows typically worn by a hunter or soldier also carrying a bow. Early images from Mesopotamia depict soldiers with a bow in one hand and a cluster of arrows in the other. This was a less than ideal arrangement given the fact that two hands were required to steady and fire an arrow from the bow. Therefore hunters and soldiers alike who carried a bow also began to wear a quiver in which they transported their arrows.

The very simple appearance of the ancient quiver does not do justice to the careful design of this tool, which included a number of tradeoffs required to meet the following design criteria. To be of value, the quiver had to be large enough to carry a reasonable number of arrows, but it could not add an inordinate amount of weight to the gear being carried. It had to remain close to the archer's body, neither restricting his mobility nor interfering with his firing motions, yet it had to be accessible, allowing the archer to quickly draw an arrow without fumbling. The container had to be long enough to securely hold the arrows in place yet not swing freely so as to catch on brush or other obstructions. The result of all these tradeoffs was a quiver approximately four inches in diameter and slightly shorter than the thirty-two-inch arrows it carried. Quivers were primarily made from leather or cloth with some wood or metal components. And they included a strap to secure the quiver to the back of the archer.

The quiver is mentioned incidentally in two Bible passages. When Isaac perceived his life drawing to a close, he choreographed the day for giving the blessing of the firstborn to Esau. It began with a meal of wild game secured and prepared by his oldest son. Isaac directed Esau to get his "quiver and bow" and head into the open country to hunt (Gen. 27:3). The second incidental mention of a quiver is in the description of a horse ridden into battle. In illustrating for Job just how meager were the powers of mortals, the Lord called Job's attention to the fierce-looking war stallion. God provided this creature with strength and abilities that Job could barely imagine, much less provide. The impressive sight

An archer from the palace of King Darius the Great of Persia carries an ornate quiver.

Erich Lessing/Art Resource, NY

of this animal was enhanced by the weapons that bristled from its flanks, including the quiver that rattled against its side (Job 39:23).

The other rhetorical passages that mention the quiver can be divided into three categories, beginning with the metaphor in Psalm 127. In the culture of God's people, all children were considered a blessing from the Lord, but the birth of a son was considered a special gift, particularly when sons were born to a father when he was young himself: "Like arrows in the hands of a warrior are sons born in one's youth. Blessed is the man whose quiver is full of them. They will not be put to shame when they contend with their enemies in the gate" (Ps. 127:4–5). Many sons assured greater economic well-being for the family and also were a source of security. Like many arrows in the quiver standing at the ready, so maturing sons born during one's youth stood ready when danger of any kind threatened at the gate.

The quiver of Babylonian soldiers is mentioned in two places. In a portion of Isaiah that addresses one judgment speech after the next to a wide array of nations, we find just such a speech directed at covenant-breaking Israel. Although the day of foreign invasion had not yet arrived, Isaiah saw soldiers taking up their quivers, a sure sign that battle preparations in Babylon were under way (Isa. 22:6). Jeremiah carried the same message of judgment to the people of his day. In response to an array of sinful words and actions, the Lord would bring a distant nation to make war on his chosen people: "Their quivers are like an open grave; all of them are mighty warriors" (Jer. 5:16). Given the skills of the Babylonian archers, an empty quiver meant that many Israelites would have died in the hail of arrows fired. The play on words naturally follows. An empty quiver is not just like an open grave but also is the tool that fills a grave. All in all, bad news was on the horizon for rebellious Israel.

Finally, the divine quiver is pictured in two passages. The voice rising from Lamentations has a different take on the arrows that had been flying about Jerusalem. To be sure, the Babylonians did empty their quivers, but the Babylonian archers were but agents; it was the Lord who "drew his bow and made me the target for his arrows. He pierced my heart with arrows from his quiver" (Lam. 3:12–13). Nevertheless, the divine quiver also contained a special arrow carefully kept for deployment long after the time of the Babylonian siege of Jerusalem.

This was not an arrow bent on destruction but one bent on healing and restoration. In Isaiah's description of the Servant, we hear the Messiah likening himself to a polished arrow: "He made my mouth like a sharpened sword, in the shadows of his hand he hid me; he made me into a polished arrow and concealed me in his quiver" (Isa. 49:2). In the poetic parallelism of this verse, the quiver is a staging area, a place in which the Messiah would rest until the time was fully come for him to be launched into this world (Gal. 4:4). Thus the same divine quiver that produced arrows of destruction also carried an arrow that would bring about redemption.

R

Rain

In the Promised Land, the year essentially divides into two seasons, a summer without rain and a winter with rain. The winter season further divides into three subseasons, each with a unique pattern of rainfall that makes a distinctive contribution to the maturing of the critical grain harvest. The early rains follow the rain-free summer months with showers and thunderstorms that soften the soil for plowing and planting. The early rains occur from October through November, providing approximately 11 percent of the annual total. The middle rains that follow provide 75 percent of the annual rainfall; these are the cold and heavy rains of December to February that mature the grain fields. A return to showery rains occurs in March and April when the late rains provide approximately 14 percent of the annual total. The average year sees little

variation from this cycle, so it becomes a way of marking the passage of time through the year (2 Sam. 21:10; Eccl. 12:2; Song 2:11–13).

The importance of rain in the Promised Land becomes evident when we compare it with Egypt or Mesopotamia. Successful farming and survival in these regions depend on the predictable flow of the large rivers that bisect them. In contrast to such regions with a river-based hydrology, Israel has a rain-based hydrology. Prior to the Israelites' entering the Promised Land under the leadership of Joshua, God made it clear that life there would look very different from the life they had known in Egypt. Irrigation channels of the Nile would be replaced by a "land of mountains and valleys that drinks rain from heaven" (Deut. 11:10–11). The autumn through spring rains would mature the wheat, green the pastures, fill the cisterns, and give the summer fruit

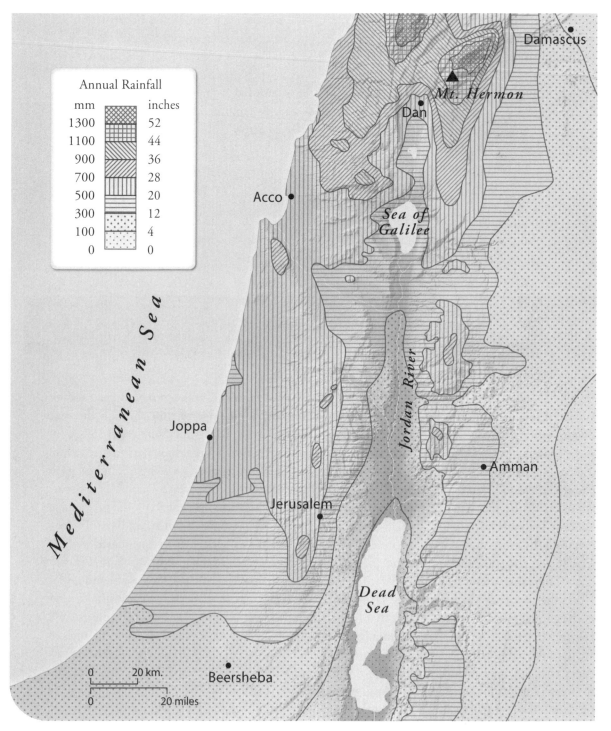

Annual rainfall in Palestine.

such as grapes and olives a healthy start (Deut. 11:14 – 15; Isa. 55:10 – 11).

Consequently, the connotations associated with rain are generally positive. So if you are accustomed to hearing the forecast of rain delivered with a formal or veiled apology, and if you perceive rain negatively as something that ruins picnics and spoils parades, you may have a hard time understanding the mind-set of the people in the biblical world who regarded rain as a blessing. People living in the Promised Land welcomed and celebrated the coming of rain and all that it meant. Its images fill songs of praise: "Sing to the LORD with thanksgiving; make music to our God on the harp. He covers the sky with clouds; he supplies the earth with rain and makes grass grow on the hills" (Ps. 147:7 – 8). Rain assumes a negative connotation in only two instances. The first is when the cold winter rains fall on those who have insufficient clothing or shelter to avoid getting chilled to the bone (Ezra 10:9, 13; Job 24:7 – 8). The second is when the rain is unleashed in such powerful torrents that it sweeps away structures (Ezek. 13:11 – 13; Matt. 7:25, 27).

The biblical authors further emphasize the important relationship between the rain and the Father in heaven who supplies it. The ancients did not have the science that allowed them to see that winter rains were caused by a steady march of low pressure into their region. They were good, however, at making the connection between clouds forming over the Mediterranean Sea during the winter months and the prospects of rain (Luke 12:54). Yet well beyond the observations of the modern meteorologist or the ancient cloud watcher, the biblical authors point us to God as the maker and supplier of rain. This connection is made repeatedly in the Bible because God's people were surrounded by false deities like Baal who claimed they provided the rain (Job 38:28; Pss. 135:7; 147:8; Jer. 10:13; 14:22; Matt. 5:45; Acts 14:17). Apart from offering rain in the months and in the places where it was expected, God could put his divine signature on an unexpected victory or mark a moment in time as special by causing rain to fall in unexpected places and at unexpected times of the year (Judg. 4; 5:4; 1 Sam. 12:17 – 18; Ps. 68:8).

The rain further played an important role in the covenant agreement the Lord had made with Israel. This relationship is mentioned both early and often in the Old Testament, starting with these words: "If you follow my decrees and are careful to obey my commands, I will send you rain in its season, and the ground will yield its crops and the trees of the field their fruit" (Lev. 26:3 – 4; cf. Deut. 11:13 – 17; 28:12, 24; 1 Kings 8:35 – 36). With the troubled days of the divided kingdom when God's people defaulted on their promises again and again, we read of rains that are either too late, too little, or absent all together, virtually guaranteeing food shortages and faltering water supplies. The prophets turn our eyes to theology rather than meteorology for the explanation. When God's people failed, so did the rains; when they were faithful, the rain fell (1 Kings 17:1; 18:1, 41, 45; Isa. 5:6; 30:23; Jer. 3:3; 5:24 – 25; 14:4; Ezek. 22:24; Hos. 6:3; Joel 2:23; Amos 4:7).

Finally, rain also appears in both positive and negative figures of speech. On the negative side, an oppressive ruler and an invading king are likened to a torrential, destructive rain that ruins crops and wipes out flowers (Prov. 28:3; Isa. 28:2). On the positive side, God's Word is likened to life-giving rain: "As the rain and the snow come down from heaven, and do not return to it without watering the earth and making it bud and flourish, so that it yields seed for the sower and bread for the eater, so is my word that goes out from my mouth" (Isa. 55:10 – 11; cf. Deut. 32:2). Wise and helpful counsel is likened to the spring rain (Job 29:23); and of the ideal king, his subjects sing, "He will be like the rain falling on a mown field, like showers watering the earth" (Ps. 72:6).

Ram's Horn (*Shofar*)

The most frequently mentioned musical instrument in the Old Testament is the ram's horn (Heb., *shofar*). Unfortunately, English translations of the Bible often obscure mention of this instrument by using the word "trumpet" to represent two different musical instruments, both the ram's horn and the true trumpet. The discussion here focuses on the *shofar*, or ram's horn. The *shofar* is typically made from the hollow, curving horn of a ram, which has a larger opening on one end and a smaller opening on the other. The one sounding the ram's horn blows into the small opening of the instrument, causing the column of air within to vibrate and produce a sound that is somewhere between that of the modern trumpet and French horn. Although this instrument is capable of only a limited number of notes, the loud and far-reaching signal sounded by the *shofar* is encoded by varying the sequence of the notes played and by reproducing those notes with a staccato, sustained, or quavering tone.

The ram's horn was used in military, worship, and political contexts. In the absence of radio communication, the *shofar* was used in a military context to communicate with soldiers and civil-

The *shofar* is the most frequently mentioned musical instrument in the Bible.
© Dana Rothstein/www.BigStockPhoto.com

ians alike. When the lookout saw a hostile army approaching, the ram's horn carried the news to those in harm's way (Jer. 4:5, 21; 6:1; Joel 2:1; Amos 3:6; Zeph. 1:16). The haunting tones of the *shofar* called to mind not just the approaching army but all the harm the soldiers would cause: "Oh, the agony of my heart! My heart pounds within me, I cannot keep silent. For I have heard the sound of the trumpet (*shofar*); I have heard the battle cry" (Jer. 4:19). The ram's horn was also used to summon God's people to a particular location to rally for battle (Judg. 3:27; 6:34; 1 Sam. 13:3; 2 Sam. 20:1; Jer. 51:27). And while one sound propelled Israel's soldiers into battle, yet another called for them to withdraw from battle (2 Sam. 2:28; 18:16; 20:22; Ezek. 7:14).

In addition to its role in a military context, the ram's horn was also sounded in connection with religious and political events. It was deemed an instrument particularly appropriate for praising the Lord (Pss. 98:6; 150:3). Its sound marked the start of the Feast of Trumpets (Lev. 23:24), the New Moon celebration (Ps. 81:3), and the Day of Atonement in the Year of Jubilee (Lev. 25:9). When David brought the ark of the covenant up to Jerusalem, the sounding of the ram's horn called attention to its progress toward the capital city (2 Sam. 6:15; 1 Chron. 15:28). As the penetrating tone of the *shofar* called attention to religious events, so it was used by kings to announce their accession to the throne (2 Sam. 15:10; 1 Kings 1:34, 39, 41; 2 Kings 9:13).

The very first time we hear the ram's horn sound in the Bible, it is not a mortal but a divine *shofar* that fills the air around Mount Sinai, signaling that the Lord has come down to meet with his people: "On the morning of the third day there was thunder and lightning, with a thick cloud over the mountain, and a very loud trumpet (*shofar*) blast. Everyone in the camp trembled" (Ex. 19:16; cf. 19:19; 20:18).

In at least two other instances, the biblical authors emphasize the sounding of the ram's horn as a way of linking subsequent events with this signature sound of the Lord's presence. The first narrative where we find repeated mention of the ram's horn is the fall of Jericho (Josh. 6). All fourteen instances in which a ram's horn is mentioned in Joshua occur in this chapter. Clearly this was an important military operation, the first operation conducted by Joshua and the Israelite army on the west side of the Jordan River. As the biblical author describes the special tactics used to put Jericho under siege, the ram's horn is mentioned again and again, not just as a signaling device but also as a way of putting God's signature on the victory. As the horn marked the Lord's presence on Mount Sinai, so it marked his presence at Jericho.

The second time we find repeated mention of the ram's horn is during Gideon's operation against the Midianites, Amalekites, and other eastern invaders who had overwhelmed the land (Judg. 7). In this case, the Lord also used special tactics to reduce the number of Israelite soldiers who would fight to the ridiculously small number of three hundred. But by using a nighttime attack and the haunting sound of three hundred rams' horns, God again put his signature on this victory.

The ram's horn also appears in the Bible as a metaphor for the words of his prophets that were like the warning sound emitted by this instrument. Isaiah is told to shout his message aloud, raising his "voice like a trumpet" (*shofar*; Isa. 58:1). The same image is found in Jeremiah 6:17 and Hosea 8:1; but the most sustained use of this metaphor comes to us in Ezekiel 33:1–6. Here the prophet is likened to a lookout with ram's horn in hand. In the metaphor it becomes the responsibility of the lookout to sound the warning that calls God's people to repentance. When the prophet has done so, his responsibilities have been met: "If anyone hears the trumpet (*shofar*) but does not take warning and the sword comes and takes his life, his blood will be on his own head" (Ezek. 33:4). However, if the prophet fails to give clear and adequate warning with the "ram's horn," he will be held accountable.

Ring

People from all rungs of the social ladder wore jewelry during Bible times. This included the three types of rings mentioned in the Bible: nose rings, finger rings, and a special type of finger ring called the signet ring. The finger or nose rings varied in style and composition from a single loop made from bronze, silver, or gold to very ornate designs that included precious stones. No matter their style, such rings were worn as a form of personal decoration. But in this era when precious metals had not as yet been pressed into coins, rings had another role to play; they made personal wealth portable. For example, when the Israelites were getting ready to leave Egypt, they were not to leave empty-handed but were to ask for silver and gold that they could carry with them (Ex. 3:22). A portion of this precious metal came into Israelite hands in the form of rings (35:22).

The signet ring was a special type of finger ring with a distinctive shape and function. The lower portion of the ring had a stirruplike shape that terminated in a flat upper surface. That upper surface was etched so that when the ring was pressed into damp clay or warm wax, it would leave behind an impression. The impression was unique to the ring's owner, making the seal impression the rough equivalent of a signature today. Thus the seal produced by the signet ring assured the readers of contracts and laws that the document had been properly authorized. Furthermore, kings and other wealthy individuals who needed to delegate authority to others could do so by giving them their signet ring to use. Agreements and orders marked in this way by the surrogate had the full authority of the signet ring's owner.

In two passages the presence of a ring clearly introduces the connotation of wealth. When Abraham's servant was sent to find a bride for Isaac, Rebekah proved herself a worthy candidate at the well. Before a marriage contract was even proposed to her family, the servant of Abraham demonstrated the wealth of his master by giving Rebekah a gold nose ring (Gen. 24:22). A suitor from a wealthy family was always welcome news; this signal was not lost on Laban who

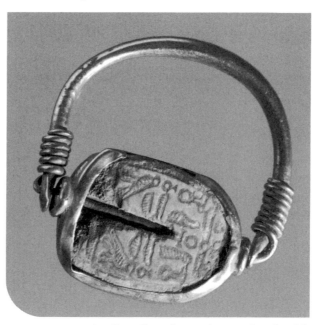

An Egyptian signet ring made of gold.
Z. Radovan/www.BibleLandPictures.com

quickly invited the man to dinner after seeing the nose ring (v. 30). The ring also conveys the image of wealth in James 2:2. Here the inspired writer urges his readers to welcome all who have come to their worship service no matter what their social status. A man wearing a "gold ring and fine clothes" should feel as welcome as the poor man without jewelry, wearing shabby clothes.

A signet ring appears in several Bible stories where a reversal of fortune is marked by the reception of a signet ring. Joseph had endured many hardships in Egypt, including a lengthy stay in prison. After he interpreted the dreams of Egypt's leader, "Pharaoh took his signet ring from his finger and put it on Joseph's finger" (Gen. 41:42). A signet ring appears in Esther, marking the movement of the plot from crisis to resolution. At first the Persian king gives Haman the royal signet ring (Esth. 3:10). This was horrible news for the Jews, because Haman had convinced the king to annihilate God's people from his realm. The king signed a law to that effect and marked it with his signet ring (3:12). Things completely reversed when Haman was executed and the signet ring was removed from the finger of Haman and given to Mordecai (8:2). This Jewish man in turn used his newfound authority to write a decree that allowed the Jews to gather, defend themselves, and even strike preemptively at those who threatened their existence. Mordecai sealed the dispatched decree with the king's signet ring (8:10). The third instance of reversed fortune is found in the parable of the lost son. Although this son had squandered his wealth in wild living, his father welcomed the return of his penitent child, directing his servants to "put a ring on his finger" (Luke 15:22).

The biblical authors also make figurative use of the ring. A nose ring used to enhance the beauty of a woman does nothing to improve the appearance of a pig. This truism can be found in Proverbs: "Like a gold ring in a pig's snout is a beautiful woman who shows no discretion" (Prov. 11:22).

A groom might well give his bride both finger and nose rings as symbols of his affection for her. Two passages from the Prophets lean on this image. Ezekiel pictures Jerusalem as a woman wooed by the Lord. He lavished many gifts on her, including a nose ring (Ezek. 16:12). Yet his bride used her beauty and fame to become a prostitute. She turned this loving gift of jewelry into "male idols and engaged in prostitution with them" (v. 17). A similar image surfaces in Hosea, only this time the unfaithful wife used the rings given to her by her husband to attract other lovers: "She decked herself with rings and jewelry, and went after her lovers, but me she forgot" (Hos. 2:13). In both instances the symbol of God's love was abusively turned against him.

Finally, we encounter two passages where the Lord himself is said to have a signet ring. Because God had promised David an eternal dynasty (2 Sam. 7:12–13), the descendants of David who led Israel could be pictured as the Lord's signet ring, an affirming signal that the promise was alive and well. Because of Jehoiachin's failures,

the Lord threatened to pull Jehoiachin off his finger like a signet ring (Jer. 22:24), an image that appeared to put God's promise to David at risk. But this threat was reversed, as he later assured Zerubbabel, "I will make you like my signet ring, for I have chosen you" (Hag. 2:23).

Road

Roads begin their life as paths that develop when people move between frequently visited locations. In Bible times people moved between home and the market, between home and the family fields, between towns and cities, and from one country to the next. As they moved, they made the pathways that became the roads of Bible times. Of course the route of choice was always the most direct route, but more often than not, other factors caused detours from that direct route. Because most people of Bible times walked from one place to the next, they felt every foot of elevation change in their calves and thighs. Consequently, routes that minimized elevation change were favored even if they were longer. Natural features like swamps, lakes, and high mountains were circumnavigated. And in a landscape that offered few water resources, there was always a concern to chart a course that brought travelers into regular contact with fresh drinking water.

With all these factors in view, those traveling from place to place began to wear a path that developed as necessary to accommodate the amount and kind of use it received. Virtually all of the local and inter-regional roads of Bible times were little more than well-worn footpaths, some wider some narrower, but not dramatically different than the pathway through a vacant lot between one's neighborhood and the local school. Yet because Israel was a natural land bridge linking Asia, Africa, and Europe, some road segments served international travelers. Such roads could be fifteen feet wide in order to accommodate the large number of users, including camel trains, donkey trains, carts, and chariots. When Israel enjoyed a strong central government, these roads could be improved particularly if they were to host the travel of the royal family. Such improvements are alluded to in the Bible and consist of straightening, leveling, and removing obstructions (Isa. 40:3–4; 57:14; 62:10). But improvements on rural roadways did not include paving stones, as we find used in some city streets of the Old Testament. Eventually that changed with the arrival of the Romans and the extension of the Roman road system into the Promised Land. Roman roads had carefully excavated and filled roadbeds designed to keep the road stable and dry. They culminated in a level, paved surface that allowed for quick deployment of Roman soldiers and that facilitated trade.

As today, frequently used roads were given names. In Bible times the names were often associated with the destination toward which the road reached, for example, the desert road

The typical road of Bible times was little more than a path.

(Ex. 13:18), the Mount Seir road (Deut. 1:2), or the road to Silla (2 Kings 12:20). The people of Bible times traveled on such roads, certainly much more frequently than acknowledged by the biblical authors. So when a road is formally mentioned and particularly when a named road is mentioned, we would do well to ask what rhetorical contribution that road is making. We find a good example in Israel's exodus from Egypt. Here the biblical author mentions two roadways, both of which would have led Israel out of Egypt. One was strategically chosen and the other not. The Lord intentionally avoided the "road through the Philistine country" (Ex. 13:17). This well-known ancient road was the shortest route between Egypt and the Promised Land that captive Israel had longed to see. But it was also the primary invasion route into Egypt from the north, so it bristled with Egyptian military outposts. The use of this road virtually guaranteed that Israel would face a fight sooner rather than later. As Israel's true leader, the Lord had other plans: "God said, 'If they face war, they might change their minds and return to Egypt.' So God led the people around by the desert road toward the Red Sea" (Ex. 13:17–18).

At other times, mention of a road without specifically identifying its name plays a role in the message. In these instances, the common experience of traveling on a road becomes a way to honor the Lord. Parents are instructed to share the truths of God with their children through all phases of their day, including the times when they are walking "along the road" (Deut. 6:7; 11:19). Various laws call God's people to honor his instructions on any road they travel and no matter how urgent their business. If they saw a brother's draft animals fallen on any road, if they came across a bird's nest fallen beside any road, or if they heard of someone leading the blind astray on any road, God's people were to act in the way he directed (Deut. 22:4, 6; 27:18). When Jesus sent out the Seventy-two to every town in Judea to announce the coming of his kingdom, he urged them to forgo lengthy greetings on the roads they traveled so as not to delay their important mission (Luke 10:4).

Finally, roads are mentioned figuratively in a number of Bible passages, such as when a road appears where no road should exist. The miracle of the Red (Reed) Sea crossing is referenced poetically in this rhetorical question of Isaiah: "Was it not you who dried up the sea, the waters of the great deep, who made a road in the depths of the sea…?" (Isa. 51:10). But perhaps the most striking figurative use of a road comes as Isaiah anticipates the coming of the Messiah. Here the image of improving a road becomes a metaphor for preparing one's life to meet the Messiah. "Build up, build up, prepare the road! Remove the obstacles out of the way of my people" (57:14; cf. 40:3–4).

Rod

"Rod" (NIV) represents tools of various sizes and shapes designed to deliver a blow, operate a loom, or measure a building project. As a tool designed for striking, the rod found application in three settings. A thick yet springy branch was used to deliver a stinging blow to those who had disobeyed one in authority: "A whip for the horse, a halter for the donkey, and a rod for the backs of fools!" (Prov. 26:3; cf. 10:13). A rod was an effective deterrent, but its use was restricted among God's people (Ex. 21:20). Paul should have been protected from this form of punishment by virtue of his Roman citizenship, yet he was beaten with rods on three occasions (2 Cor. 11:25). A similar type of branch was used to thresh fragile caraway seeds, which would have been damaged if threshed with more aggressive equipment (Isa. 28:27). And a rod that was more substantial in size and weight was carried by a shepherd to deliver blows against predators intent on harming the flock.

In addition to these tools used for striking, the Bible mentions the weaver's rod, elsewhere known as the heddle rod. The heddle rod was a flat piece of wood that was woven in and out between threads on a loom. When the weaver adjusted the angle of the heddle rod, the threads of the warp separated, creating a gap through which the shuttle could quickly pass. (*See* Loom.)

The third type of rod is a straight branch or reed used by a builder to secure measurements when cutting and fitting components of a building. In the visions of Ezekiel and John, we see this kind of rod used to measure projects that are already complete. It is used to take measurements of the temple complex and components of the temple seen in Ezekiel's and John's visions (Ezek. 40:3–8; 42:16–19; Rev. 11:1) and of the New Jerusalem (Rev. 21:15–16).

The punitive rod, shepherd's rod, and weaver's rod are all used as metaphors by the biblical authors. When more powerful nations use their might to make the lives of God's people difficult, that oppression is likened to the punitive rod that brings physical discomfort to those on whom it falls. The oppression of Midian, Assyria, and Babylon are all likened to the pain delivered by a punitive rod (Isa. 9:4; 10:24; 14:5; Mic. 5:1; 6:9).

The Lord is also said to wield a punitive rod. Job associated the pain that filled his life with such a divine rod (Job 9:34). And God promised that the descendants of David who wandered from the covenant-guided path would find their sins punished by a divine rod (Ps. 89:32), a reality not lost on at least one Israelite who made this observation while sitting in the ruins of Jerusalem: "I am the man who has seen affliction by the rod of his wrath" (Lam. 3:1). Yet even when the Lord used a nation like Assyria as the rod in his hand, that nation faced divine judgment if it presumed to become the hand wielding the rod rather than the rod residing in the hand of God (Isa. 10:5, 15).

The punitive rod also is used as a metaphor in Proverbs for various forms of discipline that might be used to shape the attitudes and actions of children: "He who spares the rod hates his son, but he who loves him is careful to discipline him" (Prov. 13:24). This passage and others like it (22:15; 23:13–14; 29:15) interpreted in a literalistic way would suggest that corporal punishment is an absolute necessity. But we would do well to keep in view all appropriate forms of correction that parents might use to shape the godly nature of their children.

The shepherd's rod is mentioned twice as a metaphor. In the familiar verses of Psalm 23, we are reminded that the Lord's flock wanders a world filled with danger just as the flock of David walked through terrifying terrain. Yet the flock found comfort in the shepherd's presence expressed poetically by the presence of the shepherd's tools. The rod and staff reminded the flock that they did not travel through this dangerous country alone but always superintended by the guidance and protection of their shepherd symbolized by those tools: "Even though I walk through the valley of the shadow of death, I will fear no evil, for you are with me; your rod and your staff, they comfort me" (Ps. 23:4). The second example finds the sheep passing beneath the rod of the Lord. From time to time, the shepherd required his flock to do just that so that he might affirm each animal as his own and designate every tenth animal as holy to the Lord (Lev. 27:32). The

Lord extends this image as he speaks of reclaiming his people from exile: "I will take note of you as you pass under my rod, I will bring you into the bond of the covenant" (Ezek. 20:37).

Finally, the spear of Goliath is likened to a weaver's rod (1 Sam. 17:7; for a similar use of this same metaphor, see 2 Sam. 21:19; 1 Chron. 11:23; 20:5). Perhaps the biblical author is attempting to describe a unique spear with this metaphor. The heddle had a leash that allowed the weaver to manipulate it more easily; the same may have been true of Goliath's spear. By wrapping the leash around the spear and using it when throwing the spear, the heddlelike spear would rotate and so be stabilized in flight. With this image, the author of 1 Samuel was helping the reader picture a weapon whose range and accuracy posed a great risk to anyone who stepped on the field of battle with such a warrior.

An Egyptian beating a slave with a rod.
Erich Lessing/Art Resource, NY

Roof

A wide variety of structures sported roofs in Bible times, including private homes, royal palaces, and temples (Judg. 16:27; 2 Sam. 11:2; 1 Kings 7:6; 2 Kings 4:10; Mark 2:4). Roofs were composed of natural materials carefully organized to create a strong and waterproof cover. The foundation layer of the roof consisted of large limbs from the tamarisk or sycamore trees that spanned the standing walls. These limbs were not positioned so as to create a perfectly flat roof; rather, they were set at a slight angle so that the surface of the roof would direct runoff rainwater into the family cistern. With the larger beams in place, the builder then added smaller branches placed at right angles to the larger roof beams. On top of this network of branches, reeds, palm fronds, and bundled grass were layered to close up the remaining openings in the roof; but the builder was not finished yet. A final layer of mud or clay was spread over the roof as a shield against water penetration. This topcoat further guaranteed that the roof would be the color of its surrounding landscape, even turning green with the fields as grass seeds in that soil began to sprout during the rainy season (2 Kings 19:26; Ps. 129:6; Isa. 37:27). Once completed, annual maintenance on the roof included a fresh layer of mud to keep the roof watertight. The end product was a strong and watertight shield; yet it was a surface that could be dug through by an insistent group of Jesus' followers who were bent on getting their disabled friend past the crowds to see their Lord (Mark 2:4).

The roof was more than a precipitation shield; this flat surface became the open-air room of the house where a variety of daily activities took place. It was a place to sleep on a summer night, to dry flax (Josh. 2:6), to carry on a private conversation (1 Sam. 9:25), to quietly pray (Acts 10:9), and to privately worship the Lord (Neh. 8:16). So much activity took place on the roof that the builders were required by divine law to build a parapet (a raised border) around the edges of the roof to prevent someone from accidentally falling over (Deut. 22:8). People spent so much time on the roof that it merited special mention as Jesus warned about the coming "abomination that causes desolation." "Let no one on the roof of his house go down to take anything out of the house" (Matt. 24:17).

When the biblical authors mention a roof rhetorically, they often draw our attention to

violation of expected norms. For example, a well-built roof should not leak. When it does, it is a source of great annoyance, a constant dripping likened to the irritation associated with a quarrelsome wife (Prov. 19:13; 27:15). People would spend time on the roof but not their entire day; that is, unless going into the house had become an unpleasant experience: "Better to live on a corner of the roof than share a house with a quarrelsome wife" (21:9; 25:24).

The roof was linked with quiet worship, prayer, and reflection. It appeared David was

A roof in Bible times was composed of natural materials carefully organized to create a strong and waterproof cover.

headed for such a moment one night when he had trouble sleeping. He went to the roof of the palace, but instead of filling his night with prayer, he filled it with unwholesome viewing and thinking that led to adultery and murder (2 Sam. 11:2). In an ironic twist, Absalom set up a tent on the same roof after he had driven his father from the royal throne. Absalom used that tent to sleep with his father's concubines, dishonoring his father and showing just who was in charge (2 Sam. 16:22). A further disturbing trend surfaced during the time of the divided kingdom. The roof, which offered the ideal place for private worship of the Lord, became the place where God's people built altars, poured out drink offerings to pagan gods, burned incense to Baal, and bowed down to the starry hosts (2 Kings 23:12; Isa. 22:1; Jer. 19:13; 32:29; Zeph. 1:5). What a relief to hear that the returning exiles got it right, building booths on the rooftops to celebrate the Lord's prescribed festival rather than worship pagan gods (Neh. 8:17).

Roofs are further associated with quiet conversations and happy family moments. Against that norm, the prophets call our attention to the deep grief felt in Moab by pointing us to their rooftops: "On all the roofs in Moab and in the public squares there is nothing but mourning, for I have broken Moab like a jar that no one wants" (Jer. 48:38; cf. Isa. 15:3). In the Gospels, a different kind of shout is coming from those usually quiet rooftops. When sending out the Twelve, Jesus encourages them to spread the news about him boldly and openly: "What I tell you in the dark, speak in the daylight; what is whispered in your ear, proclaim from the roofs" (Matt. 10:27).

Finally, the biblical authors expect their readers to be aware of the cultural connotations associated with coming under someone's roof. A guest entering the home was assured the protection of his or her host. When a crowd bent on evil pounded at his door, Lot appealed to this principle, insisting that these men "have come under the protection of my roof" (Gen. 19:8). Second, coming under the roof of another meant acceptance; this is illustrated by the centurion at Capernaum who seemed to know that Jesus' kingdom would include Gentiles but was too humble to assume that Jesus would find him acceptable. In asking for help, his humility showed through in his words to Jesus: "Lord, I do not deserve to have you come under my roof" (Matt. 8:8).

Root

The root of a plant or tree lives a quiet and unassuming life beneath the surface of the soil, performing its vital yet unsung roles. It provides the plant or tree with a solid foundation so that as the young plant reaches upward and outward toward the life-giving sun, it is less likely to be upended by its exposure to abusive elements. Second, the roots provide nourishment, mediating life to the plant from the soil. As it reaches outward in ever-growing circles, the root system of a tree searches out the vital water and nutrients that will support its continued growth and survival.

The people of Bible times were keen observers of their surroundings and noted the important relationship between the health of a plant and its root system. Those observations led directly to the images of the healthy, harmful, or damaged roots that appear in the Bible. First, a healthy plant was one whose root system had access to freshwater. The one who is blessed is like a tree "planted by the water that sends out its roots by the stream" (Jer. 17:8; cf. Job 29:19); and the country experiencing great success is like the cedar tree whose "roots went down to abundant waters" (Ezek. 31:7). On the other hand, pagan idolatry, sinful conduct, and ungodly attitudes are all likened to roots that deliver poison rather than nourishment to the plant above (1 Tim. 6:10; Heb. 12:15). Moses cautioned the Israelites, "Make sure there is no root among you that produces such bitter poison" (Deut. 29:18). Withered, dried, and decayed roots mark a dying plant. Such images are used to describe individuals who reject God's law (Isa. 5:24) and nations who oppose his divine plan (Isa. 14:30; Amos 2:9). The root of rebellious Ephraim is withered (Hos. 9:16) as is the root of new believers whose faith succumbs to trouble or persecution. Likening such a person to a seed that has fallen and sprouted on rocky ground

An uprooted tree with withered roots.
© Bhupendra Singh/www.BigStockPhoto.com

with limited soil, Jesus said, "Since he has no root, he lasts only a short time" (Matt. 13:21). In addition to dried and withered roots, we have the image of the plant whose roots have been forcefully torn from the soil. The apostasy of Israel in the Promised Land would find them uprooted by a sweep of God's hand (Deut. 29:28; 1 Kings 14:15). Although the Lord had planted Jerusalem in good soil with abundant water, Jerusalem sent out its "roots" in the direction of the Egyptians, seeking a forbidden political alliance. As a result the Lord would permit the Babylonians to enter the Promised Land and "uproot" Jerusalem (Ezek. 17:5–9).

Those living in the biblical world also observed that a tree that had been cut down would begin to grow new shoots from its roots: "Its roots may grow old in the ground and its stump die in the soil, yet at the scent of water it will bud and put forth shoots like a plant" (Job 14:8–9). Thus the root was also associated with survival and restoration. In the face of an Assyrian siege, God promised Hezekiah that "once more a remnant of the house of Judah will take root below and bear fruit above" (2 Kings 19:30; cf. Isa. 27:6; 37:31). And in the fateful dream of Nebuchadnezzar that spoke of his humiliation, there was also this symbol of renewal: the stump and the roots would remain, signaling a time when this towering tree of a ruler would be restored (Dan. 4:15, 26).

The image of the root also appears in three metaphors that liken the root to the base of the mountains, to the Messiah, and to the message Abram and his family received. Although mountains do not literally have a root system, the biblical authors do speak of the mountains as having "roots." Miners who make it their business to tunnel into the base of the mountains are said to "lay bear the roots of the mountains" (Job 28:9). Jonah saw those rocky roots during his near-drowning experience in the Mediterranean Sea as he sunk ever deeper into the water (Jonah 2:6).

The image of the root is frequently connected to the Messiah as well. Although the day of exile was coming for God's people, one in which the tree of this nation would be felled by its adversaries, the stump of Jesse would remain. Isaiah saw the day when the "roots" — the descendants of Jesse — would produce a special Branch (Isa. 11:1). Within just a few verses, this messianic Branch is recast as the Root of Jesse (11:10; cf. Rom. 15:12). The root of most plants is not the most attractive part of the plant; the Messiah is likened to "a root out of dry ground. He had no beauty or majesty to attract us to him, nothing in his appearance that we should desire him" (Isa. 53:2). Yet it is the title Root of David that remains an important title for Jesus even as he reigns in heaven (Rev. 5:5; 22:16).

Finally, God's chosen people are likened to an olive tree with some very special roots — the message given to Abram's family. This image helps to define relationships in the early Christian church during a time when there was an increasing influx of Gentiles into what had been a very Jewish church. The question of how Gentile Christians ought to regard their Jewish brothers and sisters is addressed in Romans. Here the Gentiles are described as a "wild olive shoot" grafted into the vine of ancient Israel, who "now share in the nourishing sap from the olive root" (Rom. 11:17). That image comes with this important reminder to Gentile Christians about their relationship to God's chosen people: "You do not support the root, but the root supports you" (v. 18).

S

Sackcloth

Sackcloth is a coarse fabric typically woven from the dark hair of a goat or, less frequently, from the stiff hair of a camel (Rev. 6:12). In contrast to the textiles woven from wool or flax, the darker sackcloth was coarser in texture and similar to the tightly woven burlap of today. It was very durable but not very attractive. Because sackcloth could take a great deal of abuse and was also very breathable, it became the ideal fabric for tents. These same qualities made sackcloth the fabric of choice for sacks used for carrying grain and toting provisions when traveling (Gen. 42:25; Josh. 9:4). Sackcloth was not particularly soft to sit or sleep on, but it was better than a rock; thus the tireless watch of Rizpah over the bodies of Saul's

sons and grandsons was slightly softened by her use of a sackcloth bedroll (2 Sam. 21:10).

Clothing was typically sewn from wool or linen fabric, yet the most frequent mention of sackcloth in the Bible is a reference to people wearing sackcloth clothing. The donning of this unique apparel was a cultural signal announcing to other mortals, to the Lord, or to both that the wearer was in some form of distress. Individuals mourning the loss of a family member put on such clothing during the time of their grieving (Gen. 37:34; Joel 1:8; Amos 8:10). When the opposition's general, Abner, defected to the side of David, he was murdered in cold blood. David called on all his people to show respect for this fallen warrior by putting on sackcloth as they walked in mourning before his body (2 Sam. 3:31). Dressing in sackcloth could also symbolize that one was powerless to respond to his or her circumstances. As the Aramean army faced defeat, they declared their submission to Ahab by dressing in this fabric (1 Kings 20:32). Joram expressed his powerless frustration by wearing such a garment when the citizens of his besieged Samaria resorted to cannibalism (2 Kings 6:30). And this is how people dressed when they were faced by the threat of an overwhelming enemy (Isa. 15:3). When people dressed in this clothing of distress, the expectation was that others would not only recognize their emotional state but also treat them in a more kindly fashion. David was appalled when his dressing in sackcloth did not afford him this expected courtesy: "When I put on sackcloth, people make sport of me" (Ps. 69:11).

The message of distress sent by wearing sackcloth was also one that could be directed at the Lord. Faithful leaders like Hezekiah, David, and Mordecai dressed in sackcloth when facing circumstances that were well beyond their control. In each case the distress illustrated in their attire was attended by a call for help from their powerful and merciful God (2 Kings 19:1–2; 1 Chron.

People dressed in sackcloth as a signal to others that they were in deep distress.
Gary Ombler © Dorling Kindersley

21:16; Esth. 4:1–4). As Job expressed frustration over his circumstances, he acknowledged his powerless position in the way he dressed: "I have sewed sackcloth over my skin and buried my brow in the dust" (Job 16:15).

A crisis of conscience could also lead to the wearing of sackcloth. When the burning reality of sin seared the conscience, penitence filled the heart. A change of heart was signaled by a change in clothing to garments made of sackcloth. Even the heart of wicked King Ahab was subject to moments of spiritual unrest. Faced with the horrific details of Elijah's condemnation, "he tore his clothes, put on sackcloth and fasted. He lay in sackcloth and went around meekly" (1 Kings 21:27). God recognized and honored that penitence in Ahab, just as he did the repentant hearts he found in Nineveh. Jonah had declared an end to this wicked city, and the city responded quickly, hoping that the Lord might relent. Everyone from the greatest to the least dressed in sackcloth, including the king, who ordered that not only the people dress in garments of repentance but the animals as well (Jonah 3:5–8). The attire of repentance is what Jesus longed to see but failed to see in the cities where he did the majority of his miracles,

Korazin and Bethsaida (Matt. 11:21; Luke 10:13). The connection of sackcloth to repentance may also explain why this kind of clothing was typically worn by the prophets (Isa. 20:2; Rev. 11:3). The coarse garments of Elijah and John the Baptist not only linked the ministry of these two men, but it may also be a symbol of the message they regularly carried to God's people, the call to repent (2 Kings 1:8; Matt. 3:4).

The call to put on sackcloth thus became the equivalent of the call to repent. This is particularly evident in the language of Isaiah and Jeremiah. "Tremble, you complacent women; shudder, you daughters who feel secure! Strip off your clothes, put sackcloth around your waists" (Isa. 32:11; cf. 22:12; 58:5). "So put on sackcloth, lament and wail, for the fierce anger of the LORD has not turned away from us" (Jer. 4:8; cf. 6:26; Joel 1:13).

Only one thing can bring comfort to the conscience in distress — the message of forgiveness from the Lord. Once again a change in clothing marks the moment when the pain of sin is replaced by the peace of forgiveness: "You turned my wailing into dancing; you removed my sackcloth and clothed me with joy" (Ps. 30:11).

Salt

For those living in the Promised Land, salt was available locally and used in many facets of day-to-day living. Although the art of extracting salt from seawater via evaporation was known, this

Salt along the shore of the Dead Sea.

time- and labor-intensive method of harvesting salt would not have been necessary for those living so close to the Dead Sea (also known as the Salt Sea). In the Dead Sea basin, naturally occurring salt could be mined or gathered and then transported throughout Israel for both domestic and industrial use. Of course the salt that made its way into the homes was not like the table salt of today. The ancients would not have recognized the small white grains of nearly pure sodium chloride found in our salt shakers; their salt came to them in chunks that were a mixture of the tasty sodium chloride and other impurities that either lacked taste or carried a bitter taste.

Five cultural uses of salt are either directly mentioned or alluded to in the Bible. First, our bodies require salt to maintain the appropriate balance of water; too much or too little salt can cause health problems. This is particularly the case for those living in a warm, dry climate, because salt plays a critical role in fostering the perspiration that keeps the body cool. Like the ancients, we crave salt in our food because we need a certain amount of salt in our diet (Job 6:6). Second, salt was used to preserve meat, which bacteria could quickly degrade in a culture without refrigeration. The salting of meat inhibits the growth of bacteria by removing the watery environment it needs to survive. The salt that was harvested along the Dead Sea was transported north to Magdala (Tarichaea) where it was used to preserve fish caught in the Sea of Galilee. A third use of salt was associated with the birth of a child. On the day a child was born, he or she was washed and rubbed with salt (Ezek. 16:4). The reason for this practice is unmentioned and has been assigned both medical and religious motivations. Fourth, salt was mixed with manure (Luke 14:34–35), as it is today by rural Palestinians. In a land with precious little lumber, the residents

have a long history of burning dried manure as fuel for cooking and heating. The addition of the salt is thought to produce a fuel that burns at a higher temperature than manure alone. Finally, salt was also employed as a weapon of war in various ancient Near Eastern cultures. When a city was defeated and the conquerors had no plans to occupy the city, their efforts to make such a place a permanent ruin included damaging the agricultural fields around it. One way to do so was to spread salt on the arable land to compromise its ability to produce food. Without arable fields nearby, a city was less likely to be resettled (Judg. 9:45).

Three connotations associated with salt lie behind the symbolic use of salt in biblical culture and Bible communication. First, because salt is used as a preservative, it is symbolically linked to things that will last a long time. For instance, the Bible authors speak of the "salt of the covenant" (Lev. 2:13; Num. 18:19; 2 Chron. 13:5). Those in the ancient Near East who were entering into an agreement would eat a meal that included heavily salted food as a way of stating that their agreement with one another was one destined to endure. Thus a salt covenant was one meant to be "everlasting" (Num. 18:19). This application of salt may well lie behind the frequent use of salt in the worship system designed by the Lord for Israel. Salt was used to make the special incense for the tabernacle and temple and was also used for virtually every sacrifice (Ex. 30:35; Lev. 2:13; Ezek. 43:24). This repeated use of salt may well be yet another way to link the regular worship of Israel with their covenant with the Lord. The link between covenant and salt may also provide the best explanation for Elisha's use of salt in healing the spring at Jericho (2 Kings 2:20–21).

Second, the connotation of ruin or desolation is associated with salt. Like a city that has been made unlivable, so the Lord can act against a person or a place to bring either to ruin. Lot's wife became one with the decimated landscape around Sodom and Gomorrah when she hesitated to leave the life she had known. "She became a pillar of salt" (Gen. 19:26). As an invading army might ruin the arable land, so God promised that those who challenged him would pay with the devastation of their land. The language is often reminiscent of what happened to Sodom and Gomorrah: "The whole land will be a burning waste of salt and sulfur—nothing planted, nothing sprouting, no vegetation growing on it" (Deut. 29:23; cf. Ps. 107:34; Jer. 48:9; Zeph. 2:9).

Finally, the role of salt in making food more palatable is used as a metaphor for righteous living, particularly in the language of Jesus (Matt. 5:13; Mark 9:49–50; Luke 14:34). "Salt" is good, but it is possible for salt to lose its saltiness. The chunk of salt a family struck to break free grains of pure salt lasted just so long before it produced more byproduct than pure salt, and once the chunk of salt reached that point, there was no turning back. It was not good for anything—not even for use with the manure. Therefore Jesus encourages us to "have salt in yourselves, and be at peace with each other" (Mark 9:50). Picking up where Jesus left off, Paul writes, "Let your conversation be always full of grace, seasoned with salt, so that you may know how to answer everyone" (Col. 4:6).

Salt Sea. *See* Dead Sea.

Samaria (City of)

The Old Testament city of Samaria was built on a prominent hill approximately twenty-five miles inland from the Mediterranean Sea and forty miles north of Jerusalem. Given the advantages the site promised, an important city was destined for this location. The hill on which Samaria sat rose some three hundred feet above the surrounding valleys, providing its residents with a degree of natural security from attack. A short walk down that hill brought one into a large basin filled with farm fields capable of producing an abundance of food. Samaria was also favored by its position alongside natural travel corridors that provided access to the interior of the country and to the world via connections to the Jezreel Valley and Phoenicia, Israel's strong international trading partner.

The hill that once belonged to Shemer became the capital city of the northern kingdom in the ninth century BC during the tenure of King Omri (1 Kings 16:24). In the fifty years prior to this, the capital of the northern kingdom had moved three times, but once Omri purchased this hill and founded Samaria here, it remained the capital of the northern kingdom for 150 years. Starting in the days of Omri and continuing through the rule of his son Ahab, Samaria became a showplace. It was surrounded by casemate walls twenty to thirty feet thick and contained a large palace and administrative complex with architecture that rivaled the buildings of Solomon in Jerusalem. All indications from the Bible, ancient Near Eastern history, and the archaeological record suggest that Samaria enjoyed a healthy economy, reflected in its expensive imports and high living (1 Kings 22:39; Amos 6:4).

But this rosy picture of life in the capital city of the northern kingdom is not the one painted most frequently by the biblical authors. There are bright moments, mostly connected with the ministry of Elisha (2 Kings 2:25; 5:3; 6:19–20). Yet it is the darker moments and negative publicity that overwhelm the Bible reader, leaving Samaria enveloped in negative connotations. The majority of the time, it is a city given over to pagan worship, social abuses, and shaky leadership. King Ahab built a temple to Baal in this city, erected an Asherah pole, and supported a large number of Baal priests who led worship there (1 Kings 16:32–33; 18:19). By all appearances, Baal worship had become the state religion of the northern kingdom: "Among the prophets of Samaria I saw this repulsive thing:

They prophesied by Baal and led my people Israel astray" (Jer. 23:13). And when Jehu finally brought an end to this Baal worship facility (2 Kings 10:18–28), lingering connections to Asherah and calf worship continued (2 Kings 10:31; 13:6; 14:23–24; et al.). Separated from the love of the Lord, the love for one another quickly grew cold, leading to the abuse of the poor, sexual abuse, gluttony, and corruption in the legal system (Amos 2:6–8; 3:9–10; 4:1; 5:10–13; 6:4–6). And when the prophets called

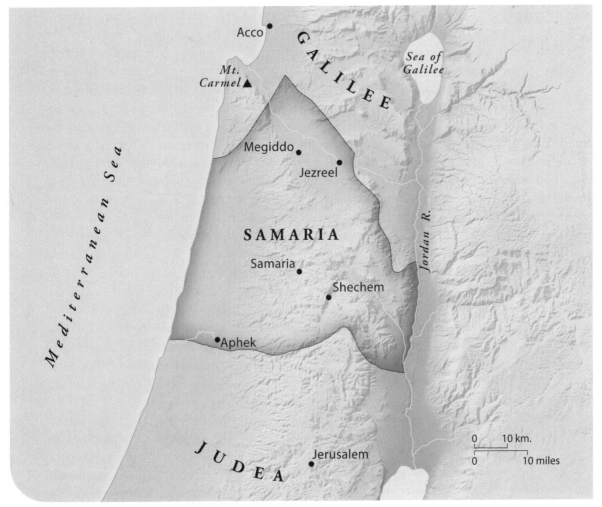

Samaria.

Samaria to repentance, their preaching was met with an unhealthy dose of misplaced pride and arrogance (Isa. 9:9). Where were the leaders of God's people in all this, the kings who were to keep their subjects connected to the Lord and make justice known in the streets? They took the lead in the debauchery, at least as long as they were in office, which in the closing days of Israel was not every long. As the morality of the capital city eroded, we see palace intrigue increasing and the time spent in office diminishing until the Lord had had enough, allowing the city to fall in 722 BC (2 Kings 17:1–6). It happened as Hosea had foretold: "Samaria and its king will float away like a twig on the surface of the waters" (Hos. 10:7). Pagan worship, social decay, and unstable and ungodly leadership clung to the capital city and permanently damaged the connotations associated with it.

The deserved reputation of Samaria subsequently became a tool in the hands of the prophets who were directing their words of correction toward Jerusalem. They urged the kings and capital of the southern kingdom to learn the lesson that Samaria had not. The measuring line that was used to evaluate and subsequently condemn the capital of the north was now being stretched to measure the righteousness of those in the south (2 Kings 21:13). As the Lord did so, he asked the poignant and penetrating question, "Shall I not deal with Jerusalem and her images as I dealt with Samaria and her idols?" (Isa. 10:11).

Samaria also became personified in the language of the prophets. Hosea addressed the city as if it were the culprit: "Throw out your calf-idol, O Samaria! My anger burns against them. How long will they be incapable of purity?" (Hos. 8:5). But it is Ezekiel who portrays the city of Samaria as a young woman, the sister of Jerusalem (Ezek. 16; 23). In this extended analogy, Jerusalem, the younger sister, is contrasted with Samaria, the older sister. The older sister, named Oholah, had regularly engaged in prostitution with other pagan kingdoms, filling herself with their idols. In the end Oholah was not favored but destroyed by her lovers (Ezek. 23:5–8). "They stripped her naked, took away her sons and daughters and killed her with the sword. She became a byword among women, and punishment was inflicted on her" (v. 10). Jerusalem had gone the unfortunate way of her sister and so would find herself meeting the same fate as her sister city to the north (vv. 32–35).

Sandal

Sandals, the ordinary footwear of Bible times, consisted of a leather or fiber sole attached to the moving foot of the owner by a leather thong. An ordinary pair of sandals must not have been particularly expensive, because Abram lists a sandal strap as the least valuable item in the pile of booty he had taken from the kings who had captured his nephew, Lot (Gen. 14:23). With sandals available at a reasonable price, ordinary men and women could afford to wear them every day when they were working outdoors or traveling (Ex. 12:11; Acts 12:8). Of course some sandals were destined to be more expensive than others, noteworthy for the way they graced one's foot and for the high-quality material used in making them (Song 7:1; Ezek. 16:10).

The role of the sandal in society was much more complex than this simple footwear might suggest. The biblical authors mention sandals rhetorically either because they conform to social expectation or defy it. For example, there was every expectation that sandals that had been in service for a time would wear out. This expectation was used by the Gibeonites who displayed worn sandals to support their claim that they had come a great distance (Josh. 9:5, 13). But sandals did not wear out when God intervened. As an example of the Lord's care, Moses reminded God's people that the Lord had kept their sandals from wearing out despite being worn for forty years in the wilderness (Deut. 29:5). In an ominous echo, Isaiah warned rebellious Israel that God would permit distant nations to invade their land. Tireless soldiers were on the march unhindered by as much as a broken

sandal thong (Isa. 5:27). Because sandals would wear out, those embarking on a longer trip might take along an extra pair. However, Jesus told the Twelve as he was sending them out to rely on their listeners for the extra support they might need; that meant leaving behind a spare tunic and sandals (Matt. 10:10).

Those of lower social standing could be assigned the undignified task of removing the footwear from their masters' feet and carrying their sandals for them. John uses this image to contrast his station with that of Jesus'. One more powerful than John was about to take the stage, and John was unworthy of removing or carrying the sandals of this great Teacher (Matt. 3:11; Mark 1:7; Luke 3:16; John 1:27). In one of Jesus' teaching stories, he spoke about a disobedient son who wasted the inheritance he had

demanded. When the impoverished, sandal-less son returned to his father, he looked more like a slave than a son. His father quickly remedied that notion, calling for sandals to be brought for his feet (Luke 15:22). Just the opposite message is sent in the Psalms when the sandal is not given to someone but thrown at him as an owner might toss his sandal at a slave: "upon Edom I toss my sandal" (Pss. 60:8; 108:9).

In several situations people had their sandals forcibly removed from their feet. In ancient Assyrian reliefs, we see captives of war forced to walk barefoot. That is why God directed Isaiah to remove his sandals and go without them for three years as a symbolic prophecy of the fate awaiting Egypt and Cush (Isa. 20:2–4; cf. 2 Chron. 28:15). The man who refused to live up to the Levirate marriage obligations also faced sandal removal. This law required a man to marry his sister-in-law should her husband die without having a son to carry on his father's name. If the living brother refused, the widow would take off one of his sandals and spit in his face. And from that time on that brother's family line would be called "The Family of the Unsandaled" (Deut. 25:5–10). The last thing a poor person might have to sell or offer as collateral for a loan was his or her sandals. Amos roundly criticized the abusive behavior of some who would "sell the

An ancient sandal found at Masada in Judea.

righteous for silver, and the needy for a pair of sandals" (Amos 2:6; cf. 8:6).

Sandals were also removed voluntarily when circumstances called for it. Going about barefoot was a sign of mourning. That is why David climbed the Mount of Olives only after removing his sandals, one of the ways he displayed his grief as he was driven from his capital by Absalom (2 Sam. 15:30). And that is why the Lord directed Ezekiel not to remove his sandals when his wife died. He was not to display any of the typical signs of mourning as a criticism of Israel who would fail to mourn the ruin of the Lord's sanctuary (Ezek. 24:17, 23). The wearer would also remove his shoes when it became clear that God was present. Because sandals were ordinary and because they tracked in dirt and filth, it was improper to wear them when standing in the Lord's presence. Both Moses and Joshua were quick to remove their footwear when it became clear that they were standing on "holy ground" (Ex. 3:5; Josh. 5:15). Sandals were also removed when real estate exchanged hands. Apparently the perimeter of the property being sold was walked by the one who either owned the property or who owned the rights to it. The sandal that had surveyed the property line was then given to the one who wished to gain ownership when the deal was done. When Boaz wished to marry Ruth, he recognized that a closer relative had first rights not only to Ruth but to the property that had belonged to her deceased husband. This closer relative had an interest in the property but not in Ruth and so was willing to transfer the right to purchase that property to Boaz. The deal was finalized when he removed his sandal (Ruth 4:7–8).

Scale

Before coins were minted, those wishing to purchase property or goods might do so with precious metals. This kind of business transaction required the use of a scale to certify that the amount of metal being exchanged was equal to the amount of metal agreed upon. The scale that stood at the heart of this transaction was a balance scale. It consisted of a straight beam that was split into two equal halves by a cord tied around the middle. Two pans of equal weight were suspended from each end of the beam with cords of equal length that were tied to the beam at an equal distance from the pivot point.

This scale functioned on a principle taught today in grade school—the weight of an object multiplied by its distance from the pivot point (arm) produces a value

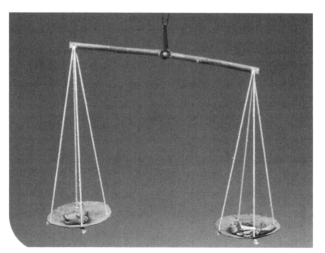

A Roman Period balance scale.
Z. Radovan/www.BibleLandPictures.com

(moment) that represents the force exerted by the object. When an equal amount of weight was placed in each pan, an equal amount of force was exerted, causing the suspended balance beam to rest in a neutral position rather than tip toward one pan or the other. With this principle of physics at work, it was possible for a merchant to put a stone or metal weight of known value in one pan and then have the purchaser add his or her precious metal to the other pan until the beam moved to a neutral position, indicating that the amount of metal in one pan was equal to the known weight in the other pan.

We see this procedure at work when the Lord directed Jeremiah to purchase a field. With the deed signed, payment was made after the agreed upon amount of silver was weighed out using a balance scale (Jer. 32:10). Isaiah alluded to this practice in mocking the pagan practice of weighing out silver and gold on a scale to pay the goldsmith to make a god from that same metal (Isa. 46:6). This is also the type of scale Ezekiel used to weigh his own hair. During this symbolic prophecy, God directed Ezekiel to shave off and then divide the hair of his beard and head into three equal parts; he did so using a balance scale (Ezek. 5:1). This same kind of scale is carried by the rider on the black horse in Revelation. Here the scale is used to illustrate just how outrageous the price of grain had become during famine (Rev. 6:5–6).

The balance scale seems quite primitive by our standards and was subject to all kinds of errors; but God called for those who owned such a scale to do the best they could to assure it produced unbiased indications. The law of God directed his people to "use honest scales and honest weights" (Lev. 19:36). This principle is reaffirmed in various proverbs: "The LORD abhors dishonest scales, but accurate weights are his delight" (Prov. 11:1; cf. 16:11; 20:23). A dishonest scale could be rigged by moving the pivot point on the balance beam, using pans of differing weight, attaching the pans by cords of unequal length, or by using weights that did not represent the value stamped on them. These techniques of rigging a scale to favor the owner must have become more prevalent during the time of the divided kingdom, for the prophets use it to illustrate the downward moral drift of God's people: "The merchant uses dishonest scales; he loves to defraud" (Hos. 12:7; cf. Ezek. 45:10; Amos 8:5; Mic. 6:11).

The biblical authors also speak of a metaphorical scale that is used to evaluate and illustrate moral integrity. In this case God's immutable law becomes the known weight used to check how well mortal deeds compare with divine commands. Frustrated that others were not recognizing his innocence, Job called for God to get out this divine scale: "Let God weigh me in honest scales and he will know that I am blameless" (Job 31:6). The Babylonian leadership had been placed in just such a scale; but the results were not what the boastful Belshazzar had hoped to hear: "You have been weighed on the scales and found wanting" (Dan. 5:27).

Metaphorical scales are called upon not just to weigh people but also to weigh a variety of other things en route to making a rhetorical point. After his first exchange with Eliphaz, Job felt that his friends did not understand the depths of his pain, so he resorted to this image: "If only my anguish could be weighed and all my misery placed on the scales! It would surely outweigh the sand of the seas—no wonder my words have been impetuous" (Job 6:2–3). Just as this scale illustrated how incomprehensible Job's suffering was, so another scale was used to indicate just how incomprehensible God is. Isaiah sought to comfort his readers with this rhetorical question: "Who has held the dust of the earth in a basket, or weighed the mountains on the scales and the hills in a balance?" (Isa. 40:12). His readers had measured the volume and weight of small, manageable items, but only the living God had the ability to weigh something as unwieldy and immense as a mountain.

In just a few verses, Isaiah returns to this image. The scales of Bible times were used in environments that guaranteed they would collect a small amount of dust. While this would introduce some inaccuracy into the weighing process, the user never bothered with this insignificant dust. The nations that seemed so powerful and so capable of disrupting the life of little Israel were of insufficient weight and influence to disrupt the plans of the Almighty. Isaiah says that these nations amounted to nothing more than the neglected dust that had gathered on the scales (Isa. 40:15).

Sea of the Arabah. *See* Dead Sea.

Seal

The seal was a carefully guarded piece of personal property used to make an impression on wet clay or wax. It was so precious that it was always kept on one's person either in the form of a signet ring worn on the finger, flat stamp seal, or cylinder seal worn around the neck on a leather cord. The young woman in the Song of Songs longed to have the intimacy with her lover that a seal had with its owner: "Place me like a seal over your heart, like a seal on your arm" (Song 8:6). If the seal was given to another, it signaled a close relationship between the holder and owner. Tamar asked for the seal of Jacob to create that connection and safeguard her life (Gen. 38:18, 25).

Seals were handmade by artisans (Ex. 28:11) who incised a wide variety of designs into stone, metal, rock, ivory, or clay. Each design was unique to the owner and could include such images as geometric shapes or scenes from everyday life, as well as personal names or phrases. The artist had to make the design in reverse so that it would appear correctly when the stamped design was transferred to an impressionable medium.

Seals were applied to vessels of various sizes to indicate the owner, origin, or contents of the container. But when literal seals are mentioned in the Bible, they are almost always being applied to letters, official decrees, or contracts (1 Kings 21:8; Neh. 9:38 – 10:1; Esth. 3:12; 8:8, 10; Jer. 32:44). Once the writing on a scroll was completed, the scroll was rolled up and tied with a cord. A blob of wet clay was placed on the knot, and the seal was pressed into the clay. When the clay dried, the enduring personal mark of the owner remained on the document. In the case of a contract, two copies of the agreement could be made. One was left unsealed and so could be easily referenced; the other was sealed only to be opened if a dispute arose about the integrity of the unsealed copy of the agreement (Jer. 32:10 – 11). This is likely the image in view when we read that a prophecy of future events is sealed for a time. After Isaiah had written down a forward-looking prophecy, he directed his disciples to roll up the scroll and seal it (Isa. 8:1, 16). When the events transpired as promised, the scroll could be opened and the untouched details perused for the accuracy of what Isaiah had foretold. (For a similar use of this imagery, see Dan. 9:24; 12:4.)

A seal could also be placed on something other than a document to prevent tampering. After Daniel was put in the lions' den, the king sealed the stone that blocked the entrance "so that Daniel's situation might not be changed" (Dan. 6:17). The stone that blocked the entrance to Jesus' tomb was sealed for the same reason; the religious leaders feared that his disciples would remove Jesus' body and claim that he had risen from the dead as he had promised (Matt. 27:66).

Whether the seal was on a contract, decree, or stone, it could be opened only by the one authorized to do so. In the book of Revelation the scroll that revealed the events of the last days had seven seals that could be broken only by one deemed worthy (Rev. 5:1–4). For a time no one in heaven or on earth was so authorized; but John's disappointment gave way to excited expectation when one of the elders pointed to Jesus who was "able to open the scroll and its seven seals" (v. 5). This led the heavenly choir to sing, "You are worthy to take the scroll and open its seals, because you were slain" (v. 9).

These images and connotations associated with the seal make figurative appearances in the artful wordplay of the biblical authors. For example, a seal marked an item as one's own. God's ownership of the world is certified by the fact that it jumped to life when his metaphorical seal touched it (Job 38:14). The Lord not only claims ownership of the world but also of the believers who live here. The Epistles often speak in this way. "Now it is God who makes both us and you stand firm in Christ. He anointed us, set his seal of ownership on us, and put his Spirit in our hearts as a deposit, guaranteeing what is to come" (2 Cor. 1:21–22). "Having believed, you were marked in him with a seal, the promised Holy Spirit" (Eph. 1:13; cf. 4:30; 2 Tim. 2:19; Rev. 7:1–5). The seal is also a sign that access has been denied. Job celebrated the fact that the

Seals stamped in clay found at Lachish. Such seals were applied to vessels in order to indicate the owner, origin, or contents of the container.
Todd Bolen/www.BiblePlaces.com

sins that put him at eternal risk were put into a container and sealed (Job 14:17).

Metaphorical seals also demonstrate authenticity. In that regard Jesus urged people not to look first and foremost at the miracles he did but at the fact that "God the Father has placed his seal of approval" on him (John 6:27). Paul notes that the righteousness of Abraham is not caused by his circumcision, but rather that circumcision is evidence of his righteousness. Circumcision thus is the seal that gives external evidence of an invisible quality, just as the visible seal gives authenticity to the contents hidden in a document (Rom. 4:11). In a second simile, Paul likens the Christians in Corinth to a seal of authenticity. Some had questioned his authority as an apostle. To the Corinthians he said, "Even though I may not be an apostle to others, surely I am to you! For you are the seal of my apostleship in the Lord" (1 Cor. 9:2).

Seat (Chair)

Following a long afternoon of traveling on foot, transporting grain from the fields, or guiding home the family flock, it felt good to sit down, particularly if your home was one that had chairs. The ordinary chair of Bible times was a simple piece of furniture resembling a four-legged stool. While some chairs had backs and armrests, surviving depictions of ordinary chairs from the ancient Near East suggest that this piece of wooden furniture was more like a stool, rectangular in shape with a flat, flexible top made from fabric or leather. This is the type of seat or chair we might typically find in a family's living quarters (2 Kings 4:10). However, if one were to take a seat in the synagogue or in the city gate, that seat was a stone shelf cut high enough to allow the average adult male to sit with his feet touching the floor.

There is no evidence to suggest that biblical culture prescribed a seating order for ordinary meals around the family dinner table. Joseph's brothers clearly were not accustomed to sitting in a specific pattern, for they were astonished by the fact that their Egyptian host knew their birth order and had them seated in the order of their birth (Gen. 43:33). Today, even when the seating order at a dinner table or in a classroom is not prescribed, we tend to return to the same seat as a matter of habit. David likewise had a customary seat at the dinner table of Saul. When it was vacant, Saul knew exactly who was missing (1 Sam. 20:18, 25).

The Bible also knows of special seats—seats of honor or judgment—that carried special connotations and that are thus used rhetorically by the biblical authors. On more than one occasion

A woman sitting on a four-legged stool.

Z. Radovan/www.BibleLandPictures.com

and in more than one testament, we read about the seat of honor at a meal or banquet. In the Old Testament, we find this kind of seat given to a king-to-be, an honored citizen, a deported king, and a royal adviser (1 Sam. 9:22; 1 Kings 21:9, 12; 2 Kings 25:28; Esth. 3:1; Jer. 52:32). The custom of establishing a hierarchy of seating is also noted in connection with New Testament banquets and wedding feasts. Observing how the guests at a meal were grabbing up the more honorable seats at the table, Jesus attacked this pride-filled, self-importance with a parable. He encouraged his listeners to cultivate the kind of humility that would lead them to select the seats of least importance at the table rather than try to muscle into the seats of honor: "But when you are invited, take the lowest place, so that when your host comes, he will say to you, 'Friend, move up to a better place.' Then you will be honored in the presence of all your fellow guests. For everyone who exalts himself will be humbled, and he who humbles himself will be exalted" (Luke 14:10–11). Behind Jesus' parable lie the words of the psalmist who speaks of God doing the unexpected: "He raises the poor from the dust ... he seats them with princes" (Ps. 113:7–8).

Although most of the seats in an ordinary synagogue were simple stone benches, certain seats carried the connotation of greater honor here as well. These may have been the upper tier of stone benches that faced those gathered to worship. More than a few Pharisees and teachers of the law basked in the glory of those seats. And in response Jesus roundly criticized their seat selection as further evidence of self-absorbed pride (Matt. 23:6; Mark 12:39; Luke 11:43; 20:46). At least in some instances, the practice of honorary seating in worship must have carried over into the New Testament church as well, for James warns about favoring a rich man over a poor man by ushering him to a place of honor (James 2:3).

One seat in the synagogue appears to have been more honorable than any other—the seat of Moses. The name of this seat clearly links it to the authoritative teaching of Moses and his role in settling disputes among the Israelites (Ex. 18:13). When the teachers of the law and Pharisees sat in this special seat, they claimed to be speaking with the authority of Moses. Insofar as they spoke for God, Jesus directed the people to heed their words: "The teachers of the law and the Pharisees sit in Moses' seat. So you must obey them and do everything they tell you. But do not do what they do, for they do not practice what they preach" (Matt. 23:2–3).

Once God's people had built cities and city gates in the Promised Land, special stone benches located along the sides of the gates were occupied by the elders of the city. These unassuming seats were honored seats from which the elders administered city affairs and carried on their judicial responsibilities (Job 29:7–8; Prov. 31:23). During the period of the monarchy, capital cities like Samaria and Jerusalem had a special seat in the gate where the king would normally sit and hold court (2 Sam. 19:8). Only against this normal scene with Israel's king and elders sitting in the gate can we appreciate this horrible news shared by Jeremiah: "All the officials of the king of Babylon came and took seats" in the gate (Jer. 39:3).

When Rome controlled the Promised Land, they installed a Roman governor who held court at a Roman judgment seat. Here there was no jury, just the Roman governor who heard the evidence and levied a verdict that could only be overturned by the emperor himself. Jesus heard Pilate deliver such a verdict from this seat during his trial (Matt. 27:19; John 19:13). Perhaps the image of a Roman judgment seat was in Paul's mind when he spoke about the judgment seat of God (Rom. 14:10; 2 Cor. 5:10).

Seed

The seed is a marvel of nature of vital importance to those living in Bible times. It consists of a protective shell and the plant embryo within it. The protective shell shields the embryo from harm while allowing it to be transported to a favorable growing medium. In addition, this protective jacket often houses a supply of food that keeps the embryo viable while awaiting conditions suitable for germination. Scientific inquiry has allowed us to better understand the processes at work within the seed, but in many respects, the ability of the seed to produce a full-fledged plant remains as much a mystery for us as it was for the ancients (Mark 4:27). Behind it lies the powerful hand of the Lord who designed, initiated, and now sustains this miraculous transformation that happens billions upon billions of times each year to beautify our world and provide us with food (Gen. 1:11 – 12, 29).

Today the vital connection between the miraculous sprouting of the seed and our daily meals can get lost between farm, factory, grocery store, and kitchen, but that was much less likely for those living in Bible times who personally planted their own seeds in hope of a harvest. Virtually everyone planted grain seeds that provided flour for making bread and seeds for sow-

Biblical authors often used the seed as a metaphor for descendants, both physical and spiritual.

ing in subsequent seasons (Isa. 55:10). No matter what else beckoned, the sowing of this seed was given priority time (Eccl. 11:6), because a field not sown was a field of no value (Gen. 47:19). The grain or seed that was harvested could be eaten, bartered for other products, or used to pay taxes (Gen. 47:23–24; 1 Sam. 8:15). In fact, seeds were so important that God provided legislation specific to planting, ritual contamination, and tithing (Lev. 11:37–38; 19:19; 27:30; Deut. 14:22; 22:9). Additionally, it was an area of life that God promised to bless or touch with catastrophe, depending on the covenant faithfulness of his people (Lev. 26:16; Deut. 28:38; Hag. 2:19). Obedience meant "the seed will grow well" (Zech. 8:12); disobedience might find "the seeds are shriveled beneath the clods" (Joel 1:17).

The seeds that were so much a part of daily living also were used figuratively by the biblical authors. Because the seeds were the natural offspring of the plant, the plant seed became a metaphor for mortal descendants or offspring (as it is often translated in the NIV). To speak of someone's seed is to speak of their descendants, family line, offspring, or child (Gen. 16:10; 19:32, 34; 1 Sam. 1:11; 2 Sam. 4:8; 2 Kings 5:27). In the Pentateuch, mention of a person's seed often takes on a narrower and more technical meaning. The seed of Abraham, Isaac, and Jacob participated in a special covenant relationship with the Lord. Consequently, the word "seed" is intimately linked to the promises that Abraham's family would grow to become a great nation, be given a special land as their own, and become a blessing to all nations (Gen. 12:7; 13:15; 15:5, 18; 17:7–10, 19; 21:12; 22:17–18; 24:7; 26:3–4; 28:13–14; 32:12; 35:12; 46:3–7; 48:4; Ex. 32:13; 33:1; Deut. 1:8; 10:15; 11:9; 34:4). In this way God's entire plan to redeem the world is intimately linked to the image of

the seed. Thus the prophets could call to mind the entire set of promises linked to the covenant by using shorthand that referred to the seed of Abraham, the seed of Jacob, or the seed of David (Pss. 18:50; 22:23; Isa. 41:8; 45:19; Jer. 30:10; 33:22, 26).

But even before we read about these "seeds" of the patriarchs and only shortly after we hear about the creation of seed-bearing plants, we hear about another special Seed. When sin entered the world, God promised that a seed of Eve would come into the world to set things right (Gen. 3:15). The field of possible families was narrowed to the family of Abraham and even further when God revealed to David that it would be one of his seeds who would be that special seed (2 Sam. 7:12). And Jesus, the seed of Abraham and the seed of David, is subsequently recognized as the long-promised Seed who provides salvation (Rom. 1:3; Gal. 3:16, 19).

In the New Testament, the image continues and matures. In the parable of the sower, Jesus describes a farmer who is sowing seed. As he casts the seed, the wind carries it to different types of soil (Matt. 13:1–23; Mark 4:1–12; Luke 8:4–10). Here the seed is a metaphor for good news about Jesus. Paul makes use of the same image (1 Cor. 3:6; 9:11).

The seed can also be the people who are part of the kingdom. That is the case in the parable of the weeds where the good seed represents the believers (Matt. 13:24–30, 38). Here as throughout the New Testament, the seed has grown from those who are the physical seed of Abraham to all who acknowledge Jesus as their Lord (Gal. 3:29). That is also the case in the parable of the mustard seed where the unassuming mustard seed grows to become a large tree: "Though it is the smallest of all your seeds, yet when it grows, it is the largest of garden plants and becomes a tree, so that the birds of the air come and perch in its branches" (Matt. 13:32).

Finally, the seed is used as a metaphor for the body. When Jesus announced his plans to die on the cross, he used the analogy of a seed to illustrate the necessity of this extreme move. Unless the seed of grain falls into the ground and dies — that is, stops being a seed — that single seed will never be able to become many seeds (John 12:24). Paul also uses the image of the dying seed to illustrate how our present body will be changed at the time of the resurrection: "When you sow, you do not plant the body that will be, but just a seed" (1 Cor. 15:37).

Serpent. *See* Snake.

Shechem (Sychar)

Shechem is located along the well-worn Ridge Route thirty-five miles north of Jerusalem in the hill country of Ephraim. Because of the natural advantages of this location, a city existed here even before the time of Abraham. Both fresh water and rich farmland were readily available. A number of natural roadways connected Shechem with the rest of Canaan, making it a regional center. And because it was situated in a pass between two significant mountains, Mount Ebal and Mount Gerizim, the city provided its visitors with a natural amphitheater where it was possible for thousands to hear and participate in a public event.

The Bible history associated with this city causes two very different connotations to linger around Shechem. On the one hand, it is a city linked with worship of the Lord and with hope. On the other hand, it is a city linked with failed kingship and disappointment. Jesus made use of both connotations when he selected this city (called Sychar during the New Testament) to make a rare and powerful announcement about himself (John 4:5–6).

The connotations of worship and hope became intimately linked to the city at the time of Abram and grew through the time of Joshua. When the Lord called Abram to leave his former homeland for a new land, he did not reveal the destination (Gen. 12:1; Heb. 11:8). The moment of revelation came when Abram reached the Canaanite city of Shechem where the Lord appeared to Abram and said, "To your offspring I will give this land" (Gen. 12:7). Abram quickly responded by building a memorial altar that marked the spot where he received this revelation, allowing his descendants to visit this place to worship and to recall the important message linked with Shechem. His grandson Jacob not only visited this place but purchased land here, built his own altar, and dug a well to support longer stays at the site, which now resonated with the hope-filled promises of God (Gen. 33:18–20; John 4:5–6).

The memory of this important worship site was so strong that it lasted throughout the hundreds of years Abraham's family was displaced from the Promised Land and was living in Egypt. When Joshua led the Israelites into the land, he brought them to this location for a worship service that included rededication to the Mosaic law (Josh. 8:30–35). And when the conquest of the land was complete, the amphitheater that had hosted this rededication was used once again (24:1). Before the tribes were dispersed to their individual homelands, Shechem echoed with words of commitment and hope as Joshua raised a monument to bear witness to this second rededication service (vv. 26–27). Before it ended, the bones of Joseph, which had been

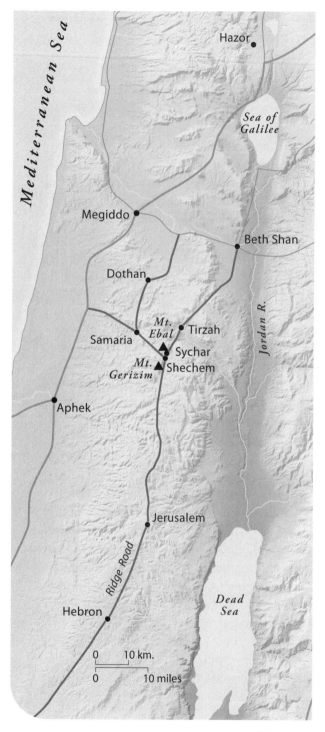

Shechem.

carried from Egypt and through the wilderness, were buried on the very tract of land Jacob had purchased (v. 32), bringing history full circle and linking the hopes of the patriarchs with the hopes of their descendants who now would stake their claim to this land. To top it off, Shechem was made a Levitical city (21:21). A portion of Israel's clergy would live in this city to care for these memorials, to encourage people in their worship, and to keep the hope of a coming Messiah alive. So it was through centuries of history that Shechem became a place associated with worship and hope.

But in the days that followed, Shechem also became a city associated with failed kingship and disappointment. During the time of the judges, the people of Shechem were so taken by the leadership of Gideon that they asked him to be their king and establish a dynasty that would perpetually rule their city (Judg. 8:22). Gideon refused, but his son Abimelech was all too happy to oblige. He proposed the idea and then forced its implementation via murder and intrigue; for the first time in Israel's history, a king was crowned (9:6). The people saw this as a solution to the persistent problem of foreign invasion, but instead, this coronation initiated a series of events that turned the citizens of Shechem against their king and the king against his citizens (9:22–23). In the end the city became a smoldering ruin (9:45), a witness to failed kingship.

That connotation informs another coronation ceremony that also went terribly wrong. Following the death of Solomon, Rehoboam was to become king in his father's place. But the problems he faced quickly become apparent when we see him traveling to Shechem to be recognized as king (1 Kings 12:1). Rehoboam traveled to Shechem, a city that was not his capital and that was associated with failed kingship, in a desperate bid to hold together his father's crumbling kingdom. His efforts were to no avail; kingship failed once again at Shechem as the northern tribes gave notice that they were seceding from the union (vv. 16–17).

These two contradictory connotations of hope and discouragement likely play a pivotal role in the selection of Sychar as the place where Jesus makes a distinctive announcement about himself (John 4:1–26). In the Gospels we almost never hear Jesus say in so many words that he is the Messiah; but he does so at Sychar, the Old Testament location of Shechem (4:25–26). Although Sychar was a Samaritan city in Jesus' day, the declaration of his true identity rings powerfully in a place that had hosted altars, memorials, and worship services in hope of his coming. And in this place where kingship had been known to fail, Jesus declared himself to be the eternal King whose rule would never fail.

Sheep Pen (Sheepfold)

The sheep and goats that were absolutely vital to the well-being of the average family had a very low capacity for defending themselves. Lacking the strength to fight or speed to flee, sheep and goats were no match for the large predators of the Promised Land. Therefore families developed a series of strategies designed to safeguard their animals. Each flock was assigned a shepherd whose sight, strength, and cunning compensated for the vulnerability of the flock. Throughout the daylight hours, the shepherd would keep the animals tightly configured in a close-knit group and usher stragglers back into the flock. With the need for food and water met, lengthening shadows signaled the coming of more dangerous hours for the flock. From dusk to dawn, even the presence of the shepherd did not guarantee the security of the flock, so the animals were taken into a hard-sided enclosure that put stone and thorns between predator and prey.

Such sheep pens or sheepfolds were located either near the village or in the open countryside. During the wet winter season, pastures for the flock were available closer to the village, which meant it was possible for the shepherds to lead their animals to sheep pens associated with the village complex. But the drier late spring and summer forced the shepherds to move their flocks farther and farther away from the village. These pastures were often too far away to allow a return to the village sheep pens before dark, so the shepherds built sheepfolds in the open countryside in the vicinity of those remote pastures.

In either case the sheepfold was not an enclosed barn or shed with roof and doors that turned on hinges. Instead, a sheep pen could be configured by enhancing a natural cave, closing off the cave's open side by stacking fieldstones to create an artificial fourth wall for the shelter. When a cave was not available, the shepherd could build an elliptical wall of fieldstone that could be topped with a layer of thorny branches. Both types of sheep pen insulated the flock from predators with solid walls that deterred their access to the sheep and goats. Of course it was necessary to create an access point to either sheepfold. The gate that guarded this entry was not a wooden door but the shepherd himself or herself who sat in the opening and controlled who could enter and exit.

This is the kind of sheep pen that receives both literal and metaphorical mention in the Bible. After the Israelites had secured the land east of the Jordan River, the descendants of Reuben and Gad approached Moses with a request. They asked that they be given their land inheritance on that side of the Jordan before sending their men into the battles that would win the west side of the Jordan River for the rest of the tribes (Num. 32:1–15). They asked for and received permission to build the necessary infrastructure that would allow their women, children, and herds to live securely—fortified cities and pens to secure their livestock (vv. 16, 24). David's dramatic change in station from shepherd to shepherd-king is described by referring to his old habit of building sheep pens: "He chose David his servant and took him from the sheep pens; from tending the sheep he brought him to be shepherd of his people Jacob, of Israel his inheritance" (Ps. 78:70–71).

The familiar sheep pen is also used rhetorically in the Bible. Zephaniah describes the ruin of the large and powerful Philistine cities by observing that the land they occupied would return to its earlier, rustic character. The places that teemed with thriving trade and urban sprawl would become "a place for shepherds and sheep pens" (Zeph. 2:6). Israel would also face the judgment of God as the Babylonian armies crisscrossed their land. Normal life would cease, a fact emphatically pictured by the prophet who looks in the direction of the sheep pens but finds them void of any animals (Hab. 3:17). That is because God's people were deported from the Promised Land. Yet there would be a return, a return that Micah envisioned with this metaphor: "I will surely gather all of you, O Jacob; I

A shepherd with sheep in a pen walled with fieldstone.

will surely bring together the remnant of Israel. I will bring them together like sheep in a pen, like a flock in its pasture; the place will throng with people" (Mic. 2:12).

The most extended and well-known metaphor that employs the image of the sheep pen comes from John 10. Jesus had healed a man who was born blind. When the Pharisees took up an investigation of this matter, they threatened this man and his family with excommunication from the synagogue; no one who acknowledged Jesus as the Christ was permitted to remain a member (John 9:22). When they made good on this threat, Jesus went to the man who had lost his membership in the synagogue to reassure him (vv. 35 – 38). In the metaphor that followed, the sheep pen was the true Israel. Jesus made it clear that he was the "gate" of this sheep pen; he and he alone was the one who controlled or denied access: "I am the gate; whoever enters through me will be saved" (10:9). But lest his listeners think of the kingdom of God in terms that were too narrow, Jesus added, "I have other sheep that are not of this sheep pen. I must bring them also. They too will listen to my voice, and there shall be one flock and one shepherd" (v. 16). The flock of Jesus' followers was much too large for one sheep pen. Gentiles from every corner and culture of the world would also be called to join the flock of the Good Shepherd.

Shepherd

While today it is unusual for a person to know a shepherd personally, in Bible times it was unthinkable that you would not know a shepherd personally. Sheep and goats were in high demand, providing every family with food, clothing, and shelter as well as animals required for worship. That meant shepherds who cared for such animals were common and came in one of two varieties: family shepherds and hired shepherds. Abel, Abraham, Rachel, Jacob, Joseph, and David were shepherds who cared for the family flock, a job that often fell to the younger teens of the family (Gen. 4:2; 13:7 – 8; 29:9; 37:2; 46:32 – 34; 1 Sam. 16:11). Royal families and those who had accumulated significant wealth hired shepherds (1 Sam. 21:7; 25:7; John 10:12). The rabbinic writers who lived after the time of the New Testament had little good to say about such hired shepherds. They urged parents to discourage their children from pursuing this despised trade since those who dedicated their life to it were prone to immoral living (*Qiddushin* 4:14; *Baba Qama* 10:9). Since this was the common perspective in the first century, we can appreciate why shepherds were the first to hear the news of Jesus' birth. On the one hand, they are later-day representatives of those who first heard the promise of a coming Savior — shepherds like Abraham, Isaac, Jacob, and David. On the other hand, the Christmas shepherds become representatives of the despised classes of new Testament society who so desperately needed to hear about a Savior from sin (Luke 2:8 – 20).

The biblical authors give us a very clear idea of what was expected of a good shepherd as they speak directly or metaphorically about them. The flock required water on a daily basis, but during certain months of the year, many regions had little surface water available. Consequently, the shepherd had to lead the animals to a spring or to a well at which the animals could be watered (Gen. 29:3; Ex. 2:16 – 17). In a similar way, changes in the season meant finding different food venues for the flock. The shepherd had to lead the flock to grasslands growing on public land or contract for the use of agricultural fields near a village where the sheep and goats would be welcomed after the harvest (Ps. 23:2; Luke 2:8). And once established in a pasture, the shepherd could not sit for an extended time but had to keep the animals moving to prevent overgrazing that would ruin a pasture for years (Jer. 12:10). Furthermore, it was the shepherd's job to keep the flock gathered in a group. A flock that became spread out made it too easy for predators or thieves to pick off stragglers. Despite the shepherd's efforts, it was inevitable that at least one of the animals in the flock would sometimes wander off and become lost. In this case, the good shepherd set out to reclaim the lost sheep (Matt. 18:12). Travel from pasture to pasture through rugged terrain also meant that there would be

injuries. No matter the time of day, the rough but kind hands of the shepherd went to work soothing the injured animal and tending its wound. What is more, the good shepherd never let this difficult work cause him or her to become jaded toward the animals. Isaiah likened the Lord to a good shepherd, saying, "He tends his flock like a shepherd: He gathers the lambs in his arms and carries them close to his heart; he gently leads those that have young" (Isa. 40:11). The sheep recognized the kind tone in the voice of the shepherd as he or she called them by name and even demonstrated a willingness to put his or her own life at risk should a predator threaten the flock (1 Sam. 17:34–36; Isa. 31:4; John 10:3, 11).

Shepherds keep close watch over their flocks.
Todd Bolen/www.BiblePlaces.com

The role of the shepherd was so familiar to people of Bible times that this image is frequently used as a metaphor for human leaders and for God. Because the role of the shepherd is characterized by leading, the human leaders of various nations who interact with God's people are called shepherds (Isa. 44:28; Jer. 6:3; 50:44). The same is true of the great King David who first led the sheep of his family but became the shepherd of God's people, Israel (2 Sam. 5:2). His godly model of leadership was not always followed by the political and religious leaders who followed him. That is why the prophets often spoke of such leaders as bad shepherds. These were men who lacked understanding, sought their own gain, and scattered the flock (Isa. 56:11; Jer. 23:1–2; 50:6). Ezekiel 34 contains the most concentrated criticism of such leaders, laying bare the failure of Israel's leadership with images of cruel shepherds.

The metaphor of the kind shepherd is used to describe the Lord in both the Old and New Testaments. The first time we find this figure coming to life is at the close of Genesis where Jacob credits the Lord with being his guiding shepherd (Gen. 48:15; 49:24). As inviting as that language is, nothing matches the simplicity and depth of Psalm 23, arguably the best-known passage of all Scripture, which builds on this image: "The LORD is my shepherd, I shall not be in want" (Ps. 23:1). When the leaders of his people failed to lead like a good shepherd should, the Lord promised a messianic leader who would get it right: "I will place over them one shepherd, my servant David, and he will tend them; he will tend them and be their shepherd" (Ezek. 34:23).

This imagery that links the Lord to the kind shepherd continues in the New Testament where favorite illustrations of Jesus involve the image of the good shepherd. As a good shepherd will leave the ninety-nine and search until finding the sheep that has wandered away, so the "Father in heaven is not willing that any of these little ones should be lost" (Matt. 18:14). Faced again by leaders who did not put the members of God's flock first, Jesus spoke out against the abuses while speaking of himself as the anticipated "good shepherd" (John 10:1–18). Distancing himself from the leaders who were like robbers and poorly disciplined hired workers, Jesus declared, "I am the good shepherd. The good shepherd lays down his life for the sheep" (10:11). This image again comes to life in the closing books of the New Testament as the inspired writers lift our eyes to "Jesus, that great Shepherd of the sheep" (Heb. 13:20), who not only rose from the dead but promised to return in glory. Heaven waits with this inviting scene: "The Lamb at the center of the throne will be their shepherd; he will lead them to springs of living water" (Rev. 7:17).

Shield

Those facing the lethal blows delivered by ax, mace, and sword as well as those subject to a shower of enemy arrows quickly came to appreciate the value of their shield. In many respects, the beauty of the ancient shield is found in its simplicity. Such shields consisted of a wood or wicker core over which multiple layers of leather were stretched. The only maintenance required of the owner was rubbing the shield with oil to keep the leather supple and thus more resilient (2 Sam. 1:21; Isa. 21:5).

The biblical authors are familiar with two types of shield, the smaller round shield and the larger rectangular shield. The well-equipped army had soldiers who carried both (2 Chron. 14:8). The round shield protected a smaller area, generally one-half to one-third of the body; but its lighter weight improved the maneuverability of the soldier who carried it. The small round shield was worn on the hand opposite the one wielding the offensive weapon whether that was a sword or ax. The larger shield was upward of four feet in length and in some cases sported a small shelf at the top to deflect arrows angled from above. This rectangular shield offered protection to a larger portion of the body but was heavier and more cumbersome. For champion fighters like Goliath or for the archers who needed both hands to aim and fire their weapon, a shield bearer would carry and carefully position this larger shield (1 Sam. 17:7, 41). We also find this larger shield depicted in ancient artwork illustrating the siege of a city. Here a number of these larger shields are overlapped to form a protective roof over those attacking the foundation of the city's wall.

The shield functioned in a number of different ways in biblical culture. We expect to find them in the hands of soldiers who used this tool to ward off blows that otherwise were destined to maim and kill, but shields also became symbols of leadership and expensive art pieces. Following the defeat of the king of Zobah, David took into his custody "gold shields that belonged to the officers of Hadadezer and brought them to Jerusalem" (2 Sam. 8:7). In more than one instance, we find special shields like this seized as plunder and placed into the victor's treasury (1 Kings 14:26–28; 2 Chron. 32:27). Whether locked down in storage or displayed on a tower (Song 4:4), such shields were clearly art pieces of some value. Solomon himself had two hundred large shields of hammered gold that he kept in his Palace of the Forest of Lebanon (1 Kings 10:16–17). It is unclear whether these shields were mounted as decorations or if they were used in royal processions as they were during the days of Solomon's son Rehoboam. The Egyptian Shishak took away those gold shields, requiring Rehoboam to make new ones of bronze. They were given to the commanders on duty at the royal palace, and "whenever the king went to the LORD's temple, the guards went with him, bearing the shields, and afterward they returned them to the guardroom" (2 Chron. 12:11).

While literal shields were more common in society, it is figurative shields that we find most often in the Bible. And most often they are used as metaphors for God's protection. Immediately after the first reported military action of Abram, God appeared to him. The very first thing he said to this man who had just returned from war with plunder in hand draws on military imagery: "Do not be afraid, Abram. I am your shield, your very great reward" (Gen. 15:1). In a striking echo of this language, at the end of the Torah we find Moses likening the Lord to a shield just before the Israelites cross the Jordan River to begin the conquest of the Promised Land (Deut. 33:29). The first two instances of this metaphor are followed by dozens more, surfacing particularly in the Psalms: "You are a shield around me, O LORD: you bestow glory on me and lift up my head" (Ps. 3:3), and "The LORD is my rock, my fortress and my deliverer; my God is my rock, in whom I take refuge. He is my shield and the horn of my salvation, my stronghold" (18:2).

The king was not only the political leader of God's people, but he was perceived to be the one who would go out before them and fight their battles, thus providing protection for his subjects (1 Sam. 8:20). It naturally follows that the image of the shield attaches itself to the king who functions as a representative of the Lord: "Indeed, our shield belongs to the LORD, our king to the Holy One of Israel" (Ps. 89:18).

The coming of the Messiah will culminate in a time of great peace. This peace will become so pervasive that the shields once so necessary for protection will be destroyed: "He makes wars cease to the ends of the earth; he breaks the bow and shatters the spear, he burns the shields with fire" (Ps. 46:9). But before that peace takes hold, the believer will face continuing warfare as satanic forces pursue control of his or her soul. The one and only time a shield is mentioned in the New Testament finds it serving as a metaphor for faith. In his letter to the Ephesians, Paul urges the Christian warrior to put on the full armor of God. With the picture of the large, rectangular shield carried by the Roman legionary soldier in mind, Paul urges his readers to "take up the shield of faith, with which you can extinguish all the flaming arrows of the evil one" (Eph. 6:16).

This model shows both the round shields and the rectangular-style shields being used to cover a group while attacking a city wall.

Ship. *See* Boat.

Sling

Like the bow and arrow, the sling and slingstone were the long-range weapons used by many armies of the ancient Near East. Although the word *sling* sounds similar to the more familiar *slingshot*, the two have little in common except for the pocket used to hold the projectile. The ancient sling consisted of two cords that were made from animal sinews, leather, or cloth. We will call one the retention cord because it was retained in the throwing hand with a loop, and the other the release cord because it was the end

Sling and slingstones found at Lachish, Judea.
William L. Krewson/www.BiblePlaces.com

of the sling released when the projectile was thrown. Both cords joined company at a cloth or leather pouch designed to hold the slingstone, often a rounded stone two to three inches in diameter weighing in at a half pound or more.

The sling used to hurl the slingstone was held and swung by the dominant hand of the slinger. That is what made the slingers who joined David worthy of special mention; they were able to sling stones with either hand (1 Chron. 12:2). The user would place the loop of the retention cord around one of the fingers of his throwing hand while pinching the release cord between the thumb and index finger. After loading the projectile into the pocket of the sling, the user would slowly rotate the sling to seat the slingstone. Centrifugal force pulled the slingstone to the outside of the orbit, tightening the cords of the sling as the slinger rotated this weapon either above his head or alongside his body. In either case it took only one good rotation to achieve the speed needed to fire the weapon. That happened when the slinger let go of the release cord, allowing the projectile to fly from the pocket at speeds well over one hundred miles per hour. The damage this weapon could do was stunning. The slingstone was capable of killing at a range of one hundred yards. And those who were particularly practiced in its use could "sling a stone at a hair and not miss" (Judg. 20:16).

Although the sling was used by shepherds in guarding the flock, the Bible connects the sling to combat more often. Apparently, ancient armies had specialized units, including a corps trained and equipped to use the sling (Judg. 20:16; 1 Chron. 12:2; 2 Chron. 26:14). When a city was brought under siege, this unit was called upon to use its long-range weapons to pick off enemy soldiers who were firing from the top of the wall. Even those hiding behind the city walls were at risk, because the slingstone could be fired using a trajectory that caused it to travel upward from the slinger and then back toward those behind the wall.

Like other implements used for making war,

the sling is also used rhetorically by the biblical authors. In two instances God is pictured as using a sling. In both he is not hurling a physical projectile but is metaphorically hurling people away with great force and intensity. The first example comes from the mouth of Abigail. She was the wife of Nabal, who had foolishly rebuffed a request of David. As David was about to draw his sword in response to this slight, Abigail showed up with provisions, an apology, and a word of encouragement for David. Seeking to turn David's attention from her husband's poorly chosen words, she told David that the Lord would hurl his enemies away "as from the pocket of a sling" (1 Sam. 25:29). God's sling comes out again in Jeremiah, but this time it is not the enemies of God's people who are being hurled away; rather, it is the Israelites themselves whom God is prepared to hurl from the Promised Land because of their sinful behavior (Jer. 10:18).

The sling appears twice in the poetry of Job and Proverbs. As Job describes the dreaded leviathan, he notes that this beast is not afraid of the weapons that terrorize mortals: "Arrows do not make him flee; slingstones are like chaff to him" (Job 41:28). The inspired poet of wisdom also points to this weapon in order to further disparage the fool: "Like tying a stone in a sling is the giving of honor to a fool" (Prov. 26:8). While everyone using a sling would place a projectile into the pocket, no one would be so foolish as to "tie" this projectile into place. If the weapon were used with the slingstone tied in place, it would cause more damage to the operator than the intended target!

Perhaps the most famous sling is the one carried by David and used to fell Goliath. This particular weapon is not just mentioned in the narrative (1 Sam. 17:40) but assumes a rhetorical role in the summary: "So David triumphed over the Philistine with a sling and a stone; without a sword in his hand he struck down the Philistine and killed him" (v. 50). As it turns out, this weapon choice has something to say about Israel's up-and-coming king. First, it says that David was smart. When we consider the list of weapons carried by Goliath (vv. 4–7), we can see that he intended to engage his Israelite competitor in close-range combat. While David had briefly considered the use of a sword (v. 39), he quickly abandoned it in favor of the sling. In doing so David betrayed his intentions; he was not planning to get anywhere near the Philistine fighting machine but rather to dispatch him from a distance. While this reveals his thoughtful intelligence, it also says something about this faith in the Lord. David took only one weapon into the fight, counting on the Lord to guide his aim and the stone toward his bellicose target. Thus the author of 1 Samuel directs us to the sling because it was the smart choice and because it was the choice that marked David as a leader after God's own heart.

Snake (Serpent, Viper)

The biblical authors use up to fourteen different Hebrew and Greek words to make reference to the thirty-six species of snake native to the Promised Land. Unfortunately, in all but a few cases, the clear assignment of a species to a specific term is not possible. The staff-turned-snake of Moses was likely a cobra (Ex. 4:3–4; 7:8–13). This species of snake was an important symbol of the pharaoh's power, artistically depicted in the crown he wore; thus the image of the Lord's ability to manipulate the cobra/Egypt lies at the heart of this miracle. The "venomous snakes" of Numbers 21:6 that ravaged the Israelites in the wilderness were likely carpet vipers. These twenty-four-inch snakes bury themselves in the sand to await the passing of prey. Known for their aggressiveness, disturbed carpet vipers will strike from hiding and unleash a highly toxic poison that causes massive internal hemorrhaging and death. In most other instances, we are left to understand the biblical snake or serpent in a more generic way.

Snakes can be found throughout the Promised Land in deserts, woodlands, and marshes. But given snakes' secretive nature, even people who traveled about in the open country were unlikely to see them. Encounters

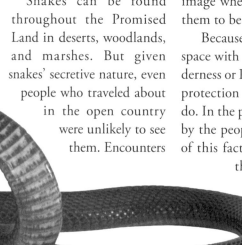

The staff-turned-snake of Moses was likely a cobra.

that are noted are always negative and typically are linked to one of the six poisonous species of snake native to this land. Such snakes would rather flee the presence of people than strike out at them. But when startled by a horse along the road, by someone breaking through a wall, or someone resting their hand on the wall of a home (Gen. 49:17; Eccl. 10:8; Amos 5:19), snakes could be expected to defend themselves by delivering a venomous bite.

In the larger setting of the ancient Near East, the snake appears in myth and art that celebrate its power, ability to heal, fertility, and wisdom.

The biblical authors seem most impressed by the exotic locomotion of the snake (Job 26:13; Prov. 30:19) and by its storied wisdom. The first time a snake is mentioned in the Bible, it is dubbed "more crafty than any of the wild animals the LORD God had made" (Gen. 3:1). The presence of a snake during the temptation of Adam and Eve may have led Jesus to select this image when encouraging his disciples. He told them to be "as shrewd as snakes" (Matt. 10:16).

Because the Israelites often shared their living space with poisonous snakes whether in the wilderness or Promised Land, God generally offered protection from the harm those snakes might do. In the psalm that details the security enjoyed by the people of God, we find specific mention of this fact: "You will tread upon the lion and the cobra; you will trample the great lion and the serpent" (Ps. 91:13). Jesus said believers would "pick up snakes with their hands" (Mark 16:18); and when a venomous snake came out of the brush and attached itself to the hand of Paul, he was unaffected by the bite (Acts 28:4–6). This is exactly the kind of divine protection Moses had in mind when he urged the Israelites to remember that God had led them safely "through the vast and dreadful desert ... with its venomous snakes and scorpions" (Deut. 8:15).

But rebellion against the Lord could lead to a time when this divine protection was switched off (Deut. 32:24). The most notable example of this occurred as the Israelites made their way around Edom. When they spoke against God and Moses, "the LORD sent venomous snakes among them; they bit the people and many Israelites died" (Num. 21:6). When the Lord turned off this protection, the carpet vipers took aim at the Israelite camp. This protection was only restored after the people repented and Moses provided them with a bronze snake on a pole; those who looked to it after they were bitten lived (Num. 21:8–9).

That the metaphors associated with the snake are negative throughout the Bible is likely a result of the negative encounters with venomous snakes and the Devil's appearance in the form of a snake in Genesis 3. Wine is mesmerizing to look at while it is in the cup, but when abused, "it bites like a snake and poisons like a viper" (Prov. 23:32). Rulers who judge their people unjustly are likened to snakes whose ungodly actions flow like poisonous venom through the lives of the people they are supposed to be helping (Ps. 58:4). Personal enemies may use slander to better their lot in life while destroying the life of another. Their "tongues [are] as sharp as a serpent's; the poison of vipers is on their lips" (Ps. 140:3). In the New Testament the corrupted leaders of the Jewish faith are called a "brood of vipers" (Matt. 3:7; 12:34), an image clearly designed to mark the threat they posed and to portray them as offspring of the satanic serpent of Eden (2 Cor. 11:3). And when Jesus sends out the seventy-two, he tells them that they have been given the "authority to trample on snakes and scorpions" (Luke 10:19), likely a metaphor for the evil spirits who also trace their origins to the Devil.

A day is coming when the ancient serpent, that is, the Devil or Satan, will be hurled down and bound (Rev. 12:9; 20:2). This will lead to a time when snakes no longer paralyze people with fear. There will be a new world order in which "the infant will play near the hole of the cobra, and the young child put his hand into the viper's nest" (Isa. 11:8).

Sodom (and Gomorrah)

The efforts to accurately place Sodom on a map require judicious use of the Bible and archaeology. The Bible suggests that Sodom and Gomorrah were significant cities located in the Jordan Valley (Gen. 13:10) but outside the traditional boundaries of Canaan (v. 12), marking the eastern or southeastern extent of that region (10:19). As archaeologists have searched this area for evidence of major cities, several possibilities have emerged. The sixth-century Medeba map places Zoar, a village located near Sodom (19:22), at the southern end of the Dead Sea. Not far from here two Early Bronze sites have emerged, Bab edh-Dhra and Numeira, large cities that were destroyed and abandoned. While the association of these two sites with Sodom and Gomorrah is tempting, they have yet to produce evidence that links them to the traditional time of Abraham. Others have turned their attention farther north where a large oval plain at the north end of the Dead Sea has been linked with the "plain of the Jordan" (13:10). Here the Jordanian Tall el-Hamman has produced evidence of a destroyed Middle Bronze city that is more closely linked with the date of Abraham. For the moment, certainty remains on hold as this robust discussion continues.

Whatever its location east of the Jordan River, the Bible does make it clear that Sodom was awash in natural resources. Before the Lord destroyed it, the area was favorably compared to "the land of Egypt" and the "garden of the Lord" (Gen. 13:10). When given the choice, Lot selected this rich area over Canaan, which he left to Abram (v. 12). Only a few verses later, we read that invaders were attracted to the prosperous cities fed by these rich natural resources (14:1–4).

However, unlike other well-placed cities that faced foreign invasion, Sodom developed a reputation and a legacy. The evidence stacks up against

Sodom, marking it as a city of unchecked immorality: "Now the men of Sodom were wicked and were sinning greatly against the LORD" (Gen. 13:13). Their conduct was so reprehensible that the Lord sent a spiritual delegation to determine if the grievous sinning was as bad as the reports suggested (18:20–21). Not even ten righteous people could be found in this city characterized by sexual perversion as well as by a host of other sins (v. 32; 19:5–9). "Now this was the sin of your sister Sodom: She and her daughters were arrogant, overfed and unconcerned; they did not help the poor and needy. They were haughty and did detestable things before me" (Ezek. 16:49–50).

The public sins of this public place were so outrageous that this pagan city's destruction would not be delayed until the time of Joshua but was implemented immediately. The nature of its destruction was unforgettable. The Lord personally rained down "burning sulfur" on the city, wiping out all living things, including the vegetation (Gen. 19:24–25; Deut. 29:23). Only the family of Lot received warning, so the sudden and horrific destruction overtook people as they went about their daily routines (Lam. 4:6; Luke 17:28–29). This destruction was not only to be a witness for those living in that time, but the ruin was to endure as an ongoing lesson to all people of the Lord's unwillingness to compromise on lifestyle; it would be a "wasteland forever" (Zeph. 2:9; cf. Jer. 49:18).

Though physically destroyed, the memory of Sodom has lived on as a symbol of rank immorality, a symbol of the destruction rebellion earns, and a benchmark for measuring the serious nature of rejecting God's Word. When the outrage of the prophets rises to meet the outrage the Lord feels over the rebellion of his own people, these prophets give the rebels a new and ominous name, one that recalls the immoral conduct of Sodom: "Hear the word of the LORD, you rulers of Sodom; listen to the law of our God, you people of Gomorrah!" (Isa. 1:10). They have reached new depths as they "parade their sin like Sodom" (Isa. 3:9) and become "like" Sodom and Gomorrah (Jer. 23:14). "As surely as I live, declares the Sovereign LORD, your sister Sodom and her daughters never did what you and your daughters have done" (Ezek. 16:48).

The horrific destruction of Sodom and Gomorrah lived on in the landscape and so became a paradigm for the havoc the Lord might

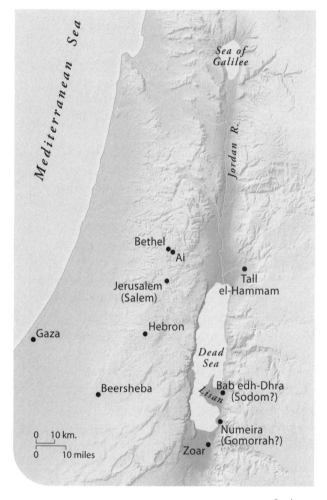

Sodom.

bring both upon his own people and upon the nations. When Israel's covenant with the Lord was still fresh, he warned them that the consequences of disobedience were severe, including a destruction that would resemble that experienced by Sodom and Gomorrah (Deut. 29:23–25). The prophets speak of a similar fate for Babylon, Moab, and Edom (Isa. 13:19; Jer. 49:18; 50:40; Zeph. 2:9). The fiery judgment of Sodom is even likened to the eternal fires of hell (Jude 7).

The last point is particularly in view when warning is given about opportunities squandered. When Jesus sent out the Twelve and the Seventy-two, he warned that those villages that were not receptive to the gospel would face a fate far worse than the one experienced by Sodom and Gomorrah (Matt. 10:15; Luke 10:12). Capernaum, the city in which Jesus spent so much time, received special censure: "If the miracles that were performed in you had been performed in Sodom, it would have remained to this day. But I tell you that it will be more bearable for Sodom on the day of judgment than for you" (Matt. 11:23–24).

A Samaritan high priest with his staff, a symbol of status and authority.
Library of Congress, LC-matpc-01861/www.LifeintheHolyLand.com

Staff

A branch became a staff when its owner carefully selected it from a sturdy tree and cut it to length. The branch could then be personalized either through special shaping, distinctive carving, writing one's own name on the staff, or by giving the staff a personal name (Num. 17:2; Zech. 11:7). By personalizing a staff using one or more of these methods, the owner could always be linked to the staff even if separated from it for some time (Gen. 38:18, 25).

For people whose day was filled with walking and frequent encounters with uncertain footing, the staff was considered standard equipment.

Like modern walking poles, the staff could be used to check one's balance and to transfer some of the weight from the knees onto the arms. Walking with a staff was considered the norm. The personal injury law of the Old Testament defines a return to normal life after an injury as one in which the injured party "gets up and walks around outside with his staff" (Ex. 21:19). Even when Jacob was forced to flee quickly and travel lightly because of the anger of his brother, he took his personal staff along (Gen. 32:10). And when Jesus sent out the twelve disciples, they were urged to leave just about everything else behind except for a staff (Mark 6:8). It was considered so fundamental that it was the first thing you put into your hand when you were getting ready to travel; therefore the Israelites were to eat the first Passover meal with staff in hand (Ex. 12:11).

The shepherd's staff and the staff marking political position expanded the function of the staff and added symbolic value to it. Certainly the shepherd used the staff for walking, but it also extended his or her reach when guiding animals, disciplining them, or protecting them from harm. Political or religious leaders might also carry a staff. This staff was often highly stylized, because its primary function was not for walking or herding animals but to mark those who carried it as people with authority (Ex. 7:11–12; Num. 17:2; 21:18; Judg. 5:14).

Staffs that are mentioned frequently or that appear unexpectedly in the narrative can carry rhetorical force. At the time Moses was called to be the leader of God's people, his staff became a symbol of the divine authority he represented. The staff was not a magical wand but was called the "staff of God in his hand" (Ex. 4:20). In the chapters that follow, the staff is used in connection with the imposition of divine plagues, opening the sea, producing water from a rock, and giving Israel victory over the Amalekites (9:23; 10:13; 14:16; 17:5, 9). Aaron also had a staff that appears frequently in the deliverance of Israel from Egypt (7:19; 8:5, 16). But its shining moment comes in a portion of the narrative where questions have arisen regarding the legitimacy of a Levite-only clergy. To set matters straight, God had directed each of the twelve tribal leaders to put his name on his own personal staff; this included Aaron who put his name on the staff of Levi. When those twelve staffs were put into the Tent of Meeting overnight, God marked the Levites as his chosen leaders by causing Aaron's staff to sprout, bud, blossom, and even produce

almonds (Num. 17:1–11). Then there is the matter of Jonathan and David's staffs, which appear in 1 Samuel 14 and 17. Note that with the failure of Saul as Israel's king becoming ever more apparent, the biblical authors do not put a staff in his hand. Rather, we find staffs in the hands of his son Jonathan and of David (1 Sam. 14:27, 43; 17:40). In both cases the seemingly incidental staff may well be carrying a symbolic message about who was and who was not fit to lead Israel.

The staff, which is a symbol of political power, can also become a symbol of political weakness when the staff is made from a less-than-stout material or is splintered or broken. The Egyptian pharaohs carried a variety of symbolic staffs, but in the Bible the staff of Egypt is pictured as a "reed" or, worse yet, a "splintered reed" (2 Kings 18:21; Ezek. 29:6). In a judgment speech against Moab, the prophet calls for all to mourn the "glorious staff" that now is broken (Jer. 48:17).

A symbolic staff is also associated with the Lord. The divine shepherd in Psalm 23 carries a staff that comforts the flock (v. 4). This image encourages Micah to lift this prayer to the Lord: "Shepherd your people with your staff" (Mic. 7:14). The prophet Zechariah was summoned to enact prophecy through the use of two named staffs: Favor and Union. To warn of the misfortune that will accompany the rejection of the Messiah-Shepherd, Zechariah is instructed to break Favor, a sign that the Lord would allow the nations to bring harm to Israel. The subsequent breaking of Union anticipated the break in relationship between Israel and Judah (Zech. 11:7, 10, 14).

Finally, a special staff is associated with the rule of the Messiah. When Jacob spoke of the legacy of Judah, he said, "The scepter will not depart from Judah, nor the ruler's staff from between his feet, until he comes to whom it belongs and the obedience of the nations is his"

(Gen. 49:10). As the first king of Israel descended from the tribe of Judah, David certainly took the first step in fulfillment of this prophecy. But a greater descendant of David was also in view. And despite the fact that Jesus was mocked and beaten with a fake ruler's staff (Matt. 27:29–30), his victory over sin and death placed him on an eternal throne with a real ruling staff in hand.

Straw. *See* Chaff.

Sword

The word *sword* appears more than four hundred times in the pages of the Bible, referring to one of three weapons: the dagger, the sickle sword, or the straight sword. To determine which type the author has in view, we need to use context and what we know about the evolution of this weapon. The dagger is the shortest of the three at approximately sixteen inches in length. It is essentially a large, straight-bladed knife with one or both sides of its blade sharpened. This weapon was used for stabbing or cutting. The sickle sword was present throughout the earlier history of the Old Testament. It was approximately twenty-one inches in length, consisting of a handle, a straight unsharpened segment, and a crescent-shaped blade that was sharpened on the outside edge. This weapon was deployed by using a hacking or slashing motion. Later in the Old Testament and into the New Testament, "sword" likely refers to the straight sword. It, too, was approximately twenty-one inches in length but had a straight blade extending from the handle with one or both sides sharpened. It was typically deployed by thrusting.

These various types of swords were made of the most durable material that maturing tech-nology and political expediency allowed, starting with flint and moving from bronze to iron (1 Sam. 13:19). No matter what material was used to make the sword, its edge would eventually dull, requiring that it be sharpened. Apart from polishing, this was the only attention this weapon needed (Ps. 7:12; Ezek. 21:9–10). By the time of David, every able-bodied soldier carried this weapon in a sheath tied to his waist, where it remained until duty called for its use (2 Sam. 20:8; 24:9; Song 3:8).

Real swords are brandished in the Bible both with and without divine approval. For example, Simeon and Levi took their swords in hand to attack an unsuspecting city, an attack delivered without divine encouragement (Gen. 34:25–26). The same can be said of Balaam who threatened his donkey with a sword and Saul who fell on his own sword (Num. 22:29; 1 Sam. 31:4). However, it is much more common to see mortals lifting the sword in divine service guided by divine direction; such swords become the sword of the Lord. This is repeatedly the case in Joshua where the sword is used to conquer Canaanite opposition in the Promised Land (Josh. 6:21; 8:24; 10:11; et al.). In the days of the Judges, Ehud made a double-edged dagger that delivered a "message" from God to Eglon, king of Moab (Judg. 3:16, 20–22). In that same light, the soldiers with Gideon shouted, "A sword for the LORD and for Gideon!" (7:20). And in that spirit, David used Goliath's own sword to deliver a fatal blow to the Philistine warrior (1 Sam. 17:51). Assuring Elijah that all was not lost, the Lord said, "Jehu will put to death any who escape the sword of Hazael, and Elisha will put to death any who escape the sword of Jehu" (1 Kings 19:17). The Bible even knows of occasions when a divinely sponsored sword is directed at God's own people. The Lord promised that there would be a penalty for sustained covenant violation

A sickle sword.
Copyright 1995-2011 Phoenix Data Systems

(Lev. 26:25, 33; Deut. 32:25), and he made good on that promise when circumstances called for a strong response (examples include Ex. 32:27; Jer. 9:16; 14:12; Ezek. 5:1–2; 21:3–5; Hos. 11:6).

In some instances the sword of the Lord is not in the hands of a mortal but on display before the eyes of mortals. A flaming sword guarded access to the tree of life following Adam and Eve's expulsion from the garden of Eden (Gen. 3:24). The angel of the Lord stood with drawn sword in hand before Balaam, Joshua, and David (Num. 22:23, 31; Josh. 5:13; 1 Chron. 21:16). In each case the message delivered was being supported by this symbol of divine force.

The sword also became a metaphor for violence, spoken words, and capital punishment. The close connection between violence and the sword makes it possible to use the sword as a symbol for violence. In contrast to the peace that comes with beating swords into plowshares, those who "live by the sword," who are told that "the sword will never depart" from their household, who are "destined" for the sword, or who find the sword "awake" to attack them (Gen. 27:40; 2 Sam. 12:10; Jer. 15:2; Zech. 13:7) are those destined to experience violence. As swords have the capacity to harm, so do words spoken by mortals. When a trusted companion proves unfaithful, "his words are more soothing than oil, yet they are drawn swords" (Ps. 55:21). The wicked who conspire to bring harm "sharpen their tongues like swords" (64:3). "Reckless words pierce like a sword, but the tongue of the wise brings heal-

ing" (Prov. 12:18). Because God's Word is the weapon used to defeat satanic opposition, the sword becomes a metaphor for the Word of God. The servant of the Lord has a mouth "like a sharpened sword" (Isa. 49:2). The Christian possesses this "sword of the Spirit" (Eph. 6:17), which is "sharper than any double-edged sword" (Heb. 4:12). Finally, the sword is also used as a metaphor for capital punishment handed down by the government (Ex. 18:4; Rom. 13:4).

The sword appears numerous times in the language and life experiences of Jesus as a sign and symbol of hostility to his message. He warns his followers that the eternal peace associated with his message would inspire such a response: "Do not suppose that I have come to bring peace to the earth. I did not come to bring peace, but a sword" (Matt. 10:34). In the closing days of his life, he told his disciples to sell their cloaks and buy swords if they did not have one. The disciples interpreted this symbolic statement quite literally, quickly pointing out that they already had two (Luke 22:36–38). As the detachment dispatched to arrest Jesus showed up at Gethsemane with swords in hand, the disciples asked if they should use those two swords. Impetuous Peter struck without waiting for a reply (vv. 49–50). But Jesus commanded him, "Put your sword away! Shall I not drink the cup the Father has given me?" (John 18:11).

Sychar. *See* Shechem.

T

Table

The flat surface of ancient tables was used for writing and money changing, but the activity most often connected with the table was eating. In Bible times the dining table could take a number of forms. For example, it could be a square of leather spread on the ground in the same way we might spread a picnic blanket. The food was placed on a plate in the middle, and the diners would either squat or recline around it. Wooden tables were also in use, though they were much lower than the conventional tables of today, because they were designed to accommodate those who were either reclining or sitting on low stools. Wooden table remains from Old Testament Jericho indicate that such tables could be much more than a slab of wood on makeshift legs. These Jericho tables had a rectangular top and ornately carved legs, and they even used mortise-and-tenon joinery. During the New Testament the *triclinium* table was becoming popular. Viewed from above, the surface of this table resembled a squared-off U, which allowed diners to recline around the outside of the table while leaving the middle of the U open for those serving the meal. The well-furnished guest room likely had such a table, making it the kind of table around which Jesus reclined with the disciples when introducing them to a special New Testament meal (Luke 22:12, 14).

Special connotations are associated with the table no matter if it is found in a home, guest room, palace, or sanctuary. The connotations of acceptance, trust, and protection encircled the family table and were extended to guests who were invited to join the family for a meal. Thus David was expressing more than just appreciation for food when he said to the Lord, "You prepare a table before me in the presence of my enemies" (Ps. 23:5). The matter of acceptance was what troubled those religious leaders who saw Jesus sitting around a table with public sinners and social outcasts (Luke 15:2). And when

A triclinium table with guests reclining while eating their meal.
Mary Evans Picture Library

Table   250

they invited Jesus to eat with them, they were shocked when Jesus turned this invitation into an occasion to criticize their character (Luke 11:37–45). People assumed they could trust those at the table with them. No wonder the disciples around the table in the upper room were so troubled when Jesus said, "I tell you the truth, one of you will betray me — one who is eating with me" (Mark 14:18).

The Bible also makes frequent mention of the "king's table." Everything said above about the family table would apply here, but we must add the connotation of honor. As the leading national figure, the king controlled who was permitted to eat from his table (1 Kings 2:7; 2 Kings 25:29; Dan. 1:5). It was an honor to receive this invitation, an honor David extended to Mephibosheth, Jonathan's son. And lest we miss the point, it is mentioned four times in seven verses (2 Sam. 9:7–13). This very positive image of national healing and loyal friendship stands in contrast to the one that comes to mind when we hear that 450 Baal prophets were regular invited guests of Jezebel (1 Kings 18:19). When invited by the king to enjoy this honor, it was unthinkable that one would be absent. That is why it proved to be a good test of Saul's attitude toward David. A reaction from Saul to David's chair being empty at the meal could be expected, but his overreaction was unexpected (1 Sam. 20:18–33). And while eating at the king's table was a great honor, it was a sign of humiliation to eat what fell from the king's table (Judg. 1:7). This same connotation extended to those who ate under the table of the well-to-do (Mark 7:28; Luke 16:21).

A very special table was also present in the Lord's sanctuary. Prior to the building of the tabernacle, the Lord gave Moses specific instructions about the worship furniture, including the wooden table overlaid with gold that held the bread of the Presence (Ex. 25:23–30). The priests were to provide a fresh set of twelve loaves of bread each Sabbath so that this bread was always "before the Lord" (Lev. 24:6, 8). When the loaves were replaced, Aaron and his sons were to eat the loaves in a holy place (v. 9). Please note that this piece of furniture is not called an "altar" but a "table." Given all the implications associated with such a table and the Lord's directive that this bread be eaten by the representatives of the people, we can see a beautiful picture emerging.

The table is also used in figurative ways. For example, the table can stand for the wonderful food that is on it. In the poetic summary of the people's rebellion in the wilderness, the psalmist recalls the willful complaining of the people about food in this way: "They spoke against God, saying, 'Can God spread a table in the desert?'" (Ps. 78:19; cf. 1 Kings 18:19; Neh. 5:17). The banquet table set by wisdom is not filled with literal food but with the knowledge that leads to successful living (Prov. 9:2). Godly knowledge was in short supply at Corinth. Paul upbraided Christians there for the confusing message they sent by participating in conflicting worship rites: "You cannot drink the cup of the Lord and the cup of demons too; you cannot have a part in both the Lord's table and the table of demons" (1 Cor. 10:21). Here the "Lord's table" stands for the Lord' Supper (Holy Communion) while the "table of demons" stands for pagan altars. Finally, as the disciples were gathered with Jesus around the table in the upper room, Jesus criticized their struggle to gain the honored seats around the table. Instead, he urged them to focus on the honor they would know when they would eat and drink at his table in his eternal kingdom (Luke 22:30), a banquet table that symbolized life in heaven.

Tent

Even for those who have enjoyed the experience of vacationing in a tent, there is still much to learn about the nature of sustained life in a tent and the use of the tent as a figure of speech by the biblical authors. The large sheets of material used for building a tent were woven from goat's hair. Having a somewhat looser weave, this material allowed air to circulate between the fibers, improving ventilation in the tent. When it rained, the individual goat hairs would swell, making the dwelling water resistant. Because the fabric, ropes, and stakes used to erect the tent were all organic and so lost from the archaeological record, we need to rely on the continuity of culture among the bedouin of modern times to get images of just how that tent may have looked. The tents of the bedouin consist of fabric stretched over a set of poles. Ropes attached to the tent fabric and tent poles were pulled taut and staked to the ground. This process allowed the ceiling and sidewalls of the tent to take shape. Fabric curtains are hung to provide walls that can be left in place when it is cold or pulled to the side to allow direct ventilation of the interior when it is warm.

During the time of the patriarchs and during Israel's wandering in the wilderness, a tent or number of tents provided each family with shelter (Gen. 13:5, 18; 31:33; Ex. 16:16; 33:8; Num. 1:52). Those who did not live in cities or villages and moved regularly took advantage of the portability of this shelter. And when God's people did settle into cities and villages, the shepherds

A tent made of goat's hair was perfect for wilderness wandering.

moving about with their flocks and the soldiers traveling with their weapons still used tents as their shelter.

The Bible speaks of a variety of activities associated with the tent. On a warm summer day, the tent provided a cool spot to sit sheltered from the harsh rays of the sun (Gen. 18:1). And when a general needed a place to hide, he chose a woman's tent, not suspecting that she would soon end his life by driving a tent peg into his temple (Judg. 4:17–21). The tent was also the setting for a variety of immoral activities, from drunkenness to illicit sex (Gen. 9:21; Num. 25:6–8; Josh. 7:21–24; 2 Sam. 16:22). It would not have been unusual for a person to return to his or her tent. But when the biblical authors call attention to this fact, it often has military connotations. The soldiers who would not accompany Gideon into battle were sent to their tents, signaling that they would not participate in the fight against Midian (Judg. 7:8). In that light the call for soldiers to return to their tents became code language for abandoning the ruling king to join those who opposed him (2 Sam. 20:1; 1 Kings 12:16).

Figurative use of the tent and tent living is also found throughout the Bible. With some frequency, the biblical authors remind us that Abraham's family and descendants lived in tents (Gen. 12:8; 13:3; 26:25; 33:19; Heb. 11:9). Although the land of Canaan had been promised to this extended family, a firmer grip on this land would have to wait for another day. The moving tents of the patriarchs are a subtle but powerful reminder that the promise of life in the Promised Land was still maturing.

As the people of Israel used tents during their wilderness wandering, so the Lord also used a tent during this time in their history. God made his presence known visibly to his people by using a tent called the tabernacle (Ex. 40:35). And

God elected to meet and speak with his people at a "tent of meeting" located outside the camp (33:7–11). Both of these rich Old Testament images find a counterpart in the New Testament. With a Greek verb developed from the noun for tent, John says, "The Word became flesh and set up a tent among us" (John 1:14; NIV has "made his dwelling among us"), just as God "tented" with his people in the tabernacle. Peter may have had the "tent of meeting" in mind on the day of Jesus' transfiguration. He longed to set up tents (NIV "shelters") that would allow this special revelation to continue (Matt. 17:4; Mark 9:5; Luke 9:33).

The image of the tent also became a metaphor for the human body, the heavens, Jerusalem, and heaven itself. The presence of sin means that the body, like a tent, will wear with age and eventually need replacement with something new; thus the tent is used as a metaphor for the human body (Job 4:21; Ps. 52:5; Isa. 38:12; 2 Cor. 5:4; 2 Peter 1:13). This image is particularly meaningful when it comes from Paul, a tentmaker by trade: "Now we know that if the earthly tent we live in is destroyed, we have a building from God, an eternal house in heaven, not built by human hands" (2 Cor. 5:1). The inspired poets of Scripture speak of the heavens stretched out like tent material over its poles by a divine hand (Ps. 104:2; Isa. 40:22). Jerusalem is also imagined to be "a tent that will not be moved; its stakes will never be pulled up, nor any of its ropes broken" (Isa. 33:20). Isaiah uses similar imagery to tell how Zion will be enlarged to accommodate the influx of Gentiles who will join Israel there: "Enlarge the place of your tent, stretch your tent curtains wide, do not hold back; lengthen your cords, strengthen your stakes" (54:2). And in contrast to the lives of those who lived in ordinary tents and experienced their share of pain and disruption, those who join the Lord in heaven can look forward to a time without the hardship and pain of ordinary tent living, because "he who sits on the throne will spread his tent over them" (Rev. 7:15).

Thorn

Thorns are present on more than seventy species of flora that grow in the Promised Land; these plants vary in size from low-growing weeds to briars, brambles, bushes, and trees. Thorns are mentioned more than fifty times by the biblical authors, who use twenty-two Greek or Hebrew words in the pro-

cess. In most instances, however, it is impossible to know which thorn-wielding plant is being referenced in a Bible passage.

The general distaste for plants with thorns grew from their lack of value, their obstruction to travel, and the painful sting they delivered. At best these plants and trees made a very meager contribu-

The general distaste for plants with thorns grew from their lack of value, their obstruction to travel, and the painful sting they delivered.
© William D. Mounce

tion to the well-being of those living in Bible times. They were quick to fill untended land and were always fighting the fruit trees and grain for nutrients, water, and sunlight. Furthermore, they blocked movement from one place to another, particularly when they formed thickets that entangled travelers (Prov. 15:19; Hos. 2:6; Nah.

1:10). When people attempted to remove them from the arable fields or pathways, they were thanked for the effort with a handful of pain.

Nevertheless, thorns were permitted to grow and were gathered for three reasons. First, because thorns did such an effective job of deterring animals and people from trespassing on farmland, farmers allowed them to grow and form a hedge around their agricultural plots (Ex. 22:6). Second, dried thorn branches burned quite quickly, but in a landscape that lacked trees, they were carefully gathered to make cooking fires (Pss. 58:9; 118:12; Eccl. 7:6). Third, thorns were also used to inflict pain on those being punished (Judg. 8:7, 16). Thus thorns became part of the cruelty imposed on Jesus as the soldiers "twisted together a crown of thorns and put it on his head" (John 19:2).

The connotations and symbolism associated with thorns in the Bible are always negative, something for which we are conditioned in the very first pages of Genesis. Life changed in a dramatic way once sin entered the garden of Eden. The land that had willingly yielded its food was cursed and subsequently was pictured as resisting the efforts of hungry mortals, producing "thorns and thistles" (Gen. 3:17–18). Such literal thorns would combine with metaphorical thorns, such as the mysterious "thorn in [the] flesh" with which Paul wrestled (2 Cor. 12:7), to create a life of hardship.

A landscape full of thorns is an image with very negative connotations. This is particularly the case with a vineyard, because it indicated that something was amiss: the owner was a sluggard (Prov. 24:31), had purposely abandoned the plot (Isa. 5:6), or had been deported from the land (Isa. 7:23–25). In announcing the day of judgment, the Lord urged the women of Jerusalem to beat their "breasts for the pleasant fields, for the fruitful vines and for the land of my people, a land overgrown with thorns and briers" (Isa. 32:12–13). Edom was warned of the coming judgment that would leave its strongholds and citadels overrun with thorns (Isa. 34:13). And Hosea spoke of the ruin that would come to the abhorrent high places whose altars would be covered with thorns and thistles (Hos. 10:8).

The metaphors that mention thorns also have negative associations. People are likened to thorns in a number of places, beginning with the Canaanites, whose theology would become a terrible stumbling block for the Israelites. When walking about the countryside, it was easy to get into thorns that might stick in one's side, or worse yet, catch an eye. The Lord uses this image as he directs the Israelites to drive out the inhabitants of the land so that they will not become "barbs in your eyes and thorns in your sides" (Num. 33:55; cf. Josh. 23:13; Judg. 2:3). Although Abimelech was an Israelite, biblical authors have little good to say about this man who longed to be the first king in Israel; they liken him to a worthless thornbush (Judg. 9:14–15). Jesus said that a false teacher from any culture was recognizable by the fruit produced: "Do people pick grapes from thornbushes, or figs from thistles?" (Matt. 7:16). And those individuals who caused the followers of the Lord and his prophets trouble are

likened to thorns (Ezek. 2:6; 28:24; Mic. 7:4; Luke 6:44). "Evil men are all to be cast aside like thorns, which are not gathered with the hand. Whoever touches thorns uses a tool of iron or the shaft of a spear; they are burned up where they lie" (2 Sam. 23:6–7).

In addition to a metaphor referring to a person, the thorn is also likened to the woes and difficulties that attend a sinful lifestyle. The inspired poet seizes upon an image taken from travel along the roads of the Promised Land. Pathways were generally clear of thorns, but a shortcut might find one caught in a mess: "In the paths of the wicked lie thorns and snares, but he who guards his soul stays far from them" (Prov. 22:5).

Perhaps the most familiar use of the thorn in a metaphor is in the parable of the sower. As the seed of the gospel is spread, the faith of a young believer takes root. But thorns threaten to choke the faith of the new believer just as thorns in a farm field attempt to crowd out the young grain plants. In this parable the thorn is a metaphor for "life's worries, riches and pleasures" which can, over time, extinguish a growing faith (Luke 8:14).

Threshing Floor

A threshing floor is a flat, open area of bare stone or compacted earth established near the agricultural fields where grain was grown. In Israel threshing floors were typically located on the east side of rising terrain, just below the crest of the ridge, so that the predictable westerly winds that flow over the ridge could be used during the winnowing process. If the threshing floor were located directly on top of the hill, the wind might well blow the grain around and remix it with the chaff. But by locating it just beneath the crest, the wind affected only the grain-chaff mixture thrown up into the air and not the materials that had fallen back to the floor.

This installation plays a key role in providing the residents of the Promised Land with an ample supply of grain. The harvested grain was hauled uphill to the threshing floor where the first task was to break the bond between the kernel of grain and the husk. The goal was achieved either when draft animals pressed the grain between their hooves and the threshing floor or when they pulled a threshing sledge over it. A threshing sledge was a weighted, wooden sled with sharp rocks embedded in the bottom that also crushed the grain plant. Once the bond between kernel and husk was broken, the farmer would make use of the sea breeze that reached the inland mountains early in the afternoon. The mixture on the threshing floor was thrown up into the wind, which blew the chaff farther downwind than the heavier grain. The grain, which was swept into piles on the threshing floor, was eventually moved to village and home for storage.

This literal use of the threshing floor is rarely mentioned in the Bible. Instead, the biblical authors speak of many other activities taking place there. A number of events made use of the open space offered by the threshing floor.

A threshing floor with a threshing sledge.

Todd Bolen/www.BiblePlaces.com

For example, when Joseph and his brothers fulfilled their promise to bury Jacob in the Promised Land, their trip came to a temporary halt at the "threshing floor of Atad" (Gen. 50:10). The large entourage, which included many dignitaries from Egypt, used this threshing floor to hold "a solemn ceremony of mourning" (v. 11). In contrast Gideon used a threshing floor like a stage to demonstrate to the gathering army that the Lord and not Baal was truly God. Gideon was already persuaded of this fact (Judg. 6:28–32), but many in Israel were not. To win the soldiers to his conviction, Gideon developed a test involving the manipulation of dew, something both the Lord and Baal claimed to control. The threshing floor provided a large, open stage that allowed hundreds to see the miracle involving dewfall that demonstrated the Lord was the one true God (6:36–40).

A threshing floor was also used from time to time by the kings of God's people when they held court (1 Kings 22:10). Thus we can appreciate why two other events involving divine judgment are linked to threshing floors. In the first instance, the Lord delivered punishment at the threshing floor of Nacon over irreverent touching of the ark of the covenant (2 Sam. 6:6–7). The second instance followed an imprudent move by David to count the number of fighting men in his kingdom. The ensuing plague that had ravaged other villages in his kingdom was about to ravage his capital. As the angel of the Lord was at the threshing floor of Araunah the Jebusite, God made the decision to end the punishing ordeal (24:15–16). In time this very threshing floor on which David erected an altar became the soil above which Solomon's temple rose (2 Sam. 24:18, 24–25; 2 Chron. 3:1).

In addition to the threshing floor functioning as an open space for such events, it also became a place of privacy where a bold marriage proposal took place. Because the threshing, winnowing, and gathering of grain took more than one day, the farmer would typically sleep on the threshing floor to protect his hard-earned grain piles. Naomi chose this time and location for Ruth to approach Boaz to learn of his willingness to become her husband (Ruth 3:1–14).

The threshing floor is further used as a figure of speech to describe the pain of divine judgment and to criticize the spiritual prostitution of Israel. Seen from the viewpoint of a grain plant, the processing that occurred on the threshing floor was a violent and painful affair. Isaiah likens the experience of God's people in exile to that of a grain plant on the threshing floor when he addresses them with these words: "O my people, crushed on the threshing floor" (Isa. 21:10). Micah adds that a similar fate awaits the nations who oppose God's kingdom (Mic. 4:11–13). The personified threshing floor feels the pain of the threshing process. The Daughter of Babylon is said to be "like a threshing floor at the time it is trampled" (Jer. 51:33). The coming of the Messiah introduced the era in which the ultimate judgment of God would occur; consequently, John the Baptist seized on this imagery: "His winnowing fork is in his hand, and he will clear his threshing floor" (Matt. 3:12).

Finally, Hosea uses the threshing floor to highlight both the nature of Israel's spiritual prostitution and its consequences. Prostitutes frequented the threshing floors in the evening when the men lay down to protect their grain piles. Hosea likens unfaithful Israel to women who "love the wages of a prostitute at every threshing floor" (Hos. 9:1). And because of this spiritual wandering, God planned to curtail the harvest so that "threshing floors and winepresses will not feed the people" (v. 2).

Throne

The thrones of ancient Near Eastern kings were ornate versions of the ordinary wooden chairs of Bible times. Artwork from the ancient world provides us with pictures of these thrones. Some have high backs, others low backs, and still others no backs. Whether upholstered or not, these thrones were carved with beautiful figures and inlaid with ivory and precious metals. The Bible gives us a detailed description of Solomon's throne. It was inlaid with ivory, overlaid with gold, and had a rounded back. One ascended this throne by six steps that were flanked by twelve lions, two to a step (1 Kings 10:18–20). The unique design and height of a throne was less about comfortable seating and more about sending a message regarding the social status of the one who sat on it (Ex. 11:5).

The person we expect to be sitting on such a throne is the king or queen of a nation, whether the throne is in Egypt, Assyria, or Persia (Gen. 41:40; Esth. 1:2; Jonah 3:6). When God yielded to Israel's request for a king, he also established clear guidelines that governed the behavior and attitude of the king, distinguishing him from his ancient Near Eastern counterparts (Deut. 17:14–20). The king of Israel was permitted to have a throne

A throne from Knossos in Crete. The throne is flanked by griffins — mythical beasts viewed as sacred by Minoans.

(17:18), but he was never to forget that his throne, no matter how ornate, was overshadowed by the Lord's throne (1 Kings 22:10, 19). Perhaps as a helpful reminder of that fact, Solomon's throne is not called the throne of Solomon but "the throne of the LORD" (1 Chron. 29:23).

The unmistakable message sent by this ornate piece of royal furniture was clear: the one who sat on the throne was the one in charge. That is why the priest Jehoida rushed the young Joash to the throne as quickly as possible after seeing to the execution of the wicked queen Athaliah (2 Kings 11:19). From the throne the king would conduct the business of his kingdom, which included judging his people. When a king ruled his people with integrity, he need not fear being deposed: "If a king judges the poor with fairness, his throne will always be secure" (Prov. 29:14).

The spiritual realm was also a place with thrones. Visions that allowed human beings to see past the mortal realm into the spirit world reveal a glimpse of such magnificent thrones (Isa. 6:1; Rev. 4:1 – 11). Ezekiel saw a sapphire throne (Ezek. 1:26) and John a dazzling white throne (Rev. 20:11). Jesus promised the twelve disciples that they each would have a throne to sit on from which they would "[judge] the twelve tribes of Israel" (Matt. 19:28). John saw twenty-four thrones occupied by twenty-four elders (Rev. 4:4; 11:16). Yet it is God who consistently is pictured on the great throne of heaven from Genesis through Revelation. We will personally see this throne when the Son of Man comes in his glory and takes his seat there (Matt. 25:31). But whether seen or unseen, this divine throne also sends a message. The one who sits on it rules not just one nation but all nations (Ps. 47:8), and his rule will not be temporary but eternal (93:2).

While the throne in the Bible may be a literal throne, it can also be a figure of speech standing in for the concepts of royal authority or dynasty. Pharaoh elevated Joseph from prisoner to second-in-command of Egypt using this language: "Only with respect to the throne will I be greater than you" (Gen. 41:40). Here the throne represents the ruling authority of the monarch. Thus when the throne is transferred from one king to the next, it is less about the furniture than the responsibilities and privileges it represents. In 1 Kings 1 – 2, which describes the transfer of rule from David to Solomon, the word "throne" appears repeatedly. For example, "As the LORD was with my lord the king, so may he be with Solomon to make his throne even greater than the throne of my lord King David!" (1 Kings 1:37). This was not about the furniture but the legacy of royal authority. The same can be said of those instances where a foreign king sets up a throne on the soil of a defeated enemy; the throne stands for the ruling authority now extended into new territory (Jer. 1:15; 43:10).

The throne can also be a metaphor for dynasty (2 Sam. 3:10; 1 Kings 2:45; Ps. 89:4). David received the amazing promise that his throne—that is, the rule of his family—would last not just for a few generations but forever (2 Sam. 7:13, 16). The Messiah would be a member of this royal household: "He will reign on David's throne and over his kingdom" (Isa. 9:7). This hope lived in the faithful of Israel through one foreign occupation after the next until finally the angel brought news of its fulfillment to a young Mary in the village of Nazareth. In describing the role of her special son, the angel said, "The Lord God will give him the throne of his father David" (Luke 1:32).

Two other figures of speech are used less frequently but powerfully, the throne of honor and the throne of grace. When the beleaguered Hannah was blessed with a son, she broke into song, praising God for his goodness: "He raises the poor from the dust and lifts the needy from the ash heap; he seats them with princes and has them inherit a throne of honor" (1 Sam. 2:8). Finally, the writer to the Hebrews urges us to storm the seat of God with prayer, because on it sits someone who knows what it is like to live where we do: "Let us then approach the throne of grace with confidence" (Heb. 4:16).

Tomb. *See* Grave.

Trap. *See* Net.

Trumpet

English translations in general and the NIV in particular use the English word *trumpet* to represent two different instruments, the true trumpet and the ram's horn. Here our description and references will be only to the true trumpet. While the horn is literally made from an animal's horn, the trumpet is made of hammered silver or bronze (Num. 10:1). Surviving trumpets from the ancient Near Eastern world give us a sense of how they looked. The trumpet was a straight, metal tube less then two feet in length, with one end flared into a bell or cone shape. Like a modern trumpet, the ancient trumpet was played by pressing one's lips to the small end of the tube and blowing air through the chamber. Unlike the modern trumpet, there were no valves to play. This meant that the ancient trumpet was capable of fewer than six notes. But as a signaling device, the player could alternate not only the tone but also the duration of the blast to encode the signal being sent to livestock, soldiers, or a large group of people.

Ancient literature suggests that the trumpet had a variety of applications. Shepherds used the trumpet as a tool in gathering their flocks.

Funeral processions employed trumpets, as did religious celebrations. The trumpet was used by a watchman to signal the arrival of danger. And it was particularly used in military contexts as a way of directing the soldiers to organize into a particular battle formation, to begin the fight, to pursue the fleeing enemy, or to retreat.

The Bible mentions the trumpet being sounded in similar ways. The most detailed account of the trumpet's application in Israel is found in Numbers 10:1 – 10. Moses was instructed to make two silver trumpets and put them to use in various ways. Given the practical problems of communicating with the thousands

St. Jerome Hears the Last Trumpet.
St. Jerome by Jusepe de Ribera/Colegiata de Santa Maria Church/
© Paul Maeyaert/The Bridgeman Art Library International

of people he was leading, Moses used the trumpet to call meetings of the people. When both trumpets sounded, the entire community was to gather. When just one trumpet sounded, only the heads of the clans were to gather. Trumpet blasts were used to signal who was to take the lead in breaking camp and in the face of military operations and when they were to do so. The trumpet as a signal in battle is known from other ancient Near Eastern cultures. But Israel was to blow the trumpet in battle not only to communicate directions on troop movement, but also so that they would be "remembered by the LORD [their] God and rescued from [their] enemies" (Num. 10:9; cf. 31:6; 2 Chron. 13:12, 14; Hos. 5:8). Finally, the trumpet was also used as a call to attention and reflection. It was blown during the daily offerings and to mark the start of festivals (Num. 10:10; cf. 1 Chron. 16:6, 42; 2 Chron. 20:28).

The tones of the trumpet also filled the air on special occasions that called for celebration (Ps. 98:6). During the days of David and Solomon, the trumpets heralded those special days when the ark of the covenant was moved to Jerusalem and into the completed temple (1 Chron. 15:28; 2 Chron. 5:12–13). The coronation of a king, particularly one expected to lead Israel in faithful obedience to the Lord, was celebrated with the sound of trumpets (2 Kings 11:14; 2 Chron. 23:13). Days of religious renewal that followed a season of wandering from the Lord were also marked by the jubilant blast of the trumpet (2 Chron. 15:14; 29:26–27). And trumpets sounded celebratory notes as the foundation was laid for the new temple in Jerusalem and as the new wall that surrounded Jerusalem was completed (Ezra 3:10; Neh. 12:35, 41).

The joy of such events will be eclipsed by the joy of Jesus' return, which also will be marked by the sound of the trumpet. As ancient armies were set in motion by a trumpet call, so the celestial army of angels will be sent to gather the elect with a loud trumpet call (Matt. 24:31). There will be no missing that day, for the sights and sounds of its coming will be unmistakable: "For the Lord himself will come down from heaven, with a loud command, with the voice of the archangel and with the trumpet call of God, and the dead in Christ will rise first" (1 Thess. 4:16; cf. 1 Cor. 15:52; Rev. 8:2–11:15).

In three instances, the trumpet is used in a figurative rather than literal fashion. In the Sermon on the Mount, Jesus encourages giving to the needy, but giving that is unmarked by ostentatious fanfare: "So when you give to the needy, do not announce it with trumpets, as the hypocrites do in the synagogues and on the streets, to be honored by men" (Matt. 6:2). There is no evidence to suggest that the literal sounding of trumpets was ever used in connection with such a gift, so Jesus must be using the trumpet blast as a metaphor for other ostentatious words or actions that would draw attention to the gift. Paul also uses a trumpet metaphorically in his discussion on speaking in tongues in 1 Corinthians. He urges the congregation to provide interpretation of the special language so that everyone can benefit from the message. If not, the value of the message will be lost: "Again, if the trumpet does not sound a clear call, who will get ready for battle?" (1 Cor. 14:8). In the third instance, John likens the voice of Jesus to a trumpet. As John begins his journey of the world beyond our own, he is guided by a "loud voice like a trumpet" (Rev. 1:10). This powerful guiding voice is that of Jesus himself. Perhaps this metaphor is mentioned by John because it recalls the loud blast of the horn that preceded the revelation of God on Mount Sinai (Ex. 19:16).

V

Vat. *See* Winepress.

Veil

The veil was a piece of cloth typically worn by a woman, who draped it over her head and wrapped it around her face so as to cover all of her face except for her eyes and the upper part of her cheeks. While the veil appears to have had little practical value for the wearer, the wearing of a veil had powerful social implications. The evidence for those social implications comes to us both from the Bible and from other ancient Near Eastern literature, but here we must be cautious lest we press slender evidence too far. In the Bible we have less than two dozen instances of a person wearing a veil, often with little commentary on why that veil was being worn. This interpretive problem is compounded by the fact that the reason for wearing a veil varied between ancient cultures. For example, in one era Assyrian law permitted a wife to wear a veil but made it a crime for that same veil to be worn by a concubine or by a slave. In certain cultures it was illegal for a prostitute to wear a veil, yet among the Canaanites it appears that the veil was normally worn by Canaanite shrine prostitutes. What we can say with confidence is that the veil functioned as an indicator of social status and marital eligibility. This was particularly the case in regard to betrothal. When a marriage contract was made between two families and a young woman became betrothed, she would wear a veil as a sign that she was spoken for.

These and other cultural signals make their appearance in familiar Bible stories. After Abraham's servant had made a marriage contract with Rebekah's family, she traveled to Canaan to wed Isaac. In the closing moments of the trip, she saw a man approaching them; and upon learning it was Isaac, she immediately secured her veil as appropriate for a betrothed woman (Gen. 24:65). Although a veil is not formally mentioned in the narrative, Leah clearly wore one on the night she wed Jacob, for Jacob presumed that he had married Rachel only to find in the morning light that he actually had married her sister, Leah (29:25). The veil was meant to add a sense of mystique to the romance. In the Song of Songs the young man waxes poetic about the young woman he longs to marry, praising what he can see; and by extrapolating beyond the folds of the veil, he even celebrates features of this young woman that he cannot clearly see (Song 4:1; 6:7): "Your lips are like a scarlet ribbon; your mouth is lovely. Your temples behind your veil are like the halves of a pomegranate" (4:3).

Among the perversions rampant in Canaanite religion, we find the practice of religious prostitution. When Tamar was slighted by Judah, she sought to circumvent this slight by tricking Judah into a sexual liaison by assuming the role of a prostitute. She deliberately removed the garments that marked her as a widow and put on a veil, both to disguise her true identity and to mark her assumed identity as a prostitute (Gen. 38:14, 19). This is the cultural practice that likely lies behind the rhetorical question of the young woman in the Song of Songs who begs her beloved to tell her where he is shepherding the flocks: "Why should I be like a veiled woman beside the flocks of your friends?" (Song 1:7).

Ezekiel alludes to another overtone associated with the veil—its use in magic arts as a tool to manipulate others. The Lord directs his prophet to approach the Israelite women who had invested themselves in this pagan practice. He tells those who "make veils of various lengths for their heads in order to ensnare people" that the Lord plans to tear off those veils (Ezek. 13:18, 21).

The veil as a marker of elite social status is mentioned twice in judgment speeches in Isaiah. In the first, Zion's pride-filled women are told that the jewelry and clothing that are signature items of their social status, including veils, will be snatched away (Isa. 3:19). The same message is directed to the high-society women of Babylon who will be forced to remove the veils that mark their social status en route to the veil-free life of a servant (47:2).

The only male in the Bible formally described as wearing a face-covering veil is Moses (Ex. 34:33–35). When he returned with a new set of tablets on which the Lord had written the Law, there was something different about his appearance; his face was literally glowing as a result of his being in the Lord's presence. It became his practice to wear a veil on all occasions to conceal

A Bedouin woman covers her head, except for her eyes, with her *hijab*—a veil.

the fact that the radiant glow would fade. But whenever he was in the Lord's presence or when he returned from the Lord's presence to speak to the people on the Lord's behalf, he removed the veil. Paul uses this very unusual practice of Moses rhetorically in 2 Corinthians to describe the way in which the good news about Jesus exceeds the "old covenant." Jesus is the key to unlocking the message of that earlier literature. Those without Jesus who read what Moses wrote will find that a "veil covers their hearts," making it impossible to see how the promises about messiah are fulfilled in Jesus. And unlike Moses, Paul did not need to wear a "veil" when speaking about Jesus for fear that the "radiance" of his face might fade. Because once Jesus had lifted the "veil," those with "unveiled" faces constantly reflect the unfading glory of Jesus (2 Cor. 3:13–16, 18).

Vineyard

The Promised Land is blessed with a climate that favors the growing of grapes. In Bible times everyone either had a vineyard of his or her own or had ready access to one. The vineyard was so important to this culture that the peaceful life was defined as one in which people sat beneath grapevines they could call their own (Mic. 4:4; Zech. 3:10). Thus it is no surprise that the precious vineyard was superintended by various laws that provided for restitution if a vineyard was damaged, that offered release from military service for those who had recently established a vineyard, that directed the fallowing of the vineyard every seven years, and that made provisions for the needy who did not own their own vineyards (Ex. 22:5; 23:11; Lev. 19:10; Deut. 20:6; 23:24; 24:21).

The amount of work required to establish and maintain a successful vineyard is nothing short of phenomenal. Because the plains and broad valleys were the favored environment for growing grain, farmers turned to the hillsides for growing grapes. This meant establishing terraces, no small job in and of itself. First a fieldstone retaining wall was put in place along the contour of the slope. Then the farmer had to haul soil that had eroded from the slope back up the hill, dumping it behind the retaining wall to create a flat, shelflike surface between fifty and one hundred feet wide. In addition to the retaining wall, the farmer constructed a garden wall several feet high around the vineyard to discourage animals from encroaching on the growing vines. Because plants were not grown from seeds, the farmer then had to obtain cuttings from successful grapevines and tenderly nurse them through the trauma of being planted in a new location. And lest you think the job was over when the transplanted vines began to grow, realize that six years of additional labor were required before one could expect to get usable grapes from the vineyard. During those years it was necessary to carefully prune the vines so that the nutrients were directed to that part of the plant where the grapes were maturing and to remove the weeds that competed for water and nutrients. If the vineyard was a great distance from the village, the farmer would also build a watchtower among the grapevines. This stone structure one or two stories high became the temporary shelter in which the farmer lived when the vineyard was about to produce its long-awaited fruit. He did so to prevent others from harvesting the grapes he had worked so long to bring to maturity. There is little doubt that the vineyard required more time and attention than any other fruit or field crop raised during Bible times.

The most famous literal vineyard in the Bible is that of Naboth of Jezreel. King Ahab offered to purchase or trade royal property for

Naboth's vineyard because it was close to his palace. Naboth refused the offer because he saw the vineyard as more than a place to grow grapes. For him the vineyard was land that God had given to his family as part of the larger promise he had made to give the Israelites a land of their own (1 Kings 21:3). Naboth's refusal to surrender the vineyard bespeaks a wonderful piety set in stark contrast to the godless greed evident in the royal family. The simple vineyard became part of a political scandal that illustrated just how godless Ahab and Jezebel had become (21:1–16).

In Proverbs the fate of the sluggard is illustrated in connection with the vineyard he has failed to tend. In stark contrast to the owner who gave the vineyard the attention it needed, this owner allowed the vineyard to fall into disrepair. "Thorns had come up everywhere, the ground was covered with weeds, and the stone wall was in ruins" (Prov. 24:31). The state of the vineyard foretold the fate of the man who was destined for poverty.

The vineyard is used as a metaphor as well. Twice in the Song of Songs the inspired poet lays a literal and a figurative vineyard side by side. The young woman asks the daughters of Jerusalem not to stare at her because long hours in the vineyard have left her without time to care for her own "vineyard"—her body (Song 1:6). In the closing chapter a similar figure of speech is used. Here the young woman compares the vineyard of her body to the literal vineyards of Solomon. As Solomon can "let out his vineyards to tenants" so the "vineyard," which is her body is hers to give away (8:11–12).

The vineyard also is used as a metaphor for God's people. The leaders of Israel are harshly criticized for failing to care for God's people who have ruined his "vineyard" (Isa. 3:14; Jer. 12:10). But Israel is not off the hook either; the song of the vineyard (Isa. 5:1–7) carefully catalogs the intense care the Lord has shown his people. He established his vineyard on a fertile hillside, cleared the stones, and planted the choicest of cuttings. He built a watchtower and winepress. "Then he looked for a crop of good grapes, but it yielded only bad fruit" (5:2).

A well-constructed and well-maintained watchtower used to guard the vineyard.

www.HolyLandPhotos.org

God had done all he could for his vineyard, and now his judgment was about to fall. He would break down its wall and stop pruning, weeding, and watering it (vv. 4–6). Ironically, this metaphor turns to literal reality just a few verses later. When God delivers judgment against "his vineyard," their vineyards produce a ridiculously small amount of wine (cf. v. 10).

Matthew contains a flurry of parables involving a vineyard that line up one after the next. The parable of the workers in the vineyard (Matt. 20:1–16) is followed by the parable of the two sons (21:28–31), which is followed by the parable of the tenants (21:33–41). In each case, Jesus is addressing workers in his kingdom (or those who claim to be so) and comparing them to workers in a "vineyard." Expectations are set and attitudes criticized as Jesus confronts those who work in his vineyard.

Viper. *See* Snake.

Wall

People living in Bible times were familiar with a variety of walls that were used to confine, protect, and create boundaries. Walls enclosed sheepfolds and vineyards, sheltered people in homes and public buildings from the elements, and surrounded fortified cities to delay and discourage attackers. The construction materials used to make such walls depended on what was locally available and the amount of money one had to spend on the building project. Particularly in the southern portions of the Promised Land where stone was harder to find, walls were built by interlocking sun-dried mud bricks on top of a fieldstone foundation. In areas where fieldstones were readily available, the builder would collect stones of mixed type and shape and assemble them like pieces of a jigsaw puzzle either with or without the aid of mortar. When a strong central government was in place, public buildings and fortifications were made of quarried limestone. Large rectangular blocks of stone called ashlars were moved from the quarry and then fitted together on site to create impressive walls whose foundations can still be seen today. In the case of ashlars, no further treatment was necessary. But fieldstone and mud-brick walls required a coat of plaster to prevent weather from eroding away what the builder had erected.

While all the walls mentioned above can be found in the Bible, the one wall found most often is the fortification wall that surrounded capital cities and strategic fortresses. Some of these walls were solid, but others took a special form called casemate. Building a casemate wall saves on material by constructing two thinner walls five to eight feet apart. These two walls are connected to one another by short, transverse walls built between and at right angles to the outer and inner wall. During a time of peace, the space created between outer and inner walls could be used for storage. But when threatened, the residents of the city could fill this space with rubble and so effectively thicken the wall. Whether the wall was of solid or casemate style, the function of the city wall was the same: it provided a ring of protection around its citizens and offered them an elevated firing platform to rain down blows upon their attackers.

Special connotations are associated with city walls that are collapsed or collapsing and city walls that are rising or being restored. City walls provided the citizens within with a sense of pride and autonomy. Walls in ruin were a disgrace, signaling that the city and its residents were defeated and subject to the whims of their enemies (Josh. 6:5, 20; 2 Kings 14:13; 2 Chron. 26:6; Neh. 2:17). The sight of Jerusalem's ruined walls was enough to make Nehemiah sit down and weep (Neh. 1:3–4). On the other hand, a city whose walls were being built or restored breathed the air of power and independence (1 Kings 3:1; 2 Chron. 8:5; Ezra 4:12–13; Mic. 7:11).

As the Lord led his people out of Egypt, he opened a path of escape through the Red Sea so that there was a wall of water on their right and on their left (Ex. 14:22, 29; 15:8). One would think that this image would have remained in the minds of the Israelites and strengthened their faith as they approached the conquest of Canaan. But in an ironic twist, the image of the wall of water gave way to city walls that reached "up

A fieldstone wall like this was constructed without the aid of mortar.

© William D. Mounce

to the sky" (Deut. 1:28). With their eyes set on man-made walls rather than on God's miraculous walls of water, God's people lost heart and failed to go up into the Promised Land.

Both mortals and God are likened to walls in Scripture. The servants of Nabal described David and his men as "a wall around us all the time" (1 Sam. 25:16). The returning exiles recognized the Lord as one who provided "a wall of protection in Judah and Jerusalem" (Ezra 9:9). And those in the new Zion will call their walls "Salvation" (Isa. 60:18), for the Lord will be a "wall of fire" that protects them (Zech. 2:5).

These metaphors associated with a well-built wall stand in sharp contrast with a weak and leaning wall. David gave voice to his frailty by calling himself a "leaning wall" (Ps. 62:3). In condemning the false prophets who claimed to preach a sturdy message, the Lord repeatedly refers to their message as a "flimsy wall" coated in "whitewash" (Ezek. 13:10–16). Just as whitewash does nothing to strengthen an otherwise poorly constructed wall against the onslaught of the elements, so their unauthorized preaching about an enduring peace would collapse under divine judgment. In the end both the wall and those who whitewashed it will be gone.

Finally, there is a special wall alluded to in Ephesians 2:14. In the temple complex enhanced by Herod the Great, there were a variety of separate courtyards. Each of these courtyards signaled another layer of restricted access as one approached the temple proper. The outer courtyard was as far as Gentiles were permitted to go. And a low stone wall with warning inscriptions made it clear that Gentiles attempting to cross that barrier risked their lives (*Ant.* 15.11.5). In speaking of the unity of Christ's church, Paul alludes to this wall when saying about Jesus, "He himself is our peace, who has made the two one and has destroyed the barrier, the dividing wall of hostility" (Eph. 2:14).

Watchtower

Two very different structures with very different cultural roles were known as watchtowers—one was for agricultural use and the other for military use. The agricultural watchtower was built by families and landowners on rural hillsides that were terraced for the growing of grapes and olive trees. For those who wished to bring their grapes to a successful harvest, this watchtower was as important as the walls that were built around the vineyard and the winepress constructed nearby (Matt. 21:33). The agricultural watchtower was a round fieldstone structure

fifteen to twenty feet tall. The first floor was completely enclosed except for the door used for entry and exit. An external stairway led to the second floor, which was like a porch. There were no walls on this porch, only a roof made of branches that provided shade. The purpose of this rural shelter was to give a family a place to live, to temporarily store their harvest, and to keep an eye on their harvest during the close of the summer growing season. The time for the ripening of the grapes and other summer fruit was also the time when wild animals and thieves would visit the hillside fields full of ripening food. The agricultural watchtower was a shelter that allowed a family to live near their fields during this part of the year; its elevated second floor became the lookout platform as they kept a close eye out for unauthorized harvesting.

The purpose of the military watchtower was security. It might be a singular tower within a

An agricultural watchtower with steps on the outside provides a great view for keeping watch over the fields.

Todd Bolen/www.BiblePlaces.com

walled city (Judg. 9:51) or a tower built into the city wall (2 Kings 9:17). In either case, such towers could be round or rectangular, were built higher than an agricultural watchtower, and were fortified to withstand a military assault. If the city walls were breached by the enemy, the watchtower could serve as a refuge of last resort. But on a daily basis, the artificial elevation provided by this watchtower allowed the watchman or lookout a good view of the surrounding countryside so that an early warning could be given of approaching danger. The daily task of watching an unchanging landscape could easily lead to boredom (Isa. 21:8), but the watchman had to fight the malaise and be ready to deliver urgent news: "When the lookout standing on the tower in Jezreel saw Jehu's troops approaching, he called out, 'I see some troops coming'" (2 Kings 9:17).

The biblical authors mention the watchtower in a number of rhetorical settings. The agricultural watchtower was such a common feature of the rural landscape in the Promised Land that it came to stand for the rural countryside in distinction from the urban setting. So when the apostasy of the Israelites is said to be evident "from watchtower to fortified city" (2 Kings 17:9), the point is that apostasy was common everywhere. Addressing a very different topic with the same formula, we learn of the pervasive success King Hezekiah enjoyed in his war with the Philistines (2 Kings 18:8).

"The song of the vineyard" in Isaiah 5 is an extended metaphor that compares the in-depth care a farmer gives to his vineyard with the wide-ranging care God had shown Israel. Among the many time-consuming tasks of the farmer mentioned is the building of an agricultural watchtower (Isa. 5:2). Sadly, the depth of care does not lead the "vineyard" to produce good grapes, and

judgment follows. The failure of Israel anticipated in this song of Isaiah brings about horrific days for God's people; and devastating foreign invasion leaves the military citadels and watchtowers of Jerusalem abandoned (Isa. 32:14). But in the end, there would be restoration. Micah pictures that restoration by likening Jerusalem to a watchtower: "As for you, O watchtower of the flock, O stronghold of the Daughter of Zion, the former dominion will be restored to you" (Mic. 4:8).

In other Bible passages, the agricultural watchtower is not formally named, but it is presumed in the imagery. The agricultural watchtower provided both an elevated viewing platform and shade. The Lord is likened to the unmentioned watchtower. "Indeed, he who watches over Israel will neither slumber nor sleep. The LORD watches over you — the LORD is your shade at your right hand" (Ps. 121:4–5). The Lord is also pictured as the one who does what the farmer would do from the watchtower but in a way that far exceeds any mortal: "Sing about a fruitful vineyard: I, the LORD, watch over it; I water it continually. I guard it day and night so that no one may harm it" (Isa. 27:2–3).

Well

The availability of water can never be taken for granted in the Promised Land, so a considerable part of any month was spent identifying, developing, maintaining, and defending a water source. The best source was a natural spring, a location where the groundwater and surface of the earth existed at the same depth. But water was needed where springs were not found. Consequently, underground chambers or cisterns were dug to collect runoff water and wells were dug through the upper levels of earth until they reached the natural water table. Given the fact that wells were converted to cisterns and cisterns into wells, this terminology remains a bit fluid in the hands of the biblical authors.

Wells were located where natural springs were unavailable and where underground water was available at a reasonable depth. We read about wells associated with rural herding stations (Gen. 29:2–3), wells located along well-traveled roadways (Gen. 16:14), and particularly about wells associated with cities and villages. The latter may be located within the walls of the city (e.g., Gezer and Lachish) or near the city gates (Gen. 24:11; 2 Sam. 23:15–16).

The well was an installation that claimed considerable time and energy. The process began when a likely spot for sinking the well was identified and a vertical shaft between seven and ten feet in diameter was hand dug. A narrower well was easier to dig but was of lower quality because it had a smaller chamber in which the groundwater might collect. If necessary the excavators would dig to a depth of more than one hundred feet to reach the water table. To prevent the walls from collapsing, they were lined with fieldstones that also helped narrow the opening of the well so as to allow a cover to fit over the top that would limit contamination and prevent

A well with a cover to limit contamination and prevent evaporation.

evaporation. Water was typically obtained by lowering a ceramic vessel into the well opening with a rope, although mention is made of a wheel that fostered the lifting of water to the surface (Eccl. 12:6). Troughs were also provided so that the water drawn from the well might be shared with animals (Gen. 24:20; Ex. 2:16).

With the infrastructure in place, the job was still not done, for the well components required maintenance; and given the scarcity of water in the region, water rights issues had to be negotiated and water sources had to be defended (Gen. 21:25; 26:15, 19–21; Num. 20:17; 21:21–22). In a number of instances, we find such wells given specific names, such as Beer Lahai Roi (Gen. 16:14) or Shibah (26:32). In most cases where such a name is mentioned, we find the naming of the well helped recall a special event or agreement that was reached in the vicinity (Gen. 21:25–31; 26:22; Num. 21:16–18).

The well became a symbol of home, hope, and divine blessing. For David the well at Bethlehem became the way he thought of his hometown. When he longed for home, he spoke of his desire to taste once again water drawn from the well at Bethlehem. A number of his brave followers took his words literally and broke through the Philistine lines to draw water from that well (2 Sam. 23:15–16). The well also was a symbol of hope. On two occasions when Hagar and Ishmael fell into disfavor with Sarah, God used a well to save their lives and lift their spirits (Gen. 16:13–14; 21:17–19). For Isaac, Jacob, and Moses, a meeting at a well proved the first step in the direction of marriage as well as a step out of what had been very difficult circumstances (Gen. 24:12–51; 29:10–20; Ex. 2:15–22). In addition to home and hope, the well was a symbol of blessing. God not only led Israel to places in the wilderness where there was water, but he also promised to give them wells in the Promised Land, wells that others had dug (Deut. 6:11).

The well is further used as a metaphor for a wife, wickedness, and salvation. In the Song of Songs, the attractive bride-to-be is likened to "a garden fountain, a well of flowing water" (Song 4:15). Husbands are urged to shun the advances of the adulteress and remain faithful to their brides: "Drink water from your own cistern, running water from your own well" (Prov. 5:15). Wives who fall into sexual sins are characterized as "a narrow well" (23:27), likely a reference to the less desirable kind of well that could collect less water. Both men and women who abandon their righteous living for ungodly living are likened to a "polluted well" (Prov. 25:26). Unfortunately, the residents of Jerusalem did not heed the warning. "As a well pours out its water, so [Jerusalem] pours out her wickedness" (Jer. 6:7).

The well was a joyful place because it linked a person to the liquid on which life depended; thus it is no surprise that the well is also linked to salvation. We see it first in Isaiah's words: "With joy you will draw water from the wells of salvation" (Isa. 12:3). But it is at Jacob's well where this receives the most memorable mention. Here the Samaritan woman hesitated to give Jesus a drink of water and even poked fun at his offer to give her "living water": "Sir, . . . you have nothing to draw with and the well is deep" (John 4:11). She used a special term for the well, marking it as one that refilled very slowly—that is, a well that was too slow to replace the water drawn from it. In reaffirming his offer and making sure she understood his words as a metaphor, Jesus in his response to her used the term for a well that recharges quickly, producing a more desirable drink of water: "Everyone who drinks this water will be thirsty again, but whoever drinks the water I give him will never thirst. Indeed, the water I give him will become in him a spring of water welling up to eternal life" (John 4:13–14).

Wheat. *See* Grain.

Wild Goat. *See* Ibex.

Wind

Wind occurs when changing temperatures produce differential pressure in the atmosphere, yet biblical authors point us to the Lord as the one who controls the force, direction, and even dramatic cessation of the wind (Job 28:25; Jer. 51:16; Amos 4:13; Mark 4:41). The biblical world knows of at least four different types of wind, each with its own cause, season, and attending benefits or threats.

The summer season is the season of the sea breeze and the Etesian winds. During the sunny summer months, the land warms quickly, causing the air above the land to rise. Cooler air that had remained over the Mediterranean Sea flows inland behind that rising air, impacting the coast by 9:00 a.m. and arriving in Jerusalem by 1:00 p.m. For the farmer this was the predictable wind that could be used for winnowing the grain, and for everyone it was the natural air conditioning that brought a break from the sweltering heat of summer. The summer months were also the season for the Etesian winds that affected the Aegean and eastern Mediterranean. These moderate northwesterly winds were well known to the sailors and merchants of the Mediterranean. They generally marked the good weather that allowed ships to sail directly across the open sea

rather than using the longer routes that skirted the coastline. Such winds allowed Paul to travel quickly between Europe and Israel, shortening the eastward journey to as little as three days when conditions were right.

The winter season also had its own winds, strong and gusty winds that were associated with the low pressure areas that took aim at the Promised Land. These weather makers charged off the Mediterranean Sea, bringing with them the wonderful rainfall that revitalizes the landscape (1 Kings 18:45). But they also could bring damaging winds that collapsed structures and brought havoc to the shipping industry (Ezek. 13:13–14; 27:26; Jonah 1:4; Acts 27:13–44).

The transitional weeks between the winter and summer seasons brought the notorious khamsin wind to the Bible lands. This wind blows from the desert areas east or southeast of Israel, filling the air with a yellow haze and every hiding place with fine dust. The discomfort of the khamsin wind is intensified by a sudden rise in temperature and plummeting relative humidity (Luke 12:55). The land quickly sheds its greenery in the face of this assault (Ps. 103:15–16), and people learn to keep their mouths closed, even limiting their conversation so as to ingest as little dust as possible. Thus the question of Eliphaz: "Would a wise man answer with empty notions or fill his belly with the hot east wind?" (Job 15:2).

Then there is the unpredictable sharqiya wind that churns the Sea of Galilee. This wind forms during temperature inversions when air over the lake basin is kept warm by the water while air on the ridges above the lake cools more quickly. Cold air suddenly rushes down the 1,300-foot ridges, turning the quiet Sea of Galilee into a death trap for boaters, with waves up to six feet high. This is the kind of wind that caught the experienced fisherman among Jesus' disciples off guard and that Jesus calmed (Matt. 14:22–36; Mark 4:35–41).

The wind is used by its divine authors in a number of different ways. The Lord is said to soar on the wings of the wind (2 Sam. 22:11; Pss. 18:10; 104:3). The biblical authors composed those words centuries before air travel became known. Thus it was one way of expressing the transcendence of the Lord over his creation. In a few instances, the wind plays a role in the delivery of God's people from harm (Ex. 10:13, 19; 14:21; Num. 11:31). But with much greater frequency, we find the divine wind at work in figurative expressions, driving away those who oppose him and the coming of his kingdom like the wind drives chaff, a leaf, fine dust, smoke, or a tumbleweed (Job 21:18; Pss. 1:4; 18:42; 35:5; 68:2; 83:13; Isa. 17:13; Jer. 13:24). The fierce khamsin wind is often used as a metaphor for the empires that lay east of Israel in Mesopotamia and "blew violently" into the Promised Land and decimated its population at the Lord's direction (cf. Jer. 4:11–13; Hos. 13:15; Hab. 1:9, 11).

Three qualities of the wind also are used in the wordplay of the Bible. First, we observe that the wind lies completely outside the control of mortals. This quality of the wind is in view as Job says his "dignity is driven away as by the wind" (Job 30:15) and as Isaiah laments that "we all shrivel up like a leaf, and like the wind our sins sweep us away" (Isa. 64:6). Restraining a quarrelsome wife is like trying to restrain the wind (Prov. 27:16). And the impossible quest for satisfaction among the things of this world is characterized again and again in Ecclesiastes as "chasing after the wind" (Eccl.1:14, 17, 2:11; et al.).

The wind also stands in figures of speech for those things that are considered to lack substance or value. Job criticizes his friends for treating the words of a despairing man like wind (Job 6:26), while Job's friend Bildad characterizes Job's words as a "blustering wind" (8:2). "He who brings trouble on his family will inherit only wind" (Prov. 11:29). Pity the man who toils all day only to be repaid with wind (Eccl. 5:16); and pity the woman who goes through the difficulty of labor only to give birth to wind (Isa. 26:18).

As wind is uncontrollable and lacks substance, so it also changes quickly and without warning. Jesus likens this aspect of the wind to the work of the Spirit: "The wind blows wherever it pleases. You hear its sound, but you cannot tell where it comes from or where it is going" (John 3:8). It is no surprise then that on Pentecost the Holy Spirit came with "a sound like the blowing of a violent wind," giving birth to the church (Acts 2:2). Yet we remain a church that aspires to a wind-resistant existence; we don't want to be "blown here and there by every wind of teaching" (Eph. 4:14).

Window

Our ability to accurately construct images of ancient windows is hampered at several levels. First, the archaeological remains of buildings from Bible times rarely rise high enough to provide indication of how windows were incorporated into the structure. Ancient artwork, like the Phoenician "woman in the window," is somewhat stylized. And where windows are mentioned by the biblical authors, description of those windows is all but lacking. What we can say for sure is that windows were rectangular openings found in various types of buildings, including palaces (1 Kings 7:4), private homes (Josh. 2:15; 1 Sam. 19:12), and temples (1 Kings

6:4; Ezek. 41:16, 26). These windows must have been modest in size, given the criticism of the king who planned to construct a great palace for himself that included "large windows" (Jer. 22:14). To provide some privacy, it appears that either permanent stone latticework or movable wooden lattices could be placed over the window opening (Judg. 5:28; 2 Kings 1:2; Prov. 7:6).

Despite the extra effort required to insert a window into a wall, the effort paid off in a variety of ways. In an era without air conditioning, it was necessary to ventilate the home using natural air currents. Windows were placed in the home to take advantage of prevailing winds that provided that ventilation. In the process they also brought natural light into the home and allowed the smoke from cooking or heating fires to leave the dwelling (Hos. 13:3). Windows installed on the second or third floor of a building had the added benefit of providing the occupants with an elevated viewing platform. When windows are mentioned in the Bible, we often find them functioning in this way (Gen. 26:8; Judg. 5:28; 2 Sam. 6:16; 2 Kings 9:30). Windows also offered a wonderful place to sit while enjoying the flow of fresh air. Yet in at least two cases, a terrible accident proved fatal when those doing so fell out

"Woman in the Window" ivory.
Todd Bolen/www.BiblePlaces.com

of a window (2 Kings 1:2; Acts 20:9; but note that when Paul put his arms around the young man, he came back to life).

Three distinct connotations are associated with the windows mentioned in the Bible: expectation, escape, and aloofness. The first time we hear about a window, it is of the small windows that Noah built into the ark. These windows that provided light and ventilation are further associated with expectation. With the ark perched in the mountains of Ararat, Noah opened the window to release a raven in hopes of finding dry land (Gen. 8:6). Sisera's mother waited nervously at the window of her home, peering into the distance to catch a glimpse of her son's chariot, which would not be coming home (Judg. 5:28). The young man in the Song of Songs gazed longingly at the window of his beloved's home, hoping to catch a glimpse of her (Song 2:9). And following the kings' decree that made worship of the one true God a capital offense, Daniel went to the upstairs room with windows that faced Jerusalem to pray (Dan. 6:10).

The connotation of expectation is joined by that of escape. Windows were not designed to function as portals for people, but when danger threatened, they became escape hatches. When Jericho's officials searched intently for the

Israelite spies, Rahab hid them and eventually lowered them to the ground on a rope that trailed from her home's window (Josh. 2:15). Later a scarlet cord dangling from that same window would spell escape for all who had gathered in that home when the Israelites attacked the city (Josh. 2:18). David and Paul also escaped their pursuers by exiting through windows (1 Sam. 19:12; 2 Cor. 11:33).

In two instances the connotation of aloofness is associated with queens who were looking out a window. Michal, the daughter of Saul who had married David, had grown apart from her husband and from his passion to advance the Lord's cause in Jerusalem. At no time was that marital tension more evident than when she stood in the window watching the ark of the covenant making its triumphal entry into Jerusalem (2 Sam. 6:16). Rather than joining the celebration, she remained aloof from it, watching it all unfold below her window and despising the way her husband had tarnished his and her royal image with his antics (6:20). Later in time another queen, Jezebel, assumed the same position in the palace at Jezreel. After Jehu had eradicated most of the royal family and their Baal connections, he headed for Jezreel to finish the job. Jezebel painted her eyes, arranged her hair, and struck a royal pose in the window, perhaps hoping that Jehu would respect the office. But her aloof pose in the window was ineffective; she met her death as she was thrown from that very window (2 Kings 9:30–33).

Finally, three figures of speech include the image of the window. Jeremiah describes the horror of foreign invasion with this startling image: "Death has climbed in through our windows and has entered our fortresses" (Jer. 9:21). In Proverbs wisdom is pictured as standing at the window keeping watch over the young people whose walk through life is threatened by many moral landmines (Prov. 7:6). And in Ecclesiastes the inspired poet waxes poetic about the increasing physical debility that accompanies the aging process. The inspired writer encourages all to remember their Creator before "those looking through the windows grow dim" (Eccl. 12:3), an apparent reference to failing eyesight.

Winepress

The Lord has blessed the Promised Land with a combination of climate and soil that favors the growing of grapevines. Thus grapes and wine were not regarded as luxurious extras in Bible times but were perceived as fundamental to the daily diet. This becomes clear when we see the biblical authors linking the threshing floor that processed the wheat and the winepress that processed the grapes as paired facilities vital to the well-being of every family (Deut. 15:14; 2 Kings 6:27). The wine produced in connection with the presses was used medically and in religious rites, but primarily it was consumed daily in a land where potable water was scarce and where water quality was always a concern.

The winepress played a key role in bringing this beverage to the people of the Promised Land. Once the grapes ripened, they were spread in the sun for up to a week to increase their sugar content. Then the grapes were taken to the winepress where they were crushed beneath bare feet so that their precious juice might be collected. The winepress consisted of two basic parts—a gently sloping, flat floor on which the grapes could be stomped and one or more collection vats connected to the stomping floor by the natural pitch of the floor or hewn channels.

Archaeology suggests that two basic forms of

the press were in use during Bible times. The first form of the press required less altering of the natural landscape. The farmer would create a recessed stomping floor by scraping away at a stone ledge and then carve a vat on the lowest side of the floor so that gravity would pull the extracted juice into this collection basin. A winepress could also be constructed using fieldstones and mortar. A short wall was built up around the stomping floor and sealed with plaster to create a liquid-tight stomping area; one or more smaller vats for collecting the juice were made in the same way. Both these forms of the winepress were located either within the vineyard itself or within a nearby city (Isa. 5:2; Matt. 21:33); they typically were of such a size that many feet could be put to work at one time.

Connotations of both blessing and distress are associated with the winepress. Grapes were harvested only once a year and the season of processing those grapes was marked by great joy, celebration, and singing (Joel 2:23–24). Given the importance of wine to the well-being of a family, a season of great blessing was defined as one in which "your barns will be filled to overflowing, and your vats will brim over with new wine" (Prov. 3:10).

There was a normal rhythm to the agricultural year, and there were normal activities and

A winepress with a flat floor and a collection vat.

Todd Bolen/www.BiblePlaces.com

expectations associated with the winepress. Times of distress were marked by deviation from that norm. For example, it was quite normal for people to stomp grapes in a winepress, but it was not normal for them to process grain in such a facility. Yet that is what Gideon did when the Midianites invaded the land and raided the threshing floors. Winepress installations were not designed for threshing wheat, and when forced into this role, they made the process very inefficient. Thus the distress of God's people during the days of Gideon was evidenced by his "threshing wheat in a winepress" (Judg. 6:11). It was normal for winepresses to be buzzing with joy-filled activity during the pressing season. Yet in the judgment speeches against Moab, the prophets warn that joy and gladness will be absent and that no one will be treading out wine at the presses (Isa. 16:10; Jer. 48:33). The processing of grapes at the winepress was a collective enterprise. It was normal for a number of farmers to share a winepress and even to work together in the stomping of the grapes. Therefore it was abhorrent that the poor would be forced to stomp grapes but still suffer from thirst (Job 24:11). And it was normal for the presses to be flowing with juice and the vats to be full during the pressing season. Empty vats and processed juice that was hijacked by another were signs of the Lord's displeasure with his people (Hos. 9:2; Mic. 6:15; Hag. 2:16).

Perhaps the most vibrant images associated with the winepress are those that have to do with divine judgment. The harm that comes to the grapes is likened to the harm that will come to those who oppose the Lord. The grapes will be pressed with such force that they will burst apart and surrender their juice. Isaiah pictures the conquering Messiah with garments stained red like the garments of those who stomp red grapes: "Why are your garments red, like those of one treading the winepress? I have trodden the winepress alone; from the nations no one was with me. I trampled them in my anger and trod them down in my wrath; their blood spattered my garments, and I stained all my clothing" (Isa. 63:2–3). This is the same image we find in Lamentations when the inspired author wishes to express the horror of what had happened to Jerusalem (Lam. 1:15). And this is the picture of the last days that we find in Revelation: "The angel swung his sickle on the earth, gathered its grapes and threw them into the great winepress of God's wrath. They were trampled in the winepress" (Rev. 14:19–20). For people who stained their garments year after year in the winepress, these images were a graphic reminder of the judgment to come.

Wolf

Visitors to Palestine in the 1800s reported seeing wolves in all parts of the region. Today fewer than four hundred wolves survive in the wild there despite government protection. Two subspecies of the gray wolf are indigenous to the land, the Iranian (Asiatic) wolf and the Arabian wolf. The Iranian wolf stands between eighteen and thirty inches tall at the shoulder and weighs between fifty-five and seventy pounds. This is the larger of the two wolves in the region but is markedly smaller than the North American and Eurasian wolves that can easily exceed one hundred pounds. The Iranian wolf is typically found in the northern reaches of Israel, in contrast to the Arabian wolf, which is lighter in color and prefers the southern desert regions. The Arabian wolf is only twenty-six inches tall at the shoulder and weighs forty pounds. Its small size is set in contrast to its larger-than-expected ears, which improve this wolf's ability to dissipate the heat of the desert day.

The Iranian and Arabian wolf share a number of characteristics. For instance, they are opportunistic predators who prefer to hunt in the early evening hours, taking small mammals and occasionally a gazelle. In pursuing their prey, they stalk to within striking range and then seek a quick kill with a speed burst that can reach forty miles an hour. That failing, the wolf's remarkable endurance can be put to work, allowing it to pursue its more easily wearied prey at a relentless lope. The fatal blow is delivered by powerful jaws that are twice as strong as those of the domestic dog. Like their North American cousins, they are pack animals but rarely if ever howl. Thus this quality often mentioned in other literature is never mentioned by the biblical authors.

In contrast to the bear and the lion, the wolf is not pictured by the biblical writers as a direct threat to mortals. Rather, when they picture the wolf, it is preying on the sheep or lambs of the family flock (John 10:12). In the various metaphors that speak of the wolf, these inspired writers assume the perspective of the vulnerable lamb. Thus the wolf is characterized as fierce, violent, blood-thirsty, ravenous, aggressive, and savage (Gen. 49:27; Ezek. 22:27; Acts 20:29).

Almost every time a wolf is mentioned in the Bible, it is being used as a metaphor to describe a tribe or nation or their leaders who bring harm. The first mention of a wolf in the Bible likens the tribe of Benjamin to this remarkable predator: "Benjamin is a ravenous wolf; in the morning he devours the prey, in the evening he divides the plunder" (Gen. 49:27). The efficiency of the Benjamite warriors is in view here; they were as fierce and efficient in their military operations as the hunting wolf. Note that this nocturnal hunter did not only have food during the evening when the kill was made, but that this food (that is, plunder) lasted into the morning and the next evening. In subsequent chapters, we read of the remarkable success of Benjamites like Ehud, Saul, and Jonathan (Judg. 3; 1 Sam. 11–15).

An Iranian wolf.
Todd Bolen/www.BiblePlaces.com

The wolf is also used as a metaphor for people who threaten believers with harm. In the first two instances, it is the Babylonians who are in view. The reckless rebellion and backsliding of God's Old Testament people brought divine judgment upon themselves in the form of the Babylonian army. Jeremiah likens the Babylonian soldiers to three large predators of the Palestinian countryside, including the wolf, which will "ravage them" (Jer. 5:6). Habakkuk notes that their "horses are swifter than leopards, fiercer than wolves at dusk" (Hab. 1:8).

Furthermore, the Old Testament prophets level sharp criticism at the politicians and clergy of Israel who are charged with caring for the well-being of God's people. Instead of treating them with respect and kindness, they treat them like a wolf treats a lamb. Speaking of Jerusalem, "Her officials within her are like wolves tearing their prey; they shed blood and kill people to make unjust gain" (Ezek. 22:27). And again of Jerusalem, "Her officials are roaring lions, her rulers are evening wolves, who leave nothing for the morning" (Zeph. 3:3). Those leaders were long dead, but the threat of opposition continued as Jesus warned the Twelve and the Seventy-two whom he sent out that their mission would take them into hostile confrontations: "I am sending you out like sheep [or lambs] among wolves" (Matt. 10:16; Luke 10:3). This concern remained into the time of Paul. Upon taking leave of the church in Ephe-sus, Paul expressed this concern: "I know that after I leave, savage wolves will come in among you and will not spare the flock" (Acts 20:29).

The turmoil of these earlier ages will eventually give way to the eternal peace of the messianic era. The two places in which a real wolf is mentioned describe an animal remarkably different than the one the rest of the biblical authors know. Isaiah pictures the age to come as one in which the wolf will live with the lamb rather than kill it (Isa. 11:6) and one in which the wolf will feed with the lamb rather than on it (65:25).

Cedar of Lebanon.
Z. Radovan/www.BibleLandPictures.com

Wood

Wood is a natural product with qualities that allow it to play a variety of roles in society. It is strong yet can be shaped, cut, and bent for many applications. It is enduring and beautiful, and some wood, such as cedar, even offers a pleasant aroma. When burned, wood produces heat that can easily consume a sacrifice, warm a home, cook a meal, or smelt metals.

The challenge of putting wood to work in the Promised Land is related to its availability. Current evidence suggests that the mountains of this land were heavily forested prior to 1200 BC when a dramatic increase in regional population put a great deal of stress on this natural resource. Acres of timber were cut and replaced by farm fields. Hillsides were harvested to make room for cities and to make lumber available for construction. Families used wood to stoke their cooking and heating fires, which on their own consumed between one and two tons of firewood per year per family. And that does not begin to account for the wood fires that were kept glowing to smelt and forge metals as well as heat the kilns of ceramic factories. Repeated military invasion also took its toll on the natural forests, as trees were used to build siege ramps and to build fires designed to topple the walls of fortified cities (Deut. 20:20). Through it all, iron tools developed during this era made the harvesting of forest more efficient. Imprudent clear-cutting with those tools and the unchecked grazing of flocks all too quickly removed the trees and plant communities that held the top-soil in place. The erosion of the hillsides to bed-rock spelled the end of the great forests, leaving behind olive, fig, sycamore, almond, and pome-granate trees that could survive in less hospi-table growing conditions. Thus, from the time the Israelites entered the Promised Land under Joshua through the New Testament era, high-quality wood was becoming an increasingly scarce natural resource.

Wood is mentioned incidentally by the biblical authors in a number of settings that illustrate its wide range of applications in biblical culture. Wood was used to make household items, including water containers, furniture, doors, and roof rafters (Ex. 7:19; Hab. 2:11). Various farm implements were shaped from wood, such as carts, yokes, and threshing sledges (1 Sam. 6:14; 2 Sam. 24:22; Jer. 28:13). The oars, masts, and decks of trading ships and fishing boats were composed of wood (Ezek. 27:5–6). Archaeology has even produced evidence of hinged, wooden writing tablets overlaid with bee's wax that were inscribed with a stylus (Ezek. 37:16–17).

Wood is mentioned frequently by the biblical authors in connection with three subjects: wood in the sanctuaries, wood for offerings, and the wood of pagan idols. In each case, a rhetorical point is being made. As one way of distinguishing the unique nature of the tabernacle and temple, we read about significant use of wood in the construction of sanctuaries and their furniture (e.g., Ex. 36:15–20, 31, 36; 37:1, 4, 10, 15, 25, 28; 38:1, 6; 1 Kings 5:10–18; 10:11–12). Both tabernacle and temple were built in regions where construction-grade lumber was scarce. Thus the widespread use of wood in these sanctuaries helped to distinguish them and their unique role in the Israelite culture.

The same may be said of the sacrifices. Beginning with Leviticus 1:7–8 and continuing throughout the law codes God gave to Israel, we find that all offerings burned on the altar were to be burned using a wood fire. As wood became less and less available, ordinary cooking and heating fires used other products, such as straw or dried manure for fuel. That was not the case at the temple. Despite the hardship, wood alone was gathered and used to burn the sacrifices at the sanctuary (Neh. 10:34; 13:31).

Wood is also mentioned again and again in connection with pagan idols. The Lord warned the Israelites that when they entered the Promised Land they would worship wooden idols (Deut. 4:28), and because they did not heed God's warning, they faced the prophets' censure throughout their history. While many idols were composed of stone or precious metals, a wooden idol was the choice of the poor who did not have the resources to commission a more expensive idol (Isa. 40:20). The rhetoric heated up as the prophets pointed out the remarkable incongruity of harvesting wood for a fire and then using a portion of that wood to make an idol. "It is man's fuel for burning; some of it he takes and warms himself, he kindles a fire and bakes bread. But he also fashions a god and worships it; he makes an idol and bows down to it" (Isa. 44:15). Those caught in this pagan web assigned values and hopes to idols that were unthinkable: "They say to wood, 'You are my father'" (Jer. 2:27), and "Woe to him who says to wood, 'Come to life!'" (Hab. 2:19). Note how in these cases "wood" is used as the equivalent for a pagan idol to emphasize its ordinary origins.

Wood also is found in proverbs and figures of speech. The use of wood as fuel gives us the following: "Without wood a fire goes out; without gossip a quarrel dies down. As charcoal to embers and as wood to fire, so is a quarrelsome man for kindling strife" (Prov. 26:20–21). Wood is also used as a metaphor for the people who will face the fire of divine judgment. The Lord tells Jeremiah, "I will make my words in your mouth a fire and these people the wood it consumes" (Jer. 5:14; cf. Ezek. 15:6).

Y

Yoke

The yoke is a wooden device that allows the energy of two or more animals to be transferred from their shoulders to the mechanism they are pulling. It consists of a stout horizontal crossbar that lies across the shoulders of the draft animals and two vertical staves aligned over their shoulders. When the animals pull forward with powerful strides, the force of each stride is transferred first to the yoke, then to the tongue that stretches between the flanks of the animals, and finally to the plow, threshing sledge, or the cart being pulled. The use of donkeys, heifers, and oxen as draft animals was common in Bible times, so we find mention of yokes in a number of places (Num. 19:2; Deut. 21:3; 1 Sam. 6:7; 2 Sam. 24:22; 1 Kings 19:19, 21).

Several different connotations are associated with the yoke. First, those hitched to the yoke were consigned to work long and rigorous days; thus the yoke is associated with hard service. Second, the draft animals hitched to the yoke did not have the freedom to wander on their own, eat as they pleased, or lie down at will. Thus the yoke also became a symbol for the loss of freedom. Third the image of being yoked together carried the connotation of great intimacy. Draft animals were carefully matched to one another both in temperament and in strength. The goal was always to yoke animals who were able to combine their energy rather than waste it by pulling in different directions or by pulling the cart or plow in a serpentine path. That is why it made no sense to plow by yoking together a donkey and an ox (Deut. 22:10). And that is why the yoke is used as an image of the illegitimate intimacy between God's people and a pagan world (Ps. 106:28; 2 Cor. 6:14).

The most common mention of the yoke in the Bible is in a variety of figurative expressions that take advantage of these connotations. In this light the yoke became a symbol of social inferiority often associated with servants or slaves (Gen. 27:40; Isa. 58:6, 9): "All who are under the yoke of slavery should consider their masters worthy of full respect" (1 Tim. 6:1). The figurative wearing of a yoke is similarly a symbol of political oppression. When the citizens of the northern tribes met Solomon's son Rehoboam, they described his father's administrative policies as a "heavy yoke" and urged Rehoboam to lighten it in exchange for their loyalty (1 Kings 12:4). When Rehoboam responded by telling them that his policies would become a yoke heavier than his father's (vv. 10, 11, 14), the kingdom divided.

Both the imposition of foreign rule and the relief from exile are illustrated by images of the yoke (Deut. 28:48). "Ephraim is a trained heifer that loves to thresh; so I will put a yoke on her fair neck" (Hos. 10:11). "In that day their burden will be lifted from your shoulders, their yoke from your neck; the yoke will be broken because you have grown so fat" (Isa. 10:27). This imagery is associated with the exodus from Egypt (Ex. 6:6–7; Lev. 26:13) as well as the exiles imposed by Assyria and Babylon (Isa. 14:25; 47:6; Jer. 30:8; Nah. 1:13). But it is in the enacted prophecy of Jeremiah where this image gets special attention. Here the Lord directed Jeremiah to make a wooden yoke, put it on himself, and wear it about in order to call attention to the message he was sent to deliver. All nations who bowed their necks under the yoke of the Babylonian king would remain in their own land (Jer. 27:8, 11–12). The false prophet Hananiah announced

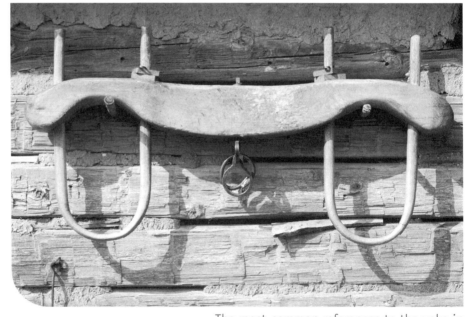

The most common references to the yoke in the Bible are connected to figurative expressions.
© Nancy Nehring/www.istockphoto.com

the opposite message and said God would break the yoke of the Babylonians from their necks (28:2, 4). To counter Jeremiah's enacted message, Hananiah then literally broke the wooden yoke on Jeremiah's neck (vv. 10–11). The Lord responded by saying, "You have broken a wooden yoke, but in its place you will get a yoke of iron" (v. 13). The wood of the yoke had to be strong to absorb the pulling force of the draft animals without breaking, but the use of an iron yoke was unthinkable and so symbolized an unimaginable burden.

The Lord's goal was to connect his chosen people to himself in a most intimate relationship. The law is pictured as the yoke that keeps the two in step. Jeremiah pictures rebellious Israel as a draft animal that has thrown off this yoke (Jer. 2:20; 5:5). Life under the law was difficult, but disobedience to the law was even more burden-some, as the guilt over sin became the oppressive yoke to be carried: "My sins have been bound into a yoke; by his hand they were woven together. They have come upon my neck and the Lord has sapped my strength" (Lam. 1:14).

The gospel message brought freedom from the threats of the law and freedom from the guilt of sin. Jesus offers this compelling invitation: "Take my yoke upon you and learn from me, for I am gentle and humble in heart, and you will find rest for your souls. For my yoke is easy and my burden is light" (Matt. 11:29–30). Those who found new life under Jesus' yoke did not have to return to life under the old yoke (Acts 15:10). This was a matter of no small importance to Paul, who wrote to the Galatians, "It is for freedom that Christ has set us free. Stand firm, then, and do not let yourselves be burdened again by a yoke of slavery" (Gal. 5:1).

Dictionary of Biblical Prophecy and End Times

J. Daniel Hays, J. Scott Duvall, and C. Marvin Pate

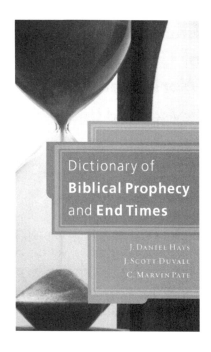

All you ever wanted to know about biblical prophecy from A to Z, the *Dictionary of Biblical Prophecy and End Times* is a comprehensive reference tool. It is written for those who truly desire to understand prophecy and the end-times. Starting with "Abomination of Desolation" and continuing through hundreds of articles until "Zionism," this book provides helpful and interesting discussions of the entire range of biblical prophecy, all at your fingertips.

This exhaustive work contains articles on a broad sweep of topics relevant to the study of biblical prophecy and eschatology. The articles are based on solid scholarship, yet are clear and accessible to the lay reader, illuminating even the most complicated issues. The authors balance their presentation by laying out differing positions along with each position's strengths and weaknesses. They do not push any specific theological or interpretive agenda, but have a firm commitment to seeking to understand the Scriptures. This is a valuable tool you will refer to time and again.

Encyclopedic Dictionary of Cults, Sects, and World Religions

Revised and Updated Edition

Larry A. Nichols,
George A. Mather,
and Alvin J. Schmidt

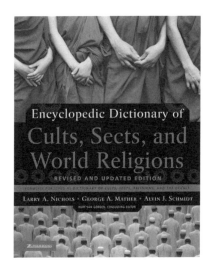

Up-to-date, well-documented, comprehensive coverage of cults, sects, and world religions, from the historical to the contemporary including: Jehovah's Witnesses, Mormons, Islam, and Baha'i and other groups with a significant North American influence.

REVISED, UPDATED, AND EXPANDED TO INCLUDE NEW ENTRIES AND NEW INFORMATION

- Updated information on Islam and its global impact
- New entries: the Branch Davidians, Native American religions, Heaven's Gate, Aum Supreme Truth, the Boston Movement, the Masonic Lodge, and many others
- Developments in the world of cults and the occult

Formerly titled *Dictionary of Cults, Sects, Religions, and the Occult*, this book provides reliable information on the history and beliefs of nearly every form of religion active today. This extensively revised edition includes new topics, updated information, and a brand-new format for a clearer, more organized approach. You will also find group histories, numerous illustrations, charts, current statistics, websites, bibliographies, and other useful information.

Available in stores and online!

Zondervan Illustrated Bible Dictionary

J. D. Douglas and Merrill C. Tenney;
Revised by Moisés Silva

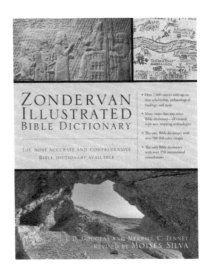

The *Zondervan Illustrated Bible Dictionary* provides a visually stimulating journey for anyone interested in learning more about the world of the Bible. Through the articles, sidebars, charts, maps, and full-color images included in this volume, the text of the Old and New Testaments will come alive for you as never before.

As a condensation of the recently updated *Zondervan Encyclopedia of the Bible*, the information contained within this reference work is solid and biblically sound. The material contains over 7,200 entries; 500 full-color photographs, charts, and illustrations; 75 full-color maps; and a Scripture index ... making this wonderful Bible study resource a must-have whether you are a general reader of the Bible, a pastor, or a student.

Available in stores and online!

Share Your Thoughts

With the Author: Your comments will be forwarded to
the author when you send them to *zauthor@zondervan.com*.

With Zondervan: Submit your review of this book
by writing to *zreview@zondervan.com*.

Free Online Resources at
www.zondervan.com

Zondervan AuthorTracker: Be notified whenever your favorite
authors publish new books, go on tour, or post an update
about what's happening in their lives at www.zondervan.com/
authortracker.

Daily Bible Verses and Devotions: Enrich your life with daily
Bible verses or devotions that help you start every morning
focused on God. Visit www.zondervan.com/newsletters.

Free Email Publications: Sign up for newsletters on Christian
living, academic resources, church ministry, fiction, children's
resources, and more. Visit www.zondervan.com/newsletters.

Zondervan Bible Search: Find and compare Bible passages in
a variety of translations at www.zondervanbiblesearch.com.

Other Benefits: Register yourself to receive online benefits
like coupons and special offers, or to participate in research.

ZONDERVAN.com/
AUTHOR**TRACKER**
follow your favorite authors